Praise for *Blood of Others*:

"In his introduction to *Blood of Others*, Rory Finnin writes that he aims to 'realign our intellectual horizons,' to refocus our attention on the cultural crossroads that is the Black Sea. He succeeds: using Russian, Ukrainian, Tatar, and Turkish sources, and with the tragic history of the Crimean Tatars as his focus, he shows how writers in the region influenced and enhanced one another's work. A brilliant book by the UK's most important scholar of Ukraine."

> **Anne Applebaum,** Staff Writer, *The Atlantic*, Senior Fellow, Johns Hopkins School of Advanced International Studies, and Pulitzer Prize-winning author of *Gulag: A History* and *Red Famine: Stalin's War on Ukraine*

"Finnin scrutinizes how collective guilt over the deportation of the Crimean Tatars was processed or denied in Crimean Tatar, Russian, Ukrainian, and Turkish literature, in particular poetic literature and cinema…. [T]he book ought to be on the reading list of all experts and students of Soviet and post-Soviet studies, as well as general readership, since it is a feast of comparative literature in the Black Sea region, beautifully written with great empathy for the suffering of indigenous peoples there."

> **Filiz Tutku Aydin,** *Europe-Asia Studies*

"In this thoughtful, nuanced study of the literature of Crimea, Rory Finnin exposes the seams connecting the nations and empires that have coexisted in the Black Sea. *Blood of Others* corrects a significant lacuna in English language scholarship on Eurasian history and literature."

> **Amelia Glaser,** Associate Professor of Literature and Endowed Chair in Judaic Studies, University of California San Diego and author of *Jews and Ukrainians in Russia's Literary Borderlands: From the Shtetl Fair to the Petersburg Bookshop*

"Finnin's research is on the cutting edge of Crimean studies … and offers a new way to examine Crimean national identity. *Blood of Others* is a fine example of comparative literary research and a valuable contribution to the field of human rights discourse."

> **Katya Jordan,** *Modern Language Review*

T0385536

"Rory Finnin has written the definitive account of cultural responses to a still-hidden atrocity: the deportation of the Crimean Tatars. Through new research and sensitive interpretations, *Blood of Others* shows how the Crimean Tatar experience is deeply connected to global themes of colonialism, dispossession, and survival. It is a record of cultural resilience against astounding odds and a detailed portrait of art and memory in action."

Charles King, Professor of International Affairs and Government, Georgetown University and author of *The Black Sea: A History*

"*Blood of Others* is an astonishing account of the entanglement of Russian, Crimean Tatar, Turkish, and Ukrainian cultural life with the political and social history of the Crimean Tatars. Rory Finnin's work is an impressive navigation among the languages and religious confessions of the Black Sea region, cultural works from poetry to film, centuries of imperial domination, and methodological toolkits, revealing the historical effects and ethical burdens of cultural expression in a fraught, multiply colonized territory."

Kevin M.F. Platt, Edmund J. and Louise W. Kahn Term Professor in the Humanities, University of Pennsylvania and editor of *Global Russian Cultures*

"The deportation of the Crimean Tatars from their ancestral homeland in 1944 was not only one of the crimes of Stalinism. It was also a triumph of settler colonialism that opened the door to the Russian annexation of Crimea in 2014. In *Blood of Others* Rory Finnin shows the power of literary texts to forge ties of solidarity with an oppressed people across national, ethnic, and linguistic lines, ties of solidarity that would not exist otherwise. It is a book about the tragedy of the past that inspires optimism about the future, and an essential read for anyone interested in the literature, history, and politics of the Black Sea region."

Serhii Plokhy, Mykhailo S. Hrushevs'kyi Professor of Ukrainian History, Harvard University and author of *The Frontline: Essays on Ukraine's Past and Present*

"The book rightfully deserves to be celebrated for the author's efforts to bring together literary exchanges in four languages, for pioneering the deep intertextual analysis of the Crimean Tatar literature, for illuminating previously obscured intercultural relations, and above all, for giving justice to centuries of Crimea's colonial condition.... [T]he book should be read by everyone who is not indifferent to the plight of others – academics and nonacademics alike."

Mariia Shynkarenko, *Nationalities Papers*

Blood of Others

*Stalin's Crimean Atrocity
and the Poetics of Solidarity*

RORY FINNIN

UNIVERSITY OF TORONTO PRESS
Toronto Buffalo London

© University of Toronto Press 2022
Toronto Buffalo London
utorontopress.com

Printed and bound by CPI Group (UK) Ltd, Croydon, CR0 4YY

Reprinted in paperback 2023

ISBN 978-1-4875-0781-7 (cloth)   ISBN 978-1-4875-3701-2 (EPUB)
ISBN 978-1-4875-5825-3 (paper)   ISBN 978-1-4875-3700-5 (PDF)

Library and Archives Canada Cataloguing in Publication

Title: Blood of others : Stalin's Crimean atrocity and the poetics of
   solidarity / Rory Finnin.
Names: Finnin, Rory, author.
Description: Paperback reprint. Originally published 2022. |
   Includes bibliographical references and index.
Identifiers: Canadiana 20230554296 | ISBN 9781487558253 (paper)
Subjects: LCSH: Ukrainian literature – 20th century – History and
   criticism. | LCSH: Russian literature – 20th century – History and
   criticism. | LCSH: Turkish literature – 20th century – History and
   criticism. | LCSH: Ethnic relations in literature. | LCSH: Literature
   and society – Ukraine – Crimea – History – 20th century. |
   LCSH: Crimean Tatars – Relocation – History – 20th century. |
   LCSH: Crimean Tatars – Ukraine – Crimea – Social conditions –
   20th century. | LCSH: Crimea (Ukraine) – In literature. |
   LCSH: Crimea (Ukraine) – Intellectual life – 20th century. |
   LCSH: Crimea (Ukraine) – Ethnic relations – History –
   20th century. | LCSH: Crimea (Ukraine) – History – 20th century.
Classification: LCC PG3906.C75 F56 2023 | DDC 891.7/909800904 – dc23

Cover design: Will Brown

The Ethics of Memory by Avishai Margalit (Cambridge, MA: Harvard
University Press), copyright © 2002 by the President and Fellows of Harvard
College. Used by permission. All rights reserved.

We wish to acknowledge the land on which the University of Toronto Press
operates. This land is the traditional territory of the Wendat, the Anishnaabeg,
the Haudenosaunee, the Métis, and the Mississaugas of the Credit First Nation.

University of Toronto Press acknowledges the financial support of the
Government of Canada, the Canada Council for the Arts, and the Ontario Arts
Council, an agency of the Government of Ontario, for its publishing activities.

To Anne and Shane

Solidarity wavers when the memory of a strong feeling of solidarity fades away.
Avishai Margalit

Contents

Illustrations

Preface to the Paperback Edition

In August 2022, six months into Russia's full-scale invasion of Ukraine, President Volodymyr Zelensky recorded a video address from his desk on Bankova Street in Kyiv. Flanked by two furled flags, he spoke to his fellow citizens with a forthright but intimate style that has become his trademark. His subject was Crimea, Ukraine's Black Sea peninsula under Russian occupation. "This Russian war against Ukraine and against all of free Europe began with Crimea," he said. "And it will end with Crimea – with its liberation."

Zelensky's bold prediction was also an urgent reminder. Crimea is the ground zero of Russia's war of aggression against Ukraine, the largest and most dangerous armed conflict in Europe since the Second World War. In February 2014 Russia's war began with the military seizure of Crimea; in February 2022 it escalated with a full-scale invasion launched in part from Crimea. At an unbearable cost, the people of Ukraine have since withstood an avalanche of Russian war crimes and countered the Kremlin's neo-imperialism with acts of defiant resistance and self-defence that have gripped the world. Today the Ukrainian Armed Forces are fighting metre by metre to expel from Ukraine's sovereign territory thousands of Russian occupiers tasked with genocide. As I write these words, they are also doing something that many Western pundits thought improbable or even impossible only months ago: striking strategic Russian military assets across Crimea and placing the question of the peninsula's deoccupation on the global agenda.

Blood of Others went to press days before the beginning of the full-scale invasion. Beyond the foreword, this paperback edition does not retrofit content or analyses in any way. The third section of the book, which focuses on Crimea and Ukrainian-Crimean Tatar relations after 1991, senses the coming escalation but senses more the forces of solidarity in Ukraine that can overcome it.

Solidarity is a formidable weapon, and the prospects of Crimea in a free Ukraine will depend on it. As this book explains, Ukrainian-Crimean Tatar solidarity is a driver of contemporary Ukraine's vibrant civic national identity, which may be the most powerful force defending liberal democracy today. In September 2023, the Crimean Tatar role in this defence took centre stage when President Zelensky tapped Crimean Tatar businessman, activist, and public servant Rustem Umerov as Ukraine's Minister of Defence. Like Zelensky, Umerov tempers bold predictions with urgent reminders. Addressing Ukraine's parliament upon his appointment, Umerov declared: "As a child I lived through the hardships brought about by Russian colonialism, which sought to make the indigenous Crimean Tatar people feel as though they were aliens on their own land. They did not succeed back then, and they will never succeed."

Rory Finnin
Cambridge
September 2023

Note on Translation, Transliteration, and Terminology

With some exceptions, I quote from Crimean Tatar, Russian, Turkish, and Ukrainian documentary or critical sources by giving an English translation only. Quotations from imaginative literature, due to their importance, are often given in the original language with a simple English translation. All translations are my own, unless indicated otherwise.

For quotations from Russian and Ukrainian texts, I follow the Library of Congress transliteration system, with some modifications. References in the notes and the bibliography hold to the LOC system, but in the body of the text I dispense with the apostrophe that marks the soft sign, render the *–yi* and *–ii* endings of proper names of individuals as *–y*, and replace the initial iotated vowels *ia-*, *iu-*, and *ie-* with *ya-*, *yu-*, and *ye-*. As for Turkish texts, the most distinctive characters have the following orthographical and phonological features:

c   *j* as in *jam*
ç   *ch* as in *church*
ğ   silent, lengthens preceding vowel
ı   *e* as in *open*
ö   *oeu* in French *oeuvre*, or German ö
ş   *sh* as in *shape*
ü   *u* in French *tu*, or German ü

The modern Crimean Tatar language has two (often competing) orthographical systems: Cyrillic and Latin. For quotations from Cyrillic-based Crimean Tatar–language texts, I convert to the Latin-based system, which largely corresponds to Turkish orthography with these exceptions:

â   *a*, with the preceding consonant palatalized
ğ   voiced velar fricative [ɣ]

h   voiceless velar fricative [x], similar to the Cyrillic *kh* or the *ch* in *loch*
ñ   velar nasal [ŋ], similar to the Polish ń
q   uvular stop [q]

For Crimean place names, I deliberately problematize usage. Crimea is legally a part of Ukraine occupied by the Russian Federation and cherished by the Crimean Tatars as their ancestral homeland; to apply one standard to its toponyms is to whistle past this contestation and enforce a uniformity that does not exist. Unless it risks confusion, I therefore tend to use the form that accords with the linguistic and cultural focus of the chapter or chapter section. The former capital of the Crimean Tatar khanate can be Bağçasaray (Crimean Tatar), Bahçesaray (Turkish), Bakhchisarai (Russian), or Bakhchysarai (Ukrainian), depending on the context. As an exception to this general rule, I privilege the traditional Crimean Tatar names for towns and villages that were assigned Russian toponyms after 1944 in Stalin's ethnic cleansing and "discursive cleansing" of the peninsula.

Finally, for the sake of consistency with sources, I use "Crimean Tatar" instead of the increasingly accepted "Qırımlı" to refer to the largest indigenous people of Crimea. I also avoid the shorthand "Tatar" in favour of "Crimean Tatar," even when context may make it obvious. The term "Tatar" can refer to many distinct ethnic groups and nations across Europe and Eurasia, and Soviet authorities attempted to leverage this fact to de-territorialize Crimean Tatar national identity after 1967, referring to them as "Tatars, formerly resident in Crimea." Given this history, and with thousands of Crimean Tatars now displaced after Russia's 2014 annexation of Ukraine's Autonomous Republic of Crimea, I consistently underscore the specific territoriality of this identity.

BLOOD OF OTHERS

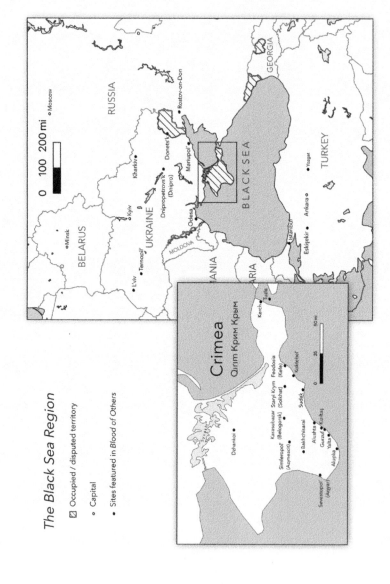

The Black Sea Region

☒ Occupied / disputed territory

○ Capital

• Sites featured in *Blood of Others*

1. Map of the Black Sea region

Introduction

In 1963 Liliia Karas attended a poetry reading in the centre of her home-town of Kharkiv, in eastern Soviet Ukraine. The venue was the city's central lecture hall near Televev Square, today's Maidan Konstytutsiï (Constitution Square). Its seats were filled to capacity. Only months earlier, Liliia had returned to Kharkiv from Siberia, where her Jewish family had settled upon Hitler's invasion of the Soviet Union in 1941. Simple chance and a vague longing for home brought her back to the place of her birth toward the end of Nikita Khrushchev's Thaw. And curiosity brought her to Kharkiv's *lektorii* to hear a group of local poets, one of whom was eliciting excited whispers from the crowd. His name was Boris Chichibabin (Boris Polushin, 1923–1994).

Liliia would later save this poet's life.[1] In 1967 she would become his wife, his best friend, his muse. But on this evening in 1963, Liliia Karas and Boris Chichibabin were strangers. He strode on stage at the end of the evening, a tall man with a striking red beard, facing what had become a tired crowd. He proceeded to take their breath away. "People were not breathing," recalled writer Renata Mukha in 2008. "And Boris was not breathing either. There was not one pause between one poem and the next. Not one second."[2] He recited his verse from memory in loud but lissom tones, his head nodding to and fro to keep pace with each metrical foot. His only pause came at his conclusion. Shaking his gaze from a distant point in space and steadying it on the audience, Chichibabin met complete silence. "I had often read in books how peo-ple fail to applaud or speak when they are staggered by something they see," said Mukha. "I only witnessed such a thing once in my life. And that was then." Seconds later, the auditorium erupted in applause. As Mukha put it, "it was a kind of liberation of the soul."[3]

Liliia Karas felt shivers up her spine during Chichibabin's per-formance. In a volume of reminiscences, she recalls a particular unpublished poem "searing itself into her memory" that evening. It was called "Krymskie progulki" (Crimean strolls, 1959–60).[4] Despite its innocuous title, the work confronts one of the most indelible crimes of the Stalinist period: the brutal 1944 deportation of the Crimean Tatars from their ancestral homeland along the Black Sea, an event that ultimately claimed the lives of tens of thousands of victims – mostly women, children, and the elderly. It was Stalin's Crimean atrocity, an act declared "barbaric" by the Supreme Soviet of the Union of Soviet Socialist Republics (USSR) itself in 1989.[5] Today, especially after Russia's annexation of Crimea from Ukraine in 2014, the demographic, political, and cultural fallout from the deportation blankets the entire Black Sea region in ways both seen and unseen.

At the time of Chichibabin's performance in 1963, the deportation of the Crimean Tatars – a Sunni Muslim national minority numbering nearly 170,000 at the time – was deeply shrouded in silence and secrecy. Soviet authorities had officially vilified and blacklisted the *entire* Crimean Tatar people as collaborators with Nazi occupiers during the Second World War. In the so-called Secret Speech at the Twentieth Congress of the Communist Party in 1956, Khrushchev exposed Stalin's mass deportations of the Chechen, Karachay, Kalmyk, Ingush, and Balkar peoples and condemned them as "heinous" (vopiiushchie) acts.[6] He also decried the sweeping accusations of treason used as justification for their punishment. As Party member Fedor Burlatsky recalled, the revelations were like a bomb detonating in the Soviet consciousness.[7] But there was unexploded ordnance as well. Speaking in Moscow, Khrushchev made absolutely no mention of the Crimean Tatars (or the similarly exiled Meskhetian Turks and Volga Germans), who were still languishing in far-flung, restrictive "special settlement camps" in Central Asia and Siberia. They were Soviet "unpersons": expelled, forgotten, effaced from society.[8]

Chichibabin railed against this injustice in Kharkiv on that evening in 1963. He was a Red Army veteran and a Gulag survivor whose moral compass could quiver but never break. "He read 'Krymskie progulki' with such rage," remembers Liliia. His poem condemned as perverse the Soviet presentation of the ethnically cleansed peninsula as a "Russian riviera." It defiantly declared Crimea a land nourished by the "blood of Others," the Crimean Tatars. After his performance a woman from the audience rushed to the stage with accusations of treason. According to Liliia, Chichibabin was unfazed. "But I was shocked by the poem," she recalls. "I knew nothing about the deportation of the Crimean Tatars. *No one* knew anything about it."[9]

"Krymskie progulki" did more than simply inform Liliia and the audience about the deportation. "One of the first things the poem roused in me was tremendous empathy [*ogromnoe sochuvstvie*] for the Crimean Tatar people, who endured such terrible suffering."[10] It ignited a solidarity in Liliia Karas-Chichibabina that would endure for four decades, as the Crimean Tatars fought for social and cultural recognition and for the right to return to Crimea, mobilizing in the process "a mass movement unprecedented in Soviet history."[11] While her husband read "Krymskie progulki" in studios and gatherings in Kharkiv and Moscow, she circulated the poem in manuscript copies throughout the Soviet underground. Today, well after Chichibabin's death, "Krymskie progulki" appears in news articles and social media posts, a clarion call with new relevance after the 2014 annexation.[12] Liliia Karas-Chichibabina worked to secure a lasting place in cultural and social discourse for this appeal to conscience. Her encounter with literature inspired her to take action in the world, not without personal risk.

1.

This book is about the possibility of such encounters. It is about the way literature can reach us, change us, and make us actively disposed to the welfare of strangers, often against all odds. That literature presumably possesses such power has been an eternal refrain of writers and readers since Aristotle. It even became an early talking point in the 2020 campaign for the United States presidency.[13] Artists in war-torn countries equate it to a "moral vitamin."[14] But what makes this power possible, if it exists at all? How can poetry and prose help engender solidarity with Others who are distant and removed from us?

In recent decades, scholars outside the traditional bounds of literary studies – where, in fits and starts, prominent names from F.R. Leavis to Wayne Booth have advanced "ethical criticism" for generations – have answered such questions by variously positing that literature stretches the nets of kinship through a unique capacity to "manipulate sentiments," as Richard Rorty memorably put it.[15] They claim that its expansion and inflation of an "empathy circle" have facilitated the rise of human rights and led to a precipitous decline in cruelty and violence in the modern era.[16] They argue, in other words, that reading stops bleeding.

But what kind of reading? Much of this research rests on a series of observations of historical co-emergence rather than on close textual analysis. Steven Pinker, for instance, observes that the humanitarian revolution of the seventeenth and eighteenth centuries unfolded when Europe witnessed an explosion in book production and literacy.[17] Lynn Hunt connects the dots between the birth of human rights and the publication of epistolary novels like Richardson's *Pamela* and Rousseau's *Julie*, whose sympathetic and vividly drawn "ordinary" characters captivated readers across Europe.[18]

With a wide-angle lens, such historical-cum-sociological studies pan over centuries of intellectual history to reveal intriguing intersections between literature, law, and ethics. But they do not tighten focus enough on the dynamics of style, genre, and rhetoric to explain what makes these intersections possible. Part of the reason for this neglect is disciplinary, a product of what has come to be known since C.P. Snow as putatively discordant academic "cultures."[19] Scholars in the social sciences are trained in the structures and institutions of human relations; they are at home in the world of the empirical and the verifiable. Scholars in the humanities are trained in the vagaries of culture and the mechanics of artistic form; they are at home in the world of the imaginary and the unverifiable. Shuttling between these worlds – between text and reader, word and deed, artifice and affect – is a journey fraught with methodological and practical pitfalls.

Among the scholars who have undertaken this journey with a sense of purpose is Martha Nussbaum. In *Love's Knowledge: Essays on Philosophy and Literature* (1990) and *Poetic Justice: The Literary Imagination and Public Life* (1995), among other works, she ascribes to literature a central role in the cultivation of our moral imaginations. Matters of literary technique, structure, and style – from narrative voice in Beckett's *Molloy* trilogy to characterization in Henry James's *The Golden Bowl* – are never far from her field of view. Following Aristotle, she holds that the literary text offers the reader emotionally rich "patterns of possibility – of choice, and circumstance, and the interaction between choice and circumstance – that turn up in human lives with such a persistence that they must be regarded as *our* possibilities."[20] Following Adam Smith – who investigated the relation of sympathy to the imagination well before the relation of the market to human labour – Nussbaum explains that literature enlists us in exercises of entering into the perspective of literary personae, which in turn prepare us to step inside the shoes of Others in the real world.[21] Such perspective-taking is critical to the development of civil society, she argues, not without a penchant for the categorical.[22] For Nussbaum, literature "develops moral capacities without which citizens will not succeed in making reality out of the normative conclusions of any moral or political theory."[23] It is a space of what she calls, after Henry James, "projected morality."[24]

This space is largely narrative space in Nussbaum's work. In fact, in most research on the interplay between literature and ethics, there is little attention paid to anything beyond the novel or the short story.[25] This book attempts to redress the imbalance by including as an analytical concern the ethical potentialities of lyric poetry, which Nussbaum, with some exceptions, sets aside.[26] This avoidance of lyric poetry is understandable. Unlike the novel and the short story, lyric poems do not package instructive plots for our consumption or fashion characters for our emulation or disdain. They do not offer us a seat as an "impartial spectator," to use Smith's term, or promote perspective-taking in any conventional sense.[27] Taking presumes giving, and lyric poems do not give perspective per se. More often than not, they suspend it, they disguise it, they mourn its futility or question its very possibility.

Literature, in other words, *obscures* morality as much as it projects it, subjecting it to a play of revelation and concealment that provokes a reader's search for meaning. The outcome of this search – even its very perpetuation – is never a given. The reader can come and go as she pleases, and many stars must align to light the way toward prosocial destinations.[28] What this book seeks to understand are the textual conditions for those moments – inconsistent, infrequent, even rare, but precious all the same – when the work of the imagination makes us more attuned and responsive to the welfare of strangers. In pursuit of this understanding, I neither suggest that literature has an innate, unidirectional, autonomous connection to the ethical nor wish to imply that the value of literature and art is dependent on ethical outcomes. A key verb in this book is *invite*. Literature can just as well invite our boredom, feed our indifference, indulge our sensation-seeking, or impede our prosocial behaviour. In fact, as coming chapters will show, literary texts can co-opt readers in the legitimation of imperial conquest (chapter 1), spout state propaganda (chapter 3), and promote cultural stereotypes with militant fervour (chapter 6).

At the heart of this study, however, is a corpus of poems, novels, and short stories that work differently. These texts are the protagonists of the book, and they engage in heavy lifting. They strive to summon the better angels of our nature and to cultivate – however imperfectly – bonds of solidarity with Others, often where and when they are least expected. Like Chichibabin's "Krymskie progulki," many of these texts were transcribed privately, recited publicly, and passed hand to hand underground by the hundreds, when such activity could lead to arrest, imprisonment, or exile. Some were published with official sanction, only to attract controversy upon their release. As we will see, most of them are recognized as having been *effective* in the work of solidarity.

Their real-world consequences are not a matter of conjecture or thought experiment. They were cited in court cases, military correspondence, and memoranda of the Komitet Gosudarstvennoi Bezopasnosti (KGB, Committee of State Security). Especially among Stalin's victims, these texts are remembered as *having mattered*. So what makes this efficacy possible?

The experiences of readers like Liliia Karas-Chichibabina – who chanced upon a poem and then undertook the risks of its circulation to support the rights of a group to which she did not belong – demand new approaches to such questions. To this point, our prevailing practice has been to attempt answers by sampling on the dependent variable. We tend to cherry-pick canonical English-language texts to substantiate claims without much cultural or historical context, a kind of interpretative reverse engineering. Nussbaum, for instance, gestures to a variety of pregnant moments of literary perspective-taking in the canonical works of Dickens, Ellison, and Henry James and then uses these moments as evidence of literature's utility as "moral technology," to use Pinker's term.[29] Rorty selects Nabokov – and through Nabokov, Dickens – to argue that literature short-circuits human cruelty "from the inside," inviting the reader to re-examine and "redescribe" herself.[30] Scholars in the growing field of cognitive poetics, which seeks to apply insights from cognitive linguistics and cognitive science to the study of works of literature, often operate in a similar fashion, peppering their conceptual models with emblematic and supportive passages from Shelley to Keats, for example.[31]

Blood of Others, by contrast, attempts an answer by exploring a diverse array of both canonical and non-canonical literary works across different languages but within an organized territorial and temporal frame. Rooted in the traditional tactics of comparative literature studies, it seeks to understand what I call the poetics of solidarity by following the cultural repercussions of a historical event wherever they lead. These itineraries may be unpredictable, but they are not without logic or structure. Imagine for a moment the breathtaking experiments conducted in the field of cymatics, which reveal the effects of vibrations on physical surfaces.[32] In controlled agitations of grains of white sand on acoustic plates, they make manifest the power of a sonic frequency to move and organize or reorganize matter in space. Sound a frequency, and the sand grains race across the plate to create a pattern, from rudimentary ovals to elaborate forms reminiscent of mandalas or zodiac wheels. Adjust the frequency, and a new pattern emerges.

Historical events behave in much the same way. They push us toward and away from each other, crafting our understandings of self and Other, in-group and out-group. As Hayden White explains, historical events "shock" the system and "spread out" across time and space, swaying individuals and groups and their interrelationships.[33] Their vibrations at once scatter and shape forms of human attachment, which materialize at a fundamental level in cultural expression.[34] This book accordingly envisions historical events as vibrational phenomena organizing or reorganizing human relationships across cultural surfaces. It not only tracks vibrations as artistic allusions, intertexts, and representations across linguistic and national borders – thereby mapping what Rilke, a poet enamoured with the idea of artistic expression as vibration, might call a "vibration-sphere" (Schwingungs-Sphäre)[35] – but also considers via close reading the responses of implied readers to these meetings of text and event, to these intricate patterns of grains of sand.

My approach seeks to pre-empt two persistent habits in the study of literature and culture. The first is our recourse to dichotomies of canonical versus non-canonical, official versus unofficial, high versus low, centre versus periphery. Entailing the study of any literary text through which a particular event lingers and resounds – regardless of standing, prestige, or position – this methodology is cold to such Manichaean enthusiasms. The second habit is our delimitation of analytical itineraries at the borders of the nation-state, our tether to national predicates.[36] By exploring a vibration-sphere over, under, and through national borders, I seek to avoid methodological nationalism and combat what René Wellek memorably called the "false isolation of national literary histories."[37] At the same time, sensitive to the multidimensionality of cultural exchange, I do not dismiss or discount national borders in a postnational or cosmopolitan reverie. Behind my approach is an acknowledgment that the need to perforate and transcend such boundaries is always and already a measure of their ubiquity and political and cultural force.

In this book I explore a region of the world where borders and boundaries are disproportionately unsettled, a "wobbly geography" where the political condition of "in-between" is never very far from home.[38] At the centre of our attention is the historical event whose repercussions were powerfully felt in the first encounter between Boris Chichibabin and Liliia Karas in Kharkiv: the deportation of the Crimean Tatars in May 1944. As we will see, this Stalinist atrocity has coursed through Russia, Turkey, and Ukraine to reveal a vibration-sphere with particular urgency today, a cultural space broadly shaped, as the geographers of antiquity once mused, like a Scythian bow. This space is the Black Sea region; its nexus is Crimea.

2.

Strabo was among the first to envision the Black Sea according to the contours of the fabled weapon of the ancient Scythians, who ruled the lower Dnipro delta and the Crimean peninsula with legendary ferocity in his lifetime. They "ate the flesh [of their enemies]," Strabo intones, "and used their sculls as drinking-cups."[39] In his colourful imagination the Scythian bow evoked the shape of the Black Sea by way of its four key components. The wooden stave of the bow is formed of two arcs, with a handle inset between them; for Strabo, it mirrored the two undulations of the Black Sea's northern shore – today dominated by Ukraine and Russia – which are joined by the "protruding" (προπίπτω, propipto) peninsula of Crimea (fig. 2). For Strabo, the bow's string followed the "straight line" of the Anatolian coast, which is now the northern border of the Republic of Turkey.[40] This seminal conceptualization of the Black Sea focuses our attention on the territories of Ukraine, Russia, and Turkey – which are today "the major players in the region by all important measures of power"[41] – and refashions their boundaries as interdependent elements of one cohesive apparatus, with Crimea as their fulcrum. In other words, it integrates what has been conventionally disconnected in academic work, divided between the fields of Slavic Studies and Middle Eastern Studies. This book adopts Strabo's vision, conceiving of the Black Sea as a site and a source of connection and exchange for Russia, Turkey, and Ukraine – in contrast to a prevailing scholarly practice that, as Charles King notes, situates its shores in several different regional specializations but at the centre of none of them.[42]

Such a realignment of our intellectual horizons is long overdue. The Black Sea sits "at the crossroads of the main axes of interaction across Eurasia."[43] It has long been considered "one of the cornerstones of Euro-Asian stability," and today the stone has been shaken. Not far from its shores are no less than six controversial breakaway polities – from criminogenic no man's lands to Kremlin puppet statelets – vying for diplomatic recognition from the international community. Since 2008 alone the Black Sea region has seen two wars, a revolution, and an audacious Anschluss. Russia's illegal seizure and annexation of Ukraine's Autonomous Republic of Crimea in 2014, which has produced "an international armed conflict between Ukraine and the Russian Federation," according to the International Criminal Court, has drawn back the Scythian bow, subjecting relations between the three countries to increasing tension.[44] Today, engaged in an undeclared war with Moscow, Ukraine calls on Turkey to close the straits of the Bosporus and the

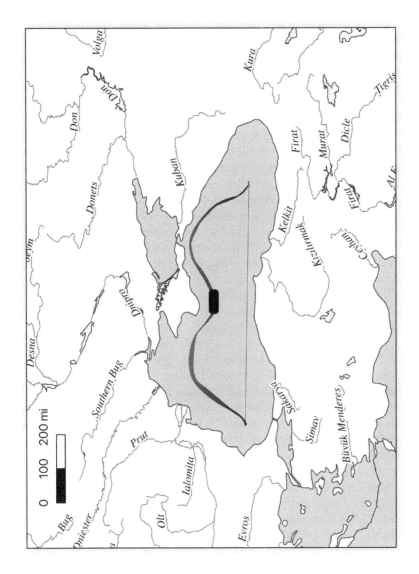

2. Map of the Black Sea and the Scythian Bow

Dardanelles to Russian vessels; Russian generals celebrate a new dominance over the Turkish navy while masking and denying aggression against Ukraine; Turkey fires on Russian jets and partners with Ukraine in exercises of the North Atlantic Treaty Organization (NATO).[45] In the words of Neal Ascherson, "the world has learned to worry about the Black Sea region."[46]

These developments grab occasional newspaper headlines and spark the industry of think-tanks and geopolitical forecasters, but we direct little study to the transnational sociocultural factors that may drive and underpin them. Indeed, what Georges Bratianu once termed the *"Question de la mer Noire"* remains overwhelmingly the domain of economics, ancient history, and international relations – but not the study of literature and culture.[47] Behind this book is a conviction that more comparative humanistic inquiry must be brought to bear on our understanding of this complex, unstable region, which only coheres as such due to a network of human relationships and to the individuals who seed and cultivate them: region makers. Over one hundred years ago the Azerbaijani poet Ahmad Cavad forever bound the Black Sea to one verb – *çırpınmak* (to convulse).[48] As the region convulses today in fits of fellowship and fear, we need now more than ever to chart and navigate the flows of ideas, narratives, and identities between Russia, Turkey, and Ukraine. We need what the Ukrainian historian Mykhailo Hrushevsky called a deeper "Black Sea orientation" – a more dynamic interdisciplinary field of Black Sea Studies.[49]

Literature is fertile soil in such a field. Traditionally, in the region of the Black Sea, literature has been or has been thought to be serious business. "The business of literature," wrote the Russian critic Vissarion Belinsky in 1841, should "not be some respite from life's troubles, a nap in plush armchairs after a rich meal ... but a *res publica*, a public thing, powerful and significant."[50] In a similar vein, the Ukrainian writer Panteleimon Kulish called on readers in the journal *Osnova* (The Foundation) in 1860 to view literary texts "not as written trifles but as a part of our common public life."[51] The leading Ottoman intellectual Namık Kemal, writing in the pages of *Tasvir-i Efkâr* (Interpreter of Ideas) in the 1860s, put the matter more succinctly and with Romantic flourish: "Literature should be the soul of a nation" (Edebiyat, bir milletin ruhu ... olmalıdır).[52]

What Eric Hobsbawm calls the "short twentieth century" thus began in Russia, Turkey, and Ukraine with dictatorships vigorously positioning literature as an instrument of policy. The Soviet Union and the early Republic of Turkey each embarked in the 1920s on ambitious top-down reform agendas designed under one-party rule to delegitimize imperial pasts and to secularize and modernize "backward" societies.

Vladimir Lenin called for the popular distribution of "serious and valued literary material [and] the best classical fiction" ahead of agricultural and industrial textbooks to facilitate the passage "from capitalism to Communism."[53] Soviet Ukraine's Commissar for Education Mykola Skrypnyk, meanwhile, greeted a prominent literary conference by saying that "in Ukraine, where not long ago virtually every political activist was also a writer ... *belles lettres* bears tremendous significance in the elevation and development of the wide working masses."[54] Across the Black Sea, Mustafa Kemal Atatürk designed his Ministry of Culture in the belief that literature was "one of the most fundamental teaching tools" (en esaslı terbiye vasıtalarından) in the project "to protect and preserve the present and future" of the young republic.[55] He celebrated the figure of the poet as one "who hears *and enables others to hear* delicate, lofty, deep, and pure emotions."[56] To this day, Turkish verse celebrating the state and its progenitor often falls under the name Atatürk şiiri (Atatürk poetry).[57] Nazım Hikmet, arguably the greatest Turkish poet of the twentieth century, was a devoted Communist at ideological loggerheads with Atatürk, but on the subject of the place of literature in society the two men saw eye to eye. In a poem dedicated to Ukraine's godfather Taras Shevchenko, Hikmet declares, "Şiir düşmeli [...] halkın önüne" (A poem should always lead the people).[58] Times have changed, but literature still bears unique political and social currency in the region. In 1999, years before becoming prime minister of Turkey, Recep Tayyip Erdoğan went to prison for five months in western Thrace. His purported crime was reading a poem that, in his words, made "the people spirited."[59]

The Russian language has a term for this central standing of literature in society: *literaturotsentrichnost*. "Literature-centrality" both reflects and promotes a role for literature in key processes of social integration and interaction, and it makes the Black Sea region a unique laboratory for the study of the poetics of solidarity. For the Crimean Tatars, one of the indigenous peoples of the Black Sea region, literature has been a cherished but besieged source of social cohesion, as we will see in chapters 2 and 3. The Crimean Tatar poet Şakir Selim describes its pivotal significance by way of two vibrant metaphors: "The homeland and poetry [*vatan ve şiiriet*] are twins of the same blood," while "the homeland without poetry is a stone lying in the road."[60]

3.

The modern history of the Crimean Tatar *vatan* (homeland) is a story of cycles of displacement, expulsion, and resistance. It takes place against the backdrop of settler colonialism in Crimea, a defining historical and political phenomenon too often swept under the academic rug and ignored in political discourse. Descended from an array of ethnic groups with roots in antiquity and from the Mongol nomads of the thirteenth-century Golden Horde, the Crimean Tatars are an indigenous people of Crimea whose khanate wielded significant political and military control over the peninsula and the inland steppe region for more than three centuries (1443–1783).[61] In 1783, after invading Crimea four times between 1772 and 1782, Catherine II annexed the peninsula to the Russian Empire. The demise of the khanate triggered an infusion of Russian imperial subjects and foreign colonists and a slow-burning physical and cultural displacement of the Crimean Tatars from their homeland. Successive waves of Crimean Tatars fled to the Ottoman Empire during the nineteenth century, with migrations spiking after the Crimean War, when the Crimean Tatars were falsely accused, not for the last time, of mass treason.[62] In 1857, Tsar Aleksandr II spoke explicitly of "the cleansing [ochishchenie] of the Tatars from the entire Crimean peninsula" and their replacement by "peasants from internal provinces" of the empire.[63]

By the turn of the twentieth century the Crimean Tatars had dwindled from the majority to a minority on the Black Sea peninsula. A glimmer of hope for a recovery of lost sovereignty and independence came in the winter of 1917, when young activists led by Noman Çelebicihan convened a national assembly, the Qurultay, which sought to govern as a national parliament for all Crimeans amid the chaos of revolution. The demise of the Qurultay and the rise of Bolshevik power in 1918 soon unleashed mass killings and eventually famine on the peninsula. Clouds started to lift, however, from 1921, when the Soviet government began to foster the development of Crimean Tatar institutions within the bounds of a newly declared Crimean Autonomous Soviet Socialist Republic (ASSR) in accordance with its broader policy of korenizatsiia (indigenization).[64] Under the leadership of Veli İbraimov as chairman of the Crimean Central Committee (1923–8), Crimea saw a "Tatarization" of political culture, a redistribution of land to Crimean Tatar villagers, and a growth of new Crimean Tatar–administered schools and cultural production.[65] Yet the halcyon days of the İbraimov era were soon brought to an abrupt end by Stalin, who used the slightest pretext to arrest and execute İbraimov in 1928.[66]

The entire Crimean Tatar nation was subjected to Stalin's violence after the three-year Nazi occupation of the peninsula during the Second World War. Beginning on the night of 18 May 1944, the Crimean Tatars were given minutes to collect their belongings, ordered from their homes at gunpoint, and herded onto the cattle-cars of waiting trains bound for destinations in Central Asia and the Ural Mountains by thousands of officers of the Narodnyi komissariat vnutrennikh del (NKVD, People's Commissariat of Internal Affairs).[67] According to witnesses, the sick and injured who were not fit for transit were "liquidated."[68] Those who openly defied the deportation order were shot.[69] This act of ethnic cleansing, which also engulfed Crimea's Greek, Armenian, and Bulgarian communities, came at the prompting of NKVD chief Lavrenty Beriia, who noted on 10 May 1944 the "undesirability [*nezhelatelnost*] of the continued residence of the Crimean Tatars in the border areas of the Soviet Union," and at the order of Stalin, whose secret Decree 5859ss of 11 May accused "many Crimean Tatars" (mnogie krymskie tatary) of collaborating with Nazi occupiers during the Second World War and then mandated the expulsion of "all of them" (vse tatary).[70]

Like all ethnic groups in Crimea – including Russians, Ukrainians, and even Jewish Karaites – a number of Crimean Tatars did collaborate with Nazi forces during the war.[71] The scholarly consensus places this number at roughly twenty thousand, or 10 per cent of the Crimean Tatar population at the time.[72] In Crimea, as elsewhere in the war-torn Soviet Union, the reasons for this "betrayal" were various: forced conscription; a legacy of arrests, executions, and artificial famines under Stalinist rule; and provocations and offences committed against Crimean Tatar communities by Soviet partisans during the Second World War.[73] Nevertheless, the large majority of Crimean Tatars fought on the Soviet side and "put their lives on the line in the struggle against Nazi invaders both on Crimean soil and on other fronts."[74] Thousands won medals and orders from the Soviet state for their service in the Red Army; six became Heroes of the Soviet Union.[75] Among the Soviet partisans fighting the Germans in the Crimean underground, the Crimean Tatars were the second largest ethnic group after the Russians.[76] Stalin's decision to exile the entire Crimean Tatar nation – largely women, children, and the elderly, given that most of the Crimean Tatar Hilfswillige (or Hiwis, "helpers") had already retreated westward with the Wehrmacht by the time of the deportation[77] – therefore seems to have been less about punitive retribution than about contingency planning for future military conflict. As Beriia implies in his communiqué of 10 May 1944, the Crimean Tatars were seen as an "undesirable" Muslim fifth column, particularly in a potential war with Turkey over control of the straits of the Bosporus and Dardanelles.[78] Geostrategic anxiety was the real reason for the deportation.[79]

Stalin's Decree 5859ss was enveloped in such secrecy that the NKVD soldiers who carried out the deportation learned of it only moments before the victims themselves did.[80] The operation was directly overseen by leading NKVD commissars Bogdan Kobulov and Ivan Serov, whose telegrams to Beriia document its rapid execution: an average of nearly seventy thousand men, women, and children were "loaded" (pogruzheny) onto trains each day between 18 May and 20 May 1944.[81] According to witnesses, this loading was often preceded by the forcible separation of children from their parents. "Between the threshold of their home and the door of the train car," observes historian Valery Vozgrin, the Crimean Tatar deportees all considered "the violent separation of families the greatest tragedy of all."[82] Because the order of train cars was reconfigured and redirected along the routes eastward, families initially divided by only one railway coupling were often divided forever, scattered between the Urals, Siberia, Uzbekistan, and Kazakhstan.[83]

What Beriia, Kobulov, and Serov term *the operation* in their internal communication is now remembered as Sürgün (The Exile) in the Crimean Tatar language, an event of brutal dispossession and mass death.[84] Train cars marked for "40 people or 8 horses" were packed with roughly 150 men, women, and children.[85] The doors to the cars did not open for eighteen days.[86] There were no toilets. There was no drinking water: deportees survived on rain run-off collected through gaps and holes in the cars. As a result, thousands of the deportees died over the course of the journey from inhumane conditions, lack of water and food, and vicious treatment by the NKVD.[87] Even after their arrival, thousands more perished from hunger, exposure, and disease in *spetsposeleniia* (special settlement camps).[88] Many Crimean Tatars believe that half of the entire population died in the first years of exile.[89]

This ethnic cleansing of Crimea had two other co-conspirators: "discursive cleansing" and "ethnic cloning," both of which are explored in chapters 3 and 7. Traces of the Crimean Tatars were wiped off the map and torn from encyclopaedias, their dwellings and property redistributed to the Slavic settlers recruited by the Soviet state to replace them. In 1944 Crimea also fell in the Soviet administrative hierarchy from an ASSR to a mere oblast of the Russian Soviet Federative Socialist Republic (RSFSR), where its economy languished without the Crimean Tatars.[90] It became "poorer, wanting, confused."[91] According to Dmitry Poliansky, who served as head of the Communist Party in Crimea from 1953 to 1954, Khrushchev believed that "Russia had paid little attention to Crimea's development" and that "Ukraine could handle it more concertedly."[92] In February 1954 the Presidium of the Supreme Soviet accordingly announced the formal transfer of the Crimean oblast from Soviet Russia to Soviet Ukraine, with Russian politician Mikhail Tarasov opening discussion of the decision by describing Crimea as a "natural continuation of Ukraine's southern steppe," whose economy was "closely tied" to that of Ukraine.[93]

Meanwhile, thousands of miles away from their homeland, the Crimean Tatars responded to the trauma of their displacement by mounting the largest, most organized, and most sustained movement of dissent in Soviet history. It was a highly disciplined campaign for recognition and repatriation founded on principles of non-violent resistance against state injustice and oppression, and its influence on the organizational infrastructure and moral direction of Soviet dissent as a whole was indelible and profound. Crimean Tatar "information bulletins" documenting state abuses were the inspiration behind the meticulous and clinical *Khronika tekushchykh sobytii* (*Chronicle of Current Events*), for instance, while their "initiative groups" were the model and the eponym for the Initiative Group for the Defense of Human Rights in the USSR, the "trailblazing" collective hailed as the first autonomous non-governmental organization (NGO) in the Soviet Union.[94]

Among the leaders guiding the Crimean Tatar movement in this period was Mustafa Dzhemilev (Mustafa Cemiloğlu, aka Mustafa Abdülcemil Qırımoğlu). Although short in stature, Dzhemilev is a giant. As an infant, he survived the deportation to Central Asia. As a young man, he survived the Gulag, enduring a 303-day hunger strike in the mid-1970s that garnered headlines around the world and prompted false pronouncements of his death. His leadership helped the Crimean Tatars prevail over the Soviet system and win the right to return to Crimea in the twilight of Mikhail Gorbachev's rule. In 1989, Dzhemilev settled in the homeland that he fought his entire life to reclaim for his people.

The dissolution of the Soviet Union, however, offered few "happily ever afters." It brought poverty and a new struggle against local political and cultural chauvinism on the peninsula. Dzhemilev and the elected assembly of the Crimean Tatar people, known as the Mejlis (or Meclis), responded by working with newly independent Ukraine and with Turkey to facilitate their reintegration into Crimean life. Despite many flaws and frustrations, the relationship between the Mejlis and Kyiv after 1991 was a "unique, almost singular example in the entire post-Soviet ethno-political space of a small nation's loyalty to a young independent state," as Svetlana Chervonnaia explains.[95] But by 2013 it still had not led to a key desideratum of the Crimean Tatar movement: formal recognition as an indigenous people of Ukraine. That would only occur in March 2014, after Russian forces had taken control of the peninsula – after it was too late.

Russia's breakneck annexation of Crimea changed everything. Almost overnight, activists associated with the Mejlis began to endure arrests, detentions, and expulsions at the hands of de facto Russian authorities. Public commemorations of the deportation on 18 May were banned. Tens of thousands of Crimean Tatars fled Crimea for mainland Ukraine, becoming the largest group of internally displaced persons (IDPs) in the country. Dzhemilev and his compatriot Refat Chubarov, chair of the Mejlis, were forbidden to set foot on the peninsula. Others like Ilmi Umerov, deputy chair of the Mejlis – who declared to Russian security services in May 2016 that "I do not consider Crimea part of the Russian Federation" – were subjected to forced treatment in a psychiatric hospital.[96] These new crackdowns on Crimean Tatar civil society have become arrows in the Scythian bow, tensing ties between Russia, Turkey, and Ukraine.

4.

For the Black Sea region as a whole, Stalin's Crimean atrocity may be considered the most enduring *centripetal event* of the twentieth century. No other historical event has fixed the attention of publics and political actors in Russia, Turkey, and Ukraine and directed them to a single regional problem with such geopolitical, ethical, and religious import for as long.[97] Its peculiar force was evident on the world stage during the 2016 Eurovision Song Contest, when Crimean Tatar singer Jamala and her song "1944" represented Ukraine and became an international *cause célèbre*. The song is a galvanic ballad interspersing indirect English-language references to Stalin's Crimean atrocity – "When strangers are coming / They come to your house / They kill you all" – with Crimean Tatar–language lyrics from the Soviet-era lament "Ey Güzel Qırım" (O beautiful Crimea) that mourn a life and a home stolen: "Men bu yerde yaşalmadım / Yaşlığıma toyalmadım" (I could not live in this place / My youth was taken from me).[98] Jamala's victory at Eurovision caused Crimean Tatars and Ukrainians to rejoice, Russian state television to cry foul, and Turks, led by President Erdoğan, to applaud.[99] It was a pop cultural manifestation of the way in which the deportation and its legacy have long ensnared Crimean Tatar civic activists, Ukrainian national democrats, Russian neo-imperialists, and Turkish secular and Islamist interest groups in pitched battles over public memory, human rights, historical reparation, and political representation.

Powering this centripetal force has been a perennial push and pull over the very issue of *possession* of the Crimean peninsula. After centuries of colonial rule, Stalin's attempt to efface Crimea's indigenous population was a paroxysm of ontopolitical insecurity that sought to settle this issue once and for all. As we shall see, it did the opposite, exacerbating rather than exorcizing these anxieties of possession. The deportation sacralized the territorial nationalism of the Crimean Tatars, sparked outrage among the Turkish military, and – by becoming a symbol of rot at the roots of Soviet society – mobilized readers like Liliia Karas-Chichibabina in protest against crimes of the state. In other words, the deportation represents a key source of what Gwendolyn Sasse describes as Crimea's "structural predisposition" to conflict.[100] It is a kind of originary fault in the design of Crimean sovereignty to which contemporary fissures directly or indirectly refer.

Today, three decades after the fall of the Soviet Union and over eight years since Russia's annexation, Crimea remains a territory upon which possessive pronouns clamber. Russian writer and filmmaker Arkady Arkanov satirized this condition by proposing a video game called *Chei Krym?* (Whose Crimea? Or to whom does Crimea belong?)[101] Since 2014, despite the clear international legal consensus that Crimea is sovereign Ukrainian territory under Russian military and political occupation, many Russians have replied to the question "Chei Krym?" with a defiant meme – *KrymNash* (Crimea is ours) – whose very ubiquity and ipse-dixitism betray a fundamental uneasiness about possession of the "fateful peninsula." As Edward Said observes, "if you belong in a place, you do not need to keep saying and showing it, [but] colonial appropriation requires such assertive inflections."[102] The anxiety behind such assertive inflections has sparked a widespread contestation of identities. When Jamala was producing "1944" in advance of Eurovision, for instance, the Simferopol band Undervud released a radically different song whose bouncy, even maudlin whistling melody clashes with a telling chorus: "Tell me who Crimea belongs to, and I will tell you who you are."[103]

Possession and its conceptual siblings, dispossession and repossession, help to structure the chapters of this book into three parts, which traverse three centuries and explore artistic works in four languages to offer a unique cultural history of the Black Sea. Part 1, "Possession," delves into the past to explain the cultural conditions of the very possibility of Stalin's Crimean atrocity and of its ultimate failure. Solidarity is about overcoming distance, and here I take care to establish the historico-cultural framework that allows us to measure distances across the literary landscapes of Russia, Turkey, and Ukraine. My points of orientation are representations of and by the Crimean Tatars, a people caught in 1783 between an expanding Russian Empire and a contracting Ottoman Empire. These two imperial powers antagonized and repelled each other, but they were kept in contact by a Russian project of settler colonialism in Crimea that turned the Black Sea into a highway of migrants and refugees.

Settler colonialism occurs when an empire displaces and replaces a conquered native population. In our study of Crimea it is a historical phenomenon rarely acknowledged outright, but its legacy is responsible for making the peninsula a geopolitical flashpoint. I explore this legacy through the operation of what I call a *dialectic of imperial possession* in Russian, Turkish, Ukrainian, and Crimean Tatar literatures – in classics by such writers as Aleksandr Pushkin, Namık Kemal, Lesia Ukraïnka, and Üsein Şâmil Toktargazy. As we will see, the texts engaged this dialectic by conceptually de-Tatarizing or re-Tatarizing Crimea. In spite of their differences, they all proceeded from the same starting point: the idea that Crimean territory and Tatar culture were bound together. How these canonical texts then treated this bond can teach us a great deal about national imaginations across the shores of the Black Sea.

Part 2, "Dispossession," represents the book's centre of gravity. It is the untold story of responses in Crimean Tatar, Russian, Turkish, and Ukrainian literatures to Stalin's attempt to eviscerate the human, material, and cultural traces of Crimea's indigenous population through acts of both ethnic cleansing and discursive cleansing. Many of these texts, such as the *samizdat* or *samvydav* (self-published, in Russian and Ukrainian respectively) poetry of Boris Chichibabin and Ivan Sokulsky, were produced clandestinely and circulated at risk of arrest under Article 70 of the Soviet Criminal Code. Other texts, like the novels of Cengiz Dağcı and his imitators, became assigned reading for students and recommended literature for soldiers in the Turkish military. Nearly all of them, I argue, seek to foster relations of solidarity with the Crimean Tatars by inviting readers to confront and process reparative guilt rather than avoidant shame. This literary "guilt-processing" is a vital agent of the poetics of solidarity. As I define it, solidarity is an active convergence of interests and fellow feeling between groups that bridges a distance. It is achieved, not given – a dynamic physics of human connection that can turn outsiders into insiders. The story of these texts in the service of solidarity is vivid evidence of a productive intervention of art into socio-politics and a reminder of the power of culture to transform, as Timothy Snyder would put it, "bloodlands" into "brotherlands."[104]

Part 3, "Repossession," surveys the politico-cultural landscape of the Black Sea region after the return of the Crimean Tatars to their ancestral homeland and in the aftermath of Russia's annexation of Crimea. Following the collapse of the Soviet Union, this landscape was especially bumpy and uneven. Due to a failure to acknowledge and address the unique demands of its decolonization, Crimea became a space of ad hoc political strategies and fitful cultural activity, where a Crimean Tatar, Ukrainian, and Russian interliterary discourse did not evolve. Over time, however, one potent selective affinity emerged from this space: Ukrainian–Crimean Tatar solidarity. From the prose of Şamil Alâdin to the poetry of Serhiy Zhadan, from the poetic cinema of Oles Sanin's *Mamai* (2003) to the nostos drama of Nariman Aliev's *Evge* (*Homeward*, 2019), I follow its development through discourses of *encounter* and *entanglement* to a discourse of *enclosure*, of home. As we will see, this relationship has helped secure civic nationalism as the main driver of Ukrainian politics, turning a small Sunni Muslim people into a shaper of national identity in the largest country within Europe – and advancing a promising model of interethnic co-operation for the entire region of the Black Sea.

PART ONE

Possession

Chapter One

Imperial Objects

In May 1787, Russian empress Catherine II strode solemnly into what had been for centuries the palace of the Crimean Tatar khan in Bağçasaray, nestled in the Çürük Suv valley in southern Crimea. She ascended the throne of the *hansaray*, we are told, with "satisfaction."[1] After repeated invasions and abortive treaties Catherine had subdued the Crimean Tatar khanate and annexed its territory to the Russian Empire only years before, in 1783. It was a hotly contested land grab. Across the Black Sea, Ottoman Sultan Abdülhamid I still considered himself suzerain over Crimea. He refused to acknowledge Russian control. Months after the annexation, his new grand vizier, Koca Yusuf Paşa, hurriedly summoned a brain trust to Neşatabad Palace along the banks of the Bosporus in Istanbul to discuss, belatedly, "the determination of the Russians to take over Crimea completely" (Rusyalunun Kırım'ı bi'l-külliye zabt etmek iradesi).[2] An account of the deliberations at Neşatabad reveals that the Sublime Porte had not accepted the loss of Crimea – "*ma'azallahu*" (God forbid) – or come entirely to grips with the threat of a Russian Empire scheming to extend its borders "from the Baltic Sea to the Mediterranean Sea."[3]

In Bağçasaray, Catherine indeed personified an empire on the march. Her storied journey from Saint Petersburg was an event intended in its grandeur to "add something to the history of Crimea," as the Latin American revolutionary Francisco de Miranda recalled her words.[4] Accompanying Catherine was a vast imperial retinue that included Belgian Prince de Ligne (Charles-Joseph Lamoral) and French diplomat Louis Philippe, comte de Ségur. The retinue was not short on pomp or pedigree, but its arrival in the former seat of Crimean Tatar power in Bağçasaray failed to elicit the expected awe and wonder from many local residents. As Ségur recalls in his memoirs, some Crimean Tatars averted their gaze and even turned their backs on Catherine's procession, "preserving their stupid pride [*orgueil stupide*], even when they are conquered."[5]

Acts of defiance among communities of the colonized are too often absent in the pages of such chauvinistic imperialist writing. If only fleetingly and unwittingly in his memoirs, Ségur cedes space for them. In one vivid episode, the Crimean Tatars of Bağçasaray – who remain mostly entrapped in his account as "subjugated" (soumis) imperial objects deprived of agency – did more than look away in resistance; they confronted him with force. At Ligne's invitation Ségur had set out on a hunt outside of town to find uncovered Crimean Tatar women. "What pleasure is there in touring a vast garden," Ligne said to him, "where we are not allowed to examine the flowers?"[6] After wandering for hours, Ségur and Ligne came upon three women washing their feet in a brook and positioned themselves behind a thicket of trees, ogling like schoolboys. They were quickly discovered. The women screamed, and Crimean Tatar men ran to the scene, flashing daggers and throwing stones. Catherine's foreign dignitaries, as it were, fled.[7]

Later Ségur attempts a more serious and scrupulous tone. He explains that Ligne unwisely proceeded to regale the imperial retinue at dinner with the story of this encounter to enliven the mood. Everyone erupted in laughter, save a "*sévère*" Catherine. "You are living among a people conquered by my arms [*conquis par mes armes*]," she admonished them, "and I wish their laws, their religion, their manners, and their habits to be respected."[8] She echoed her lover, fixer, and factotum Grigory Potemkin, who years before had frantically sought to stop grievous abuses of the Crimean Tatar population at the hands of Russian troops by commanding one of his generals, with abundant military circumlocution, to "allow the Tatars to feel the benefits of their current condition."[9]

Living among the Crimean Tatars provoked not only stern lectures but awkward attempts at poetry by Catherine, including a poem that did not quite model the respect she demanded of her company. In a trifle of verse sent to Potemkin, Catherine reduced the customs and practices of the Crimean Tatars in Bağçasaray to annoyances. They interfered with a good night's sleep. Resting near one of the mosques of the khan's palace, her eyes growing heavy, she was roused uncomfortably by the imam's call to prayer: "Disrupting my sleep in Bakhchisarai / Are shouts [of the imam] and tobacco smoke … Is there here not a place of paradise? [*Ne zdes li mesto raia?*]"[10]

Either by telling raucous, ribald stories or penning rhyming lines, Ségur and Catherine both make clear that the act of representing Crimea upon its absorption into the Russian Empire – at a pivotal time of political and cultural consolidation of imperial authority – was above all an exercise in observing, figuring, and even pursuing the Crimean Tatar Other. To be sure, Catherine sought to project Crimea as part of ancient Hellas reclaimed, renaming the peninsula "Tavrida" (Taurus) and towns like Aqmescit "Simferopol," as part of a broader "Greek project."[11] But this project was often little more than elite window dressing. As we shall see, the Crimean annexation captured the public imagination most powerfully as a defeat of the exotic Crimean Tatar khanate, not as a "mystical," as Potemkin put it, resurrection of classical antiquity.[12] Crimea may have been anointed in neoclassical fashion as the new Greece, but it was *consumed* with Romantic ardour as the conquered land of the Crimean Tatars. After all, empire thrives when the representations of its power to subordinate "natives," "enemies," and "barbarians" abound – when it brandishes, in the words of Edward Said, "the authority interposed between the victim of imperialism and its perpetrator."[13] In the imperial imagination the most seductive story of conquest is the story of a people conquered.

In such representations, a conquered people is an emplaced people, and a conquered place is an empeopled place – at least at first. Ségur and Ligne, for example, cast Crimean Tatar women as the "flowers" of the Crimean "garden," and Catherine alludes to the Crimean Tatar sounds and smells seizing the air and the built environment around her. No matter the language or the context, such tropes are commonplace in colonialist literature, which, as a tendency if not a rule, first promulgates a tight, intersectional bond between native cultural content – what I call *personality* – and territorial form – what I call *place* – before signalling its breakdown. Instances abound in diverse contexts across the ages. Following the Norman invasion of Ireland in the twelfth century, for instance, Giraldus Cambrensis (also known as Gerald of Wales) featured the Irish as part of the very "topography" of Ireland in his *Topographia Hibernica* (1186–8), likening them to beasts shaped from birth by the natural world around them.[14] Alexander Pope describes the American Indian in the poem "An Essay on Man" (1734) as a human being through whom the land speaks, a "poor," "untutor'd" native ensconced "in depth of woods" and attuned to whispers in the wind.[15] In colonialist literatures the world over, we can cite countless comparable examples of this seminal assertion of the bond between place and personality, in which the colonized native is shown communing symbiotically with the colonized territory – and whereby the colonizer, by virtue of this symbiosis, legitimates and confirms his efficient dominion over both.

I use the contested term *place* in the sense employed by the geographer Yi-Fu Tuan, as space endowed with affect and cast as a "center of felt value."[16] The equally fraught *personality* denotes here cultural colouring perceived to fix to a space, conducting "felt value." Personality, in other words, is the canvas in the frame, or the colour of the walls, or the arrangement of furniture in a room that attests to a particular human presence in space. The bond between place and personality is the fruit of an active process of mutual construction and affirmation that subtends our appreciation of *home*, or what Heidegger calls *wohnen* (dwelling) or being in place. Before Catherine's visit to Bağçasaray, Potemkin deliberately presented Crimea as the home of the Crimean Tatars, refurbishing the hansaray and arranging lanterns around its exterior to conjure an Oriental reverie among her retinue. Upon arriving, Catherine requested a massive company of Crimean Tatar cavalry in full regalia as her personal guard. To inflate its size, Potemkin stuffed the unit with Crimean Tatar civilians and anyone else deemed to resemble them.[17]

These gestures direct us to a paradox at the heart of the cultural politics of the Russian colonization of Crimea: namely, that an intimate bond between Crimean place and Tatar personality had to be affirmed in order to be negated. This bond was the ribbon presented to be cut at the ceremonial introduction of colonial power. Like a record or a rule, it was made to be broken. Visually, even poetically, Potemkin and Catherine brought the Crimean Tatar khanate to life in order to extinguish it – in order to fashion their imperial conquest of the peninsula as *narrative*, as a compelling story and spectacle of change. And the change was swift. As Mary Holderness noted as early as 1821, "[t]he Crim [*sic*] Tatars, now living under Russian government ... are no longer able to exercise their own customs."[18] This affirmation-negation paradox bears the mark of the colonizer's original sin; it records what jurists would call prior possession, embedding a claim to the indigeneity of the colonized and a rationale for decolonization inside the very code of empire. In a significant sense, the "structural predisposition"[19] to conflict afflicting Crimea today originates right here.

Reading Russian literature of the long nineteenth century allows us to see this paradox gradually give way to what I call *a dialectic of imperial possession*, whereby a bond between place and personality is first asserted, then ruptured, and finally reconfigured, with one element of the pair elevated over the other. In Hegelian terms, the bond is *aufgehoben* (sublated), subject to a sequence in which it is secured, abolished, and then transcended. Literatures of modern empire differ greatly in the ways they inscribe and enact strategies of domination, but this basic dialectic, I would argue, is common to most settler and classical land empires. It is a process akin to a chemical reaction in which works of culture act as either catalyst or inhibitor. In the Russian case, Aleksandr Pushkin's *Bakhchisaraiskii fontan* (*The Fountain of Bakhchisarai*, 1824) asserts the bond between Crimean place and Tatar personality only to break it and initiate an elevation of *place* over personality that will be perpetuated by his successors. This elevation of place, amounting to what Said describes as a "loss of [the native's] locality to the outsider," leads to the apotheosis of Crimea as a paradisiacal garden.[20] If Catherine searched in exasperation for a place of paradise in Crimea at the end of the eighteenth century, the trope of a Crimean place as paradise becomes ubiquitous and inescapable in Russian literature a century later. What results from this process is a progressive evacuation of Tatar personality from cultural discourse, a "de-Tatarization" so successful that two of the most prominent Russian works set in Crimea in the mid- to late-nineteenth century, Lev Tolstoy's *Sevastopolskie rasskazy* (*Sevastopol Sketches*, 1855) and Anton Chekhov's "Dama s sobachkoi" ("The Lady with the Lapdog," 1899), make no mention of Crimean Tatars at all. Such is the effect of cultural texts facilitating the politics of imperial expansion, the brutal process of seizing a place and substituting the Other's personality with one's own.

In 1787, however, Crimea marked a point not only of imperial expansion but also of imperial recession, as an Ottoman ebb accompanied the Russian flow in the Black Sea. For centuries the Crimean Tatar khanate had been for the Sublime Porte a cherished strategic asset that kept the Black Sea a "Turkish lake" (Türk gölü) in the face of such enemies as "deli Petro" ("Mad" Peter I, in Ottoman parlance, for his willingness to sacrifice scores of his troops).[21] But toward the end of the eighteenth century it had drifted quickly out of the sultan's grasp. Cascading military and diplomatic defeats at the hands of Russia were to blame, none more crippling than the 1774 Treaty of Küçük-Kaynarca, which formally severed the khanate from Ottoman space and marked the first loss of Ottoman authority over a territory with a majority Muslim population. News of Catherine's 1783 annexation decree followed soon thereafter, scrambling the sultan's advisers and precipitating new calls for war. For Istanbul, Crimea was a ground zero of geopolitical decline, a peninsula upon which the entire Ottoman Empire appeared to teeter. The prospect of "conquering" it again – "easily" (müyesser), in the words of one adviser to the sultan – remained on the table for decades.[22] Only weeks after Catherine's return to Saint Petersburg in late 1787, in fact, the Sublime Porte proceeded to mobilize its forces for yet another Russo-Turkish war. A concise Ottoman intelligence report at the time catalogued troop numbers and surveyed the geopolitical lay of the land, singling out for attention "the Tatar tribe on the Crimean island [*sic*]" (Kırım Ceziresi'nde olan kabail-i Tatar).[23] Potemkin had singled them out as well. He forcibly transplanted Crimean Tatars along the coast further inland and beyond the Perekop Isthmus into mainland Ukraine.[24]

To read Ottoman and Turkish literature over the long nineteenth century is to encounter a dialectic of imperial possession comparable to the Russian case, but with a twist peculiar to a receding empire. As we will see, the Young Ottoman intellectual Namık Kemal testifies to an intimate bond between Crimean place and Tatar personality in the novel *Cezmi* (1880) before staging an elevation of personality over place that will be taken up by Turkish nationalists like Ziya Gökalp and Mehmet Emin Yurdakul. This elevation is a movement from the specific to the general, from the unique to the diffuse, as the Crimean Tatars increasingly become referred to as "Crimean Turks" in Turkish discourse by the end of the Ottoman period. Abstracting linguistically related ethnic groups with cultural or historical links to what had been the imperial metropole – crafting and co-opting them as transnational "diasporas" – is a common tactic of receding empires or former empires, for whom lost territory fast acquires utility as "civilizational space" with irredentist potential. It is alive today, for instance, in the project of the so-called Russian World (Russkii mir). Reflective of the Kremlin's "reimperialization" impulse, *Russkii mir* seeks to connect Russian-speaking "compatriots" (sootechestvenniki) of "similar mentality," as Russian diplomat Aleksandr Chepurin puts it, across Ukraine, Belarus, Kazakhstan, and other post-Soviet states – across more than two million square miles.[25] A symbol of this project, in the view of *Russkii mir* proponents like Chepurin, is the poet Aleksandr Pushkin (1799–1837).

1.

Upon his death in early 1837, Aleksandr Pushkin – riddled with debt, tortured by gossip – was still a giant of Russian culture. Yet one painting, composed around the time of the infamous duel that took his life, presented something of a different view. *Pushkin at Bakhchisarai Palace* (1837; fig. 3) by Grigory and Nikanor Chernetsov depicts the poet as a man dwarfed by the world around him, swallowed by the space of the hansaray. The painting's foreground, framed by massive archways, is cast in shadow; its background, a play of stucco walls and flagstones, is bathed in light. The chiaroscuro nearly obscures the figure of Pushkin, who stands not far from the fountain that he helped make famous with the poem *Bakhchisaraiskii fontan*. Inviting our eyes to move from right to left along a parabola across the canvas, the brothers Chernetsov usher

3. Grigory and Nikanor Chernetsov, *Pushkin at Bakhchisarai Palace* (1837)

us from the diminutive figure of the poet, past the fountain at the centre of the canvas, and finally to a crescent atop one of the oldest and most revered sites in the khan's palace, the Demirkapı (Iron Gate).

Pushkin at Bakhchisarai Palace is a capriccio, an architectural fantasy of the kind made popular in the Renaissance, in which light and shade collide over the surface of ruins. These ruins could be those produced in the past, like the Roman Forum in the work of Giovanni Paolo Panini (1741), or imagined in the future, like the Grande Galerie of the Louvre in the canvases of Hubert Robert (1796). What the Chernetsovs give us is something else: a ruin that is not yet a ruin. In their vision, the hansaray is splendid in size and structurally impeccable; as space it shows no signs of decay. At the same time, it is eerily lifeless, devoid of human activity beyond the small, stationary poet; as place it is abandoned and empty. In *Pushkin at Bakhchisarai Palace*, the Crimean Tatar khanate is neither alive nor dead; it is suspended somewhere between disappearance and emergence, morphing from the seat of Tatar sovereignty into a museum of imperial conquest and control. Pushkin, meanwhile, looks out at us with a knowing gaze.

Grigory and Nikanor Chernetsov, in other words, place Pushkin in the flow of the dialectic of imperial possession in Crimea. Theirs is a portrait of the artist as conduit, as a vessel of exchange between what Hannah Arendt calls the "no-longer of the past" and the "not-yet of the future."[26] It is, as far as one poem is concerned, a very perceptive likeness. In *Bakhchisaraiskii fontan*, Pushkin offers the reader an emblematic performance of the dialectic of imperial possession. With Orientalist colour and sentimental appeal, his poem asserts a bond between Crimean place and Tatar personality and then severs it, elevating Crimean place as ground for Russian colonization. *Bakhchisaraiskii fontan* is, in one sense, an ekphrastic work: it siphons a vividly realized narrative from a real eighteenth-century marble fountain tucked in a corner of the hansaray. According to legend, the fountain mourns the death of Dilara Bikeç, the beloved of Khan Kırım Giray (Girei in Russian, Geray in Crimean Tatar). Above its mihrab-shaped niche, crafted in a rococo Ottoman style, is an inscription from Qu'ran 76:18, which alludes to the fountain at the centre of the Garden of Paradise named Salsabil, an etymological relation of the Arabic word *sabala* (to let fall, to shed tears).[27]

Visitors to the fountain today would be forgiven for their surprise. It defies expectations. In the mind's eye, Pushkin's poetic treatment endows the fountain with larger-than-life proportions, but in reality it is modest in size. His mythologization has helped make *Bakhchisaraiskii fontan* the work of literature with the most transnational resonance in the Black Sea region, a text to which Russian, Ukrainian, Turkish, and Crimean Tatar writers have not simply referred but also *appealed* over the course of centuries. The poem's reception in the region is profoundly ambivalent. On the one hand, Ukrainian, Turkish, and Crimean Tatar cultural figures do not ignore the poem's facilitation of the dialectic of imperial possession, its collusion with state power. On the other hand, they value what sets *Bakhchisaraiskii fontan* apart from nearly all other works of Russian Orientalist literature: its focus not on cunning Muslim tribesmen (cf. Pushkin's "Kavkazskii plennik"), chieftains (cf. Lermontov's "Ammalat-Bek"), or rebels (cf. Tolstoy's *Hadji Murat*) but on *a sovereign political precursor to the tsar*, whose dynastic line is the poem's first word: Giray.

With *Bakhchisaraiskii fontan*, Pushkin secures the Crimean Tatar khanate firmly in the cultural imaginations of the region, shielding it against eradication in history and memory. In this sense, Ukrainian, Turkish, and Crimean Tatar cultural figures see Pushkin not as a vampire "guzzling until he slides off" his victim, as Andrei Siniavsky once characterized him, but as Midas, one who casts Crimean Tatar personality as a thing of beauty with the touch of his poetic gift but hardens it into an aesthetic object with no life of its own.[28] *Bakhchisaraiskii fontan* is in fact credited for saving the hansaray from demolition in the Stalinist era; as we will see in chapter 3, it is likely the very reason the city of Bakhchisarai still exists as such in name today.

Bakhchisaraiskii fontan is therefore the Black Sea's literary lodestone. It pulls together an entire region – attracting references, allusions, and imitations across shores and across languages, providing a point of orientation for itineraries to what might be called, borrowing from Joseph Brodsky, the "second Crimea" made of Crimean Tatar, Russian, Turkish, and Ukrainian poetry and prose.[29] Its unique standing was not a matter of Pushkin reaching Crimea first, as it were, after Catherine's annexation. That distinction was won by Semen Bobrov, whose epic *Tavrida* of 1798 introduced Crimea as a literary topos to readers in the imperial metropole.[30] Yuri Lotman calls Semen Bobrov (1763?–1810) "a poet of genius" – but a poet of genius whose work is virtually forgotten today.[31]

In the words of one Russian critic, Bobrov is Crimea's literary Columbus, its "*pervopoet*" (first-poet).[32] His *Tavrida* is "a comprehensive textbook" of the peninsula, an almanac of its culture, mythology, zoology, and geology based on the idea of an intricate, imbricated bond between Crimean place and Tatar personality.[33] The bond is immediately evident at the level of form. *Tavrida* is the first poem in Russian literature to use an unrhymed iambic metre, and Bobrov accounts for his sonic experimentation as a kind of deference to the Crimean Tatars: "Dear reader! Permit me to confess in jest! I have a Crimean ear, and Crimean Muslims do not like the chimes of bells."[34] He explains that he must explore a new sound, a "Muslim" sound, in order to render Crimea in verse. Here a catalogue of assonant and alliterative Crimean Tatar river names helps him on his way, as his lyrical persona imagines himself one with the clouds, gazing down on the rivers below:

Здесь зрю я Зую, Бештерек,
Индал, Булганак и Бузук,
Что прыгают с крутого камня
Пенистой шумной стопой.[35]

(Here I behold the Zuia, the Beshterek,
The Indal, the Bulganak, and the Buzuk,
Which leap off the steep rock
In a foamy, noisy throng.)

Human life emerges from this storm in splendour as well – in the figure of Tsulma, a young Crimean Tatar princess in spiritual communion with the land. Bobrov places her in a similative relationship with the flora and fauna around her: Tsulma is as "slender as a myrtle" and as "light as chamois cloth." Above all she is the "beauty and honour" of the Crimean Tatar nobility, a woman who prays to Allah for the return of her beloved Tatar *mirza* (noble), Selim. For Bobrov, she exemplifies a deep bond between a living Tatar culture and the territorial bounty of the peninsula. His vision of Crimea as a home of the Tatars in *Tavrida* becomes an object of aesthetic pleasure to readers in the early nineteenth-century Russian Empire.

Among these enthusiastic readers was Pushkin, who admitted to "stealing" one or two lines for *Bakhchisaraiskii fontan*, which John Bayley calls his "most popular poem."[36] Its popularity was due in part to its exotic setting in the harem of the Crimean Tatar khan, where "young captives" frolic in cool pools:

Раскинув легкие власы,
Как идут пленницы младые
Купаться в жаркие часы,
И льются волны ключевые
На их волшебные красы.[37]

(Having let down their fine hair,
Off go the young captives

To bathe in the hot hours,
The waves of the fountain flowing
Over their enchanting beauties.)

The scene is highly intertextual with Bobrov's *Tavrida*. Here are Tsulma's handmaidens, seeking refuge from the heat:

В струи сребристы погружая
Стыдливые красы свои,
Руками влагу рассекают,
Играют, — плещутся, — смеются
. . . .
Купальня хладна защищает
От силы солнечного зноя.[38]

(Plunging into silvery streams
Their modest beauties,
[The girls] slash through the water with their hands,
Playing, splashing, laughing [...]
The cool bathing hut offers protection
From the power of the scorching sun.)

The male gaze of Pushkin's narrator is invasive, rendering useless the walls of the harem. But like the ogling Ségur and Ligne, Bobrov's narrator proves even more intrusive and voyeuristic by acknowledging Tsulma's fear of being seen, but nonetheless refusing to look away:

Тут — робко Цульма озираясь,
Последню ризу низлагает;
Какой красот вид обнажился!
Какой мир прелестей открылся![39]

(Here – bashfully Tsulma looks around,
Dropping the last garment;
What a vision of beauty is exposed!
What a world of delights is revealed!)

The cool waters of the bath cannot temper the "burning passion" of the Tatar princess for the distant Selim. Bobrov's Tsulma is at once desperately romantic and prayerfully modest, offering a source from which the two heroines of Pushkin's poem – Zarema and Mariia – may be seen to spring.

In *Bakhchisaraiskii fontan*, these two women are the favoured concubines of the Crimean Tatar khan. Zarema is a passionate woman who desires the khan's affections but no longer holds his attention; Mariia is a quiet and devout woman who resists the khan but appears to win his heart. In the dead of night Zarema visits Mariia to beg her to release her hold on the khan: "Return to me my happiness and tranquility, / Return my erstwhile Giray." Mariia and Zarema die after this encounter. They are simply "no more" ("Marii net," "gruzinki net"; 189–90). Did Zarema really kill Mariia, as the text intimates? Did the khan explicitly order Zarema's execution? The poem's incomplete, mysterious feel stands in contrast to its preoccupation with symmetry, which is most evident in the parallelisms oriented around the pairings of Mariia-Zarema and khan-eunuch.

Both Mariia and Zarema, for example, are beautiful captives torn from Christian homes and cast into the khan's harem. Mariia is a musical woman who is attuned to the world of spirit; Zarema is a woman celebrated in music who is attuned to the world of the flesh: "I was born for passion" (Ia dlia strasti rozhdena; 187). Mariia comes from the Polish lands to the northwest, Zarema from Georgian lands to the southeast. These geographical origins, in fact, are constitutive of the identities of the two women; they define and confine them. Pushkin establishes a tight bond between place and personality in the narrative portion of *Bakhchisaraiskii fontan*, virtually dissolving territorial form into cultural content. Mariia's corner of the harem, for instance, is a simulated piece of Poland, a holy refuge where she practises her faith unimpeded and reminisces about her homeland, "an intimate, better place." She never leaves this chamber alive. Zarema, by contrast, does move beyond her sanctioned area in the harem, eluding the eunuch under cover of darkness to confront Mariia. Yet this act is less a transgression than simple obedience to her fierce, impetuous nature, which she directly attributes to her geographical origins, in an elliptical threat to her rival: "But listen: if I have to [...] I have a dagger, / And I was born near the Caucasus" (188).

Zarema makes a point of emphasizing that her place of birth is not Crimea, for the Black Sea peninsula is the land of the Crimean Tatars, and the khan is its metonym, its contiguous relation. Often considered a "marginal" figure, a foil to the poem's two doomed heroines, the khan is in fact the main character of *Bakhchisaraiskii fontan*.[40] Compared to Zarema and Mariia, whose traits dictate their actions, he is the only character to undergo any real change in the poem. He begins the poem as potentate and ends as impotent. In the opening lines, even when troubled, he is portrayed as the fearsome, scowling scourge of Rus and Poland. The prominent caesura in the first line distinguishes his position and his station: "Girei sidel, potulia vzor" (Giray sat, looking downward; 175). The Crimean Tatar khan is literally a sitting monarch, and all look up to him, respecting his authority. Yet by the end of the poem he is a man weak and broken, especially on the field of battle:

Он часто в сечах роковых
Подъемлет саблю, и с размаха
Недвижим остается вдруг,
Глядит с безумием вокруг,
Бледнеет, будто полный страха,
И что-то шепчет, и порой
Горючи слезы льет рекой. (189)

(Often in fateful moments he would
Hoist his sabre, and with a swing
Suddenly stand motionless,
Look around senselessly,
Grow pale, as if seized with fear,
And whisper something, and now and then
Tears of sorrow would flow like a river.)

These inaudible whispers underscore the khan's silence throughout the story. He has no voice; silently (*molcha*) does he move about the harem. He communicates in glances and gestures, dismissing his court, for example, "with an impatient wave of his hand." Now that he can no longer brandish his sword, the khan becomes as mute and emasculated as the eunuch who monitors his harem. Pushkin hints at their affinity, even playing with the masculine rhyme *litsa-skoptsa* to join the two together:

Забытый, преданный презренью,
Гарем не зрит его *лица*;
Там, обреченные мученью,
Под стражей хладного *скопца*
Стареют жены. (189–90; emphasis mine)

(Forgotten, scornfully cast aside,
The harem does not see [the khan's] face;
There, doomed and tormented,
Under the watch of the cold eunuch
The women grow old.)

Both the khan and the eunuch are figures of authority who hold the lives of the harem in their hands. Their fates are closely intertwined: the eunuch's every action is determined by a command of the khan, and the khan's rule and lineage are preserved by the eunuch's regulation of his concubine.

The symmetry between them invites a reading of the poem with relevance to our understanding of the dialectic of imperial possession, because *Bakhchisaraiskii fontain* can be understood as a commentary on dynastic succession. Behind the poem's veil of harem romance and intrigue, in other words, is a story of the failure of the Crimean Tatar khan to protect his line. For Vissarion Belinsky, Pushkin's work is a simple love story: "The idea of the poem is the rebirth (if not the enlightenment) of a savage soul by way of the lofty feeling of love."[41] Yet the reader never encounters the khan in love at all. Over the course of the poem he shares no intimate moments with Zarema or Mariia. As Baudelaire once said, "in a palace [...] there is no place for intimacy."[42] The khan professes no affection for either woman. Only in Zarema's lengthy appeal to Mariia – that is, second-hand – does the reader learn that the khan and his Georgian consort once "breathed happiness in never-ending rapture" (187). Even Pushkin's narrator is unsure of the khan's feelings, repeatedly investigating the reasons for his deep malaise: "What drives this proud soul? / What thought occupies him?" (175). Is it unrequited love that has the Crimean Tatar khan brooding intensely in the poem, or fear for the stable perpetuation of his rule?

The problem of succession was not insignificant to Pushkin in this period. His historical drama *Boris Godunov* (1825), written very soon after *Bakhchisaraiskii fontan*, centres on the demise of the Riurik line during the *Smutnoe vremia* (Time of Troubles, 1598–1613). *Boris Godunov* is a famously fragmentary and "incomprehensible" play, which intrigued and alienated audiences immediately upon its appearance – and which, by Pushkin's own account, drew its inspiration from Shakespeare.[43] Crises of patrilineal succession, one of which gripped Russia at the time of the Decembrist revolt of 1825, are of course never very far from the centre of the Bard's tragedies and historical chronicles. Macbeth, to cite one prominent example, fears that "upon my head they placed a fruitless crown,/ And put a barren sceptre in my gripe, / Thence to be wrench'd with *an unlineal hand, / No son of mine succeeding*."[44]

If endowed with voice in *Bakhchisaraiskii fontan*, the Crimean Tatar khan might be heard to speak the same fear. Instead he is shown at the conclusion of the narrative portion of the poem silently pushing back against the irrevocable decline of his dynasty. He erects a monument – the fountain of tears of the poem's title – bound to the sorrow of those mourning the absence of children:

За чуждыми ее чертами
Журчит во мраморе вода
И каплет хладными слезами,
Не умолкая никогда.
Так плачет мать во дни печали
О сыне, падшем на войне. (190)

(Behind its strange characters
Water murmurs inside the marble
And falls in drops like cold tears
Without end.
Thus weeps the mother in the depths of grief
For the son fallen in war.)

In a poem whose story forges an intimate bond between place and personality, the khan symbolizes the khanate itself, a silenced and emasculated sovereign state whose only lasting traces are hand-hewn structures monumentalizing grief and loss.

Pushkin's elegiac coda, in which the narrator reveals himself as a visitor "from the north" recounting past events, is a meditation on this loss. What was joined earlier in the poem is now riven: Crimean place has lost Tatar personality. Directing his gaze over the grounds of the hansaray, the narrator encounters only a charged silence. Amid the quietude he wonders, "Gde skrylis khany? Gde harem?" (Where have the khans gone? Where is the harem?; 191) He asks these questions with an unspoken knowledge of the answer: namely, that the expanding borders of empire have consigned the khan and the other sovereigns along Russia's periphery to extinction.

Here Pushkin's narrator seems struck by an imperial melancholy, a "reflective nostalgia" triggered by the ruins that have been wrought by the advance of empire, by the seizure of place at the expense of the Other's personality. According to Svetlana Boym, citing Susan Stewart, "reflective nostalgia does not pretend to rebuild the mythical place [...] It is 'enamored of distance, not of the referent itself.'"[45] In these rhetorical interrogatives the narrator evokes the absence of the khans, of Tatar personality – not to condemn or mourn it but "to narrate the relationship between past, present, and future."[46] In spite of the absence of a living Tatar personality, Crimean place stands in full bloom, overcome by winding vines and reddening roses. Tatar personality is the vanishing past; Crimean place bears the promise of a flourishing future. Progress arrives to the sound of hoof beats:

Волшебный край! очей отрада!
Все живо там: холмы, леса,
Янтарь и яхонт винограда
. . . .
Всё чувство путника манит,
Когда, в час утра безмятежный,
В горах, дорогою прибрежной,
Привычный конь его бежит,
И зеленеющая влага
Пред ним и блещет и шумит
Вокруг утесов Аю-дага. (192–3)

(O enchanting land! O delight of the eyes!
Hills, forests, sapphire and amber of the vine:
Everything flourishes there […]
All of it seizes the senses of the rider,
As in placid morning-tide,
Amid the mountains, along the seashore,
A trusted steed carries him,
And the greening waters
Stir and sparkle before him
Around the cliffs of Aiu-Dag.)

In this last scene, the narrator projects the Crimean landscape as an object of desire, a place of beauty and vigour to be celebrated, explored, and occupied. It is open and submissive. Unlike *Kavkazskii plennik* (*The Prisoner of the Caucasus*, 1822), the narrative poem that immediately precedes *Bakhchisaraiskii fontan* in Pushkin's oeuvre and tells the story of the penetration of a Russian soldier into a Circassian mountain community, *Bakhchisaraiskii fontan* casts the dissolution of the Crimean khanate as an internal matter free of Russian interference.

Pushkin's elevation of Crimean place over Tatar personality in the coda of *Bakhchisaraiskii fontan* was epochal in its literary impact. The poet and painter Maksimilian Voloshin (1877–1932) felt it keenly. In his own verse, Voloshin – who spent a part of his childhood as well as the end of his life in Koktebel, on Crimea's southern coast – condemned his fellow countrymen for "trampling upon this Muslim paradise, / Cutting down forests, desecrating ruins, / Looting and plundering the land."[47] He also lamented how Pushkin's performance of this

dialectic of imperial possession had turned Russian artists from perceptive observers into myopic "tourists": "The relationship of Russian
artists to Crimea has been the relationship of tourists surveying notable
places with a painterly eye [*zhivopisnost*]. This perspective was given to
us by Pushkin, and after him, poets and painters over the course of the
entire century have seen Crimea only as 'O enchanting land! O delight
of the eyes!' ['*Volshebnyi krai! ochei otrada!*']. And nothing more. Such
were all the Russian poems and paintings composed throughout the
nineteenth century. They all worship the beauty of the southern shores
with poems abounding in exclamation marks."[48]

Voloshin could compile an entire anthology with texts about Crimea
that "abound in exclamation marks." The Ukrainian writer Andrei
Kurkov describes such works as Crimean "souvenir literature" today.[49]
Immediately after *Bakhchisaraiskii fontan*, Pushkin contributed to this
souvenir literature once more with "Otryvki iz puteshestviia Onegina"
("Fragments of Onegin's Journey"), which was initially intended as
canto 8 of *Yevgeny Onegin* (*Eugene Onegin*, 1825–32). Here Pushkin portrays Crimea more overtly as a locus and object of sexual longing:[50]

Прекрасны вы, брега Тавриды,
Когда вас видишь с корабля
При свете утренней Киприды,
Как вас впервой увидел я;
Вы мне предстали в блеске брачном:
На небе синем и прозрачном
Сияли груды ваших гор,
Долин, деревьев, сёл узор
Разостлан был передо мною.
А там, меж хижинок татар ...
Какой во мне проснулся жар![51]

(You are beautiful, O shores of Taurida,
When one sees you from the ship
By the light of the morning Kiprida,
As I first saw you;
You presented yourself to me in nuptial splendour:
Against a blue, pellucid sky
The peaks of your mountains shone brightly,
The design of your valleys, trees, and villages
Was laid out before me.
And there, among the Tatar dwellings ...
What a fire awoke within me!)

Just as the khan's fountain is all that remains of him, the only vestiges of Tatar personality in this poem are shacks (*khizhiny*) devoid of human life and activity. Similarly, in Vasily Tumansky's "Elegiia" (Elegy, 1824), no Tatars are found amid the poem's surfeit of vibrant flowers, trees, cliffs, and clouds. Only their huts appear, overgrown by the fruits of the land:

Вот жизнь моя в стране, где кипарисны сени,
Средь лавров возрастя, приманивают к лени,
Где хижины татар венчает виноград,
Где роща каждая есть благовонный сад.[52]

(This is my life in the land where blue cypresses,
Amid aged laurels, entice one to leisure,
Where grapevines top Tatar huts,
Where every grove is an aromatic garden.)

For Vladimir Benediktov, meanwhile, Crimea's unusual topographical features actually replace its indigenous population. In "Oreanda," which constitutes part of his 1839 cycle *Putevye zametki i vpechatleniia (v Krymu)* (Travel notes and impressions [in Crimea]), Benediktov's lyrical persona anthropomorphizes the land as natives offering visitors shelter from the rain and relief from the hot sun. He looks admiringly on the "living rock faces" near Yalta and demands a human gesture of gratitude for them: a reverent bow.[53] Such texts give us Crimea as a kind of fetish object for landscape tableaux, poetic canvases of glimmering peaks and deep ravines whose grandeur leads lyrical personae toward an implicit embrace of colonialism and toward a Romantic experience of the natural sublime.

When war descended upon the Black Sea peninsula in 1853–6, these familiar peaks and ravines became less a source of enchantment and awe than landmarks of sorrow and suffering, especially in Crimean Tatar literature. The end of the Crimean War saw tsarist officials under Aleksandr II level the Crimean Tatars with accusations of mass treason and betrayal. As Nekrich explains, "these charges were meant to divert attention from the inept performance of the tsarist government itself, and its bureaucrats, during the war."[54] Voloshin called the accusations "barbaric," a cruel assault on a "hard-working and loyal" people.[55] This assault was physical, involving a series of atrocities committed against the Crimean Tatar civilians by Russian troops. Aleksandr Herzen catalogued these crimes in his newspaper *Kolokol*.[56] The storm of pressure and persecution turned what had been a gradual, century-long Crimean

Tatar migration to Anatolia into a flood. As if in amber, Crimean Tatar folk songs trap the pain of leaving the homeland at this time: "Woe has come to Crimea! / On one side, the Muscovite surrounds us, / On the other side, we face the mighty Black Sea!"[57] On the horizon was the *ak toprak* (white land) of Ottoman Turkey.

2.

Namık Kemal (1840–1888) placed a journey of a Crimean Tatar across the Black Sea at the heart of the first historical novel in Turkish literature. Kemal was the most influential Ottoman intellectual of the nineteenth century and a writer of fiction with a penchant for melodrama. His polemical essays were sober, clear-eyed endorsements of a European liberalism with an Islamic soul – the essence of a Young Ottoman political platform – but his plays and novels expressed such effervescent feeling that they occasionally gave themselves over to caricature.[58] Compared to Pushkin, who would come to describe *Bakhchisaraiskii fontan* as the product of a younger self prone to an exaggeration of feeling,[59] Kemal was a writer who embraced a superfluity of emotion as his literary trademark. It seemed to suit his era. At a time of rapid changes that saw the introduction of the first Ottoman constitution in 1876, Kemal's passion was in many ways a barometer of societal transition and upheaval. In his literary works it was a catalyst of reform, igniting in audiences a powerful new understanding of and loyalty to *vatan* (homeland), an originally localized concept that he helped develop to encompass the entire multi-ethnic Ottoman Empire.[60]

In 1880, Kemal published a ground-breaking novel entitled *Cezmi*. Set in the sixteenth century and originally envisioned as a multivolume work in the vein of Hugo's *Les Misérables*, it bears a misleading title. Kemal only completed the first volume, which centres less on Cezmi, the eponymous scholar and poet who becomes a *sipahi* (special cavalry officer) in the service of Sultan Murad III, and more on Adil Giray, *kalgay* (heir apparent) to the Crimean Tatar khan. Like Pushkin's *Bakhchisaraiskii fontan*, *Cezmi* holds special importance in our discussion as a text that initially attests to an intimate bond between Crimean place and Tatar personality – in other words, to the status of the Crimea peninsula as a possession of the Crimean Tatars. But it then disrupts this bond, elevating *personality* at the expense of place.

Cezmi does so to advocate a transcendence of local territorial loyalties in the service of the Ottoman imperial project. The charismatic example of this transcendence is the figure of Adil Giray, who leaves Crimea and crosses the Black Sea to support the Ottomans against Persia.

Representing his elder brother and sovereign, Khan Mehmed Giray, Adil arrives at the head of forty thousand *akıncılar* (light cavalry) just as the Persians are about to rout Cezmi and an undermanned Ottoman infantry. The dramatic entrance of the Crimean Tatars lifts the Ottomans, causing the Persians to give up hope of victory. In their retreat, however, the Persians capture Adil, who is sent to the shah's palace, where he becomes embroiled in imperial intrigue and a poisonous love triangle.

Kemal derives the narrative events and existents of *Cezmi* from *Tarih-i Peçevi* (Peçevi's history), the authoritative chronicle of sixteenth-century Ottoman history written by İbrahim Peçevi.[61] But we might be forgiven for thinking that he was inspired in some way by Pushkin. *Cezmi* is a mirror image of *Bakhchisaraiskii fontan*: instead of a Crimean Tatar khan caught between two women imprisoned in his Bahçesaray harem, Kemal gives us an imprisoned Crimean Tatar khan-in-waiting caught between two women in a Tabriz palace.

The first woman in the love triangle is Şehriyar, the wife of the shah, who falls in love with Adil at first sight. She is beautiful, passionate, and vengeful – Kemal's Zarema. The second is Perihan, the young sister of the shah, who wins Adil's love and attempts to free him from captivity. She is beautiful, moral, and devout – Kemal's Mariia. Scheming to turn Bahçesaray against Istanbul, Şehriyar offers Adil full independence for the Crimean khanate and a position of authority in a new Crimean Tatar–Persian alliance. He spurns her advances. Emboldened by his love for Perihan – and by Cezmi, who reappears later in the novel to rescue the Crimean *kalgay* – Adil devises a plan to overtake the palace and overthow the Persian state. Şehriyar learns of his betrayal, however, and orders the execution of Adil and Perihan before taking her own life. Not unlike Pushkin's Zarema, she destroys the happiness of a Crimean Tatar beloved – and dies in recompense for the act.

Adil and Perihan perish united in their love. They also perish as a Crimean Tatar and a Persian princess who ultimately sacrifice their lives in service to Istanbul. Although the Crimean khanate "entered under Ottoman protection" in 1478, in practical terms it was a partially independent sovereign polity with control of the Black Sea peninsula and the adjoining northern steppe between the Kuban and the Dniester throughout the sixteenth century.[62] For a Young Ottoman like Namık Kemal, who sought to elevate a concept of open Ottoman citizenship founded primarily on allegiance to the state rather than to ethnicity or religion, the choice of Adil Giray as a hero of *Cezmi* therefore had significant political purchase.

Kemal considered imaginative literature a primary means of educating the people of the empire.[63] Writing *Cezmi* between 1876 and 1880, he likely viewed the very survival of the Ottoman Empire as hinging on the lesson of Adil Giray and his decision to sacrifice the local in defence of the imperial. The Balkans were exploding with nationalist sentiment, and in 1877 Russia declared war on the Ottoman Empire ostensibly over demands for autonomy for the latter's Bulgarian population. Even after the Treaty of Berlin of 1878, which helped staunch the excessive bleeding of territorial losses beyond Anatolia, the empire still saw Serbia, Montenegro, and Romania break away as independent states.[64] Whatever the concerns Namık Kemal had as a reformer, one who plied the sultan with calls for a Western-style constitutional and parliamentarian government that would remain true to Islamic tradition, they did not diminish his devotion to the Ottoman Empire. With the long-standing borders of the vatan beginning to crumble before his very eyes, he must have dreamt of an army of Adil Girays, impervious to the seduction of the local and to the comfort of home, coming to Istanbul's aid.

In *Cezmi*, Kemal does not understate the power of this seduction. He underscores Adil's affinity for his Crimean homeland and Tatar brethren and does so precisely to extol the heroism involved in the pursuit of an Ottoman "higher calling." Most illustrative in this regard is a long poem written in Adil's own voice, which the distinguished Turkish poet, novelist, and literary critic Ahmet Hamdi Tanpınar calls the novel's "biggest peculiarity" (en büyük hususiyeti).[65] It is, as it were, a "Bildungspoem" offering psychological insight into the life and upbringing of the Crimean Tatar *kalgay*. It takes the form of a *Terkibibend*, a poem featuring a series of stanzas composed of ten *beyts* (couplets), each of which concludes with a contrapuntal *makta* (a "cutting" or end couplet).

Adil begins by contemplating the force that brings him into the world: *kaza*. The meaning of the term *kaza* lies somewhere between its denotations as both "chance" and "calling" (or "divine judgment") – in a word, fate.[66] While in self-imposed exile in France from 1867 to 1870, Namık Kemal was an enthusiastic reader of the Romantic works of Victor Hugo, and he cast Adil Giray in this poem within the novel as a "fated" Romantic hero caught in the sweep of cosmic forces. Fate for Adil is a presence that speaks to him in the words of a relentless *hatif* (mysterious voice):

Bilmem ne sebeple vardı dâim,
Gûşumda şu hatifî terâna:
Yüksel ki yerin bu yer değildir,
Dünyâya geliş hüner değildir.[67]

(I do not know why there has always been
This mysterious voice in my ear:
"Arise! This is not your place,
There is no merit in simply being born.")

Nearly every *makta* – the concluding couplet of each stanza – begins with the imperative "Yüksel!" (Arise!) and encourages Adil to exceed himself and advance beyond his current station.

As the poem continues, Adil reflects on his upbringing in Crimea, which taught him the difference between strength and weakness and between intelligence and wisdom. At the right hand of his brother, Khan Mehmed Giray, Adil turns his attention to the affairs of the Crimean Tatar khanate: "My brother became khan of Crimea, / And drew me to the throne with him" (99). The people praise him and find "none of [his] orders contemptible":

Herkesteki hande-i neşâtın
Aksiyle açardın dilde güller.
Hükmümde safâ süren raiyyet,
Evsâfımı virdederdi yer yer.[68]

(Roses bloomed in the hearts of men,
Reflecting the joyous laughter of all.
Under my authority my subjects lived in bounty
And always applauded my qualities.)

Adil Giray feels a devotion to and an intimate connection with his home, expressing a strong resolve "not to abandon" (terketmemek) Crimea and his fellow Crimean Tatars. His life to this point – a childhood idyll, an adolescent quest for knowledge – has readied him for a position as a leader and a steward of Crimean Tatar society on the Black Sea peninsula. In other words, Adil is at home.

When the *hatif* reappears with a new appeal for ascendance, however, this bond between Crimean place and Tatar personality is shaken: "Arise! The world is base and destitute; / It is madness to be inclined toward it" (Yüksel ki cihan sefîl ü dundur, / Rağbet ona âdeta cünundur).[69] The *hatif* calls on Adil to serve his ethnic brethren in the Ottoman Empire. Kemal fashions a new home for his Crimean Tatar hero. The very next couplet testifies to Adil's submission to the interests of the broader vatan: "The Ottoman dynasty declared war against the enemy; / For those who spoke of bravery, here was its arena."[70] Adil Giray forsakes Crimean place, to which he will never return, and goes forth to fulfil his civic duty as a Crimean Tatar noble bound to Istanbul. Kemal thus decouples Crimean place from Tatar personality, elevating the latter as the condition of possibility for the *uhuvvet* (brotherhood) at the heart of this allegiance. In an era when ethnic and confessional differences began to undermine the territorial integrity of the Ottoman lands, *Cezmi* mobilized a Crimean Tatar as a symbol of unity whose support of the Ottoman state was a triumph over division. For Kemal, this loyalty was the hope of his brand of Ottomanism.

Kemal's ideas were highly contested in this period of mass migrations, fluid borders, and proliferating ideologies. In fact, the most persuasive critique of his Ottomanism came from a member of the Muslim intelligentsia in the Russian Empire. In an influential pamphlet entitled *Üç Tarz-ı Siyaset* (The three paths of policy, 1904) and published in the Cairo-based journal *Türk*, Yusuf Akçura wonders whether Kemal's Ottomanism really suits the reality of the turn-of-the-century Ottoman Empire. A Volga Tatar, Akçura deliberates the pros and cons of three political ideologies, each promising to serve the interests of an Ottoman state in crisis: Ottomanism, Islamism, and pan-Turkism. For Akçura, the prospects for Kemal's doctrine are dim, mainly because its platform of open citizenship and equal rights constitutes a surrender of political privilege for Turks and Muslims, on the one hand, and a disavowal of self-determination for non-Muslims, on the other.[71] After considering Islamism, which he argues would alienate and anger European powers with a destabilizing offer of a "more concentrated community" of Muslims across borders, he sees a potential upside in a new, less-tested ideology: pan-Turkism.[72]

Akçura describes Türkçülük as a policy of ethnic nationalism encompassing "all the Turks found scattered across a large swath of Asia and Eastern Europe and bound by the same language, ethnicity, culture, and to a significant degree, the same religion."[73] Its ambition worried journalist and politician Ali Kemal, who questioned its practical implications by citing the Ottoman loss of Crimea and the fate of the Crimean Tatars. "My God, we could not protect Crimea when it was inhabited by the Tatars, a type of Turk [*Tatarlar ile, bir nevi Türklerle*]," wrote Ali Kemal, "and now we are going to work to unify all the Turks in Asia?"[74]

This "loss of Crimea" evolved into a pregnant poetic trope in turn-of-the-century Turkish literature, albeit not quite in the way Ali Kemal had in mind. It became an event cited by poets to advocate versions of Akçura's *Türkçülük* and to stir outrage over the failure of the Ottoman state to protect Turks around the world. One such poet was Ziya Gökalp, the influential sociologist and civic activist who defined the concept of the nation according to the bonds of "culture" (hars) rather than the boundaries of territory, in his *Türkçülüğün esasları* (*The Principles of Turkism*, 1923).[75] Called "the founding father of [both pan-Turkism] and Turkish nationalism," he began his career warmly supportive of pan-Turkist ideals, which are most evidently expressed in his poetry. Later, after the Ottoman defeat in the First World War in 1918, he narrowed the focus of his political program to Anatolian Turkey.[76] His writing has since maintained a consistent salience in Turkish society. When Recep Tayyıp Erdoğan read Gökalp's poetry in public in 1997, it even earned him a trip to prison.

Gökalp's early poems deliver the ideas he puts forward in his academic writing in simplified, digestible form. They bear the steady cadence of a march and call out for memorization and oral recitation. With abundant internal rhyme, his early poem "Altın Destan" (The golden epic, 1911) begins by evoking the wider Turkic world as one of an unattended flock in need of a shepherd. His lyrical persona wanders through Turan, a mythical territory of Turkic peoples extending from Anatolia into Asia, and searches for stirrings of a new movement for unity. Instead he sees only lands "where foreign hands have built principalities," Crimea foremost among them:

Kırım nerde kaldı, Kafkas ne oldu?
Kazan'dan Tibet'e değin rus doldu.[77]

(Where was Crimea abandoned, what happened to the Caucasus?
From Kazan to Tibet, the land is stuffed with Russians.)

Turan in Gökalp's poem is a landmass so large and so abstract that it renders the concept of *place* meaningless. Its expansive borders reach Crimea, Tibet, and even the Tian Shan mountain range. This is space without a centre, with no specific *where* to invest felt value.

Originally a Persian term for Central Asia, Turan has been described as "an *undefined* Shangri-La area in the steppes of Central Asia."[78] This lack of definition is only territorial. What really defines Turan is culture, the aggregate of social, linguistic, and confessional traits privileged by Yusuf Akçura. Its borders are the borders of whatever is understood as the Turkic world. For Ali Kemal, responding to Akçura, the loss of Crimea is instructive because of its territorial specificity and proximity to Istanbul; for Gökalp in "Altın Destan," it is instructive because of its *lack* of specificity, its capacity to be emblematic of countless other losses, from the Caucasus to Kazan.

This apotheosis of personality over place is especially evident in the work of the "first nationalist poet of Turkey," Mehmet Emin Yurdakul, for whom the loss of Crimea also figures as an instrument of pan-Turkist mobilization.[79] In "Nifâk" (Discord, 1912), Yurdakul cites Crimea as an admonition. It is pluralized, a floating signifier: "O lamp of history! Give light to us [...] / And show us [...] how many miserable Crimeas there are [kaç zavallı Kırım var]."[80] In his 1914 epic "Ey Türk Uyan!" (Awake, O Turk!), whose title echoes the nineteenth-century anthem of pan-Slavism "Ej Slovane" (Hey, Slavs!), he encapsulates the central idea of pan-Turkism:

> Bu saf kanı taşıyan
> Herbir insan, aşiret;
> Türk diliyle konuşan
> Herbir şehir, memleket
> Senin birer evladın, senin birer oymağın;
> Senin birer öz yurdun, senin birer bucağın![81]

> (Every person, every nomadic tribe
> Carrying this pure blood;
> Every city, every civilization
> Speaking the Turkish tongue
> Is your descendent, your tribe,
> Your place, your true home!)

Yurdakul explicitly casts place (yurt) as wholly contingent on personality (bu saf kani taşıyan / Herbir insan). In his formulation, surrendering to the thin bonds of ethnicity, language, and culture among the Turkic peoples will lead to a discovery of a new home, a new "Türk yurdu" encompassing the Kirgiz, Tonguz, and "wet-browed Tatars" (alin terli Tatarlar).[82]

Aiding this discovery is what Yurdakul calls a new "national spirit" (milli duygu), which is conveyed by Sur, the trumpet announcing the Holy Kingdom in Qu'ran 6:73. He heralds national awakeners who have changed the map of Europe, including Russia. Armed with "national spirit," after all,

> Tatarlar'a harac veren bir Rusya
> Şark'a varis olmak için canlandi.[83]

> (Russia, which once paid tribute to the Tatars,
> Came alive to become heir to the East.)

Among these national awakeners, Yurdakul reserves a special place for Ismail Gasprinsky (or İsmail Bey Gaspıralı, 1851–1914), the Crimean

Tatar educator, journalist, and civic leader based in Bahçesaray whose journal *Tercüman* (or *Perevodchik*; The Interpreter) played a singular role in promoting pan-Turkist ideals in both the Russian and the Ottoman Empires.

The motto of *Tercüman* – "Dilde, fikirde, işte birlik" (Unity in language, thought, and action) – encapsulates Gasprinsky's mission, which was nothing less than to consolidate the interests and the resources of the Turkic communities around the world, from the Tatar to the Uzbek and Kirghiz, and to ready them for the modern age. Gasprinsky advocated *lisan-ı umumi* (the common language), a hybrid of simplified Ottoman Turkish and Crimean Tatar largely free of Persian, Russian, and Arabic influences and capable of reaching Turkic audiences across borders; he promoted the rights of women and an Islam reconciled to the secular ideals of the European Enlightenment; and he called for *usul-i cedid*, a "new method" of Muslim educational practices critical for civil society.[84] These positions became the central tenets of what is known as Jadidism.

In his "İsmail Gaspirinski'ye" (To Ismail Gasprinsky), published in 1914 in the collection *Türk Sazı* (The Saz of the Turk), Yurdakul hailed Gasprinsky not only as a national awakener but also as a unique light-bearer to the Muslim world, one who spread both *nur*, the "light" of religious faith, and *medeniyet güneşı*, the "light of civilization."[85] He wrote the poem upon the occasion of Gasprinsky's death in 1914. The two had been friends. In 1899, for instance, Yurdakul sent Gasprinsky a copy of his first collection of verse, *Türkçe Şiirler* (Poems in Turkish, 1898), which the latter received with gratitude, remarking that the poems "cheered" and "heartened" him.[86] Marking the passing of his friend in "İsmail Gaspirinski'ye," Yurdakul offered a prayer for Crimea among the poem's first stanzas:

Ta ki fatih Cengizler'in evladı
İslavlık'ın pençesinden kurtulsun;
Onun mazlum, sefil olan hayatı
Hür ve mes'ud bir tali'le can bulsun.

(Let [Crimea,] son of Genghis the Conqueror
Escape through the talons of the Slavs;
Let independence and a blessed soul
Greet its oppressed, wretched life.)

Here the loss of Crimea is the result of an egregious theft by "the Slavs." Under Russian control, Crimea is a land "kneaded with blood," "a slave to savages." This virulent anti-Russian rhetoric, in which

Gasprinsky himself did not engage, appears in a number of Yurdakul's poems from this period: in "Petersburg'a" (To Petersburg, 1916), for example, the lyrical persona curses the residents of the imperial city as ignorant idol worshippers, with imagery evoking the apocalyptic scenes of Qu'ran 81, and in "Çar'a" (To the Tsar, 1917) he warns the Romanov "Nero of Russia" (Rusya'nın Neron'u) of a coming revolutionary resurgence of Crimea.[87] Yet in "İsmail Gaspirinski'ye" this antipathy toward Russian power quickly makes way for an encomium to Gasprinsky, who "dared to do great, sacred work" on behalf of pan-Turkist ideals.

Yurdakul praises Gasprinsky as, above all, "a great Turk" (ulu Türk). He detaches Tatar personality from Crimean place and elevates it to such an extent that it loses its distinctiveness, its particular cultural and historical colouring. This move from *Tatar* to *Türk* is critical to our understanding of the cultural dynamics in the region of the Black Sea at this time. Whereas "the term *Tatar* had a specific territorial component […] the term *Türk* did not," as Uli Schamiloglu explains.[88] This terminological evolution was another deterritorialization, dilating and diluting Crimean Tatar personality. In Crimea it prompted a backlash from a new generation borne in Ismail Gasprinsky's shadow, who would soon speak a language of political authority along the corridors of the han-saray once more.

Chapter Two

Colonial Eyes

Downriver from the hansaray stand the humble premises where Ismail Gasprinsky turned *Tercüman* into "the most famous newspaper in the entire Muslim world."[1] Over the course of three decades (1883–1914), he exhausted a Skoropechatnik typesetting machine to produce a total of 1,194 issues, each one a labour of love.[2] His project was at once sweeping in scope and local in tone, both geopolitically ambitious and intensely personal. Through succinct news capsules and colourful feuilletons, Gasprinsky sought to educate and empower Muslim communities in a clear, straightforward idiom, but he also enlisted them at times in discussions about everyday life in Bağçasaray – about the efficacy of neighborhood policing, for example, or the water quality of the Çürük Suv River.[3] For all his designs to command a diverse, international audience across the shores of the Black Sea, he still referred to the newspaper in its very pages as "my" *Tercüman* and signed off on his editorials and serialized travelogues as simply "Ismail."[4] At times he even devoted entire pages to advertising his trusted Skoropechatnik for the printing of business cards and provincial circulars.[5]

Today a portmanteau captures the peculiarity of Gasprinsky's outlook: *glocal*. The concept of translation at the heart of his periodical's name was ultimately a translation between the global and the local, a give and take between the universal and the particular. Gasprinsky promoted a pan-Turkism that penetrated deeply into Central Asia while establishing sleepy Bağçasaray as a beacon of a new progressive Muslim culture. At the same time, he tied the prospect of a surge of Russian imperial power and a "heartfelt rapprochement of Russian Muslims with Russia" to the spread of local grassroots education among the Muslim peasantry.[6] Centre and periphery were not only radically interdependent for Gasprinsky; they were plural. From his modest printing house in Bağçasaray he reached elites in two mutally antagonistic imperial metropoles – Istanbul and Saint Petersburg – with high-flying visions of thriving empires, integrated populations, and "enlightened" subjects. In one breath he championed the civilizing role of Russia and, of course, called on "Russian Muslims to honour Pushkin." In another he spoke highly of the regime of Sultan Abdülhamid and lived up to Yurdakul's praise by publicly embracing the transnational ethnonym *Türk* rather than *Tatar*.[7] "Although the Turks who were subjects of Russia are called by the name 'Tatar,' this is an error and an imputation," he wrote in 1905. "Those peoples who are called by the Russians as 'Tatar' […] are in reality, Turks."[8] In other words, looking upon the destruction of the bond between Crimean place and Tatar personality, Gasprinsky did not attempt to repair or restore it. Instead, in a passionate quest for the socio-political revival of all Muslims in the region of the Black Sea, Gasprinsky heeded his own motto, "What is best for a man is that which is most useful and practical," and cast Tatar personality into the swell of both pan-Turkism and Russkoe musul'manstvo (Russian Islam).[9]

At the turn of the twentieth century Gasprinsky therefore cultivated a position for Crimea in both Russian and Ottoman imperial geographies. He serviced Russian and Ottoman claims to the peninsula, which helps explain why Russia and Turkey both attempt to lay claim to his legacy today. Turkish president Recep Tayyip Erdoğan, for instance, opened the proceedings of the 2019 Türk Konseyi (Turk Congress), a critical conduit of Turkish political and cultural power in Central Asia, by citing Gasprinsky as an inspiration behind its integrationist agenda.[10] A year earlier a Russian propagandistic documentary film entitled *Ismail and His People* (*Ismail i ego liudi*, a title that in Russian studiously avoids *ego narod*, "his people" in the sense of "his nation") premiered on Red Square thanks to state support from the History of the Fatherland Fund.[11] Even Sergei Aksenov, who is head of the de-facto Russian administration of Crimea and known in the criminal underworld as "Goblin," refers to Gasprinsky reverently as "our fellow countryman."[12]

This transnational appropriation of Gasprinsky today is not only the result of his strategic imperial bet-hedging of over a century ago. It is above all a reflection of the way in which his prolific output and visionary leadership at the helm of *Tercüman* cleared space for new views that related to but departed from his own. He blazed trails for the diverse, even divergent itineraries that would come well after him. To use Michel Foucault's vocabulary, Gasprinsky was a "founder of discursivity," a writer who propelled currents of discourse that he could not anticipate or control, a thinker whose influence spawned respectful rebels as well as loyal epigones.[13] Among the former was a motley group of poets and intellectuals who collectively became known as Yaş Tatarlar or Genç Tatarlar, the Young Tatars.

The Young Tatars pivoted away from Gasprinsky to condemn the Russian colonization of Crimea and to fight to secure a singular bond between Crimean place and Tatar personality. In reaction to the decades of rhetorical "de-Tatarization" of Crimea in Russian and Turkish discourse – which, as we saw in chapter 1, accompanied a physical and material one, particularly after the Crimean War – writers like Hasan Çergeyev and Üsein Şâmil Toktargazy pursued a re-Tatarization of the Black Sea peninsula. As we will see, their cultural and political struggle to promote the idea of a bounded territorial Crimean Tatar homeland was not theirs alone. Leading Ukrainian writers at the fin de siècle – Lesia Ukraïnka and Mykhailo Kotsiubynsky – also advanced an anti-colonial discourse invested in the fate of the Crimean Tatar Other. Their remarkably similar approaches offer us a vivid case of intertextual alignment and communion. They also direct us to the role of sight in contesting the dialectic of imperial possession and in returning fire against colonial power. In the process, they make way for something new: solidary reflection, in which the image of the Ukrainian can be seen in the image of the Crimean Tatar.

1.

If Gasprinsky's vision and leadership facilitated the emergence of voices at odds with his own, the Young Tatar newspaper *Vatan Hadimi* (Servant of the Homeland; first published in 1906) stood at the vanguard of this opposition. It was *Tercüman*'s fractious stepchild – vocal, disruptive, and unequivocal in its denunciations of autocracy. "Tsars and sultans offer nothing of value," its pages read, "other than the gilded crowns on their heads."[14] The newspaper shared *Tercüman*'s modernizing mission and its goal of unifying Muslims of the Black Sea region, employing a language akin to Gasprinsky's *lisan-ı umumi* (common language) to reach the broadest possible readership. But it could not tolerate the deep injustices of colonial rule and, like Gasprinsky, play the long game. In this way *Vatan Hadimi* was clearly and indelibly marked by the revolutionary fervour of 1905, when the prospect of republican democracy and national liberation in the Russian Empire appeared, if only momentarily, on the horizon.[15] The newspaper's political abandon brought about punitive fines and intermittent closures, all of which reduced its shelf life. Only a handful of its hundreds of issues are extant today. *Vatan Hadimi* burned brightly but burned fast, ceasing operations in the summer of 1908.

Right before its closure, *Vatan Hadimi* published a revealing poem by a learned young teacher from Simferopol named Hasan Çergeyev (1879–1946). In a sense, the poem is the newspaper's epitaph, a poignant reflection on the reason and purpose of its existence. "Your body is broken, your head held high, / Your soul paces in a cage [*Canıñ teprene qafeste*]," one of its stanzas reads, "But let fear never enter your heart." Entitled "Közyaş han çeşmesi" (The khan's fountain of tears), Çergeyev's work adopts the popular *koşma* form common to Turkic folk poetry to craft what is at once a lament and an indictment. It bemoans the consequences of the dialectic of imperial possession and does so by communicating with the talismanic literary text that helped empower it in Crimea: Pushkin's *Bakhchisaraiskii fontan*, which was translated into the Crimean Tatar language by Osman Akçokraklı in 1899.

If Pushkin may be said to have stolen the legend of Kırım Giray's fountain for Russian literature, Çergeyev steals it back in "Közyaş han çeşmesi." As we will see later in this chapter, his short poem would be adapted and recited publicly amid the tumult of 1917 in anticipation of a return of Crimean Tatar political sovereignty. Its political and cultural purchase stems from the way in which Çergeyev reappropriates the image of the khan's fountain and animates it in a new way. In the elegiac coda of Pushkin's poem, as we recall, the ruins of Crimean Tatar power provoke the lyrical persona's pensive reflections on an irretrievable past. Only place remains – a place to be filled, presumably, by imperial colonizers. Pushkin's persona wanders "among mute passages" (sredi bezmolvnykh perekhodov) of a Bakhchisarai palace enveloped in a pregnant silence: "All is quiet around me" (Krugom vse tikho).

Çergeyev's lyrical persona in "Közyaş han çeşmesi" finds something more. He too walks the vacant corridors of the hansaray, which he approaches as a site of the past political location and current cultural dislocation of the Crimean Tatars. Wandering its grounds at night, his lyrical persona turns to the fountain of tears and asks it directly, "For whom do you weep?" The fountain answers, "I have been flowing since the times of the khan":

Evel zaman çeşit sesler
Çuvuldardı bu evlerde,
Şimdi yalnız quşçuqlar
Suv içeler bu kemerde.
. . . .
Boş ... xiç bir yerden ses çıqmaz,
Ağlarım, yaş tamlar yere.[16]

(In days long gone, a host of voices
Whispered in these rooms.
Now only lonely birds
Drink from my basin. [...]
Emptiness ... there is only silence here,
I weep, my tears falling to the ground.)

The silence in "Közyaş han çeşmesi" is not the silence in the coda of Pushkin's *Bakhchisaraiskii fontan*. It is a broken silence. "When I pronounce the word silence," writes the poet Wisława Szymborska, "I destroy it."[17] Endowed with voice, Çergeyev's fountain destroys it too. Its voice is dormant agency. In the poem's concluding couplet, the fountain accordingly speaks of the possibility of a revival of Tatar personality on Crimean place: "I wait for friends to come alive."

Nearly two decades before Çergeyev, the Ukrainian poet Lesia Ukraïnka (1871–1913) had a similar vision. Stricken with tuberculosis of the bones, Ukraïnka often convalesced in Crimea, where the warmer climate provided comfort. She referred to the peninsula as "the Tatar land."[18] It was a place whose distance from home could provoke feelings of loneliness, but whose complex history and rich cultural inheritance stoked the fire of her talent. Crimean Tatar culture in particular was an object of her artistic fascination and close study. Writing to her uncle Mykhailo Drahomanov in 1891, Ukraïnka reveals that she is collecting Crimean Tatar symbols and embroidery patterns, of which "there are so many good specimens, so similar to Ukrainian ones."[19] As we will see, such similarities between Ukrainians and Crimean Tatars were not the only ones she would explore in her work.

Ukraïnka's letter to Drahomanov was written while she was composing *Krymski spohady* (*Crimean Reminiscences*, 1893), a lyric cycle closely modelled on Adam Mickiewicz's *Sonety krymskie* (*Crimean Sonnets*, 1826) and highly intertextual with Pushkin's *Bakhchisaraiskii fontan*. Over the course of her career Ukraïnka repeatedly wrote back to Pushkin to skew his wreath of laurels. Her verse drama *Kaminnyi hospodar* (*The Stone Host*, 1911), for instance, revisits the Don Juan legend that had been revisited by Pushkin in *Kamennyi gost* (*The Stone Guest*, 1830) – her title alone is a knock and a nod – by presenting Donna Anna as an ambitious, calculating tragic heroine and transforming Don Juan into a figure of defiant resistance to conservative power.[20] In the second poem of her *Krymski spohady* cycle, which is entitled "Bakhchysaraiskyi dvorets" (The palace of Bakhchysarai), Ukraïnka gestures toward Pushkin's footsteps while forging a new path. Her lyrical persona too roams the former seat of power of the Giray khans, but where her Polish and Russian counterparts see only ruins, she perceives faint, dormant life:

Тут водограїв ледве чутна мова, –
Журливо, тихо гомонить вода, –
Немов сльозами, краплями спада;
Себе оплакує оселя ся чудова.[21]

(Here the fountains barely make a sound,
The water murmurs quietly, mournfully,
And falls like drops of tears;
This special place weeps for itself.)

Ukraïnka's fountain emotes. As in Çergeyev's "Közyaş han çeşmesi," it is invested with agency, intimating that Tatar personality is not a mere vestige of the past but a seed with a future.

Çergeyev does not give an account of the events that wounded the bond between Crimean place and Tatar personality in "Közyaş han çeşmesi." The wound is simply given. But in a ground-breaking poem written a year later, he offers more detail, surveying the crimes and injustices of Crimea's colonization through an unconventional lens – the genre of the grotesque. Writing as "Anonymous" (Belgisiz), Çergeyev worked with a private publisher to release the poem "Eşit, mevta ne söyleyür!" (Listen to what the dead man says!, 1909) as a twelve-page pamphlet, slim enough to fit inside a jacket pocket. It caused a sensation. Within months of the publication of its Russian translation, the tsarist secret police identified Çergeyev as the author and placed him under surveillance, trailing the "unmarried thirty-year old who lives with his father," as police reports coldly described him, until his arrest and imprisonment in 1913.[22]

The "dead man" at the centre of "Eşit, mevta ne söyleyür!" is Ümer-oca (Ümer the teacher), a Crimean Tatar from the era of the khanate who rises from the grave and wanders across the Crimea of 1909, only to discover that his homeland, in effect, no longer exists. Crimean place remains, but Tatar personality is nowhere to be found. With satirical flourish Çergeyev adopts the literary genre of the grotesque but turns it upside down. Whereas works of the grotesque typically represent reality estranged by ghosts, monsters, and uncanny Others, "Eşit, mevta ne söyleyür!" features a living corpse estranged by the reality of Russian colonization. Ümer-oca is horrified by what he encounters across Crimea:

Yıqıldı köyler, yurt kesildi,
Mezarlıqlar yoq oldı,
Olanın da taşlarından
İlge bina quruldı.

Düştüm düşman qapqanına
Qaldım, sandım qabaatke.
Quvdılar beni, dediler:
-Poşöl tatarskiy lapatke![23]

(Villages were decimated, homes razed,
Cemeteries destroyed,
And from our tombstones
They built country estates.
I fell into the enemy's trap,
I stayed, thinking I was to blame.
They drove me away, crying,
"Get out, Tatar scum!")[24]

In this frightening land of the living, Ümer-oca discovers no traces of living Tatar culture. Only a handful of displaced, dislocated *mırza* princes remain: "One in a ditch, another in a field, / But none of them knows a homeland [*Bilinmez em Vatan yurtu*]." He sees only ignorance and poverty, mourning that "Tatar possessions in Crimea [*Qırımda tatar mülkü*] are only an illusion." The Crimean Tatars whom he does encounter have lost sight of themselves, having abandoned their distinctive dress and appearance in the throes of imperial-friendly self-fashioning to "look like Ivan." Ümer-oca's refrain echoes throughout the poem: "None of you is any different / From the dead lying in the ground."[25] Disturbed by the Crimea of 1909, he proceeds to bury himself back in the grave.

"Eşit, mevta ne söyleyür!" lacks the sliver of light of the conclusion of "Közyaş han çeşmesi." Yet even without a concluding note of optimism, Çergeyev still implies that not all is lost. After all, if the dead can come to life, then the past – once marked by a tight bond between Crimean place and Tatar personality – has a future. "What characterizes a specter," Derrida reminds us, "is that no one can be sure if by returning it testifies to a living past or a living future."[26] Throughout his verse Çergeyev suggests that Crimea's "living future" is contingent on scales falling off our eyes, on acts of looking and watching that penetrate the imperial veneer of power and authority. His protagonists preach, as it were, anti-colonial sightedness: his fountain in Bağçasaray "watches" its visitors (insanlara olup seyran) with a studied patience, biding time until there is a Crimean Tatar renaissance and rejuvenation, while his revenant Ümer-oca calls upon his interlocutors – and the reader herself – "to look upon the conditions" (Halımıznı hem baqıñız) around them and demand accountability for all the loss, suffering, and decay.

Here Çergeyev again walked in lockstep with Lesia Ukraïnka. A decade before "Eşit, mevta ne söyleyür!," she also drew attention to the role of sight in the dynamics of the Crimean Tatar encounter with Russian imperial power – but through the perspective of a Ukrainian woman. Her short story "Nad morem" (At the sea, 1901) is a tale of anti-colonial sight-seeing, a journey of intersubjective recognition in which a Ukrainian sees a Russian looking at a Crimean Tatar and, in the process, comes to see herself anew. On holiday in Crimea, Ukraïnka's nameless first-person narrator bristles at the behaviour of her fellow holidaymakers, whose only desire is to create a simulacrum of the imperial metropole on the Black Sea. She complains that their ships toss "corks, peels, old shoes, and all kinds of human misery" against the shore, while their military orchestras disrupt the tranquility of the natural environment with intrusive horns.[27]

The plot of "Nad morem" revolves around a relationship – and eventual conflict – between the highly introspective Ukrainian narrator and one of these holidaymakers, a Russian aristocrat from Moscow named Alla Mykhailivna (Mikhailovna), who is drawn to the pretensions of high society. The two spend time together strolling around Yalta's parks and promenades, but the narrator joins Alla Mykhailivna only reluctantly, unable to decline her invitations with conviction. Ukraïnka casts the Muscovite debutante as a superficial, self-absorbed Francophile who mistreats her servants and falls for a womanizer (*sertseïd*) who is seeking a casual tryst. Alla Mykhailivna is Chekhov's Anna Sergeevna without redeeming qualities – or a dog.[28]

Beneath this relatively banal plot lies not only a study of divergent conceptions of womanhood at the fin de siècle but also an incisive psychological portrait of colonialism on the Black Sea peninsula. The short story turns on a moment in which a Crimean Tatar boy, carrying a bucket of paint in one hand and a large brush in the other, bumps into Alla Mykhailivna and the narrator on the street. Reacting so suddenly that she nearly pushes the narrator off the sidewalk, Alla Mykhailivna screams for the boy to move and insults him under her breath (*"muzhlan,"* dolt). What transpires is a scene that haunts the narrator:

Хлопець трохи збочив і руку з квачем заложив за спину, щоб не зачепити панну, але при тому кинув такий погляд у наш бік, що мені стало ніяково. Не знаю, чи завважила той погляд Алла Михайлівна і чи вміла вона прочитати в ньому і зрозуміти той страшний, фатальний антагонізм, – темніший, ніж чорні очі молодого робітника. Не знаю, чи й хлопець побачив той погляд, що панна кинула йому вкупі з презирливими словами. Але я бачила обидва погляди, і мені стало страшно – в них була ціла історія.[29]

(The boy got out of the way and put the hand with the brush behind his back so as not to touch [Alla Mykhailivna], but in doing so, he cast such a gaze at us that I felt ill at ease. I do not know whether Alla Mykhailivna noticed this gaze or whether she could read it and understand that terrible, fatal antagonism – darker than the black eyes of the young worker. I do not know whether the boy noticed the gaze that [Alla Mykhailivna] cast at him or her contemptuous words. But I saw both gazes, and I was horrified – there was an entire history in them.)

Ukraïnka frames this specular confrontation, which underscores the role of sight in the production of cultural difference, as a psychological representation of the colonial relation. Alla Mykhailivna's gaze is what Frantz Fanon, expanding on Freud's work on the formation of the gendered subject, identifies as the racial "gaze," the look of the white colonizer that reifies and fixes the black colonized as dye does a chemical substance ("dans le sens où l'on fixe une preparation par un colorant").[30] For Fanon, the gaze of the colonizer objectifies the colonized and triggers a process of identification through which the latter "recognizes" himself as lacking, deficient, inferior. The gaze of the Crimean Tatar boy, meanwhile, is nothing less than what Homi Bhabha, referring to the work of Fanon, describes as "the threatened return of the look," a gesture of resistance to this colonial identification that manifests "a potentially conflictual, disturbing force."[31] Ukraïnka's narrator respects the violent power of this resistance. She envisions Alla Mykhailivna as Little Red Riding Hood chasing butterflies into a forest, oblivious to what happens to the colonizer when "the bloody scarlet of the sky overtakes the forest, the birds grow quiet [...] and amid the dark brush, the eyes of the wolf ignite with a wild fire."[32]

In this moment, Ukraïnka not only captures the "particular regime of visibility deployed in colonial discourse" but also dramatizes an encounter that exposes the narrator's identification and solidarity with the Crimean Tatar people.[33] For her narrator, this identification is abstract, implicit, and painful: "The boy had long ceased taking notice of us, but I could not stop thinking about his dark gaze [temnyi pohliad], and perhaps because of it, the vacuous affairs and carefree ramblings of my conversation partner evoked in me a kind of oppressive, almost tragic impression."[34] Toward the end of the story, while engaging in a heated argument with Alla Mykhailivna that finally spells the end of their contrived friendship, the narrator feels a building sense of frustration and anger that she cannot control. After impulsively proclaiming to Alla Mykhailivna that their conversations have been vapid and pointless, she remarks in an aside: "I did not say another word. I cast my eyes to the floor because I sensed that I had 'the dark gaze,' full of an irrepressible, fatal antagonism."[35] Like the Crimean Tatar boy, the Ukrainian woman harbours an unrealized, deep-seated antipathy to the Muscovite debutante and identifies with the "dark gaze." Explicit reasons for this identification are never given.

2.

For both Çergeyev and Ukraïnka the anti-colonial struggle is, at its core, a struggle to see and to be seen on one's own terms. It is to observe patiently, to look through and past the status quo, and to learn to view oneself as an imperial object susceptible to "an irrepressible, fatal antagonism." In time, as Fanon argues, it is also to realize that one's own sightlines are shaped by the colonizer, who even in confrontation "determines the centres of resistance" against him.[36] Only in shaking free of the imperial gaze can one cast eyes toward the horizons of decolonization and self-determination. Fanon suggests that this step necessarily involves an inward turn, an act of self-affirmation whereby the colonial relation is not merely inverted but discarded altogether. This work is, in Fanon's words, the work "to make myself known" (me faire connaître).[37]

For Üsein Şamil Toktargazy (1881–1913), every word was a conduit of such knowledge, every stanza a vehicle to answer the question "Who are the Crimean Tatars?" Born near Bağçasaray in the verdant village of Kökköz, which was the muse of such nineteenth-century landscape artists as Carlo Bossoli and Vladimir Orlovsky, Toktargazy lost his father at an early age. Formal education became an infrequent luxury. While working to provide for his family, he became a passionate autodidact who tried his hand at poems and songs. At first he could not escape Çergeyev's shadow. His poetic skills were simply not as sophisticated, scholars like Bekir Çoban-zade would later claim; even the foreword to Toktargazy's debut collection of verse made apologies for his "shortcomings" (eksiklik).[38] But what he lacked in finesse, he made up for in force, both poetic and political. As the Ukrainian polymath and Orientalist Ahatanhel Krymsky would argue in 1930, Toktargazy injected the Crimean Tatar national idea with unprecedented creative energy.[39]

He did so less by litigating the injustices wrought by the imperial dialectic of possession – injustices chronicled in Çergeyev's "Eşit, mevta ne söyleyür!" – than by promoting, even parading, a renewed equilibrial bond between Crimean place and Tatar personality. His verse not only heaves with exclamatory attestations of this bond but invests it with religious significance. In "Fi-medkh-i-Qırım" (Ode to Crimea), written in the *destan* ballad form, Toktargazy begins by gesturing to the past panegyrics to Crimean place. "Is there a poet alive who does not love Crimea?" he writes. "The great Pushkin was enchanted by it!"[40]

Almost dutifully, Toktargazy sings of the majesty of the peninsula's mountain crags, deep valleys, and cool streams, all of which offer up their beauty and form *to* Crimea. They do not define it. He ends each strophe with the word *Qırıma* (to Crimea), using the dative to underscore its position as an indirect object of virtues and affection, as a recipient of felt value. "Love of Crimea [*Qırımı hub*] is the work of the eternal Allah," Toktargazy writes, delivering a message of guidance (*hadith*) attributed to Muhammed:

«Hubb-ül-Vatan minnel iman» hadistir,
Vatanını sevmeyenler habistir,
Bu Vatana Tatar oğlu varistir,
Diğerler sahip olamaz Qırıma!
Qırım kibi Vatan var mı dünyada?
Tatarlıq kibi şan var mı dünyada?[41]

(The Prophet said, "Love of the homeland is a part of the faith,"
Those who do not love their homelands are sinners,
The heir to this homeland is the son of a Tatar,
Others will not possess Crimea!
Is there another homeland like Crimea in this world?
Is there another honour like Tatarness in this world?)

Toktargazy represents Crimea as the inheritance of the Tatars, and he does not do so casually. He speaks in the language of Islamic law, using *varis* (*warith*, "heir"), a term with standing in the elaborate system of regulations of *mawarith* (inheritance), which is informed, in part, by the fourth sura of the Qu'ran. This is a subtle move, but it is radical. No longer is the Crimean Tatar khan *varis*, the medium through which Allah bestows the gift of belonging and purpose onto his people. No longer does the khan – or the metonyms (the hansaray and the fountain) contiguous with him – embody the bond between Crimean place and Tatar personality. For Toktargazy, this bond now lives through the Crimean Tatar people themselves, who, as heirs, are responsible for its stewardship.

Toktargazy is more teacher than poet here. The *hadith* he cites– "Hubb-ül-Vatan minnel iman" (Love of the homeland is a part of the faith) – had wide currency among the Young Ottomans and Young Tatars of the era, appearing on the mastheads of Namık Kemal's Paris-based newspaper

Hürriyet (Liberty) and of the Crimean upstart *Vatan Hadimi*. Its message was efficient. Not only did it bestow religious meaning on the concept of nationalism – communicating, in effect, that being a devout Muslim meant being a patriotic Muslim – but it implied that religious obligations were due to the homeland. Toktargazy was accordingly a frequent practitioner of the obligative mood in the Crimean Tatar language. "We should love Crimea, we should face its losses, / and we should know its strengths," he writes elsewhere.[42]

Such prescriptions were only part of Toktargazy's literary agenda. Like Çergeyev, he had a taste for satire. He reserved his most effective barbs not for local Russian colonizers or authorities in the metropole but for conservative elements of Crimean Tatar society who exploited the imperial system for their own gain. In this way, both Çergeyev and Toktargazy present Crimean Tatar society as internally heterogeneous, captive to competing interests and even conflictual aspirations. In the poem "Para" (Money), for example, Toktargazy sarcastically ventriloquizes the voices of Crimean Tatars who worship wealth and instrumentalize education as a mere tool for material enrichment: "This has become the Tatar way," he writes. "You learn a trade because / Now it's all about money, money, money."[43]

Toktargazy's play *Mollalar proyekti* (The mullahs' project, 1909) was based on his own experiences campaigning for the poor and working to exorcize the influence of traditionalist clerics in Crimea. It imagines a hasty convention of mullahs debating responses to a campaign on the part of progressive Crimean Tatars – like Toktargazy himself – who travelled to Saint Petersburg to press for more educational opportunities and equality on the peninsula. In the play one of the mullahs reports on the efforts of these progressive activists to reduce the standing of the conservative *ulema* (body of Muslim religious scholars) and remarks disdainfully, "But who will perform *namaz* [prayer ritual] for the ignorant Tatar [*qara tatarğa*]?" After hearing of proposals to redistribute land from the clerics to the poor, the mullah adds, "And what are we going to live on? Should we serve [*hızmet etmeq*] for free?" Another mullah recommends petitioning the tsar with a drastic proposal: "At the very least we need to write that the Tatar people do not need freedom! Freedom is the tsar's to give away, so let other people have it!"[44]

Like Çergeyev with Ukraïnka, Toktargazy had an intertextual companion in the Ukrainian writer Mykhailo Kotsiubynsky (1864–1913). A Crimean Tatar play like Toktargazy's *Mollalar proyekti* is at stake in the novella *Pid minaretamy* (Under the minarets), which Kotsiubynsky wrote during a summer sojourn in Bakhchysarai in 1904 and published in the journal *Kievskaia starina* in 1905. The work is a study of a profound generational and ideological conflict between two camps in Crimean Tatar society at the turn of the century, between traditionalist mullahs and progressive, youthful "enlighteners." With a sustained focus on the lived experience of Crimean Tatars, *Pid minaretamy* has no room for Ukrainians per se. It makes no explicit mention of their history or culture. Yet as we will see, Kotsiubynsky nonetheless fashions the text as an effective commentary about Ukrainians – and particularly about the debate between *narodnytstvo* (populism) and *modernizm* in fin de siècle Ukrainian literature.[45]

Kotsiubynsky was a pioneer in detaching the Ukrainian language from the representation of Ukrainian life. In his effervescent modernist prose he sets the language free to address universal themes in diverse cultural settings, from Moldavian towns to Crimean Tatar villages. *Pid minaretamy* sees Kotsiubynsky at the top of his form, combining the flair for impressionistic colour of "Na kameni" ("On the Rock," 1902) – an *akvarel'* (watercolour) set in Crimea and populated with Crimean Tatar, Turkish, and Greek characters – with the kind of extensive ethnographic detail found in *Tini zabutykh predkiv* (*Shadows of Forgotten Ancestors*, 1912). *Pid minaretamy* is alive with the sights and sounds of Bakhchysarai, with the frenetic rhythms of its cafes and the heated debates of its people. At one point Kotsiubynsky takes us inside a dervish tekke and captures in rapturous prose the young novice Abibula's synaesthetic experience of *sema*, the whirling dance:

Плигає тіло в шалених рухах, хвилюють груди, і скаче голова, залита потом, а крізь заплющені очі він бачить небо, усе в огнях. Бачить троянди, червоні гранати, білі лілеї … Горять … цвітуть … літають … Цілий дощ цвітів …[46]

(His body convulses in frenzied motions, his chest billows, and his head, covered in sweat, dances to and fro. Through closed eyes he sees the sky, consumed in flames. He sees roses, red pomegranates, white lilies … They burn … They bloom … They fly … Flowers like sheets of rain …)

Scattered throughout the novella, meanwhile, are Tatar phrases left untranslated, at once estranging the reader from the text and drawing her into it with a verisimilar simulation of the experience of the foreigner. The shouts of hawkers peddling lemonade in the market bazaar, for example, are "heard" by the reader but not understood: "O-oi buzly! … pek tatly!" (Ice cold! … Quite sweet!)

Kotsiubynsky, in other words, crafts his story through the warp and weft of Crimean place and Tatar personality. Non-Tatar communities are not featured in the text, nor does the politics of colonial expansion figure centrally in its plot. As with Toktargazy's *Mollalar proyekti*, what is showcased is an internal struggle for Crimean Tatar personality itself. At the centre of Kotsiubynsky's novella is Rustem, the son of a prominent local mullah who rebels against a creeping "darkness" and a profound "regress" (vidstalist) that are overtaking the Muslim Tatar community.[47] He becomes estranged from his father and, spurning his social station, takes up work at a café run by a family rival. There he agitates against the overbearing influence of local mullahs, imams, and muftis and for the education of women and the poor, calling for enhanced literacy by way of curriculum reform. He discovers an intellectual equal in Mir'iem and dreams of making a life with her out in the wider world, free of the constricting conventions of their patriarchal society. But this dream is interrupted by violent conflict. Disciples of the Bakhchysarai religious elite confront Rustem and condemn him as a sinner and *beynamaz* (heathen). What ultimately provokes the confrontation is a work of literature, a play like Toktargazy's *Mollalar proyekti*.

Rustem is a writer, a character inspired by the likes of Toktargazy, Çergeyev, and other modernizers – or *taraqqiparvarlar* (lovers of progress) – who emulated Gasprinsky and pursued "knowledge and enlightenment."[48] Such activists oriented their pursuit in the direction of Europe, and so does Rustem. Europe is a beacon for him, a banner to take up. His earnest comrade, the merchant Dziafer, distills this Eurocentrism in a creed: "Give us a literature. Give us our Byrons, our Shakespeares, our Goethes! And then we will stand alongside all other peoples and enter the family of cultured nations! [...] A unified, strong literary language, a literature in the European spirit!"

Rustem's play is written in this European spirit. In a moment focalized through the perspective of the dervish Abibula, Rustem is described as "inciting the people against religion, writing books in which not a word is devoted to God, and mocking old traditions and even the Qu'ran." After surviving a number of false starts, his play opens in Bakhchysarai to the great curiosity of local tradesmen, workers, merchants, and even clerics, "who wish to see with their own eyes how far Rustem's courage has taken him." Kotsiubynsky tells us little about the performance, only revealing that, like Toktargazy's *Mollalar proyekti*, it skewers mullahs who misrepresent the spirit of Islam. Kotsiubynsky dwells instead on the play's reception in the Crimean Tatar community, on the critical reaction that it prompts among local religious elites and traditionalists. They denounce it as "debauchery" (rozpusta).

This scandalized reception of a new work of Crimean Tatar literature, ostensibly prompted by a concern for the moral health and harmony of the people, is strikingly reminiscent of a key moment in the history of Ukrainian culture. In 1902, less than two years before the composition of *Pid minaretamy*, the Ukrainian populist critic Serhy Yefremov published an infamous essay entitled "U poiskakh novoi krasoty" (In search of new beauty) in the journal *Kievskaia starina*. Especially outraged by the modernist prose of Olha Kobylianska, Yefremov rails against what he considers a slavish dependence on European thinkers and an elitist contempt for the peasantry on the part of the "young generation" of Ukrainian writers. He labels their literary modernism, with its focus on the psychological world of the individual, a "national pathology" (natsionalnyi marazm).[49] His populist offensive against the modernist agenda would prove intensive and prolonged – and influential. Over eight years after the publication of "U poiskakh novoi krasoty," for instance, Ivan Nechui-Levytsky would revisit the concept of modernist "shamelessness" and argue that it comes dangerously close to "pornography," in an article entitled "Ukraïnska dekadentshchyna" (Ukrainian decadence).[50]

Yefremov's sally in a conflict between *narodnytstvo* (populism) and *modernizm* brought about a series of swift responses from Kotsiubynsky. First, he wrote to the primary target of Yefremov's attack, Olha Kobylianska, with high praise for her talent: "I am simply enchanted by your short story [...] Everything about it reveals such a fresh and strong talent [...] I am so happy for our literature." He then expresses regret over the way in which Yefremov and his circle "treat modern directions in literature with such hostility."[51] Months later, Kotsiubynsky wrote Kobylianska again to celebrate her writing: "I am such a sincere admirer of your talent and your *completely European* style of writing."[52]

This positive evaluation of the Europeanness of the new modernist Ukrainian literature is something that Kotsiubynsky would advocate in a public letter written with Mykola Cherniavsky in February 1903. Nominally addressed to Ivan Franko, the document articulated a rationale for a Ukrainian modernist literature in a measured tone: "In recent years the literary movement in Ukraine has become noticeably lively. This is evident both in the increase in literary production and in the growth of publishing activity, as well as in the spread of Ukrainian books not only among the popular masses but also among the intelligentsia [...] Our intelligent reader – raised on *the better models of modern European literature*, which is rich not only in its themes but also in the techniques it employs in the construction of plot – has the right to expect from his native literature a wider field of view, a genuine portrayal of the different sides of the life of all people, not just one layer of society."[53] In *Pid minaretamy*, written only months after this letter, Kotsiubynsky's Crimean Tatar hero Rustem echoes this judgment of Europe.

In Rustem's view, Europeans "are stronger than us because their intellect is stronger." His vocal promotion of European ideals – particularly in literary form – leads to near-fatal physical conflict and the realization that "everyone is against [him]." Rustem considers giving up and leaving Bakhchysarai at the end of the novella, but the support of his friends persuades him to stay and continue the fight.

The congruencies between the Ukrainian populists and the Crimean Tatar traditionalists, on the one hand, and between the Ukrainian modernists and the Crimean Tatar modernizers, on the other, signal a profound identification between Ukrainians and Crimean Tatars that is at work under the surface of Kotsiubynsky's novella. This identification is not a metonymical relation, in which the Crimean Tatar experience stands as somehow a part of the Ukrainian whole. A relation based on such contiguity is the type presumed, for instance, by Ahatanhel Krymsky, the Ukrainian philologist and polymath who claimed Crimean Tatar ancestry.[54] Krymsky and his colleagues write that a "complete, multi-sided history of Ukraine is impossible" (usestoronnia, neodnobichna istoriia ukraïnstva nemozhlyva) without a knowledge of "oriental peoples" like the Crimean Tatars, who constitute one "side" among others.[55] While Krymsky elsewhere writes of specific parallels between the Ukrainian *vertep* (puppet theatre) and Crimean Tatar folk drama, for example, he tends to cast such resemblances as partial and particular.[56] For Kotsiubynsky in *Pid minaretamy* and for Ukraïnka in "Nad morem," by contrast, the identification between the two distinct groups is consistent, thorough, and metaphorical. Their texts are a looking-glass through which the Ukrainian comes to see herself in the Crimean Tatar. In 1917 this dynamic of cultural reflection becomes a political vision.

3.

Just over a decade after Kotsiubynsky's *Pid minaretamy*, what had been a literary campaign to "re-Tatarize" Crimea – to restore the bond between Crimean place and Tatar personality – suddenly took on urgent political purchase. The chaos of the First World War had blown open political opportunities for the non-Russian nations of the Russian Empire, turning the "national question" into an answer. Across the Black Sea, readers in Istanbul could see the world changing in the very titles of such collections as *Ukrayna, Rusya ve Türkiye* (1915), which featured a map of Ukraine as a bordered polity not unlike the one we know today, albeit without Crimea (fig. 4). It also featured the eminent historian and political activist Mykhailo Hrushevsky surveying modern Ukrainian history and culture in Ottoman Turkish translation.[57] In

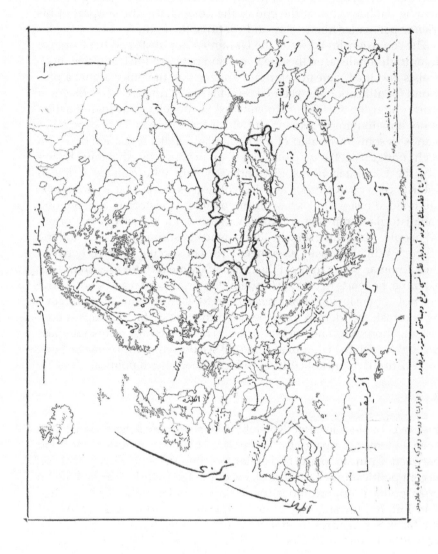

4. Map of Ukraine, in *Ukrayna, Rusya ve Türkiye* (1915)

the popular Istanbul daily newspapers *İkdam* (Effort) and *Tanin* (Resonance), Ukraine and Crimea became new geopolitical actors splashed across dramatic headlines.[58]

In the pivotal year of 1917, Ukrainian and Crimean Tatar activists had an abiding inclination to support one another in what became a gradual, uneven, and often dangerous climb toward national autonomy. In July, roughly a month after Hrushevsky's Tsentralna Rada (Central Council) had declared autonomy for Ukraine, a Crimean Tatar delegation visited Kyiv hoping to follow in its footsteps. Among their number was Cafer Seydamet, who considered an "inspection of the Ukrainian national movement [*Ukrayna milli hareketi*] a necessity."[59] Seydamet and his colleagues asked their Ukrainian counterparts "to support their aspirations for the establishment of Crimea's autonomy." More than that – according to the Simferopol-based newspaper *Golos Tatar* (Voice of the Tatars), "the Muslims expressed a desire for the territorial annexation of Crimea to Ukraine" (o territorialnom prisoedinenii Kryma k Ukrainie).[60] Seydamet found a "playful-eyed" Hrushevsky receptive to their cause; Volodymyr Vynnychenko, strangely inscrutable, "off in his own world"; and Symon Petliura, "the sincerest of all."[61]

The precise results of these deliberations are not entirely clear. Any record of them has become a casualty of political turbulence.[62] What did emerge from the July meeting was a Congress of the Enslaved Peoples of Russia hosted by the Tsentralna Rada in Kyiv in September 1917. On its first day Seydamet paid tribute to the hosts and wished "success to the Ukrainian movement."[63] Symon Petliura replied in turn, "I firmly believe that Russia stands on the brink of death when it does not turn to the living source of the nations that comprise it. All of us – Ukrainians, Tatars, Georgians, and all others – are great nations."[64] Among the Crimean Tatar leaders in attendance was Amet Özenbaşlı, who proclaimed in a passionate speech that, "just as the khans forged unions with Ukrainians […], we free sons of the Tatar people extend our hand to you."[65] He then evoked the legendary image of the fountain in the hansaray, reciting from a Russian-language adaptation of Çergeyev's "Közyaş han çeşmesi." Özenbaşlı challenged the attendees of the congress to bring the weeping fountain back to life, to rejuvenate it once more.[66]

Poems never seemed far from the lips of Crimean Tatar activists at this time. Amid the chaos of revolution, poetry often becomes a harbour of stability and clarity. Some poems were vehicles of effusive apostrophe to national identity: "I do not deny it," wrote the poet and activist Cemil Kermençikli, "I am a Tatar, a Tatar to my very core!"[67] Most were testaments to a renewed bond between Crimean place and

Tatar personality. Şevki Bektöre's "Tatarlığım" (My Tatar identity, or My Tatarness, 1913) – a poem considered "bound to the soul of the nation"[68] – refers to this bond in a mode elegiac and prayerful: "My Tatar identity, my homeland [*Tatarlığım, tuvğan yerim*], / I have loved them both since childhood. / And for them I have often / Wept and suffered."[69]

Another poem composed at this time, "Ant etkenmen" (I pledged), would become the national hymn of the Crimean Tatars, a song later sung "in KGB basements and prisons."[70] Its author was Noman Çelebicihan, who joined Özenbaşlı and Seydamet in Kyiv in 1917 and returned to Crimea determined to establish the most progressive parliament in the Muslim world. Named after ancient assemblies of the khanate period, the Qurultay foregrounded the Crimean Tatars as the titular nation of Crimea but sought to represent the interests of all inhabitants of the peninsula, committing to the rights to "freedom of identity [*svoboda lichnosti*], speech, press, conscience, assembly, housing," and more.[71] Before its first session in December 1917, the incoming members of the Qurultay recited Celebicihan's "Ant etkenmen" aloud, casting its words across the grounds of the hansaray where Catherine strode triumphantly in 1787.[72] Çelebicihan had been appointed mufti, Crimea's chief religious authority, and his verse accordingly sounds the confident, compassionate tones of the Qu'ran. His lyrical persona also speaks of "living for the sake of" his people, embracing the trope of martyrdom common to the *vatan şiirleri* of Namık Kemal, whose work Çelebicihan had read voraciously as a student in Istanbul.[73] The last stanza of his "Ant etkenmen" looks mortality in the face and speaks of the ultimate sacrifice for his nation:

> Ant etkenmen, söz bergenmen millet içün ölmege,
> Bilip, körip milletimniñ köz yaşını silmege.
> Bilmey, körmey biñ yaşasam, Qurultayga han bolsam,
> Kene bir kün mezarcılar kelir meni kommege.[74]

> (I pledged and gave my word to die for the nation,
> And knowing and seeing my nation's tears, to wipe them away.
> Even if I live a thousand years, even if I become khan to the Qurultay,
> One day the gravediggers will come to bury me all the same.)

Çelebicihan fulfilled this pledge. A recent novella by Uzbek writer Timur Pulatov (aka Timur Pulat) has him write it in his own blood on a prison cell wall.[75] In the first months of 1918, Bolshevik forces invaded Crimea, forcing the Qurultay to disband and scatter. They arrested

Çelebicihan and took him to Sevastopol's "Quarantine Bay," where ships were traditionally held before passengers came ashore. There he was tortured and shot, his clothes and belongings looted, and his body dumped in the Black Sea.[76] His murder presaged a new period of violent dispossession at the hands of Soviet power, an era indelibly marked by Stalin's Crimean atrocity.

PART TWO

Dispossession

PART TWO

PART TWO

Dispossession

Chapter Three

Ethnic Cleansing, Discursive Cleansing

"O frenzied waves, do not rise so high," wrote Crimean Tatar poet Şevki Bektöre in 1918. "Give way, release me, let me go."[1] Bektöre had crossed the Black Sea no less than three times in the months following the demise of the Crimean Tatar Qurultay. As the Treaties of Brest-Litovsk quelled hostilities between Russia and the Ottoman Empire and recognized an independent Ukrainian People's Republic, he shuttled anxiously between his home in Istanbul and his ancestral home in Crimea, a young man on a committed search for purpose amid unsettled political waters. "O frenzied waves," he pleaded, "are you resentful of my passion?" Bektöre's intrepid movements across the shores of the Black Sea, over fluid imperial and national borders, came at a time when Turks, Ukrainians, and Crimean Tatars were exploring alliances against Russian power, tensing the Scythian bow in an attempt to reverse Catherine's gains in the Black Sea region.[2] Like Gasprinsky and Çelebicihan before him, Bektöre deepened the lanes of social and political exchange in a unique zone of contact between what are today Turkey, Russia, and Ukraine. He was, in other words, a region maker.

Arriving in the port of Kefe (Feodosiia) in the spring of 1918, Bektöre witnessed first-hand the destruction wrought by frenzied waves of military advances and retreats in Crimea. He quickly learned of the downfall of the Crimean Tatar Qurultay and of the brutal murder of his friend Çelebicihan at the hands of the Bolsheviks. The tragedy came as a shock; the news had not yet reached Istanbul.[3] Communication across the Black Sea was notoriously slow. Atatürk once wrote to Lenin, "Whatever disagreements exist between us are due to the slowness of correspondence [*yazışmaların yavaşlığı*] between Ankara and Moscow."[4] In Kefe, Bektöre was therefore tasked with bringing word of the violent fate of the Qurultay back home. In October 1918 the influential

Ottoman-language periodical *Kırım Mecmuası* carried the story, placing below a photograph of the Qurultay a caption that read, "They sacrificed for the nation in blood."[5]

This abatement of Crimean Tatar political authority and autonomy under Bolshevik rule was dramatic, but it was not to last. "Frenzied waves" wax and wane. In the 1920s, with the emergence of a battery of ambitious Soviet policies known by the term *korenizatsiia* (indigenization), new currents of possibility washed upon the banks of what had become the Autonomous Soviet Socialist Republic (ASSR) of Crimea. Promoted by Lenin, overseen by Stalin, korenizatsiia was a belated concession to what had been a dangerously underestimated opponent of Bolshevism in the civil wars across the former Russian Empire: nationalism. It was an implicit acknowledgment of the swift force and deep resilience of what Stalin called the "kaleidoscope of national groups" that brought the Tsentralna Rada and the Qurultay, among many other examples, to political power.[6] In an eager attempt to reassure non-Russian nations that the Soviet project was not a retread of an empire afflicted by what Lenin termed "Great Russian chauvinism," korenizatsiia sought to "root" and nurture national languages, national cultures, and national elites in tens of thousands of national territorial units – "in their place" (na meste), as Stalin put it[7] – with the expectation that these national energies would eventually "exhaust [themselves] completely" en route to the construction of a postnational *Homo sovieticus*.[8] In a sense, the policy was a breathtakingly bold attempt to affirm the tight bond between native cultural content – what we have been calling *personality* – and territorial form – *place* – at the centre of our discussion in part 1.[9]

Korenizatsiia turned out to be fleeting, however. It was caught up among the "contradictory zigzags" of a regime lurching from one thing to the next, as Lev Trotsky memorably put it.[10] After 1927, Stalin's geopolitical paranoia slowly perverted what had been a policy of ethnophilia into a program of ethnocide. Soviet non-Russian nations along the Black Sea coast, a site of geostrategic sensitivity for Moscow, were especially vulnerable in this new order, and none more so than the Crimean Tatars. The Second World War compounded the peril, and its penultimate year brought cataclysm. When the Nazi threat receded in 1944, Stalin seized an opportunity to obliterate the bond between Crimean place and Tatar personality once and for all – not only by ethnically cleansing the Crimean Tatars from the peninsula but also by discursively cleansing them from Soviet life. It was coordinated physical and epistemic violence that aimed to erase them, and their claims of possession of a homeland, from the face of the earth.

1.

What I call *discursive cleansing* is an amplification and extension of conventional censorship, a disciplining of representation that is both retrospective and prospective in its application.[11] As we will see, it targets not simply the work of writers or artists and their textual traces but also a prevailing understanding of the world, an *idea*. Discursive cleansing is the traditional handmaiden of ethnic cleansing, from today's China, where scholarship on Uighur culture is subject to deletion, to today's Myanmar, where Facebook removes posts documenting crimes against the Rohingya people.[12] In the case of the Crimean Tatars, discursive cleansing abetted Soviet ethnic cleansing by assaulting the most essential of ideas – that a group called the Crimean Tatars existed, or had the right to exist, at all.

It hardly seemed to matter that the indigeneity of the Crimean Tatars had been a pillar of Soviet Crimea in the 1920s. At this time korenizatsiia had "drummed it into Crimea that it was Tatar, Tatar," as Aleksandr Solzhenitsyn emphatically put it. "Even the alphabet was in Arabic [script], and all its signs in Tatar."[13] This Tatarization, which established the Crimean Tatars as the indigenous people of the Crimean ASSR, may not have penetrated very deeply beyond the surface level in the political realm – ultimately, Vozgrin calls it a "Bolshevik bluff"[14] – but its effects in the realm of culture were beyond doubt, particularly between 1923 and 1928. This fleetingly golden period marked the tenure of the chairman of the Central Executive Committee of the Crimean ASSR, Veli İbraimov, a disciple of Ismail Gasprinsky who had helped operate *Tercüman's* Skoropechatnik typesetting machine as a boy and later contributed to the pages of the newspaper *Vatan Hadimi* as a young man.[15]

Under İbraimov's leadership there was an intense flowering of Crimean Tatar literature, visual art, music, and drama. This cultural renaissance was a selling point in Koç-Yardımı (Resettlement Help), a locally orchestrated initiative led by writer and dramatist Amet Özenbaşlı.[16] Koç-Yardımı sought to pull Crimean Tatar emigrés scattered across the Black Sea region into the Soviet orbit and to facilitate their organized return to Crimea. It was an entrepreneurial exercise of what Terry Martin calls the Piedmont Principle, "the belief that cross-border ethnic ties could be exploited to project Soviet influence into neighboring states."[17] İbraimov made a grave error in the process of sanctioning the project, however: he failed to secure Kremlin approval.[18] His freelancing prompted the ire of Stalin, who by the end of the 1920s was losing faith in the utility of the Piedmont Principle. Stalin had become captive to the notion that such cross-border activity could cut another way, leading not to an expansion of the borders of Soviet influ-ence but to their penetration and retraction. As Martin makes clear, the exploitation of cross-border ethnic ties – of korenizatsiia's extra-Soviet potential – came to stoke a fear in Stalin that would later lead to a vio-lent backlash against non-Russian national elites, national institutions, and national cultures.[19] İbraimov was an early victim of this backlash. He was executed in 1928.

Yet there was another backlash as well, one driven not by a fear of cross-border ties but by a fear of cross-ethnic ones. This was a backlash against what might be called, in the realm of the arts, *cross-korenizat-siia*, whereby the promotion of the work of culture in one non-Russian national space directly affirmed and promoted national consciousness in another. As evidenced in their censorial practices and their targeting of elites, Soviet authorities in the 1930s grew concerned about the work of national actors not only in the advancement of their own distinctive non-Russian national culture but also in the advancement of another's distinctive non-Russian national culture. Korenizatsiia, after all, was a massive and often confused state undertaking, and its outcomes did not always track along straight lines. While it often involved disentan-gling and differentiating national cultures from one another – especially among Central Asian peoples, where regional and tribal affiliations could criss-cross through Uzbek and Kazakh national denominations, for instance[20] – korenizatsiia also promoted an entanglement of national cultures. This intermingling did more than lay the ground for the con-flation of national cultures envisioned as the end game of Soviet policy; it did more than spark cross-cultural understanding or, alternatively, interethnic contestation and conflict.

At times, Soviet korenizatsiia empowered national cultures to *reinforce* each other in processes of solidary identification. An eloquent testament to this phenomenon can be found in the pages of the Belarusian-language journal *Maladniak* (The Young) in 1928. Commenting upon a visit to Belarus by the Ukrainian writers Maik Yohansen and Volodymyr Sosiura – who were representing the Kharkiv-based literary organiza-tion Hart (The Tempering) at a gathering hosted by the Minsk-based organization Maladniak – the Soviet comparatist Petr Buzuk describes the presence of the Ukrainians as evidence of the "common roads" of Belarusian and Ukrainian cultures.[21] In his view, these cultures nour-ish one another in the young Soviet Union not by way of a reductive, mythic East Slavic "brotherhood" but by way of a productive interplay between their "harmonies and disharmonies."[22] Soviet Ukrainian cul-ture, Buzuk proclaims, "echoes proudly in the Belarusian soul."[23]

Amplified by the policy of korenizatsiia, such echoes redounded across cultures as well as within them, making possible mutually beneficial projects of transnational solidarity among non-Russian nations in the early Soviet Union. These projects deserve more study. We understandably tend to conceptualize the objects of affective identification among Soviet citizens as a dual proposition – as identification with "the nation to which they were officially ascribed" and/or with the Soviet Union "as motherland or fatherland," as Ronald Grigor Suny frames it.[24] But a third, more supplementary and ad hoc proposition could exist as well at times, especially in the 1920s: co-identification with another non-Russian nation. It was not without risk. If korenizatsiia organized the Soviet population into thousands of national territorial units with at least some view to a strategy of *divide et impera*, then moments of incidental cross-korenizatsiia naturally represented a threat to this strategy. The Ukrainian–Crimean Tatar cultural encounter in this period offers vivid examples.

2.

As we observed in chapter 2, a process of identification between Ukrainians and Crimean Tatars had begun to percolate in the poetry and prose of Lesia Ukraïnka and Mykhailo Kotsiubynsky at the turn of the twentieth century. This process was marked by a subtle, implicit metaphorical formulation: *Ukrainians are Crimean Tatars*. In the early Soviet period this process of identification matured by way of state-sponsored cross-cultural collaboration. An emblematic case is *Alim*, a play written by Ümer İpçi in 1924. İpçi (1897–1955) was responsible for almost singlehandedly reviving Crimean Tatar drama in the early Soviet period. With Veli İbraimov's support and the winds of korenizatsiia at his back, İpçi helped develop the Crimean Tatar State Drama Theatre – "Tatteatr" – into a cultural force.[25] His dramatic works bore the mark of Toktargazy's influence, confronting problems of social equality in Crimean Tatar society, from the plight of the poor to the rights of women.[26] *Alim* was one of his most popular plays, a work that reached into the realm of folklore and breathed new life into the legend of Alim Aidamak, a nineteenth-century Crimean Tatar Robin Hood. İpçi's story of one man's defence of the downtrodden soon came to grace the silver screen. In a vibrant example of cross-korenizatsiia, İpçi's Crimean Tatar–language play formed the basis for a film project undertaken by the highly successful All-Ukrainian Photo Cinema Administration (VUFKU).[27] It was a work of drama supported by policies of Tatarization in Crimea, which made possible a work of film supported by policies of Ukrainization in Ukraine.

VUFKU billed *Alim* as a story torn from the pages of "the Crimean Tatar struggle for their own national renaissance."[28] Mykola Bazhan, a Ukrainian poet who was also editor of the film journal *Kino*, teamed up with İpçi to complete the screenplay. First-time Ukrainian director Heorhy Tasin (1895–1956) took the helm of the project, while Crimean Tatar scholars and cultural activists like Üsein Bodaninsky, director of the Bağçasaray Museum of Turko-Tatar Culture, joined the production to ensure its cultural authenticity and to protect against what Osip Mandelshtam had panned in previous cinematic works as an absurd Orientalist "sterilization" of the Crimean Tatars.[29]

Alim was an overnight success. After its release in 1926 the film began to play to audiences in France and Germany as well as across the Soviet Union – especially, as Bodaninsky notes, in the Azerbaijan SSR, Tatar ASSR, and Central Asian republics.[30] In celebrating its achievements, Ukrainian critics in the journal *Kino* highlighted one distinction above all others: the recognition among Crimean Tatars that *Alim* was "their first national film" (svoia persha natsionalna kartyna).[31] Indeed, if İpçi's *Alim* was a Crimean Tatar play that fed the success of Ukrainian cinema, then Tasin's *Alim* was a Ukrainian film that fed perceptions of a Tatar Crimea, of a tight bond between Crimean place and Tatar personality. From its opening minutes, *Alim* avails viewers of broad, visually resplendent vistas of a multicultural nineteenth-century Crimea with a clear titular nation at the centre of everything.

Its second scene is representative. In an open-air market bustling with workers in fezzes and imperial functionaries in frock coats, Tasin focuses attention on the dominant figure of a Crimean Tatar *delial* (herald) through whom, as we learn in an intertitle, all the business and news of the market moves. Crimean Tatar order, the film suggests, is what makes sense of Crimea's busy diversity. But this order has a dark side. It tolerates an exploitation of the poor and vulnerable, igniting a rebellion in the wily Alim, who retreats to the forest to hatch plans to upset the status quo. Alim is no bandit, in stark contrast to the hero of Viacheslav Viskovsky's film of 1916, *Alim – Krymskii razboinik* (Alim, Crimean brigand); in accordance with Soviet heroization, he is a social revolutionary. The villains he targets are not tsarist colonizers, who linger in the margins of the film, but local Crimean Tatar mullahs and mirzas guilty of hypocrisy and greed.

By every measure, the Crimea of Tasin's *Alim* is a land possessed by the Crimean Tatars, where Crimean place and Tatar personality dwell fully and deeply within each other. Tasin's eloquent use of

5. *Alim*, directed by Heorhy Tasin (1926)

mise-en-scène makes the point repeatedly: in one scene Alim and his love, Sara, played by husband and wife duo Hayri (Khairi) Emir-Zade and Asiye Emir-Zade, stand between two entangled trees and frame a minaret behind them in the distance. In another, the jagged rocks along the beach cast in relief the undulating lines of their national dress, Alim's *şalvarlar* (wide trousers) and Sara's *marama* veil (fig. 5). Here Tasin foreshadows the film's tragic ending, in which Sara and Alim, fleeing at night from authorities, drown in the dark surf of the Crimean coast.

As *Alim*'s artistic and scholarly consultant, Üsein Bodaninsky helped Tasin craft these poignant scenes with "authenticity" and "sincerity." He also played a pivotal role in another moment of cross-korenizat-siia, one with lasting repercussions for both Ukrainian and Crimean Tatar historical memory. In 1925, Bodaninsky joined the Crimean Tatar ethnographer, archaeologist, and philologist Osman Akçokraklı on the hunt for *cönkler*, traditional anthologies of folk and devan poetry from the era of the khanate often preserved in family homes. Their expedition had only modest success until they arrived at the village of Kapsykhor (today's Morskoe) in the Sudak region, where they stumbled upon a major discovery: a seventeenth-century *destan* by Crimean Tatar poet Canmuhammed (Dzhan-Mukhammed).[32]

When Akçokraklı and Bodaninsky's discovery began to circulate in Soviet scholarly circles, it did so by way of Ukrainian journals. Ahatanhel Krymsky alluded to it in *Studiï z Krymu* (Crimean studies), a collection of articles and resources related to Crimean Tatar culture, history, and demography that was released under his editorship by the All-Ukrainian Academy of Sciences in 1930. "Soon this Crimean poem, which is so interesting for Ukrainians," Krymsky observed, "will get to see the world."[33] What made the poem interesting was its distinctive subject matter: the military alliance between the Crimean Tatar khanate and the Ukrainian Cossacks of the Zaporizhian Host, which had helped produce out of the territory of the Polish–Lithuanian Commonwealth an autonomous Ukrainian Cossack proto-state in 1649. Krymsky assured the reader that Canmuhammed's text would be published eventually, remarking in a footnote: "The People's Commissariat for Education of Crimea has given its approval." He was correct, at least in part; only months later, a gloss of Akçokraklı's discovery appeared in the journal *Skhidnyi svit* (World of the East) sandwiched between articles on the class struggle of the nineteenth-century Nogai people and the dialects of the Greeks in the southeastern Ukrainian city of Mariupol.[34]

Only a number of excerpts of Canmuhammed's *destan* are extant today. The fragments recount the heroic exploits of Tuğaybey (Tugai-Bey, Tuhai-Bey), the military commander of the Crimean Tatar khan İslâm Giray III heralded by Mykhailo Hrushevsky as "the genuine soul of the Crimean-Ukrainian union."[35] Tuğaybey joins the Ukrainian Cossack fight against the Poles, forging a strong friendship with Hetman Bohdan Khmelnytsky, or "Meleske," as he is named in Canmuhammed's rendition.[36] He does so after Khmelnytsky's emissaries petition İslâm Giray III for assistance:

> Didiler ki, yey bizim sultanımız,
> Baş urıp, selâm qıldı atamanımız.
> Batavskiy seksen biñ asker ile,
> Kelmek içün tedrik idti bize.
> İlimizi, köyimzi yıqsa kerek,
> Cümlesini ep ota yaqsa kerek.
> Kelecek yıl em Qırıma kelse kerek,
> Qırım halqın qoymayıp alsa kerek.[37]

> (They said: "O great Sultan,
> Our ataman [Khmelnytsky] sends greetings, bowing his head.

Batavskiy [i.e., Polish commander Stefan Potocki], with eighty thousand
   troops,
Is slowly advancing upon us.
He seeks to tear down our villages and provinces,
He seeks to lay waste to everything and everyone.
He seeks also to invade Crimea in a year,
He seeks to storm and enslave Crimea's people.")

These are the first words spoken by Ukrainians in extant Crimean Tatar
literature, and they are warnings of mutual suffering. For amplificatory
and dramatic effect, Canmuhammed makes extended use of a *redif* –
literally, "a warrior who rides on the back of another's saddle" – a
word (*kerek*, in this case) that "rides on the back" of the rhyme *yıqsa-
yaqsa*, *kelse-alsa* to build momentum.[38] The prominent epistrophe turns
a Ukrainian entreaty for Crimean Tatar help into something akin to a
prayer.

Profound emphasis is also placed on the identity of the prospective
victims of the violent conflict: the people (*halq*, the folk) whom both the
khan and the hetman presume to protect. In Canmuhammed's epic,
war is not simply politics by other means; for the Ukrainian Cossacks
and Crimean Tatars, it is not a geopolitical venture to extend influence,
extract tribute, and enrich elites. It is a struggle for survival. The poet's
ventriloquy of these Ukrainian voices in the Crimean Tatar vernacular
facilitates a mingling of the first-person plural and, by extension, the
fates of both groups. Indeed, when the warning of Poland's planned
invasion of Crimea is issued at the end of the passage, any distinction
between *you* and *us* is made largely irrelevant. Canmuhammed portrays both groups as objects of foreign aggression who strike an alliance
based on an understanding of the human costs of their inaction and on
their mutual self-identification as victim.

By 1930, when Akçokraklı had begun to publicize the discovery of
the poem across the Soviet Union, Ukraine's most sensational writer
was promoting a Crimean Tatar national identity resilient in the struggle against settler colonialism. Ostap Vyshnia (born Pavlo Hubenko,
1889–1956) was Ukraine's "Mark Twain," the "king of the Ukrainian
print-run," whose fame, it was said, rivalled only two others in early
Soviet Ukraine: Taras Shevchenko and Vladimir Lenin. His sui generis
usmishky (funny vignettes or feuilletons; literally, "smiles") appeared
regularly in major newspapers, including *Visti VUTsVK*, the official
government periodical promoting *ukrainizatsiia*.[39] In a Soviet Ukraine
increasingly beset by rigid ideologization and internal censorship,
Vyshnia's satirical usmishky were a breath of fresh air: topical in content, playful and disarming in tone. Nothing escaped his wit. From

the rise of Mussolini to the geostrategic utility of canals, Vyshnia's usmishky delighted in hurtling readers between domestic and international topics with abandon. And like the simple-minded, light-hearted Ukrainian peasant narrators of Nikolai Gogol and Hryhory Kvitka-Osnov'ianenko before him, Vyshnia's persona had a forked tongue and spoke at times in the Ukrainian-Russian non-standard linguistic hybrid known as *surzhyk*.[40] There was always something subversive behind his seemingly innocent explorations of the status quo, a cagey wink in the wide eyes.

The maverick prose stylist and polemicist Mykola Khvylovy, Vyshnia's close friend and advocate, celebrated the heteroglossia of the usmishky in the pages of his journal *Prolitfront*. "I fell in love with them because of their piquancy, their delicacy, their rudeness, their humour," wrote Khvylovy, "and because of their profound tragedy."[41] Vyshnia's collection *Vyshnevi usmishky krymski* (Vyshnia's funny Crimean vignettes; literally, Vyshnia's Crimean smiles) fits Khvylovy's description perfectly. In the feuilletons, inspired by a trip to Crimea in the early summer of 1924, Vyshnia riffs on the foibles of plump tourists from Moscow and, with characteristic self-deprecation, ridicules the sedentary lifestyle of the writer. But his tone veers dramatically toward the tragic when he approaches the subject of the Crimean Tatars, an object of his sustained attention.

In "Tatarynove zhyttia" (The life of a [Crimean] Tatar), one of three usmishky dedicated to the Crimean Tatars in the collection and originally published in the weekly arts supplement of *Visti VUTsVK*, Vyshnia departs from the world of satire to deliver a searing indictment of the colonial oppression of Crimea's indigenous people. The voice of his narrator echoes the righteous anger and sarcasm of Taras Shevchenko. It also summons Shevchenko's empathy, evoking from the outset an image of a tearful Crimean Tatar elder named Akhmet, who gazes off into the distance and says, "It was better before." What changed everything for Akhmet's people, Vyshnia's narrator explains, was an invasion of Crimea by imperial forces "from the north," a "deadly whirlwind across the steppes" that "beat, ravaged, destroyed" his home.[42]

Here Vyshnia's use of "whirlwind" and verbal asyndeton (*pobyly, potroshchyly, poruinuvaly*) is an intertextual trigger. For the Ukrainian reader it can invite reference to sixteenth- and seventeenth-century Cossack *dumy*, lyrico-epic poems that thrive on characterizations of the Crimean Tatars as a fearsome horde attacking Ukrainian victims, a "black cloud"[43] whose violent actions are listed without conjunctions in breathless end-rhymed lines.[44] In "Tatarynove zhyttia," Vyshnia flips the script, transferring the role of victim from Ukrainian to Crimean

Tatar. He then exposes, with astringent wit, the imperial conceit of colonization as a "civilizing mission."

Vyshnia's narrator approaches the reader with a hand on the shoulder. "Listen, my good people, to the ways in which the tsars and his spawn united ancient 'Muslim' Crimea with 'Christian civilization'! Listen carefully!"[45] In an extraordinary move, he then gives the floor to someone else. Vyshnia quotes – at great length, and virtually verbatim – a Russian writer and historian named Yevgeny Markov, whose seminal work *Ocherki Kryma* (Sketches of Crimea, first published in 1872) followed Aleksandr Herzen in expressing an admiration for the Crimean Tatars and a sympathy with their plight after the Crimean War.[46] Markov addressed his Russian readers directly and asked them to question the benefits of empire: "Speaking frankly, did we really give the Crimean Tatar a better life?"[47] His answer: no.

Markov's message circulated widely in the late imperial period, but the Soviet era was a different story. Even though it was released in no less than four editions between 1872 and 1911, Markov's *Ocherki Kryma* was not reprinted at any point in the twentieth century in the Soviet Union. As we will see in chapter 5, the revisionist work of Soviet historians after the Second World War would eventually frame Crimea as ancient Russian territory, consigning Markov and his ilk to the dustbin of historiography.[48] Vyshnia's conspicuous recycling of Markov here – a footnote even refers readers to the third edition of *Ocherki Kryma* – was therefore a very prescient circumvention of the censor.

Vyshnia clearly appreciated Markov's own penchant for sarcasm. Translating from Russian into Ukrainian, Vyshnia quotes Markov's quip that "in order to avail Crimea of the benefits of Christian civilization, we first had to bring it low."[49] Critically, he repeats Markov's metaphor of the Russian conquest of Crimea as an act of ethnic "cleansing." Using the Ukrainian verb *chystyty* (to clean) where Markov uses the noun *chistka* (cleansing or purge), Vyshnia exposes his many thousands of readers to a history that saw Count Khristofor Minikh (aka Burkhard Christoph Graf von Münnich) in 1736 "painstakingly cleanse Crimea to such an extent that Bakhchysarai and other cities in his path became ruins, and the steppe a desert." A year later Count Petr Lassi (aka Peter Lacey) assumed Minikh's mantle, "laying waste to the cities and the steppe, with a particular German pedantry. He burned down nearly 1,000 villages – that is, those villages only left untouched by Minikh because they did not fit his itinerary."[50] In the nineteenth century this "embrace" of Christian civilization manifested itself grotesquely as a rejection and expulsion of innocent people. "At last, civilization began to engulf the Tatars," forcing "two-thirds of the entire population" to flee their ancestral homeland. Vyshnia quotes Markov drily: "the benevolence of European civilization is at least open to question."[51]

Vyshnia's cut-and-paste of Markov's text, which makes up over half of the entire usmishka, is occasionally broken up with exclamatory intrusions from his narrator: "Did you hear that? Keep listening." At the end of "Tatarynove zhyttia," however, the narrator climbs back in the driver's seat to ensure that his readers understand that this history of colonial exploitation is no thing of the past. It is alive in the Soviet present. Vyshnia's narrator explains how Akhmet, the old Crimean Tatar man whose tears of nostalgia open the usmishka, is manipulated by Soviet tourists who ask him to show them Crimea but act like he is their guest. These are tourists who profess to "love" him but pay him little for his trouble. In other words, Vyshnia deftly connects the dots between Russian imperial oppression and Soviet cultural exploitation.

Doing so marked "Tatarynove zhyttia" for deletion. After 1930, it never saw the light of day in print again. Vyshnia was arrested in 1933 and sentenced to ten years in the Gulag on absurd charges of conspiring to assassinate Pavel Postyshev, whose involvement in overseeing the Holodomor, the murderous artificial famine of 1932–3, led to his sobriquet as "butcher of Ukraine" (kat Ukraïny). Then the Second World War intervened. In a desperate move, Vyshnia was released in 1943 to rally a beleaguered war-time Ukrainian public. Nearly destroyed by Stalin, he was dusted off to serve him at a moment of need.

After Vyshnia's death in 1956, the *Vyshnevi usmishky krymski* collection remained immensely popular.[52] But "Tatarynove zhyttia" was carefully excised from every single subsequent reprinting. In fact, this cleansing of "Tatarynove zhyttia" from literary discourse has been so effective that Vyshnia's feuilleton remains largely unknown in Ukraine today. Even a recent volume entitled *Vyshnia's Funny Vignettes: Banned Works* (*Vyshnevi usmishky: zaboroneni tvory*), prepared by the Institute of Literature at Kyiv State Taras Shevchenko University, fails to include it.[53]

The film *Alim* too was banned. In a memorandum marked "not subject to disclosure," Soviet censors pulled the film from circulation in 1937.[54] Most of its copies were destroyed. It was expunged so thoroughly from Soviet cinematic history that even today Western film scholars neglect to include *Alim* in Tasin's filmography, citing his next film, *Order na arest* (Arrest warrant, 1927), as his directoral debut.[55] Osman Akçokraklı and Üsein Bodaninsky, who uncovered Canmuhammed's source material of a premodern Ukrainian–Crimean Tatar alliance, were arrested under charges of pan-Turkism, counter-revolutionary activity, and espionage. On 17 April 1938 the two were shot in Simferopol by the NKVD alongside dozens of other members of the Soviet Crimean Tatar intelligentsia. Their compatriot Ümer İpçi, who had collaborated with Mykola Bazhan on *Alim*'s screenplay, was arrested in 1937. He remained imprisoned until his death nearly two decades later, unable to protect his daughter Dzhevair from the tragedy of May 1944.

3.

In the middle of the night of 18 May 1944, Dzhevair İpçi awoke to the sound of "strong blows on the door." She was fourteen years old. Two soldiers with machine guns gave her mother fifteen minutes to gather their belongings. The family's Singer sewing machine was among the things she collected. "Leave it," they told her mother, "or we shoot." The armed men, Dzhevair remembers, treated them "like cattle" (kak skot), cursing at them while loading them onto the train. "In the train car," she says, "there was no water, no toilet. For eighteen days we endured inhuman conditions."[56] At the same time, some fifty miles away, a six-teen-year-old Russian student in Yalta named Zoia Khabarova awoke to the sounds of shooting and screaming. She rushed out onto her balcony to find "men in military uniforms pushing and shoving our neighbours – Tatars – onto trucks."[57] She grew worried about her Crimean Tatar friend Rita. In the morning of 19 May, Zoia ran to check on her: "Rita was gone. The apartment was open, everything strewn around [...] I learned that they seized all the Tatars and sent them away last night. Rita's father was a [Soviet] partisan. Why was she taken?"[58]

Why? The Ukrainian writer and journalist Vasyl Sokil asked the same question in the late spring of 1944. He remembers waiting at a remote railway crossing in Kazakhstan and seeing a hand grasping tobacco leaves through a small opening in a waiting eastbound train car opposite his own. An urgent voice exclaimed from within the car: "Bread!" Moving closer, Sokil spied an old man desperate to exchange the tobacco for food. Behind his fragile, emaciated frame stood a group of figures barely clothed. There was a frantic exchange:

Confused, I asked the old man, "What happened? What's wrong with these people?" The old man quipped with irritation, "Take the tobacco and give me some bread!" "How much?" He shot back, "However much you'll give me, just make it quick! The train's about to leave!" I rushed back and grabbed half a loaf [...] The old man nearly ripped the bread out of my hand.

The trains had not yet left the junction, so I asked once again, "Where are you going?" The old man darkened and said in a detached voice, "Wherever they take us." "But where are you from?" "What, haven't you read the papers?" he replied angrily. "From Crimea. We're Tatars [...] Now there are none of us in Crimea."

The whistle sounded, and the train went eastward with its prisoners [...] Slowly the train cars passed by me, and staring out from the narrow cracks of its doors were old women, young women, children, grey-haired grandfathers.[59]

"Ty chto, gazet ne chital?" (What, haven't you read the papers?) Sokil's encounter lays bare a central paradox of the events of May 1944: namely, that a deportation of an entire people on a peninsula of over ten thousand square miles – carried out by NKVD agents in plain sight "with the speed of a landing attack," in the words of Alexander Solzhenitsyn – was not *perceived* by the Soviet public in the years immediately following the Second World War.[60]

To an extent, this failure to perceive was wilful on the part of many Soviet citizens, particularly in Russia and Ukraine. Sokil recalls: "On my train there were many passengers [who had exchanged food for] these golden leaves of tobacco. But no one uttered a word about the encounter. They were silent. Some refused to let it in and did not understand, while others were frightened to address what was a dangerous subject."[61] For others scattered across the Soviet Union, however, this failure to perceive was the result of the Stalinist regime's perverse adherence to George Berkeley's dictum, *esse est percipi*. Removed from the field of perception, the Crimean Tatars would no longer exist.

Their discursive cleansing began suddenly. Only days before the deportation, the newspapers *Pravda* and *Izvestiia* had considered the heroism of Crimean Tatars good copy. The 12 May edition of *Pravda*, for instance, extolled the valour of Amethan (Amet-Khan) Sultan, whose reputation, the reader was told, struck fear in the hearts of the Germans.[62] Born in 1920 in Alupka, where a bronze bust now stands in his honour on a boulevard in his name, Sultan was a Crimean Tatar pilot who was twice named a Hero of the Soviet Union.[63] His exploits as an ace pilot were legendary: in 1942, for example, discovering that his guns were jammed, Sultan rammed and forced down a German aircraft before parachuting to safety.[64]

Between 12 and 18 May – between the authorization of the deportation and the first moments of its execution – *Pravda* and *Izvestiia* gave no indication whatsoever of the coming accusations of mass treason and betrayal that would be levelled against the Crimean Tatars. In fact, on Wednesday, 17 May, only hours before the NKVD began to execute Stalin's Decree 5859ss, *Pravda* ran a front-page article with a headline in large, bold typeface, "Slava geroiam Kryma!" (Glory to the heroes of Crimea!), which celebrated the Red Army's success in retaking the peninsula from the Germans, now in retreat. "Everyone," the article read, "has become a hero in our country" (Geroem v nashei strane stanovitsia kazhdyi).

One of these heroes was Şamil Alâdin (1912–1996), a Crimean Tatar poet who had commanded a Red Army platoon on the southwestern front. After the Nazi retreat from Crimea, he deserved a joyous homecoming. What he experienced instead was a nightmare. In the late spring of 1944 he made his return to Simferopol only to find strangers living in his home. His wife, Fatma, and young daughter, Diliara, had been rounded up in the deportation and exiled to Central Asia, and a family by the name of Frankovsky had taken their place. There was an altercation at the door. The poet remembers the man at the threshold becoming "amused" when he realized Alâdin was a Crimean Tatar. "He understood that in front of him was a man, albeit in the uniform of an officer, who had no civil rights, whom no law would protect."[65] Alâdin set off eastward to find his family, evading imprisonment and fleeing from Crimean authorities. He later discovered Fatma and Diliara in Uzbekistan, near death from hunger in a special settlement camp.

Not far from Alâdin's family, an eighteen-year-old poet named İdris Asanin confronted the trauma of the deportation through poetry in a special settlement camp near Samarkand. His "Menim antım" (My pledge), written in September 1944, is the first poem to resound in Crimean Tatar culture after the deportation. It is an echo of Noman Çelebicihan's "Ant etkenmen," the anthem composed in the haze of revolution and civil war that was discussed at the end of chapter 2. In 1951, "Menim antım" would be used against Asanin in a trial that sentenced him to twenty-five years in prison:

Yurtsız qalğan hor milletim, ğurbetlikte yüresiñ,
Açlıq, horluq, hastalıqtan sürü-sürü ölesiñ.
Mezarcılar yoruldılar, cenazeler qılınmay,
Dua-hatim bir yaq tursın, … olgen eske alınmay.
. . . .
Bu ğarip halq aqsız yerde mında ölip bitsinmi,
Yurtnı basqan yağmacılar körip bayram etsinmi?
Millet artıq ğayıp ola, qaldı duşman şerine.
Tatar adı tarihlardan şan-şüretsiz siline.
. . . .
Nefretlenem, göñlüm taşa, kozlerimden yaş kele,
Tek bir Niyet — Küreş yolu… irademe kuç bere.

Men ant etem, ant etkenniñ izlerinden ketmege,
Milletimniñ aqqı içün canım feda etmege![66]

(My aggrieved, homeless people, you are living in exile,
You are dying in droves from hunger, want, and disease.
The gravediggers have grown tired, our funerals are mocked,
Let alone the prayers... no one remembers the dead.
. . . .
Should this poor nation unjustly die and perish here?
Should plunderers who have raided the homeland enjoy seeing this?
Your people are now lost, captive to an evil enemy,
While the Tatar name has been expunged from history, stripped of fame
    and glory.
. . . .
My heart boils over with hatred, tears are flowing from my eyes.
Only one purpose, the path of struggle, strengthens my will:
I pledge to follow in the footsteps of those who have pledged,
To sacrifice my soul for the rights of my people!)

Like Çelebicihan's "Ant etkenmen," Asanin's poem centres on an
explicit illocutionary moment – a pledge, an oath – whose utterance
is also an act with social force. It models and performs an act of individual self-ascription to a beleaguered national community in need of
reinforcement and cohesion, addressing a "you" that is ultimately a
"we." Through an intertext with the seminal work of the leader of the
Qurultay, the poem also asserts the community's historical continuity,
restoring a circuit of memory that the event of the deportation sought
to sever. These two concerns – national cohesion and historical continuity, grounded in and guided by the concept of the Crimean vatan – are
at the heart of nearly every single work of Crimean Tatar–language literature after the deportation.

There is another notable attribute of this literature, evident only
between the lines: an avoidance of direct mention of the deportation
itself. Asanin's poem rails against the consequences of an event of which
it does not speak. There are no allusions to a fateful knock on the door,
no references to a torturous journey in crowded cattle-cars bound to
destinations unknown. This silence, as Jay Winter observes, "is a space
where nobody speaks what everybody knows."[67] In Crimean Tatar literature, with the exception of impressionistic stories by Ervin Umerov
in the late Soviet period,[68] the deportation is only present in its effects:
mass death, displacement, humiliation, despair. The exile experience

is driven underground, into subterranean coded references that are hidden, for instance, in poetry dedicated to the nineteenth-century Ukrainian poet Taras Shevchenko, who withstood years of brutal exile in Central Asia. A vibrant example is a poem by writer and teacher Yunus Temirkaya (1914–2004) entitled "Taras Şevçenkoğa" (To Taras Shevchenko, 1961):

> Şuña sıltav etip olar quvdı seni,
> Uzaqtaki yat-yabancı ülkelerge.
> Yaş başıñdan bahıtsızlıq urdı seni,
> Meşaqatlı qara künde kirdiñ yerge.[69]

> (The [tyrants] sentenced you and drove you
> To strange, alien, far-flung lands.
> Misery beat the youth from your face,
> And on that painful, black day you were exiled.)

In Crimean Tatar discourse, the deportation event is referred to as Qara Kün (The Black Day), and Temirkaya slides the term into a poem ostensibly about a Ukrainian poet in order to articulate, only obliquely, the pain and suffering of the tragedy. Such elusiveness is emblematic of much of the literature written by victims of Stalinist trauma. Reading this corpus is not unlike using sonar to plumb the recesses of an uncharted sea: we apprehend the object only by way of the disturbances and discontinuities its presence exerts on our frequency. In poems like Asanin's "Menim antım" or Temirkaya's "Taras Şevçenkoğa," the deportation is not quite absent, nor has its trauma gone unrecognized or, in the words of Cathy Caruth, "unclaimed."[70] It has been hastily entombed, its existence only evident at surface level – in a shifting of the textual ground, in pockmarks and debris.

The Crimean Tatars and countless other victims of Soviet state violence buried such trauma out of concern for survival both psychic and physical, out of an awareness that there was both no "Other to which one could say 'Thou' in the hope of being heard" and no secure public context in which this Other might emerge.[71] This is the perverse double bind of Stalinist trauma: the challenge of bearing witness, and the prohibition to try. Decades after the deportation, Şamil Alâdin was asked why he had not used the event as fodder for a short story or novel. Shrugging his shoulders in exasperation, he replied: "What for? And who would publish it? We are forbidden not only to write but also to think about the past."[72]

4.

The conspiracy between discursive cleansing and ethnic cleansing is an indiscriminate assault on the past and the future, a crime of both body and name. As the bodies of the survivors of Stalin's Crimean atrocity endured conditions in "special settlement camps," their names were effaced from the land that they had called home for centuries, as if they had never been there. Traces of their past presence on maps and signs were thrown into what Robert Conquest, after Orwell, calls "the memory hole."[73] Before the deportation there were, by one count, 1,775 towns and villages in Crimea bearing a Crimean Tatar toponym.[74] After the deportation only a small number remained.

This reterritorialization of Crimea took place at breakneck speed. In October and December of 1944 the Crimean oblast party committee and the Presidium of the Supreme Soviet of the RSFSR issued decrees calling for Crimean Tatar (and German and Krymchak) names of cities, towns, and villages to be replaced with Russian ones.[75] Pushkin seemed to have helped exempt Bakhchisarai from this process; the fame of his *Bakhchisaraiskii fontan* was a small finger in the dike of this discursive cleansing.[76] The daunting task of renaming most of the rest of the peninsula fell to a fastidious "old newspaper man," the executive secretary of *Krasnyi Krym* (Red Crimea), who came up with the new toponyms by hastily consulting a nineteenth-century fruticulture book, on the one hand, and a recent account of the Red Army's Crimean offensive, on the other.[77] Hence the descriptive and patriotic functionalism of the post-1944 onomastics: Kiçkene, a village near Simferopol with only 156 recorded residents in 1939, became Malenkoe (Small); Aşağı Camin, a small settlement in the Sak region, became Geroiskoe (Of Heroes); Bağça-Eli became Bagotoe (Rich). Some villages saw their unique place names – which could bear sacred religious meaning or allude to a founding family or a particular regional economic identity[78] – replaced by unimaginative collective ones: Alma Kerman (Apple Fortress), Savurçı (Tanner), and Yanış Taqıl (a Crimean Tatar family name) all became Zavetnoe (Cherished), for example.

These saccharine toponyms often "forgot" the many tragedies endured by local Crimean communities during the war. Qutlaq, a village in the Sudak region first cited in historical records in the fifteenth century, had a majority population of 1,636 Tatars in 1939. For assisting the Soviet partisan movement during the war, its residents had to watch as Nazi occupiers retaliated by burning the village to the ground. Qutlaq was later named Veseloe (Happy). Büyük Özenbaş, a village near Bakhchisarai, was overtaken by the Nazis one fateful dawn.

"With lashes and the butts of rifles, [the Germans] rounded up the fleeing villagers, mocking them cruelly. Many of the villagers, looking for
rescue, ran to the mosque. Once praying had begun inside, the Nazis
doused the mosque with gasoline and incinerated it."[79] After May 1944,
Büyük Özenbaş was named Schastlyvoe (Lucky).

These mawkish place names echo in Petr Pavlenko's short story
"Rassvet" (Dawn, 1945). It is an unwittingly chilling text that recounts
the distribution of Crimean Tatar homes and property to Ukrainian
and Russian Soviet settlers – without breathing a single word about the
owners who had been deported only months earlier. "Rassvet" reveals
what happened immediately after the ethnic cleansing of Crimea: *ethnic
cloning*. Soviet authorities repopulated the peninsula with Slavic peoples, describing the project of changing its demography as the task of
"making Crimea *a new Crimea with its own Russian form*" (sdeliat Krym
novym Krymom so svoim russkim ukladom).[80]

Pavlenko's story is not widely read in Russia today, but thanks to
Cengiz Dağcı, it has notoriety in Turkey, as we will see in chapter 6.
Pavlenko is typically remembered as a "Stalin cult specialist" responsible for some of the most egregious panegyrics to the General Secretary,
including his popular Stalin Prize–winning novel *Schaste* (*Happiness*,
1947) about the revival of a Crimean collective farm at the end of the
war.[81] He was an enthusiastic apologist of the Stalinist regime, who cruelly taunted an ailing Mandelshtam during an NKVD interrogation.[82]
Earlier, in the 1920s, he had also become something of an amateur Orientalist, serving as a Soviet trade officer to Turkey and penning travelogues about Central Asia and the Far East. In 1945, finding himself
in Crimea at the close of the war, he was therefore primed to see the
remnants of Crimean Tatar culture all around him. But in "Rassvet,"
Pavlenko carefully curates their absence. It is an audacious feat of discursive cleansing.

At times Pavlenko almost lets slip the truth that he strains so hard
to conceal. He describes Alushta as "quiet, truly deserted" (tikhaia,
tochno ubezliudevshaia).[83] "Orchards and tobacco plots glimmer on
warm hills" – the identity of those who cultivated them is ignored –
while across the sea, the horizon touches Turkey. His protagonist, an
elderly Ukrainian man known by his surname Kostiuk, tours a house
given to him by the head of the collective farm. It is a former Crimean
Tatar residence, although its provenance is unspoken: "The house was
small, but tidy and strong. The glass veranda overlooked a tiny, vine-
covered courtyard [...] A few strange trees with aromatic foliage stood
around the edges of the courtyard."[84] Pavlenko peppers the story with
the odd Ukrainian word to convey a sense of Kostiuk's provincial

nature and his intimate attachment to Ukraine – and to paper over, with sympathetic character traits, an act of complicity in Stalin's Crimean atrocity. Kostiuk embraces his new Crimean home, because "the local beauty stung [*uzhalila*] him and conquered him forever." Taking off his hat, he proclaims with gratitude at the end of the story, "You gave us paradise, dear Comrade Stalin. God give you strength – and good luck to us!"[85]

Pavlenko's "Rassvet" is the first portrait of Crimea as a new Soviet frontier, as red virgin soil awaiting, in the manner of a novel by Zane Grey, caravans of dewy-eyed settlers. It makes transparent the Soviet project of *settler colonialism* in Crimea, whereby tens of thousands of indigenous inhabitants were forcibly removed and replaced by tens of thousands of exogenous Russians and Ukrainians. Between 1944 and 1946 alone, over sixty-four thousand settlers from five oblasts of the Russian SFSR and four oblasts of the Ukrainian SSR were transported to Crimea, where they were allotted Crimean Tatar homes and offered state subsidies for their repair.[86] Tens of thousands more arrived in the 1950s.[87] As Patrick Wolfe explains, "settler colonies are not primarily established to extract surplus value from indigenous labour. Rather, they are premised on displacing indigenes from (or *re*placing them on) the land; as Deborah Bird Rose points out, to get in the way all the native has to do is stay at home."[88] Crimea was not only settler-colonial territory but territory freighted with particular ideological significance in the Soviet and Russian imaginaries: a homogenous space thick with rhetoric of "glory" and "heroism" divorced from, and silent about, the living past of its indigenous peoples.

A year after the publication of Pavlenko's "Rassvet," Soviet authorities finally made public mention of the deportation of the Crimean Tatars – but only vaguely. On Wednesday, 26 June 1946, *Izvestiia* published a series of decrees of the Presidium of the Supreme Soviet from the preceding day. Under the heading "Concerning the Abolition of the Chechen-Ingush ASSR and the Transformation of the Crimean ASSR into the Crimean Oblast," the following text appeared on the third page, positioned below a prosaic announcement about the formation of a ministry of cinematography at the union republic level:

Во время Великой Отечественной войны [...] многие чеченцы и крымские татары по наущению немецких агентов вступали в организованные немцами добровольческие отряды и вместе с немецкими войсками вели вооруженную борьбу против частей Красной Армии [...] [О]сновная масса населения Чечено-Ингушской и Крымской АССР не оказывали противодействия этим предателям Родины.[89]

(During the Great Patriotic War [...] many Chechens and Crimean Tatars, at the instigation of German agents, participated in volunteer brigades organized by the Germans and conducted an armed struggle against units of the Red Army together with German soldiers [...] A critical mass of the population of the Chechen-Ingush ASSR and Crimean ASSR did not show opposition to these traitors to the Motherland.)

The decree continues euphemistically that, for failing to rise up against those who presumably collaborated with German occupiers, "the Chechens and Crimean Tatars were relocated [*pereseleny*] to other regions of the Soviet Union. In these new regions they were allotted land and given the government assistance needed for their economic development."

Despite its heading, the 1946 Presidium decree has little to do with "the abolition of the Chechen-Ingush ASSR and the transformation of the Crimean ASSR into the Crimean oblast." These administrative changes had been made de facto a year before, on 30 June 1945.[90] Instead, the decree offered Moscow an opportunity to legitimate quietly the post-war deportation campaigns – the bureaucratese of its heading and its relegation to *Izvestiia*'s third page did not encourage close reading – and at the same time to advance the main elements of the narrative of mass Crimean Tatar (and Chechen and Ingush) treason, for uptake in the sphere of cultural discourse. After all, the year 1946 saw Andrei Zhdanov, the resurgent ideological boss of the Communist Party, forcefully repeat the maxim that where the state leads, literature follows. Soviet literature, he declared in an infamous rebuke of the journals *Zvezda* (Star) and *Leningrad*, "does not have, nor can it have, any interests besides [...] the interests of the state."[91] The 1946 Presidium decree articulated these interests with respect to the deportation of the Crimean Tatars, furnishing *fabula* for a *siuzhet* that would emerge on the pages of Soviet documentary and historical novels.

The negative effect of these post-war novels would be felt for decades. In a petition to the United Nations written decades after Stalin's death, Crimean Tatar activists would in fact condemn what they called a "special school dedicated to the distortion of the past and the present of the Crimean Tatars" and populated by such figures as Ivan Kozlov, whose popular novelistic memoir *V krymskom podpole* (In the Crimean underground) won a Stalin Prize in 1948, and Arkady Perventsev, whose novel *Chest smolodu* (*Childhood of a Hero*) won a Stalin Prize in 1949.[92] *V krymskom podpole*, which recounts Kozlov's exploits as a leader of the partisan underground based in Simferopol, follows the 1946 decree and declares that "the Tatars were traitors [*predateli*] from the very beginning of the war."[93] Moreover, when confronted with facts that testify to the participation of Crimean Tatars in the partisan movement against the Germans, Kozlov obscures the truth so as not to contradict the Presidium's pronouncement. He refers to the Simferopol-based underground organization of the Crimean Tatar Abdulla Dağcı (Abdulla Dagdzhi), for example, only by a Russian nickname, "Diadia Volodia" (Uncle Volodia).[94] He also catalogues a number of individuals who, judging by their surnames, were Russian and Ukrainian collaborators with Nazi forces, but he never makes explicit mention of their respective nationalities. Crimean Tatars are not afforded the same courtesy.[95] The reader encounters, for instance, "Mirka the Tatar prostitute" and the "Tatar Karabash," "leader of an [anti-partisan] retribution detachment."[96] As the scholar and activist Refik Muzafarov notes, this telling double standard calls to mind Maksim Gorky's famous remark in *The Life of Klim Samgin* (*Zhizn Klima Samgina*, 1927–36): "When a Russian steals something, they say, 'A thief stole it,' but when a Jew steals something, they say, 'The Jew stole it.'"[97]

The UN petition expresses particular scorn for Perventsev's *Chest smolodu* (*Childhood of a Hero*, 1949), which is also set during the war. The novel's protagonist and narrator, the *komsomolets* (member of the Soviet youth movement) and partisan Sergei Lagunov – whose beloved Liusia, toward the end of the novel, finds a volume of Pushkin's poetry and recites a passage from the coda of *Bakhchisaraiskii fontan* – expounds at length about an egregious "betrayal" of the Soviet Union perpetrated by the Crimean Tatar people. Lecturing his Crimean Tatar friend Fatih (Fatykh), Lagunov proclaims:

> При советской власти крымские татары получили республику, братское содружество русского и других народов СССР, свободу от эксплуатации. Советская власть подняла этот народ, поставила на ноги, дала все для развития, для настоящей жизни, а они послушались своих злейших врагов и качали массовое предательство [...] *Многие крымские татары, ты знаешь, Фатых, по наущению немецких агентов вступили в организованные немцами добровольческие отряды, ведут вооруженную борьбу вместе с немецкими войсками против Красной Армии*, против партизан. Как можно продавать свою совесть, свою страну? Ведь большинство населения крымских татар не оказывает противодействия этим предателям родины, помогает им, и тем самым весь народ теряет свою честь [...] А если потерял честь, значит потерял все...

(Under Soviet rule the Crimean Tatars received their own republic, the fraternal friendship of the Russian people as well as the other peoples of the USSR, and freedom from exploitation. Soviet authorities embraced the Crimean Tatar people, stood them on their feet, and gave everything they could for their development, for a genuine life, but [the Crimean Tatars] obeyed their own worst enemies and initiated mass treason [...] *Under the instruction of German agents, many Crimean Tatars,* you know, Fatih, *joined volunteer brigades organized by the Germans and embarked on an armed struggle together with German troops against the Red Army* and the partisans. How could they sell out their conscience, their country? *The majority of the Crimean Tatar population did not oppose these traitors to the Motherland* and helped them, and the entire nation by its own devices lost its honour [...] And if you lose your honour, you lose everything.)[98]

With care and precision, Perventsev incorporated the text of the 1946 Presidium decree verbatim into his narrative, offering evidence of the top-down, hand-in-glove working relationship between the Soviet state and its writers at the height of *zhdanovshchina* (Zhdanov era). Decades after the publication of *Chest smolodu*, Perventsev would confess to Crimean Tatar activists that his exploitation of the defamatory stereotype of the Crimean Tatar traitor came not at his own initiative but on order from above.[99]

Chapter Four

The Guiltless Guilty

While Ivan Kozlov and Arkady Perventsev were collecting Stalin Prizes, Boris Chichibabin was imprisoned in one of the largest Gulag camp systems in the Russian north, a sprawling, overcrowded "spider's web" of starvation and disease.[1] In time Chichibabin would become, in the words of Yevgeny Yevtushenko, "one of the most prominent contemporary [Russian] poets."[2] But between 1946 and 1951 Chichibabin shuttled between prisons and penal colonies before enduring forced labour in the notorious Viatlag camp complex, logging in the forests of the taiga alongside hardened criminals and political prisoners. Through it all, poetry was a companion. Fellow inmates remember him "mischievously" reciting the experimental poetry of Ilia Selvinsky and, in quieter moments, debating Vladimir Maiakovsky's views on Soviet authority.[3] The putative "crime" that brought him to the camps was "anti-Soviet agitation." Shortly after returning home from the Transcaucasian front in 1945, he had been pulled out of Kharkiv University in eastern Ukraine and arrested for a stanza warning of the dawn of a new post-war Terror.[4] What had been a warning became an example.

Chichibabin was released in 1951. Years later he sought solace in what Liliia Karas-Chichibabina called his favourite place on earth: Crimea.[5] He had been there once before the war, as a teenager. The crisp sea air, the rugged mountains, the verdant flora – Crimea's hold on him was immediate, and it never slackened. Yet the Black Sea peninsula to which Chichibabin returned after the war, after his trials in the Stalinist Gulag, was as radically changed as he was. The Crimean Tatars were no longer there. As Liliia describes it, this discovery "did not let him rest." It deeply affected him with "a feeling of guilt [*chuvstvo viny*] in the presence of the land, a compassion for another's grief."[6] Rather than shaking his head and looking away, rather than succumbing to quiet cynicism or even a sense of self-preservation, Chichibabin confronted the injustice of the deportation and foregrounded it as one of the most consistent themes of his poetry. He and Liliia circulated this verse widely in networks of *samizdat* (*samvydav*, in Ukrainian; "self-published") literature. During poetry readings, at a time when knowledge of the deportation remained confined to hushed whispers, he shouted it from stages.

Such poetry not only exposed Stalin's Crimean atrocity but also cleared space for greater exposure. It began to rouse the conscience of Soviet publics *before* appeals and open letters emerged to press for the right of the Crimean Tatars to return to their homeland. The primacy of literature here is no accident. In the Soviet Union, poetry especially was the big bang of samizdat culture; in its wake came constellations of documentary texts at odds with state agendas and practices.[7] And so it was with the deportation of the Crimean Tatars: in the revelation of the crime, the role of imaginative literature was paramount. But it was also peculiar. As we will see, these literary texts invite the reader to process an emotion that non-literary works of samizdat largely avoid: guilt.

Most of the documentary chronicles, appeals, and petitions about the deportation present it as an event whose victims are human but whose perpetrators are impersonal and distant or, alternatively, an inhuman few: Stalin, Beriia, NKVD commissar Bogdan Kobulov. They aim to spur the reader to action by enumerating the state's violations of the laws and principles set down in domestic constituent documents (e.g., the Soviet constitution) and international charters (e.g., the Universal Declaration of Human Rights). Literary texts about the deportation, however, work differently. They engender a deeper introspection, appealing to the reader's conscience rather than to externally codified law. Through the unique indeterminacies of their form, they co-opt the reader into a unique communicative circuit and approach her, in the words of the poet Aleksandr Tvardovsky, as one of the "guiltless guilty" (vinovaty bez viny).[8]

1.

For writers and poets like Chichibabin and Tvardovsky, Stalin's death marked a turning point in the relationship between literature and the state, a relationship long tumultuous in the region of the Black Sea. Under Stalin's rule the relationship in the Soviet Union had hardened into a socialist-realist orthodoxy enforced by arrests and disappearances. Writers held the Party line or suffered consequences under charges of "formalism" or "bourgeois nationalism." In the eyes of the Kremlin, as Joseph Brodsky remarked, they were either "a slave" or "an enemy."[9] In Turkey, by contrast, writers and cultural figures experienced what might be called a thaw after Atatürk's death in 1938. There, *social* realism remained a popular genre, but Turkish literature enjoyed a relative diversification and experimentation in artistic form and practice.[10] Poets like Orhan Veli discarded what Atatürk called "committed [*gayeli*] poetry"[11] for the surreal, the strange, and the sardonic, sending up *Atatürk şiirler* (or, more broadly, *milli şiirler*, "nation poetry") with the epigram "For the Homeland" (Vatan İçin, 1949): "What haven't we done for the homeland! / Some of us died; others gave speeches."[12] Veli and his compatriots brought about what the poet Ece Ayhan likens to a "golden age" in Turkish poetry.[13] In Stalin's Soviet Union, however, Party-minded writers dogged by censors (both internal and external) endured an iron age, a period of artistic rigidity, formularism, and cliché.[14]

Windows in the "communal apartment" of the USSR opened somewhat after Stalin's death in 1956 with the landmark publications of such works as Vladimir Dudintsev's *Ne khlebom edinym* (*Not by Bread Alone*, 1956) and Aleksandr Solzhenitsyn's *Odin den Ivana Denisovicha* (*One Day in the Life of Ivan Denisovich*, 1962) in the journal *Novyi Mir* (New World). At this time, writers and poets circumventing Soviet censors or shunning official publication found more and more readers in the alleys and gangways of unofficial, samizdat literature. Talent that was free of ideological fetters, of what William Blake called "mind-forg'd manacles" – either from preceding decades (Anna Akhmatova, Mykola Khvylovy) or from the contemporary moment (Joseph Brodsky, Lina Kostenko) – discovered select audiences through typewritten, carbon-smudged onionskin pages passed hand to hand.[15] According to Vladimir Bukovsky, typewriters throughout the Moscow underground were overwhelmed at this time with one task: the transcription of "poems, poems, poems."[16]

These literary texts were often transcribed in samizdat notebooks compiled by individual readers. In turn, these notebooks could become source material for unofficial almanacs published for wider networks of readers. These networks, in the words of Nadiia Svitlychna, "intersected in some places, and diverged in others," spreading texts thither and yon, as Liudmila Alekseeva put it, like "mushroom spores."[17] Aleksandr Ginzburg's Moscow apartment was one point of network convergence for what would eventually become both the Russian and the Ukrainian human rights movements. His 1959 almanac *Sintaksis* (Syntax), the first prominent exemplar of samizdat, provided an outlet for such Moscow- and Leningrad-based poets as Bulat Okudzhava and Dmitry Bobyshev. It also marked a watershed. In the words of Aleksandr Daniel, the emergence of *Sintaksis* represented nothing less than a "declaration of independence of the cultural process."[18] As if staking claim to the moment, Ginzburg printed his name on the cover, which he had adopted from his mother in a defiant protest against Soviet anti-Semitism. Two years later he was arrested for "anti-Soviet agitation."[19]

The first issue of *Sintaksis* in 1959 opened with a loose sonnet without a title by Aleksandr Aronov. Its very first words jettison the reader into an underspecified exchange between anonymous first and second persons: "I would not dare take you / Into that addled age [*zaputavshiisia vek*]."[20] Aronov's lyrical "I" is disingenuous: his words perforce "take" and seize the reader with a perplexing lack of clarity and pretext. Who is this spoken "you"? Why is the age "addled"? He continues ominously:

В это время, в это время,
Камни по небу скользят.
Им на землю падать вредно,
А не падать им —
      нельзя.

(At this time, at this time,
Stones glide across the sky.
They bring peril when they fall,
But fall they must.)

Writing or transcribing such opaque and sullen lines, distributing more political, satirical ones, or simply keeping such literature at home – this creative activity could warrant classification from the 1960s in the West and later in the Soviet Union as "dissidence." Those who undertook such diverse activity could become grouped, *nolens volens*, under the term *"dissidents"* – even they used scare quotes at times, tending to prefer instead the term *inakomysliashchye* (*inakodumtsi* in Ukrainian; "other-thinkers")[21] – who were romanticized in the West as an army of heroic activists committed to the demise of the Communist regime and vilified in the Soviet Union as a clique of deviant, disloyal "dropouts" (nedouchki).[22] The term *dissident* belonged more to the definers than to the defined.

Literature, particularly poetry, was thus a spark to the flame of Soviet dissent. It exercized a socializing function, integrated diverse readerships, and cleared ground for the cultivation of *inakomyslie* (Russian) or *inakodumstvo* (Ukrainian), "other-thinking." This foundational influence has been universally acknowledged by scholars and activists alike. In fact, Aleksandr Daniel speaks of the first generation of dissidence from the late 1950s to 1965 as *literaturotsentrichnyi* (literature-centric)."[23]

Viacheslav Chornovil, writing anonymously in the first issue of the samvydav periodical *Ukraïnskyi visnyk* (*The Ukrainian Herald*), emphasizes that the first stirrings of dissent in Soviet Ukraine were principally belles-lettres.[24] More colourfully, the Ukrainian poet Iryna Zhylenko describes the Soviet Union of this era as "Poetry Land": "Not only Kyiv (and Ukraine), but the entire Soviet Union exploded with poetry." She continues: "At this time poetry was the only form of protest. It filled an empty hole in the soul of the Soviet person."[25]

In the conventional historical account of Soviet dissent, however, literature appears much like the muse in Homer's epics. It is invoked early as a font of inspiration, often with praise for its otherworldly, "spiritual" power.[26] It then recedes into the background.[27] Natalia Gorbanevskaia describes this transition as an evolution in samizdat "from a predominant concern with poetry and fiction toward a greater emphasis on journalistic and documentary writing."[28] As a poet turned chronicler who launched the influential periodical *Khronika tekushchykh sobytii* (*Chronicle of Current Events*) – modelled after the "information bulletins" of the Crimean Tatars – Gorbanevskaia personified this transformation. She also performed it. With a simple adjustment to her portable Olympia typewriter, she replaced the type-bars that she used for her underground poetry with new ones for *Khronika* in order to avoid identification by the KGB.[29] This is often considered to be the moment when literary samizdat gave way to social samizdat, when the "cultural opposition" became the social opposition.[30] This transition was noticed in Turkey as early as 1971 by prominent legal scholar and diplomat İzmet Giritli, who remarked that the Soviet "Literary Opposition" (Edebi Muhalefet), despite ceding attention to documentary samizdat, still occupied a privileged position because it "appeals to a wider audience" (daha geniş bir kitleye hitap etmektedir).[31]

Often downplayed in the story of this social or documentary turn – which can understate the persistence of imaginative literature in samizdat culture well after it[32] – is a simple but critical question: why literature in the first instance? Why did literature overwhelmingly predominate in the decisive early years of Soviet dissent? Samizdat has been called many things – a corpus, a culture, a genre, a mode, a field – but it may be also understood (the stubborn fact of Soviet communism aside) as a market. Specifically, it was a parallel market, operating with its own means of exchange alongside, but in competition with, the state. Its prevailing product was knowledge. "Dissidents" were its brokers and entrepreneurs. What kind of knowledge did literature offer in this environment, where information was so tightly regulated and the stakes of exchange so high?

Answers to such questions seem close at hand, but they tend to have us grasping at air. Alekseeva remarks that in her youth unofficial poetry and prose helped yield "a realistic picture of what was going on in our country."[33] Her comment rests on a presumption that the unreal – anonymous lyrical personae and fictional characters and events – can engender an apprehension of the real. But how do we derive empirical knowledge about the world from imaginary sources? Such eternal questions spawn only more questions, exposing in the process a paradox at the heart of Soviet dissent: namely, that it was an influential social movement for transparency, honesty, and disclosure founded on a rhetoric of concealment, obfuscation, and implication. To live "not by the lie," as Solzhenitsyn famously put it,[34] dissidents frequently turned to something other than the truth. They turned to the imaginary.

In search of an explanation for this appeal to literature, we are tempted to resort to familiar arguments fed by our intuition. One argument relates to the content of a literary work. "Contemplating how the phenomenon of dissidence could have arisen in an isolated society," writes Andrei Amalrik, "I think first of all about the role of Russian literature [and] the passion of this literature in defence of the individual against the system."[35] Such a characterization only takes us so far. Putting aside the question of conservative collectivist or nationalist samizdat, what are we to make of underground literature in which the lines between the individual and the system are not clearly drawn, in which "everyone is guilty" and complicit in what Vasily Grossman calls "our human indecency" (nashe chelovecheskoe nepotrebstvo)?[36] What are we to make of Grossman's Anna Sergeevna in Vse techet (Everything Flows, 1961), a character who recounts her own eager, callous involvement in the forced starvation of the Ukrainian peasantry in 1932–3? Of Lidiia Chukovskaia's Sofia Petrovna, who is more willing to believe in "the system" than in her own son?[37]

Another argument is material. "Samizdat began with poems," speculates Alekseeva, "perhaps due to the ease with which we could retype them, given their modest size."[38] Her astute remark centres on the question of materiality and practical efficiency: that is, poems were used to yield "a realistic picture of what was going on" because they were relatively short, duplicable, portable, and easy to memorize.[39] In the parallel market of samizdat they could facilitate communication about the world with reach and alacrity. Here again, things are not so straightforward. After all, literature, particularly poetry, "pushes communication to the background."[40] It does not get to the point, at least not in a conventional sense. Roman Jakobson goes so far as to say that it subjects communication to a form of "organized violence" (organizovannoe nasilie).[41] His Formalist colleague Viktor Shklovsky tempers his language, but the point is still the same. Literature revels in the ambiguous and the indeterminate, notes Shklovsky, and increases "the difficulty and length of perception."[42] It is, in a word, strange.

Literature's strangeness was implicitly recognized by Gorbanevskaia in the preparation of *Khronika tekushchykh sobytii*, which adopted a dry "objective tone" that fled from ambiguity and indeterminacy. Inspired by the informational bulletins produced by the exiled Crimean Tatar community after 1965, *Khronika* avoided excessive editorial commentary and sought "to be very exact, to lay out the facts, to describe the violation of rights, to quote articles of law."[43] Arrests, court proceedings, demonstrations, and state abuses were chronicled with great precision, names and dates meticulously cited. It appeared to be the farthest thing from the work of literary intellectuals.[44] What was written was what was meant; there was little place for metaphor or allusion or play. A representative passage: "In the cell of VADIM DELONE [Delaunay], a participant in the Red Square Demonstration of 25 August [1968] and an inmate in a camp in Tiumen, authorities discovered his poem 'The Ballad of Unbelief' during a search. For this poem Delaunay was placed in solitary confinement for ten days."[45] The editors of *Khronika* do not give the text of Delaunay's poem, which had been circulating in samizdat for years. To do so would have been to mingle *Khronika*'s clinical constative rhetoric with something else: a verse form with a peculiar "expectation of meaningfulness" that exceeds a straightforward expository function.[46]

If samizdat was the "core" of Soviet dissent, as Alekseeva posits, then this core was riven: between the representation of what Aristotle called *hoia an genoito* (that which might happen) and the representation of *ta genomena* (that which did happen). In the *Poetics* this divergence is at the heart of Aristotle's discussion of *poiesis* and *historia*, which leads him to elevate the former over the latter as more "worthwhile." Here I do not mean to draw a hard and fast line between poetry and history or between the literary and the documentary. To be sure, apart from periodicals like *Khronika tekushchykh sobytii*, Soviet samizdat could often breach the boundaries between them. Documentary samizdat could mount "experiments in literary investigation," as in the famous case of Solzhenitsyn's *Arkhipelag Gulag* (*The Gulag Archipelago*, 1973). Likewise, literary samizdat could exercise a documentary function, informing audiences of harrowing events about which no one dared to speak, as in the case of Vasyl Barka's *Zhovtyi kniaz* (The yellow prince), a novel that appeared in samvydav in 1962 to confront the Holodomor, Stalin's man-made famine of 1932–3, which killed millions in Ukraine alone.

Aristotle's distinction between *poiesis* and *historia* is helpful here in its choice of time signature, which in turn clarifies, in his philosophy, the range of objects of literary and historical knowledge. The optative in *hoia an genoito* conveys a sense of potentiality, allowing *poiesis* to gesture toward universals. The aorist in *ta genomena* carries a force similar to that of the perfective aspect in Slavic languages, restricting *historia* to particulars realized in a specific place and time. Documentary samizdat, exemplified by *Khronika tekushchykh sobytii*, is time bound in this sense. It is also often, but not always, time sensitive, calling for urgent action on the part of the reader in the real world. By comparison, literary samizdat is never time bound, but it is often time sensitive. It is an open invitation to exercise the optative – to revisit the past, for instance, and make it present in the act of creative reading.

The knowledge on offer in the market of literary samizdat, in other words, was a knowledge-how, a priming of what Kant characterized as the "productive imagination," a kinetic force actively shaping the contours of human experience anew.[47] By revelling in the opaque and trafficking in the disjointed, literary samizdat challenged the reader to work through what Wolfgang Iser calls "suspensions of connectibility" and to engage in the construction of new, virtual worlds of her own. This power is the reason that literature, especially poetry, dominated the early years of samizdat and helped facilitate the rise of Soviet dissent. It was a training ground. It not only provided an outlet for critical views, defended the individual against the system, or promoted efficient communication. Above all, in an environment of restricted thought and speech, literature also exercised muscles of ideation and empowered circles of readers to forge and pursue new itineraries of meaning and action, itineraries that could provide coordinates for social opposition. As we shall see, in the case of literary responses to Stalin's Crimean atrocity, this pursuit could bear the hallmarks of lived experience and convey an emotional urgency all its own. In pockets of activity across the region of the Black Sea, it spurred prosocial action and enabled across ethnic, linguistic, and religious borders something that was never a given: a flowering of solidarity with an alienated nation thousands of miles away.

2.

Inviting readers to remake the world in conditions hostile to ideological pluralism is, of course, a dangerous undertaking. Boris Chichibabin always seemed to do so from a position on the periphery. His home in Kharkiv in eastern Ukraine, less than thirty miles from the border with

Soviet Russia, was at a physical remove from the literary circles of Moscow and Saint Petersburg and at an additional linguistic remove from the Ukrainian-language literary circles of Kyiv and Lviv. As he explains in "Rodnoi iazyk" (My native tongue, 1951), in Ukraine "I am a Russian," but in Russia "I am taken for a 'topknot'" (khokhol).[48]

In the 1960s Chichibabin led a Kharkiv poetry studio that regularly drew large crowds and proved a popular venue for up-and-coming poets: Aleksandr Vernik, Yuri Miloslavsky, Eduard Siganevich. Chichibabin used his live readings as an opportunity to reach his audiences with a "political spirit" typically exorcised in his programmatic printed works by Soviet censors.[49] "In his publications everything was purged, prepared, and selected in advance," recalls the journalist Feliks Rakhlin. "But on stage his words were much harder for the censors to monitor. The poems Chichibabin read at poetry evenings and the poems he published were often completely different works."[50]

A mainstay in his performances, "Krymskie progulki" (Crimean strolls, 1959–60) was never published in the Soviet period. Today it stands as the first non–Crimean Tatar literary work to confront the 1944 deportation. For Crimean Tatar poet Şakir Selim, Chichibabin was at the vanguard of a literary defence of their rights, the leader of a phalanx of poets "with conscience" (vicdanlılar).[51] Chichibabin's frequent recitation of "Krymskie progulki" across the Soviet Union caused friends to worry for his safety. As Rakhlin noted, "I was concerned for Boris. He was very good on stage, where he often delivered his poems directly to the people [...] And he consistently read 'Krymskie progulki,' a poem that condemned the Stalinist deportation of the Crimean Tatars and other peoples, *when it was not possible to hear about such things*."[52] He recited the poem in the 1960s at Grigory Levin's renowned Magistral literary gathering at the Railworkers' Central House of Culture in Moscow (Tsentralnyi dom kultury zheleznodorozhnikov, TsDKZh).[53] The Moscow-based poet and critic Vladimir Leonovich underscored the risk he was taking there: "The Crimean theme [...] fell under article 58–10 [of the Russian SFSR penal code] and therefore under article 70: anti-Soviet agitation, the distribution of state secrets [*gostainy*], nationalist propaganda. Chichibabin was a former prisoner of the Gulag [*lagernik*], and he knew this all too well. But you should have seen and heard how he read the poem in Moscow at TsDKZh."[54]

Transcribed and passed hand to hand without his name, "Krymskie progulki" circulated in samizdat throughout the Soviet Union for decades. As late as 1987 the poem found its way into an appeal to Mikhail Gorbachev, where it served as a powerful addendum.[55] But because of the material transience of samizdat – its capacity to be "ephemeral" and to "disappear without a trace"[56] – it is virtually impossible to follow closely the poem's journey in the literary underground. To understand its reception, we cannot turn to stores of letters from readers to a journal editor or publisher, for instance.[57] At times we are left with only glimpses. Mustafa Dzhemilev – the legendary Soviet dissident widely considered the leader of the Crimean Tatar people – remembers discovering it in Tashkent sometime in the early 1960s. "When I read 'Krymskie progulki,' the first thought I had was, 'How much time in prison will he get for this?'" he said. "Because in Soviet times, you could not write such a thing and escape punishment. Once the poem fell into my hands, we circulated it everywhere."[58]

What made "Krymskie progulki" ostensibly dangerous from the point of view of Soviet authorities? One evident factor was its treatment of the deportation and the Crimean Tatar "problem" at a time when, as Rakhlin put it, "it was not possible to hear about such things" – even after the many revelations of Khrushchev's "Secret Speech," which made no mention of Stalin's Crimean atrocity.[59] Viktor Shklovsky, for example, convinced friend and collaborator Sergei Paradzhanov not to pursue a film project based on Pushkin's *Bakhchisaraiskii fontan* for this very reason. "The theme of Crimea," he wrote, "is for us a particularly closed national theme, because *in Crimea there are no longer any Crimean Tatars*" (v Krymu net krymskikh tatar).[60] Indeed, the Soviet state continued to remain silent about the deportation operation beyond the 1946 Presidium decree buried in the dense typeface of *Izvestiia*. Even those like Kozlov and Perventsev who slandered the Crimean Tatars in literary prose declined to detail what their "punishment" actually was. Indeed, the very fact that "Krymskie progulki" could not be published at any point in the Soviet era attests to the deportation's particular radioactivity: it was an identifiable, ongoing crime committed by the Soviet state, an *actus reus* whose envelopment in silence and lies betrayed a *mens rea*, a guilty mind.

A samizdat work of documentary journalism exposing the brutality of the deportation could have performed the same informative function around 1960, when "Krymskie progulki" first circulated in the underground. But Chichibabin's text is a poem, and its status as a work of imaginative literature is no incidental detail. What accounts for its putative threat to the regime was its literary added value: an efficient manipulation of affect, its "notation of the heart," as Thorton Wilder would call it.[61] "Writing [in a documentary mode] about a specific injustice has clear practical importance, but great poetry can attract a wider audience," notes Dzhemilev, adding, "'Krymskie progulki' clearly had a huge emotional impact [*ogromnoe emotionalnoe vozdeistvie*] on people."[62]

The renowned Ukrainian civic activist and former Soviet dissident Myroslav Marynovych agrees. "The fact that it is poetry increases the emotionality of perception [*emotsiinist spryiniattia*]. Reading a dry list of historical facts, one works the mind, but reading poetry, one works the heart."[63] Marynovych encountered Chichibabin's poems when he was a prisoner in the Perm-36 Gulag camp complex, where fellow inmate Genrikh Altunian – a dissident and mutual friend whom Chichibabin celebrated as a "guardian of honour"[64] – often recited them by heart.[65]

In alluding to the poem's "emotional impact" and "emotionality," Dzhemilev and Marynovych do not specify any one emotion in particular. But Chichibabin does. He foregrounds guilt. In correspondence with a Crimean Tatar activist, he discusses how he agonized over Stalin's Crimean atrocity and "empathized" (sochuvstvoval) with the Crimean Tatar people. The foundational source of this solidarity was guilt (*vina*). "An individual, or a group of individuals – a people, a nation – who begin to consider themselves guilty," he explains, "think about how to rectify and expiate guilt and, if possible, about how to atone for it through good conduct."[66]

What guilt is he referring to? After all, Chichibabin took no part in the deportation operation; in May 1944 he was at the Transcaucasian front with the Red Army. The guilt he has in mind is less a consequence of any action in the service of Stalin's regime than a consequence of inaction and ignorance in the wake of Stalin's death – a consequence of what Lidiia Ginzburg described as "adaptation, excuse, and indifference."[67]

Karl Jaspers calls this guilt "political."[68] In contrast to "criminal guilt" – in this case, the guilt of those whose actions directly contributed to the deaths of thousands of Crimean Tatar deportees – political guilt, for Jaspers, blankets all the citizens of a given state, making them fundamentally complicit in its misdeeds. Most of the Soviet writers and artists featured in this book grapple with the implications of political guilt. They evidence an "ethic of moral seriousness"[69] that accommodates political guilt as an idea and as a condition, a feeling. Some run to it, like Chichibabin, while others struggle to fix its radius and reach.

Indeed, for Chichibabin, burying or forswearing this guilt was deeply destructive. His friend Petro Grigorenko agreed. A Ukrainian former Red Army major-general, Grigorenko was a critical link between Russian and Ukrainian dissident circles and the Crimean Tatar movement. His ardent defence of the Crimean Tatars came at great personal cost. It led to his imprisonment, beating, forced feeding, and – as the Turkish press put it – confinement in the "madhouse" (tımarhane).[70] In Grigorenko's view, guilt was in fact the prey of a "cruel, callous" Soviet "machine" powered by "our hands and our heads." The machine "crushes us mercilessly, destroys the best people in our society, *makes everyone guiltless*" (delaet vsekh nevinovnymi).[71] Like Jaspers, Grigorenko viewed guilt and liberty as consubstantial; one proceeds from the other.[72] Accepting guilt, then, is to defeat the machine. Chichibabin went further. For him, an acceptance of guilt bore the promise of harmony and redemption. "The feeling of guilt is a feeling noble and fruitful, *even in the imagination or in representation*" (emphasis mine), he says. "I appeal to every one of you: embrace the feeling of guilt."

Clinical psychologists would agree: Chichibabin was on to something. He articulated a case for interpersonal guilt as a moral, prosocial emotion at a time when a Freudian view of guilt as aggression toward the self still had considerable currency. Nowhere in his remarks does Chichibabin refer to "shame," *pozor* or *styd*. The omission is important. Guilt and shame are related feelings that emerge out of our ability to fashion ourselves as objects of moral evaluation, but their effects are divergent. In a pioneering study, Helen Block Lewis demonstrates that guilt is an emotional response to a transgression that maintains and even strengthens the integrity of the self, whereas shame is an emotional response to a transgression that adversely affects it.[73] Guilt preserves an active, capable self; shame produces a disempowered one. The difference has real-world consequences. In the wake of wrongdoing – real or perceived – guilt provokes reparative action, whereas shame too often prompts retreat and "mobilises avoidance."[74] An embrace of guilt, Chichibabin suggests, enables efforts of repair.

The poet keenly intuited what psychologists have illustrated in a series of empirical studies over recent decades: namely, that there is a special bond between guilt and empathy.[75] This psychological research also indicates that guilt-induced empathy is as robust for individuals who only see suffering as it is for those who feel that they have caused it somehow.[76] "By its very nature," argues Judith Price Tangney, "guilt forges a natural bridge to Other-oriented empathic concern."[77] Chichibabin sensed that his art was a form of passage over this bridge. After all, in the process of coming to moral terms with wrongdoing, literature can be considered particularly conducive to guilt but relatively inimical to shame, because it is by nature "self-serving."

I am guided here by Wolfgang Iser's theory of aesthetic response. For Iser, literature stimulates the reader's world-making, ideating activity by way of its characteristic indeterminacy, which is fed by what he calls *Leerstellen*, "gaps" or "blanks" that the reader is meant to fill with the force of her imagination.[78] This process of "meaning assembly" is not a linear or uniform movement of an interpretative iron, as it were, smoothing out semantic wrinkles. It is the movement of a ratchet, a continual back-and-forth "of anticipation and retrospection that leads to the formation of [a] virtual dimension, which in turn transforms the text into an experience for the reader."[79] In creative reading, we move in two directions at once.[80] Iser describes this experience as a "repositioning" and "boundary-crossing" in which the reader dislodges preconceptions and assumptions, disrupts the prevailing demands of the social and cultural systems around her, and "stages" new versions of the self.[81]

Literature's self-serving quality is not, however, selfish. Staging new versions of the self in the act of creative reading is to leap among what Charles Taylor calls "webs of interlocution."[82] It is always an implicit act of seeing Others, of acknowledging and navigating among a multiplicity of subject positions not our own. Indeed, in the case of the literary texts in this book, there is a consistent attempt to orient the reader in the direction of the Crimean Tatar Other and to induce a feeling of guilt disposed to empathic connection. In other words, there is a consistent cultivation of *solidarity*.

Solidarity is a famously polysemous term. It has been used variously as a shorthand for *sympathy, altruism, unity, social cohesion*. It can have a universalist ("we are the world") or a particularist ("we alone") flavour. I define it here as an active convergence of interests and fellow-feeling between groups that bridges a distance. In adding to the terminological mêlée, I want to underscore two key elements. The first is convergence. Solidarity realigns the borders of an in-group and an out-group to create new avenues of trust and communality for the individual to travel – while affirming, crucially, the respective group identities at the same time. As we will see, Russian, Ukrainian, and Turkish literary expressions of solidarity with the Crimean Tatars sought to secure ethical deliverables for the respective in-groups – among them a perception, however modest, of recovered or enhanced moral authority. They also helped – demonstrably so – to consolidate Crimean Tatar identity by performing recognition of the Crimean Tatar Other and positioning him as an object of concern.

The second element is activity. Solidarity is a dynamic, searching force testifying to our need to co-operate with Others, to our desire for community. David Goodhart understands solidarity as static and given, framing it in the context of the question "Who is my brother?"[83] I would ask instead: "*When* is my brother?" Solidarity *emerges*, and it emerges to contest the atomization of human life, to bridge distances in age, gender, language, ethnicity, religion. It is fluid, not fixed. Nor is it limited to a contest in which a gain of interests and fellow-feeling *here* presumes a loss of interests and fellow-feeling *there*. In a sense, solidarity is always plural. And importantly for our discussion, it emerges through imagination and affect.

To be sure, solidarity can result from a cognitive transaction in which we infer relations with each other based on a common interest or point of reference.[84] But very often it is empathic, a product of face-to-face interaction or a real-time moment of direct observation or experience of an Other's emotions. Seeing the Other feel, in other words, is an invitation for the self to connect. But when such direct observation or experience is impossible, Adam Smith offers a prescription: "conceive it in a very lively manner."[85] By stimulating ideation and conceiving "surrogate experiences" for the reader – experiences that are live at the moment of creative reading – literature can enable solidarity to develop in circumstances in which the reader and the Crimean Tatar Other, for instance, find themselves separated by both time and space.[86] According to Iser:

> Even though the literary text has its reality not in the world of objects but in the imagination of its reader, it wins a certain precedence over texts that seek to make a statement concerning meaning or truth [...] Meanings and truths are, by nature, influenced by their historical position and cannot in principle be set apart from history. The same applies to literature, but *since the reality of a certain text comes to life within the reader's imagination, it must, again by nature, have a far greater chance of outlasting its historical genesis.*[87]

In the face of historical and physical distance, literature allows us, as Colin McGinn writes with appropriate emphasis, "to *see* and *feel* [...] in a way no [constative] tract can."[88] Among the works explored in this book, both seeing the victim and feeling guilt are at the heart of the poetics of solidarity.

3.

Literary texts active in this poetics of solidarity – like Chichibabin's "Krymskie progulki," which we will explore more closely – approach the reader with at least three invitations. The first is to endeavour to see the victim in light of the event that led to his suffering, an event previously withheld or obscured from the reader's view. I emphasize *endeavour* not only because both prose and poetry use words to paint a visual image but because they oscillate between offering and withholding a clear view of the image itself, compelling the reader to work to establish coherence and consistency on her own. Literature "enables visual practices to come into being," such that the reader sees, in this case, a victim not *in* the text but *through* the text.[89] This effort turns the reader into a stakeholder; she has to *pay* regard to an Other, who becomes an object of concern.

The second invitation pertains not to object but to subject. Literary texts that are active in the poetics of solidarity invite the reader to gravitate toward or adopt the voice of a lyrical "I" or a narrator who at times speaks a language of guilt, even modelling confession. Take this example from poet and singer-songwriter Bulat Okudzhava:

Простите меня, крымские татары!
Когда вас под конвоем вывозили,
когда вы на чужбине вымирали,
вы ведь меня о помощи просили,
ко мне свои ладони простирали.
Когда на мушку брали вас подонки,
вы ведь меня просили о защите...
Когда-нибудь предъявят счет потомки
мне одному... Я вас прошу: простите![90]

(Forgive me, Crimean Tatars!
When you were deported at gunpoint,
When you were dying in a foreign land,
You asked me for help,
You extended your palms to me.
When thugs placed you in the cross-hairs,
You asked me for protection...
Someday my descendents will hold
Me to account... I beg you: forgive me!)

Invariably this voice exposes an inconsistency between reality and a communal standard or value. It evokes the ethos of the in-group. "You cannot persuade people to feel guilty," notes Alyson Brysk. "You can only mobilize guilt by activating some underlying identity."[91] The third invitation at the heart of the poetics of solidarity is accordingly for the reader to access a meaningful framework of identification with the out-group. The literary texts under study here present this framework by way of two interdependent components: a "we-denomination" (how the "we" of the in-group primarily sees itself, as civic, national, or ethnic) and a "we-relation" (how this "we" conceives of its connection with the Other, as either "one of us," "like us," or "part of us").

In "Krymskie progulki," Boris Chichibabin unveils a framework of identification with the Crimean Tatar Other by way of an immediate reference to *empire* in the poem's first word. He places the question of the colonization of Crimea front and centre but then leaves it there like the elephant in the room:

Колонизаторам — крышка!
Что языки чесать?[92]

(The colonizers are finished!
What is there to wag your tongue about?)

This startling opening, which literally places a "lid" (kryshka) on the text, is a disorienting remark that calls attention to the poem's *désancrage* or "uprootedness" from a clear context.[93] The very condition of the poem's existence, a *pre hoc* "wagging of tongues" about colonizers and colonization, is missing. This is less an absence than a vacancy for the reader to fill. To make sense of these lines, she must make room for the assertion that colonizers are *not* "finished" but are still present and even active in Crimea. Chichibabin's onset couplet is what might be termed apopha(n)tic: it denies the existence of colonizers but, in doing so, asserts their existence by calling on the reader to supply what is not there. The poem continues:

Перед землею крымской
совесть моя чиста.
Крупные виноградины...
Дует с вершин свежо.

(Before this Crimean land
My conscience is clear.
Voluptuous grapes...
A fresh wind blows from the peaks.)

As if ticking a box, the lyrical persona ventriloquizes the poets in chapter 1 who fetishize Crimean place and celebrate the *zemlia krymskaia* as an exquisite specimen of physical, rather than human, geography. Yet couched in this celebration is something else: an implicit expression of guilt amplified by a variant, unsettled metre, *Sovest moia chista*.[94] The line's placement in the quatrain calls attention to *sovest* (conscience, moral faculty), the watchword of such Russian civic poets (*grazhdanskie poety*) as Aleksandr Radishchev and Nikolai Nekrasov, to whom Chichibabin expressed admiration throughout his career.

This intrusion of the ethical alters the trajectory of the text, displacing what was a fawning tribute to the Crimean arcadia and proffering a sudden and defensive denial of complicity in unspecified crimes of pillage and robbery:

Я никого не грабил.
Я ничего не жег.

(I have not robbed anyone.
I have not burned anything.)

This convulsive alternation between the pleasant and the unpleasant – between colonizers and refreshing winds and criminal wrongdoing – is a *minus-priem* or "minus device."[95] By calling attention to the poem's instability, it engages the reader in a heightened process of communication, one inflected by the vagaries of the lyric form. While "Krymskie progulki" seems representative of what T.S. Eliot calls poetry of the first voice – "the voice of the poet talking to himself, or nobody"[96] – the interrogative orientation of the opening couplet and the defensive tone of the last quoted lines suggest an address to an unspoken "you" by the lyrical persona's "I."

As this address is unsettled, the poem at once welcomes the reader's identification with the lyrical persona – a default identification, as it were, according to those who hold that "the lyric is a script written for performance by the reader, who, as soon as he enters the lyric, is no longer a reader but an utterer"[97] – and prompts him to explore the participant role of an interlocutor to whom the lyrical persona's questions and guarded assertions could be directed. In effect, the beginning of "Krymskie progulki" invites the reader to stage himself as a guilt-ridden and self-persuasive "I" (Chto iazyki chesat? [...] Sovest moia chista [...] Ia nikogo ne grabil) *and* as a right-behaving "you" with a concern for justice.

The remainder of the poem reveals the tragedy behind these rhetorical contortions and seeks to make sense of it as a symptom of a larger disease afflicting what Grigorenko called a "seriously ill" body politic.[98] After its disorienting beginning, it settles into a more consistent strophic and metrical pattern tending toward iambic octaves. The lyrical persona catches a stride as well. Discarding a defensive pose for a more contemplative one, he wanders from the beaches of the Black Sea into the mountains, searching for a lost Crimea:

Волны мой след кропили,
плечи царапал лес.
Улочками кривыми

в горы дышал и лез.
Думал о Крыме: чей ты,
кровью чужой разбавленный?
Чьи у тебя мечети,
прозвища и развалины?
. . . .
Люди на пляж, я — с пляжа,
там, у лесов и скал,
«Где же татары?» — спрашивал,
все я татар искал.
Шел, где паслись отары,
желтую пыль топтал,
«Где ж вы, — кричал, — татары?»
Нет никаких татар.

(Waves splashed against my footprints,
The wood scraped my shoulders.
Along crooked lanes
I clambered toward the mountains and breathed deeply.
I thought about Crimea: to whom do you belong,
You, soaked in the blood of Others?
Whose are these mosques,
ruins and place-names?
. . . .
People went to the seaside, but I left it,
And there, amongst the cliffs and woods,
I asked, "Where are the Tatars?"
I searched everywhere for them.
Off where a flock of lambs grazed,
I walked along and trampled yellow dust,
And cried "Where are you, Tatars?"
But no Tatars remain.)

The Crimea that elicited metaphysical reverie among Pushkin and the
Russian poets of the nineteenth century oppresses Chichibabin's lyrical persona: it constricts his physical movement and haunts him like
a spectre. The eerie absence of Tatar culture and society resounds in
a question – "Gde zh tatary?" – repeated as a mournful apostrophe –
"Gde zh vy, tatary?"

Here Chichibabin is intertextual with Pushkin's *Bakhchisaraiskii fontan*: "Gde skrylis khany? Gde harem?" (Where have the khans gone?
Where is the harem?) Pushkin's questions are exoticized and rhetorical;

Chichibabin's questions demand an answer. They are made urgent by a claim about Crimea and the question of possession:

А жили же вот тут они
с оскоминой о Мекке.
. . . .
Не русская Ривьера,
а древняя Орда
жила, в Аллаха верила,
лепила города.

([The Tatars] lived right here
With reverence for Mecca.
. . . .
This is not the Russian Riviera,
The ancient Horde
Lived here, worshipped Allah,
And built cities.)

Ne russkaia Riv'era – Chichibabin contests the rhetorical and physical deterritorialization of the Crimean Tatars. He portrays the settler colonial encounter in Crimea as a folly of noblesse oblige, a shortsighted "civilizing mission" that, in the words of one admirer of Russian imperial power, sought to "spread light" among "a [Tatar] population that [...] had lived in ignorance."[99] In "Krymskie progulki" this ignorance is ascribed not to the Tatars but to a collective "us":

Конюхи и кулинары,
радуясь синеве,
песнями пеленали
дочек и сыновей.
Их нищета назойливо
наши глаза мозолила.
Был и очаг, и зелень,
и для ночлега кров.

(Cooks and grooms,
Enjoying the blue [of the sea],
Swaddled in songs
Their sons and daughters.
But *their* poverty intrusively
Calloused *our* eyes.

After all, they had food, a hearth,
And a roof for a night's shelter.)[100]

This first-person plural *nash* (our) operates "vertically" here: it gathers the "I" of the lyrical persona and the unspoken "you" of the reader according to an established set of historical, linguistic, and cultural affinities that they are thought to share – in this case, as part of a Russian and Soviet in-group. It also suggests that they are not simply descendants of the colonizers who dispossessed the Tatars but colonizers themselves. In this way, "Krymskie progulki" challenges the reader to assume responsibility for a legacy of wrongdoing against the Tatars, a legacy that culminated in May 1944:

Стало их горе солоно.
Брали их целыми селами,
сколько в вагон поместится.
Шел эшелон по месяцу.
Девочки там зачахли,
ни очаги, ни сакли.
Родина оптом, так сказать,
отнята и подарена, —
и на земле татарской
ни одного татарина.
Живы, поди, не все они:
мало ль у смерти жатв?

(The grief [of the Crimean Tatars] grew bitter still.
Entire villages of them were taken,
As many as could be stuffed into a train car.
The convoy travelled for a month.
There girls withered away,
Without a hearth, without a home [*sakla*].
Their homeland was, as it were,
Taken and given away wholesale.
And now on Tatar land
There is not one Tatar.
Not all of them are alive:
After all, does death have small harvests?)

What the 1946 Presidium decree characterized as a benevolent "relocation" is chronicled here as a cruel assault on the innocent ("Devochki tam zachakhli / Ni ochaga, ni sakli") that killed thousands ("Zhivy, podi, ne vse oni"). The lyrical persona dwells on the deportation "not to disturb the dead," he says, but to urge the reader to contemplate its gravity and its meaning: "To deport an entire nation – / How could they come up with such a thing?"

Chichibabin's "Krymskie progulki" concludes with a savage indictment of the Soviet civic compact. His lyrical persona condemns a societal system bound in a corrupt "circle of mutual responsibility" (krugovaia poruka) – by lies, fear, and naked careerism. Soviet authorities sit and plot campaigns of deception, which the radio and the newspaper attentively carry out before a passive public, while bureaucrats "abandoning their honour, slither across bodies toward power and exultation." Presiding over this grotesque scene are monuments to Stalin, "before which," the lyrical persona tells the reader, "you bow."

Addressed for the first time by way of the second-person singular, the reader is directly implicated in this *krugovaia poruka* – a term for a system of enforced "all for one and one for all" mutual oversight and reliance, which "generated some of the most attractive and most unattractive features in Russian social life"[101] – as a functionary who surrenders her agency to granite idols and sacrifices her fellow citizens in the process. In "Krymskie progulki" the crimes of the Soviet state are not the fault of one man who cultivated, as Khrushchev famously insisted before the Twentieth Congress of the Communist Party in 1956, a cult of personality (*kult lichnosti*). For Chichibabin, they ultimately stem from the Soviet "we," the civic collective that abets the state or, at best, stands aside as fellow citizens are slandered and dispossessed.

4.

Boris Chichibabin never travelled to Central Asia, but "Krymskie progulki" did – swiftly. The poem reached Crimean Tatar readers in exile in the early 1960s soon after its composition. But Chichibabin left his name off the text, and his identity was largely a mystery to Crimean Tatar readers until Eşref Şemi-Zade travelled from Tashkent to Kharkiv on a research trip in 1966. A Crimean Tatar poet, literary scholar, and translator, Şemi-Zade already knew "Krymskie progulki" well, but it was in Kharkiv that he learned the identity of the man who had written it. A journalist friend introduced Şemi-Zade to Chichibabin, and their connection was immediate. The two men were Gulag survivors with a passion for poetry; they spoke for hours. Chichibabin embraced Şemi-Zade as a "wise, tender, quietly intelligent man full of pain for his people," and Şemi-Zade, in an inscription to a gifted volume of his Crimean Tatar–language poetry, called Chichibabin "the best friend of the long-suffering Crimean Tatar people."[102]

Their encounter in Kharkiv in 1966 inspired Chichibabin to write another poem about the deportation, "Chernoe piatno" (Black mark, 1966). Before Şemi-Zade returned to Tashkent, Chichibabin rushed to present it to him with a dedication. He later apologized for the hurried composition of its iambic tetrameter lines, which begin with a collision of two images:

Я видел Крым без покрывала,
он был как высохший родник.

(I saw Crimea without its veil,
It was like an arid spring.)

Chichibabin's haste, however, had an upside when it came to samizdat distribution and circulation. It led to a text with highly portable, memorizable quatrains packed with salient images and aphorisms. "Chernoe piatno" is less intertextual and lyrically variant than "Krymskie progulki," but it has its moments of unpredictability. In the second strophe, for instance, the historical fact of the deportation abruptly careens into an array of impressionistic visuals:

Росли цветы на камне твердом
и над волной клубился пар,
но в девятьсот сорок четвертом
из Крыма вывезли татар.
Сады упали на колени,
земля забыла имена.[103]

(Flowers grew on hard stone
And steam swirled above the waves,
But in 1944
From Crimea they expelled the Tatars.
Gardens fell to their knees,
The land forgot its names.)

Stalin also enters the poem, perverting its strophic pattern with an odd five-line stanza stuffed with a stretch of warped metre in the middle, an aside about his savagery:

Их всех от мала до велика
оговорил и закатал,
как это выглядит ни дико,
неограниченный владыка
и генеральный секретарь.

(All of them, young and old,
Were slandered and cast in fetters
– No matter how savage it appears –
By the insatiable master
And General Secretary.)

Chichibabin makes sure to place the Crimean Tatars first – "ikh vsekh" – and Stalin last ("the General Secretary") in the stanza's order. His lyrical persona also invites the reader to envision those persecuted in the deportation as children, reminding her that, while the Ingush and Balkar people have already returned from exile, the "evil" of Crimean Tatar dispossession is alive in the present of 1966. He then calls attention to the shattered bond between Crimean place and Tatar personality – "there can be no body without a soul" – and urges the reader to help make things right.

This restitution pivots on an assumption of guilt and an avoidance of shame:

Чтобы нам в глаза смотрели дети
без огорченья и стыда,
да будет всем на белом свете
близка татарская беда.

(So that we might look our children in the eyes
Without sorrow or shame,
Let everyone the world over
Feel the plight of the Tatars.)

The lyrical persona moves from the misery of Crimean Tatar children to the expectant gazes of "our" children, literally calling for the reader to be "close" (blizka) to the Crimean Tatars. He then proceeds to speak in a series of directives – "return this people to their homeland" and "do not cloak shameful acts in euphemism" – which project a voice of moral authority. His last command is the poem's culmination, disclosing a we-denomination that again places the "you" of the reader and the lyrical "I" under the Soviet umbrella:

скорей с лица советской власти
сотрите черное пятно!

(Now go and wipe the black spot
From the face of Soviet power!)

Such directives are the farthest thing from aesthetic detachment. After all, Chichibabin dedicated "Chernoe piatno" to Şemi-Zade but did not address it to him. As in "Krymskie progulki," its intended address-ees are Soviet citizens outside the Crimean Tatar community who are meant to envision the deportation and its victims, come to grips with its "savage" nature, and act to save face for future generations. In this sense, the poem is less an expression of solidarity with the Crimean Tatars and more a tool configured to *generate* solidarity with them, to induce guilt and spark empathic connection and prosocial action on their behalf. When Chichibabin rushed to give "Chernoe piatno" to Şemi-Zade, he did so in the knowledge that it would be reproduced and circulated in samizdat. He was handing him, as Dmitry Furmanov would put it, a weapon.[104]

It was also a salve. Like "Krymskie progulki," Chichibabin's "Chor-noe piatno" became a source of comfort for the displaced and dispos-sessed Crimean Tatar people. His work was regularly read at gatherings of the so-called initiative groups (*initsiativnie gruppy*) of the National Movement of the Crimean Tatar People in Uzbekistan, which met regu-larly to elect delegates to travel to Moscow, Kyiv, and Simferopol and campaign on behalf of their cause. The Crimean Tatar journalist and cultural activist Aider Emirov explains: "[In exile], we devoured every kind word addressed to us with hunger and excitement [...] Two poems were especially popular in those difficult years: 'Krymskie progulki' and 'Chernoe piatno.' These lines literally brought tears to listeners' eyes. We transcribed them secretly and read them at meetings of the initiative groups. The authorities reacted in a typical fashion: the KGB chased us down for distributing these poems."[105] At meetings of these Crimean Tatar initiative groups, poems were not ornamentation; they did not serve as mere ceremonial preludes or codas to political discus-sion and debate. They were declarations of existence. Read alongside Şevki Bektöre's "Tatarlığım" and Noman Çelebicihan's "Ant etken-men," two anthems of the Crimean Tatar people, Chichibabin's verse testified to the coherence and continuity of the Crimean Tatar national community and recognized the legitimacy of their struggle – from the outside.[106] Its use in such settings is striking evidence of the power of the poetics of solidarity. "Even in Uzbekistan we knew Chichibabin," remembers one Crimean Tatar activist. "I will never forget his name."[107]

5.

The Crimean Tatar initiative groups reciting Chichibabin's "Krymskie progulki" and "Chernoe piatno" in the 1960s were at the vanguard of a lawful and well-organized rehabilitation and repatriation campaign based largely in Uzbekistan. This movement was pivotal to the evolution of Soviet dissent, an unacknowledged godfather. As Ukrainian dissident and mathematician Leonid Pliushch explains, "the Crimean Tatars impressed us all with [...] their understanding of things still inaccessible to the 'average Soviet intellectual.'"[108] In the face of arrest and imprisonment, Crimean Tatar activists regularly met in large numbers in Bekabad, Angren, Fergana, and Tashkent and appealed to Soviet authorities in Moscow with massive petitions calling for their return to Crimea. In 1962, for example, they presented a letter to the Twenty-Third Congress of the Communist Party with over 125,000 signatures, or roughly the entire Crimean Tatar population at the time.[109] Between 1965 and 1967 they sent Moscow a staggering number of letters and telegrams: over 53,000.[110] Meanwhile, activist leaders like Mustafa Dzhemilev, whose repeated arrests and historic hunger strike would soon become a rallying cry for the Crimean Tatar cause, worked to instil in younger generations a knowledge of their history, language, and culture in order to sustain and refresh the movement with new energy.[111] Put simply, the Crimean Tatar movement was the largest and most organized of its kind in Soviet history.

The war of attrition waged by the Crimean Tatars against the Kremlin eventually led to a breakthrough. In September 1967 the Presidium of the USSR Supreme Soviet issued Decree 493, "On Citizens of Tatar Nationality, Formerly Resident in Crimea," which finally absolved the Crimean Tatars of the charges of mass betrayal and treason. Yet unlike the June 1946 decree that had condemned the Crimean Tatars as traitors, it was published neither in *Izvestiia* nor in *Pravda* but only in local Central Asian newspapers. It was buried there for a reason. Decree 493 was a step forward and two leaps back. While it effectively rehabilitated the Crimean Tatars as rights-bearing citizens within the Soviet system, it claimed that they were now "rooted" (ukorenilis) in Central Asia, thereby precluding the legitimacy of their right of return to Crimea.[112]

The terminology of *rooting* from the period of korenizatsiia was resurrected. Petro Grigorenko attacked it with ridicule: "What are the Crimean Tatars – seedlings?"[113] Grigorenko had been enlisted in the support of the Crimean Tatars by the writer Alexei Kosterin, whose widely distributed samizdat essay "O malykh i zabytykh" (About the small and forgotten, 1967) reflected upon the crime of Stalin's deportations. The friendship between Grigorenko and Kosterin was brief – less than three years – but it contained "an entire lifetime," in Grigorenko's words. Their relationship was deeply consequential and uniquely Soviet, involving a Russian writer who inspired a Ukrainian general to become a spokesperson for the Crimean Tatar people.[114] Especially after Kosterin's death, Grigorenko was transformed from "a rebel into a fighter."[115] With an academic rigour (he held a doctorate in military science) and a soldier's fearlessness (he wrote directly to Yuri Andropov, head of the KGB, and "respectfully" threatened the agency in 1968), Grigorenko advocated passionately for the Crimean Tatar cause and connected activists in Tashkent with counterparts and foreign journalists in Moscow.[116] When Turkish readers learned of Grigorenko at this time, he was introduced with admiration as "the stubborn Ukrainian who does not know when to shut up."[117]

Grigorenko understood well that Decree 493 represented a backhanded act of discursive cleansing that sought to sever the relationship between Crimean place and Tatar personality, because it referred to them as "tatary, ranee prozhivavshie v Krymu" (the Tatars, formerly resident in Crimea). This classification, which openly denied them their distinctive national identity, was replicated in official Soviet discourse from internal passports to the *Great Soviet Encyclopedia*. As Grigorenko observed in a speech to the Crimean Tatar community in 1968, Decree 493 was a logical cul-de-sac: "You were subjected to repressions as Crimean Tatars, but after this 'political rehabilitation,' it turns out that there is no such nation on this earth. The nation has disappeared, but the discrimination remains."[118] Leonid Pliushch had one word for the decree: "vile."[119] Across the Black Sea, Turkish periodicals reacted to it with sarcastic exclamation points: "So this is Soviet justice (!), Soviet freedom (!), and Soviet humanity (!)."[120] Another lamented: "Stalin's reign of terror has not ended. The Crimean [Tatars] still cannot live as human beings [*hala insanca yaşayamiyor*]."[121]

While Decree 493 was mainly a political concession made to appease a vocal, mobilized national minority, its knock-on effects were profound. Within days, thousands of Crimean Tatars from Uzbekistan and beyond tested this "rehabilitation" by travelling to their ancestral homeland, which had become not only a massive dacha for the Soviet elite but also a unique frontier of Soviet identity building, given the collusion of ethnic cleansing and ethnic cloning, as we saw in chapter 3. KGB memos from the autumn of 1967 reveal a scramble to track the activities of these "inflammatory elements among the Crimean Tatars" and to prevent them from settling back in Crimea. "They are looking around the homes they used to live in before the deportation, taking photographs and suggesting to locals that they will be returning soon," one KGB report reads.[122] One of the Crimean Tatar pilgrims was Timur İbraimov, son of the executed Soviet Crimean Tatar leader Veli İbraimov. "He was raised in the Russian Federation and does not even know his native tongue, which he considers a disgrace," the report continues, almost sympathetically. "For him the Crimean land is sacred."

For İbraimov and the thousands of Crimean Tatars who attempted to return to Crimea in 1967, Decree 493 brought about what Talat Halman – "Turkey's most distinguished man of letters"[123] – called in his influential *Milliyet* column a "second deportation," another tragedy of a people "beset by all manner of punishments and tortures."[124] The decree represented a crack in the mortar that held up the flimsy legal façade justifying the dispossession of the Crimean Tatars. As it crumbled, other poets joined Chichibabin in an aesthetic defence of the Crimean Tatar cause. One was the influential editor of the journal *Novyi Mir*, Aleksandr Tvardovsky (1910–1971), who is remembered today in Crimean Tatar poetry as "courageous" (cesür).[125] In 1961, Tvardovsky had composed a long poetic panorama of life after Stalin. Entitled "Za daliu – dal" ("Distance beyond Distance"), it includes a couplet that gestures to Stalin's mass deportations at the end of the Second World War:

Он мог на целые народы
Обрушить свой верховный гнев.[126]

(On entire peoples he could
Rain down pure wrath.)

After Decree 493, Tvardovsky returned to this sensitive subject in "Po pravu pamiati" ("By Right of Memory," 1966–9), a work now considered the "brother" poem of Anna Akhmatova's seminal "Rekviem" ("Requiem," 1935–40) for its cathartic mourning and heartbreaking candour.[127]

The son of a blacksmith exiled to Siberia during collectivization, Tvardovsky wrote "Po pravu pamiati" toward the end of his life. Completed in 1969, it is an intensely personal lyric meditation on the problem of political guilt as well as the tortured movement of private and public memory in the Soviet Union. While it circulated in samizdat and *tamizdat* (literature smuggled abroad for publication) soon after its composition, "Po pravu pamiati" was only published after Tvardovsky's death, in 1987 in the journals *Znamia* and *Novyi Mir*.[128] "Po pravu pamiati" consists of three main parts: "Pered otletom" (Before departure), a reminiscence of youth; "Syn za ottsa ne otvechaet" (The son does not answer for the father), an indictment of Stalinism that is rendered as a dark, terrifying psalm; and "O pamiati" (On memory), a premonitory appeal to the reader not to forget his past and sacrifice his memory on the altar of the state. In "Syn za ottsa ne otvechaet," the poem's controversial centrepiece, Tvardovsky shares with the reader a devastating personal confession of guilt: he repudiated his exiled father, labelled by the Stalinist regime as a "vrag naroda" (enemy of the people), in the service of another "father," Stalin. Twisting the language of Matthew's Jesus, the voice of the Stalinist state counsels him with a series of sinister imperatives, inserting among them an allusion to a vague injustice against the Crimean Tatars:

Любой судьбине благодарен,
Тверди одно, как он велик,
Хотя б ты крымский был татарин,
Ингуш иль друг степей калмык.[129]

(Be grateful for your fate, whatever it may be,
And swear one thing: that he is great,
Even if you are a Crimean Tatar,
Ingush, or Kalmyk, friend of the steppe.)[130]

The passage is intertextual with Pushkin's "Exegi monumentum" ("I Erected a Monument," 1836), a work that positions the national minorities of the Russian Empire as exotic vessels of memory bearing the promise of the poet's immortality.[131] The nineteenth-century Tungus and Kalmyk of "Exegi monumentum" become, in Tvardovsky's rendering, three deported nations forced to bury the memory of their homelands and express gratitude to the regime that oppresses them. His word order in the line "Khotia b ty krymskii byl tatarin," separating "Crimean" and "Tatar" with the past tense of the verb *to be*, also gestures to the effect of Decree 493, which declared them "Tatars, formerly resident in Crimea."

Tvardovsky's allusion is brief and oblique. There is no vision of the vulnerable victim, no focused exploration of guilt, no accessible framework of identification. It took a contemporary with less prominence in official literary circles to engage more directly in a poetics of solidarity: Viktor Nekipelov. Nekipelov (1928–1989) is often remembered outside of the former Soviet Union as the author of *Institut durakov* (*Institute of Fools*, 1976), a documentary chronicle of his 1974 detention in the Serbsky Institute for Forensic Psychiatry (Institut sudebnoi psikhiatrii im. V.P. Serbskogo), the most infamous of the Soviet *psikhushki*, or psychiatric hospitals, where Petro Grigorenko had also been interned.[132] Nekipelov was central in exposing what Grigorenko called the Soviet "system of Chaadaevization," which turned intellectuals (like Petr Chaadaev in the nineteenth century) into residents of insane asylums.[133] That he is, in the words of Andrei Sakharov, a "wonderful poet" is not as well known.[134] Yet it was Nekipelov's poetry, declared an instrument of "anti-Soviet agitation" under Article 190 of the Soviet penal code, that offered the regime a pretence to send him to Serbsky in the first place. His arrest in 1973 was originally prompted by the discovery of a number of his poems amid the samizdat collection of the biologist and dissident Sergei Miuge, whose literary Thursdays were popular happenings in the Moscow area.[135]

These poems included a 1968 Crimean triptych – "Chufut-Kale," "Gurzuf," and "Ballada ob otchem dome" (Ballad about the ancestral home). According to Mariia Petrenko-Podiapolskaia, who played a central role in the formation of the Initiative Group for the Defense of Human Rights in 1969, Nekipelov often gave stirring performances of these three poems in Moscow in the late 1960s.[136] At the centre of his Crimean triptych are three distinct journeys among the "cold ruins" (kholodnye ruiny) of a Crimean place devoid of living Tatar personality. In "Chufut-Kale" the lyrical persona moves through an ancient fortress situated in the rock exposures high above the valleys radiating north from Bakhchisarai. Çufut Qale was a centre of life for the Jewish Karaim (or Karaites) of Crimea, "yet another disappeared people" (eshche odin ischeznuvshii narod) in Nekipelov's words, from the late fifteenth to the nineteenth century.[137] Before the arrival of the Karaites, it served as a stronghold for what would become the first Crimean Tatar khanate. For all its vibrant history, the site strikes Nekipelov's lyrical persona as frustratingly enigmatic and distant, as inaccessible and inhospitable to memory. A past of death and sufffering marks the remnants of its honeycomb cave dwellings, markets, and temples carved from stone.

In "Gurzuf," which like Chichibabin's "Krymskie progulki" gestures to the tradition of peripatetic poetry, Nekipelov's lyrical persona wanders a space seemingly more hospitable to human life. Windswept Gurzuf seems free of the decay and the thick patina of suffering that afflict Çufut Qale. It abounds in sites of religious and social communion, from minarets to teahouses (chaikhany). His lyrical persona soon discovers that these sites are uninhabited; they are "empty amphorae" rather than vibrant human dwellings. He then encounters a mysterious doppelganger, a Crimean Tatar poet in whose weary memory "a tragic night surfaces":

Когда трусливо и послушно
Орда опричная –

`как скот,
Вдруг растолкала по теплушкам
Его талантливый народ.
И бедняков, и бонз высоких,
И виноделов, и купцов,
И седовласых, и безногих,
И звездочетов, и слепцов.[138]

(When cowardly and obediently
The horde of the new *oprichnina*
                              – like cattle,
Suddenly pushed his talented people
Into railway cars:
The poor, the esteemed clerics,
The vinters, the merchants,
The old, the amputees,
The astrologers, the blind.)

Nekipelov suspends the alliterative pair *orda oprichnaia* before a hanging indent to endow the terminal foot *kak skot* with economical ambiguity: it can either modify the antecedent *orda* (horde) or the punished *narod* (people) in the final line of the quatrain. "Like cattle," the agents of the NKVD executed their orders to deport the Crimean Tatars without a protest of conscience; they forced human beings out of their homes, prodding and corralling them onto waiting train cars, "like cattle." The conspicuous visual positioning of *orda oprichnaia* also draws attention to a pregnant metaphor that Nekipelov employs later in human rights appeals: the metaphor of the Brezhnev era as a new *oprichnina*, a twentieth-century incarnation of Ivan IV's notorious reign of terror.[139]

Like the ruthless *oprichniki* who ravage villages and towns with indiscriminate regard for human life in Ivan Lazhechnikov's verse drama *Oprichnik* (1867), the Soviet NKVD officers in Nekipelov's "Gurzuf" persecute the vulnerable and dispatch them without remorse to remote settlements in Central Asia. The proliferative catalogue of human victims, underscored by the anaphoric conjunction *i* in the previous excerpt, compels the lyrical persona to confront his own guilt:

Моё преступное молчанье
Простишь ли мне, Гурзуф-Ага?

(Do you forgive
My criminal silence, Gurzuf-Ağa?)

Ağa is an honorific in Crimean Tatar, and Nekipelov's lyrical persona uses it to model for the reader a confession of guilt before a respected authority. If "the lyric is a script written for performance by the reader," then "Gurzuf" facilitates the reader's performance of this confession in the act of reading.[140] But in the world of the poem, this confession seems destined to fall on deaf ears. Gurzuf is overcome by silence:

Теснятся мысли вереницей
Измятых чувств, безсильных слов ...
Гурзуф молчит.

(My thoughts cluster in rows
Of haggard emotions and powerless words ...
Gurzuf is silent.)

Not unlike the conclusion of Chichibabin's "Krymskie progulki," these sombre lines dangle powerlessness and silence as bait. They seek to catch the reader and spur her to respond and restore the conditions of felicity for this painful confession – to contest the discursive cleansing that silenced the voices of the Crimean Tatars and to advocate for their rightful return to Crimea.

With each poem in Nekipelov's Crimean triptych, the lyrical persona becomes progressively attuned to his physical surroundings and the human lives that imbue them with meaning. An exploration of the ruins of Çufut Qale, cold to human life, alienates the lyrical persona. In "Gurzuf," by contrast, a nocturnal stroll along the welcoming streets of the seaside town sees him increasingly sensitive to the absence of the Crimean Tatars and mournful of his passive, "silent" complicity in the deportation. In "Ballada ob otchem dome," the final poem of the triptych, the lyrical persona proceeds to identify completely with his subject, internalizing the perspective of a Crimean Tatar who visits his homeland in 1967 in the wake of Decree 493, only to be displaced from it once more:

Я — крымский татарин. Я сын этих солнечных гор,
К которым сегодня прокрался украдкой, как вор.[141]

(I am a Crimean Tatar. I am a son of these sun-drenched mountains,
Where today I must creep furtively like a thief.)

His lyrical persona is a Crimean Tatar to whom "a grumbling bureaucrat" has given a permit to visit Crimea for only twenty-four hours. He travels to the home of his forebears near the mountain of Aiu-Dag outside Gurzuf:

Поклон Аю-Да́гу и сизой, туманной Яйле́!
Как долго я не́ был на горестной отчей земле!
Вот дом глинобитный, в котором родился и жил.
Ах, как он разросся, посаженный дедом инжир!
А наш виноградник и крошечный каменный сад,
Как прежде, наполнены праздничным звоном цикад.
Тверды и упруги, темны от дождей и росы,
Как дедовы руки — бугристые мышцы лозы.
Мускат дозревает! Да мне урожай не снимать.
Крадусь по задворкам отцовского дома, как тать.

(I bow to you, Aiu-Dag, and to you, misty-blue plateau!
How long it has been since I was here in my sorrowful ancestral home.
Here is the clay dwelling where I was born and where I lived.
O, how the fig tree planted by my grandfather has grown!
And our vineyard and small rock garden are there
As before, filled with the convivial ring of cicadas.
Hard and resilient, dark from rain and dew,
The sinewy muscles of the vine are like my grandfather's hands.
And how the Muscat ripens! But it is not for me to reap the harvest,
Creeping along the back of my ancestral home like a thief.)

These lines, written in an amphibrachic tetrameter traditionally employed to express solemnity and melancholy, may be read as a poetic translation of an account written by Anatoly Yakobson in a pamphlet of 1968.[142] Entitled "The Judgment of the Crimean Tatars," it highlights the ongoing process of settler colonialism on the Crimean peninsula: *"Crimea is a forbidden zone for the indigenous [korennykh] Tatars. There is no law to this effect, but there are obviously secret instructions […] Groups and families are returning to Crimea one by one. They return only to endure the hardships of a vicious cycle: local Crimean authorities do not register them, because they have no home; and they cannot buy a home, because they are not registered [net propiski]. Yet at the same time the state sends to Crimea an unstoppable flood of settlers [pereselentsev] from Russia and Ukraine."*[143] This passage from Yakobson's pamphlet simulates for the reader an aerial perspective from which to observe the Russian and Ukrainian settlers of Crimea and the Crimean Tatars, a "they" to whom concern and sympathy should be directed.

The optics in Nekipelov's "Ballada ob otchem dome" are decidedly different. Not only does the poet present the tragedy of an abortive return to the homeland from the perspective of a Crimean Tatar "I" – grafting the reader's unspoken "you" onto his subject position – but he also gives settler colonialism a distinctly human face, displacing the state from the centre of the equation:

В саду копошится какой-то лихой отставник.
Он погреб копает (а может быть, новый сортир?).
Ах, что он наделал — он камень в углу своротил!
Плиту вековую под старой щелястой айвой,
Где все мои предки лежат — на восток головой!
Он думает — козьи, и давит их заступом в прах, —
Священные кости… Прости нечестивца, Аллах!

(In the garden an old pensioner putters about.
He is digging a cellar (or maybe, a new latrine?)
Oh, what has he done? He dislodged a stone in the corner,
An ancient slab under an old, cracked quince,
Where my ancestors lie buried, facing east!
He thinks, "Goats!" – and crushes these sacred bones
Into dust with a spade … – Forgive this inhumanity, Allah!)

In Nekipelov's poem the villain is not an impersonal, amoral state but a puttering "old pensioner," someone like Kostiuk from Pavlenko's "Rassvet" decades after the deportation. His desecration of the bones of the lyrical persona's ancestors is based on similar acts described in samizdat documentary accounts. In a letter published in the second issue of *Khronika tekushchikh sobytii* on 30 June 1968, for instance, a group of Crimean Tatars led by the physician Zampira Asanova decries "the defilement and effacement of the graves of our ancestors from the face of the earth."[144] Whereas the authors of the letter avoid attaching an agent to these acts, using past passive participles wherever possible, Nekipelov prominently features an individual responsible for such defilement, an elderly man who does not occupy the corridors of power in the Kremlin or the shadowy backrooms of the KGB. In doing so, the poet confronts the uncomfortable truth that the dispossession of the Crimean Tatars was, to an extent, a state crime enabled by ordinary Soviet citizens.

Not unlike Ukraïnka and Çergeyev, Nekipelov frames the encounter between the Crimean Tatar victim and the "everyday" perpetrator by way of an anti-colonial sightedness:

Как долго и трудно мы смотрим друг другу в глаза.
Он кличет кого-то, спуская гривастого пса.
Не надо, полковник! Я фруктов твоих не возьму.
Хозяйствуй покуда в моём глинобитном дому.
Я завтра уеду обратно в далёкий Чимкент.
Я только смотритель, хранитель отцовских легенд.
Непрошеный призрак, случайная тень на стене,
Хоть горестный пепел стучится и тлеет во мне.
Я — совесть, и смута, и чей-то дремучий позор.
Я — крымский татарин, я сын этих солнечных гор.

(How long and hard we looked one another in the eyes.
He calls someone who lets loose a rabid dog.
Don't worry, colonel! I won't take your fruit.
Go keep house in my home.
Tomorrow I go back to distant Chimkent.
I am only a custodian, a keeper of ancestral legends.
An uninvited spectre, a chance shadow on the wall,
Even if mournful ashes knock about and putrify inside me.
I am conscience and dismay, someone's great disgrace.
I am a Crimean Tatar, I am a son of these sun-drenched mountains.)

In these poignant concluding lines, the "I" of the lyrical persona laments his fate as a custodian of identity, a vessel for the ashes of past generations. His tone of resignation and defeat stands in some contrast to the rousing force of the imperative, emphasized in capital letters, that ends Asanova's letter of 1968, for example: "POMOGITE NAM VERNUTSIA NA ZEMLIU NASHIKH OTTSOV!" (Help us return to the land of our forefathers!) But the power of Nekipelov's poem resides precisely in its dour, tempered restraint. Like Chichibabin's "Krymskie progulki," Nekipelov's "Ballada ob otchem dome" leverages despair for perlocutionary ends. Rather than positioning the reader as a mere recipient of information or a follower of commands, the poet ushers her into a more active, albeit decentred enunciatory pose, inviting her to stage her unspoken "you" as a Crimean Tatar "I." This act of staging is an act of solidary identification: "Ya – krymskii tatarin."

6.

Years after the composition of the Crimean triptych, Viktor and Nina Nekipelov sent a postcard to Petro Grigorenko and his wife, Zinaida, who had travelled to the United States for medical treatment. While abroad, the former Red Army general was stripped of his Soviet citizenship. The Nekipelovs' postcard is a reminiscence of Grigorenko in happier times, of the lifelong military man reading poetry. On the front of the card is a portrait of the poet Gavriil Derzhavin; on the back, an inscription with the lines "alive in the movement of matter, eternal in the flow of time" from Derzhavin's metaphysical poem "Bog" ("God," 1784). Grigorenko had recited the poem in Nekipelov's company years earlier. It was not clear at the time whether the two men would ever see each other again, but the postcard's allusion to the "eternal" gestured to their lasting bond as friends and as citizens who had endured the Serbsky psychiatric hospital and spoken out in defence of the rights of the Crimean Tatars.

Today Grigorenko's archive is a meeting place of the Soviet Russian, Crimean Tatar, and Ukrainian dissident movements, marking the many convergences and divergences between them. It is a vivid reminder that Soviet dissent was both a mosaic and a palimpsest, a phenomenon of diverse agendas and of overlapping, often contradictory messages: unnational, national, supranational, transnational. Enclosed in the archive's folders are letters across the Russian and Ukrainian languages to and from Nekipelov, Mustafa Dzhemilev, and Ukrainian poet and activist Mykola Rudenko, whose work is featured in the next chapter.[145] In these folders are batches of poems as well – most of which were written by Chichibabin.[146]

Among the nearly fifty pages of Chichibabin's verse in Grigorenko's archive is "Sudakskie elegii" (Sudak elegies, 1974), a lyric meditation of tail-rhyme stanzas set in Sudak on the northern shore of the Black Sea, a "forsaken Eden" whose spirit courses through the blood of the lyrical persona "like a sweet infection." One passage in particular would become a refrain among Crimean Tatar activists:

Как непристойно Крыму без татар.
Шашлычных углей лакомый угар,
заросших кладбищ надписи резные,
облезлый ослик, движущий арбу,
верблюжесть гор с кустами на горбу,
и все кругом - такая не Россия.[147]

(How obscene Crimea is without the Tatars.
The delightful intoxication of shashlik on coals,
The carved inscriptions of overgrown graveyards,
The old donkey pushing its cart,
Shrub-covered mountains like camel humps, and
Everything around us – this is not Russia at all.)

As in "Krymskie progulki," Chichibabin presents the Crimean Tatars as Crimea's indigenous people, evoking in an Orientalist vein the symbols and relics of its Muslim alterity, which now stand as empty and obsolete as a "shepherd without his flock." "This is not Russia at all," he insists. Indeed, after 1954, Crimea was no longer part of the RSFSR; Khrushchev had placed it within the administrative boundaries of Soviet Ukraine, where it began to emerge from economic depression.[148]

In the twilight of the Soviet period, Chichibabin was invited to publish "Sudakskie elegii" in *Novyi mir*, the journal made legendary by Tvardovsky. There was one problem, however: the word *obscene* (*nepristoino*) in the line "How obscene Crimea is without the Tatars." It was arresting. The journal's editors politely suggested an alternative: *uncomfortable* or *distressing* (*neuiutno*). Echoing Voloshin, Chichibabin replied:

> "How uncomfortable [*neuiutno*] Crimea is without Tatars" – this is not what I want to say at all. This is *not my* feeling and *not my* word [...] Without the Tatars, Crimea is not Crimea, not the real Crimea [...] It is some kind of artificial, exotic nature reserve invented and designed especially for tourists and holidaymakers [...] [The Crimean Tatars] were the original local population of this land; they were the people who took root in this soil. Having settled on it and spiritualized it [*odukhotvorivshim ee*] with the names of mountains, tracts, villages, a mythology, a memory, a faith, and a dream, they became and were the *soul* of Crimea. And when such a soul is artificially, violently removed from the body, and the body is left without a living soul [...], not only is this tragic, sad, and frightening, but there is in it something inauthentic, false, unnatural, shameful, *obscene*.[149]

As we will see, Soviet Ukrainian dissidents felt this obscenity as keenly as Chichibabin did. "The struggle of the Crimean Tatars in a sense united Russian and Ukrainian dissidents," says Myroslav Marynovych. "We could differ in our understanding of our own Russian-Ukrainian relations, but we were aligned in our solidarity with the Crimean Tatars."[150] For Ukrainian writers active in the 1960s and 1970s, the obscenity condemned by Chichibabin was keenly felt because it was also intimately familiar. It was seen as a toll exacted by a hegemonic, "chauvinistic" state on non-Russian nations, the price of imperialism in the guise of "internationalism."

Chapter Five

Trident and Tamğa

In 1967, as the Crimean Tatars were being rebranded "the Tatars formerly resident in Crimea," a secret KGB memorandum flagged correspondence between two strangers as a matter of pressing concern for the Central Committee of the Communist Party of Ukraine (see fig. 6). The memorandum gave an account of an exchange of letters between Mansur Osmanov, a Crimean Tatar driver in Tashkent, and Borys Antonenko-Davydovych, a Ukrainian writer in Kyiv. The two had never met. "I have heard that you are a fair, progressive writer," explains Osmanov, who initiated the contact, "and that is why I am writing to you." He reviews the political state of play for Antonenko-Davydovych. "For two years our [Crimean Tatar] representatives have been in Moscow ceaselessly working toward a resolution of our national question – the return to our native Crimea." It is not long, however, before Osmanov's tone turns personal – and urgent. "What has become of my life? What awaits my children? I have three sons. My children often come home complaining that they have been called 'traitors.' Twenty-two years have gone by, and we are all still traitors." His letter closes with a note of desperation and an almost impossible question: "Dear Boris Dmitrievich, can you – as a writer – explain any of this to me?"[1]

Antonenko-Davydovych had been sentenced to death by Soviet authorities in 1935. In the 1920s he had made his career as a prose stylist by treading on sensitive terrain: namely, the psychology of intellectuals who reconciled themselves to the realities of Bolshevik power. In the novel *Smert* (Death, 1928), his protagonist reasons that "I must kill [...] And then I can say to myself, boldly, honestly, without any doubt or hesitation: I am a Bolshevik."[2] Antonenko-Davydovych escaped his death sentence only to endure forced labour in the Gulag and then exile in Siberia over the course of two decades. He knew enough not to offer

Osmanov any explanations. "I have just returned from your Crimea, to which you and your people – the true stewards of this land – are forbidden to return," he replied. (The KGB apparatchiks in receipt of this memorandum underlined *your Crimea*.) "I myself do not understand why justice has not yet been restored [...] No people should ever be punished by being deprived of their homeland."[3]

After empathizing with Osmanov's anger and frustration, Antonenko-Davydovych tries to offer him counsel. He starts in what might be considered expected territory: the realm of the political. "I can advise only this – keep sending your representatives to Moscow. Ask the Party and the Supreme Soviet to come to a fair resolution of your national question." But these political suggestions are brief. Antonenko-Davydovych's real focus is elsewhere: the realm of culture. "Protect your language and your national traditions," he emphasizes. But, above all, Antonenko-Davydovych tells Osmanov to reach out to more poets. "The poet Tvardovsky would understand you," he says, citing the lines from "Za daliu – dal" that are highlighted in chapter 4. Other poets, he continues, "would also understand you and *give vent to your grief* [...] Write to them as you have written to me. *Let them know of your suffering*."[4]

The KGB memorandum concludes with warnings about the many copies of Antonenko-Davydovych's reply that are floating around Tashkent in 1967. Its concerned tone speaks to a seriousness with which Soviet authorities approached the Ukrainian writer's advice, which included a clear call for the strategic use of literature to mobilize guilt ("*I* have just returned from your Crimea, where *you* [...] are forbidden to go") and to cultivate an empathic, solidary connection with the Crimean Tatars ("let them know of your suffering"). But there was another concern evident between the memorandum's lines – perhaps even an anxiety. After all, the memorandum was addressed not to the Central Committee of the Communist Party of Uzbekistan, where Antonenko-Davydovych's letter was circulating and where the Crimean Tatar community was actively mobilizing with growing purpose and direction. It was sent to authorities in Kyiv. What appeared to alarm them, especially after the incorporation of Crimea into Soviet Ukraine in 1954, was a Ukrainian dissident movement making increasing cause with the Crimean Tatars.[5]

As we saw in chapters 2 and 3, this worry was not without basis. Especially from the turn of the twentieth century, Ukrainian writers routinely expressed solidarity with the Crimean Tatars, rhetorically re-Tatarizing the peninsula, in a departure from Russian and Turkish literary fashion. Amid the uncertainties of revolution and civil war in

гл2.

УРСР   УССР
КОМІТЕТ ДЕРЖАВНОЇ БЕЗПЕКИ | КОМИТЕТ ГОСУДАРСТВЕННОЙ БЕЗОПАСНОСТИ
при РАДІ МІНІСТРІВ УКРАЇНСЬКОЇ РСР | при СОВЕТЕ МИНИСТРОВ УКРАИНСКОЙ ССР

"__" апреля 1967 г.   № 2/5/__

Секретно

Экз. № 1

ЦЕНТРАЛЬНЫЙ КОМИТЕТ КОММУНИСТИЧЕСКОЙ ПАРТИИ
УКРАИНЫ

ИНФОРМАЦИОННОЕ СООБЩЕНИЕ

Комитет госбезопасности при СМ УССР располагает данными о том, что в августе 1966г. писатель АНТОНЕНКО-ДАВИДОВИЧ Б.Д. получил письмо из Ташкента от ОСМАНОВА Мансура, татарина по национальности, в котором последний пишет:

"... Я житель Ташкента ОСМАНОВ Мансур, крымский татарин по национальности, шофер по специальности. Как и все крымские татары, я с нетерпением жду решения нашим Правительством нашего национального вопроса. Вот уже 2 года наши представители беспрерывно находятся в Москве и добиваются справедливого решения нашего национального вопроса - возвращения в родной Крым. Уже побывало около тысячи человек, но какого-либо положительного ответа или даже приема на высшем уровне нет.

... Что я получил в жизни? Что ожидает моих детей? У меня три сына. Мои дети часто приходят домой с жалобой, что их называют "изменниками". Ведь прошло уже 22 года, а мы все еще изменники... Где же ленинская

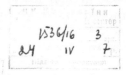

6. KGB memorandum about correspondence between Mansur Osmanov and Borys Antonenko-Davydovych (1967)

1917, Ukrainian and Crimean Tatar national leaders publicly professed support for each other, even contemplating political union. In the early Soviet period, Ukrainian and Crimean Tatar cultural figures worked in frequent symbiosis, empowered by what I call cross-korenizatsiia, with Crimean Tatar plays becoming Ukrainian films, and with Ukrainian writers acting as Crimean Tatar historians. What Ukrainian and Crimean Tatar activists shared was, inter alia, a particular concern for national "groupness" under pressure – a concern not simply for their own national identity but for the idea of national identity itself.

In the previous chapter, the lyrical personae of Chichibabin and Nekipelov spoke with little reference or regard to *national* identity or belonging beyond the Crimean Tatar context. Their we-denomination was essentially civic, governed by an affiliation between Soviet citizens. In texts like "Krymskie progulki" or "Gurzuf," the Crimean Tatars were ultimately presented as "one of us," as Soviet compatriots treated unjustly by the state. Their dispossession was also instructive in its metonymicity, in its ability in the singular to comment upon related, "contiguous" Soviet problems in the plural. By contrast, the Ukrainian texts under study in this chapter make an additional figurative move. In the poems of Ivan Sokulsky and Mykola Rudenko and in the prose of Roman Ivanychuk, the struggle of the Crimean Tatars is additionally instructive in its metaphoricity, in its ability to reflect and illuminate a Ukrainian experience of suffering and victimization. These texts cultivate an understanding of the Crimean Tatars as "(like) us." As Crimean Tatar dissident Rollan Kadyev told Leonid Pliushch in 1968, "[p]olitically Moscow does more for us than Kyiv does, but Ukrainians understand us better."[6]

1.

The distinction between metonymy and metaphor in this context may seem esoteric, but as Roman Jakobson reminds us, it is of "primal significance" for all human behaviour.[7] Here the dichotomy not only helps us understand the different ways Soviet Russian and Soviet Ukrainian writers framed Stalin's Crimean atrocity and its aftermath. It also invites us to focus on the discursive currents and schemas of Soviet dissent rather than on reductive classifications of the dissidents themselves, on forced labels like "intellectuals," "religious believers," or "nationalists," as one report of the US Central Intelligence Agency (CIA) organized them.[8] The expansive and unqualified use of the last term has been particularly unhelpful. By *nationalist*, do we mean those who advanced ethnic nationalism, which defines membership in the nation by *jus sanguinis* (law of blood), or civic nationalism, which defines membership by *jus soli* (law of the soil)? Or do we simply mean those who celebrated national culture or promoted national conscious-ness? Even today, in our study of Soviet dissent, there remains a casual inclination to tie, even fuse, *non-Russian* Soviet dissent with *nationalist*.[9] Putting aside the issue of the countless definitions of *nationalism* or the fact that the term *nationalist* has highly negative and loaded connota-tions in the region, this knee-jerk conflation obscures a dynamic spec-trum of belief and sentiment and, at worst, risks affirming the charges of "anti-Soviet nationalism" levelled at non-Russian dissidents by Soviet authorities themselves.

The suffix *-ism* tends to reach back and twist the root of its word into an end. But for most mainstream dissidents in Soviet Ukraine between the 1960s and 1980s – those who became known in the West as civic activists and prisoners of conscience – the national was, in a productive sense, less an end than a means. It was a means of self-realization, col-lective remembrance, cultural flourishing, and even the development of Soviet socialism. With some notable exceptions – Valentyn Moroz, for instance – the aim of these dissidents was less to make the nation and state congruent than to reboot the Soviet system with a view to Lenin's critique of "great power chauvinism." "For some reason Len-in's positions are forgotten," proclaimed the scholar Mykhailo Horyn in his "Final Word" before Soviet judges in 1966, "and they should not be!"[10] Standing in a closed chamber in Lviv, Horyn vigorously disputed the charges of nationalism brought against him. "I was raised as much on the works of Dobroliubov and Herzen as I was on the works of Shevchenko and Franko," he testified. "I have stated, and I state now, that nationalist views are foreign to me."[11]

When Ukrainian dissidents condemned what Horyn called Soviet "lawlessness" (bezzakonnia), they not only stood on principle like their counterparts in Moscow did. They stood on principle that in turn stood on another site of political belonging: the nation. Their denun-ciations of the Soviet state, in other words, were implicit reminders of a competing locus of ethical value and political order. This dynamic made the dissidents who were attuned to national rights especially dangerous in the eyes of Soviet authorities, and it is part of the reason why Ukrainian prisoners of conscience represented the largest group in the Gulag proportionate to their share of the Soviet population.[12] Their quest to reform Soviet authority was an insistent gesture to another authority, one whose potential membership was massive, well defined, and ready made, served up by a Soviet state system that, as Rogers Brubaker observes, "went to remarkable lengths [...] to institutionalize both territorial nationhood and ethno-cultural nationality as basic cognitive and social categories."[13] The designation "nationality" (natsionalnost), for instance, was displayed on the fifth line of all Soviet passports.

Yet condemning Soviet crimes from a national position could be like burnishing a stone in a glass house. A throw risked self-harm. "The national question poses its own moral problems," notes Leonid Pliushch.[14] He illustrates the dilemma by envisioning, among others, a persecuted Crimean Tatar. "Behind his back is his suffering people," Pliushch writes, "but behind mine is a *formal attachment to the oppressor*" (formalnaia prinadlezhnost k ugnetateliam).[15] He alludes to an unspoken, dynamic order of privilege among Soviet nationalities, to moral hierarchies related to experiences of victimization that affected certain nations or groups more than others. One's victim, in other words, could be another's oppressor. This problem has understandably complicated the work of national history and memory, especially since the collapse of the Soviet Union. It has bedevilled Ukraine in particular, and for good reason.

At the heart of the modern Ukrainian national idea – which finds its most powerful articulation in the Romantic verse of Taras Shevchenko, a serf who became a poet and a poet who, in the words of one Turkish writer, "became a flag"[16] – is a strident anti-colonial ethos. It bears a strong suspicion of state authority, conceives of political liberty and democracy as refuge from historical injustice, and sees allies in oppressed, subaltern nations. But how do adherents to this ethos reconcile themselves to historical moments when they or their compatriots ignored or abandoned it in service to a totalitarian state, "affiliating with the oppressor," especially in the crucible of total war? The stakes on the collective sense of self, on national identity, are high. How do representatives of a diverse and formerly stateless nation whose narrative of the past is a story of resistance to abusive state power – Polish aristocracy to the west, Russian and Soviet autocracy to the east – confront and process political guilt in abetting state power in the victimization of fellow citizens? Ukraine's ongoing "memory wars" boil down to the challenge of answering this question while exorcising, at the same time, a legacy of Russian cultural colonialism and Soviet historiographical distortion.

Alongside Russians and Belarusians, Ukrainians were recruited to resettle in Crimea after 1944. Like the character of old Kostiuk in Petr Pavlenko's "Rassvet," some of them directly benefited from the dispossession of the Crimean Tatars. Robert Conquest wrote in 1972 that "Ukrainians now demanding their own rights have also expressed solidarity with the [Crimean Tatars] – even though it is to Ukraine that [the

Crimean Tatars] have lost their land."[17] Conquest's comment is blind
to the longer history of Ukrainian–Crimean Tatar solidarity and obtuse
in its presentation of Khrushchev's 1954 transfer of Crimea to Soviet
Ukraine, which was clearly not Kyiv's initiative.[18] But the thrust of his
remark, which places guilt and solidarity into contact, merits our attention. How do Ukrainians process political guilt related to the plight of
the Crimean Tatars if they resemble the Crimean Tatars as victims of
Stalinism targeted on the basis of nationality?

Texts by self-professed Ukrainian nationalists avoid this question.
They invariably situate guilt inside the arched gates of the Kremlin.
But the dissident literary texts in this chapter, which are framed by a
discussion of key events and figures of the Soviet Ukrainian *rukh oporu*
(defence movement), grapple with the historical grounds for and the
contemporary implications of this question. They contemplate the conditions for a metaphorical relation of resemblance between the Ukrainian and Crimean Tatar nations, as in Ivan Sokulsky's "Bakhchysarai
(Tsykl)" (Bakhchysarai [a cycle], 1968); the tension between a history
of antagonism and a history of fellowship among Ukrainians and
Crimean Tatars, as in Roman Ivanychuk's *Malvy* (The mallows, 1968);
and the moral claims of the nation on the individual subject, as in
Mykola Rudenko's "Tataryn" (The [Crimean] Tatar, undated [1969?]).
These searching works of poetry and prose not only help account for
what will become, in the twilight of the Soviet period, a consequential
Ukrainian and Crimean Tatar political alliance, but also shed light on
its affective and empathic power.

2.

Around the time of Borys Antonenko-Davydovych's correspondence
with Mansur Osmanov in 1967 – in fact, the very day after the Presidium
of the USSR Supreme Soviet issued Decree 493 – the so-called External
Units of the Organization of Ukrainian Nationalists (ZCh OUN) drafted
a scathing statement about the "Crimean Tatar question." Decree 493,
they wrote, was tantamount to "the criminal magnanimously 'reha-
bilitating' the victim." Soviet authorities had "mumbled through their
teeth: 'sorry!' And that's all. No acknowledgment of perpetration of a
crime. No moral atonement."[19] The authors of the statement explained
that the treatment of the Crimean Tatars hit very close to home. "For
us, this is not simply a political or economic question; above all this is
a human, even emotional [*chuttieva*] issue," they claimed. "Over the
centuries, the Crimean Tatars have been our closest southern neighbor.
Our relations have been complicated throughout this period; we have

made war, and we have made peace," the ZCh OUN authors continued. "Our historical folk songs – as well as their historical folk songs – are rich with echoes of these battles [...] In Ukrainian national life, in our language and culture, there are a number of Tatar and Turkish influences. This is our historical heritage – and we do not deny it."[20] Marked up with corrections, excisions, and marginal comments, the draft of the ZCh OUN statement reflects careful preparation and a concern for historical accuracy. Its authors allude to the co-operation between the Tsentralna Rada and the Qurultay in 1917, insisting that "Ukraine never had designs on Crimea." They then recount dark moments in Crimean Tatar history, framing them awkwardly as acts in a play: "Historians of Crimea enumerate eight periods in the systematic genocide of the Crimean Tatars. For the most part, these acts align with the acts of our own Ukrainian national-political drama."[21]

What was a rhetoric of metonymical contiguity in the previous chapter – a rhetoric presenting the persecution of the Crimean Tatars as a symptom of what dissidents like Petro Grigorenko characterized as a Soviet disease – is a rhetoric of metaphorical similarity here. For all of our attention to its thirst for contrast and differentiation, nationalism has a keen eye for resemblance. The ZCh OUN statement positions Ukrainians and Crimean Tatars alongside each other and explicitly suggests their historical interchangeability. As we saw in chapter 2, such a metaphorical presentation of the Ukrainian and Crimean Tatar experiences – which pivots on the we-relation "(like) us" – has a long history. In the realm of Ukrainian imaginative literature, however, it tends to operate through much more subtle, implicit means. In the novella *Pid minaretamy*, for instance, Mykhailo Kotsiubynsky alludes to strong congruencies between Ukrainians and Crimean Tatars at the turn of the twentieth century, from a common struggle against the inertia of tradition to a common aspiration for a forward-looking "European" culture. But he does so without direct reference to historical conjunctions or without recourse to the declarative.

Kotsiubynsky's *Pid minaretamy*, which was discussed in chapter 2, marks an example of what might be called *national metaphorization*, a process of implicitly mirroring one nation in the image of another nation traditionally conceived as dissimilar. It is a world apart from Frederic Jameson's controversial concept of national allegory, which posits that in all Third World texts "the story of the individual is always an allegory of the embattled situation of the public third-world culture or society."[22] In Jameson's concept the modifier *national* is understood as intranational; in his view, the protagonist of a "third-world text" always represents his or her nation. By contrast, in national metaphorization, the modifier denotes an international relation. And whereas allegory by nature elevates the figurative subject over the literal one, metaphorization achieves a relation of resemblance or equivalence between two subjects without collapsing the difference between them. In *Pid minaretamy*, for instance, Kotsiubynsky employs national metaphorization in such a way as to invite the reader to encounter an intricately drawn world of Crimean Tatar modernizers and, at the same time, to see the more familiar world of Ukrainian modernists in a new light.

The concept of national metaphorization is not meant to shackle literary texts to the realm of the political, nor does it reduce nations to discrete, bounded objects that can be conveniently held up in a mirror for reflection. It simply seeks to account for moments when literary texts forge, sustain, or modify an image of the nation, not by turning to its own store of myths, heroes, and villains but by smuggling in, as it were, an identification with another nation altogether. The more unexpected the identification, the better. Indeed, for Aristotle, the power of a metaphor often hinges on the "foreign" (allotriou), on the extent of the estrangement between its two component parts, as in his own example of fire and seed corn in the ancient metaphor "sowing flame."[23] In Ukrainian culture, national metaphorization is fond of challenging convention and expectation in this way. It repeatedly involves, in fact, majority Muslim nations: Circassians, Kurds, and especially Crimean Tatars.

National metaphorization becomes a commonplace in the Ukrainian literary tradition with Taras Shevchenko's "Kavkaz" ("The Caucasus," 1845). Nazım Hikmet once proclaimed that Shevchenko's poetry collapsed the bounds between the national and the international, offering "a song of struggle to be sung in colonies, semi-colonial territories, and developing countries – by people shedding blood for national independence, for land, for democratic rights."[24] "Kavkaz" is one of the reasons for Hikmet's praise. The poem is a masterpiece of an anti-colonial poetics of solidarity, representing Circassions as victims of oppression at the hands of the Russian tsar and asserting a distinct *Ukrainian* national identity by way of this representation. Shevchenko draws an implicit parallel between the Caucasus and Ukraine, between the mountains and the steppe, by casting the former in imagery that he deploys throughout his oeuvre to describe the latter – that is, as a landscape of suffering where justice and freedom are crippled but not entirely defeated.[25] In "Kavkaz," the Caucasus is a land of blood ("krov"), tears ("slozy"), and woe ("hore") forsaken by God ("Za koho zh ty rozipiavsia, Khryste, syne bozhyi?") where widows weep ("v slozakh udovikh") and their sons languish in fetters ("kaidany [kuiut]"). In "Son" ("A Dream,"

1844), Ukraine is the same land of blood, tears, and woe forsaken by God ("Chy Boh bachyt iz-za khmary / Nashi slozy, hore?") where widows are abused ("rozpynaiut vdovu") and their sons languish in fetters ("syna kuiut").

Shevchenko's metaphorical alignment of the Caucasus with Ukraine exercised political force in 2013–14 during the Euromaidan protests in Kyiv, turning a couplet from "Kavkaz" addressed to Circassian rebels of the nineteenth century into an empowering refrain for Ukrainian demonstrators of the twenty-first. On signs, shields, and banners across Maidan Nezalezhnosti (Independence Square), thousands of Ukrainians protesting the corrupt regime of Viktor Yanukovych brandished the lines, "Boritesia – poborete! / Vam Boh pomahaie!" (Fight – you will prevail! / God is helping you!). In "Kavkaz" these words are explicitly directed to Muslim Circassian rebels fighting Russian imperial forces, not to Ukrainians per se. That this detail was mostly forgotten by Euromaidan protestors indicates the efficiency of Shevchenko's national metaphorization, which can address Ukrainians without addressing them at all.

Illustrative of the lasting influence of Shevchenko's "Kavkaz" is a poem by Vasyl Symonenko entitled "Kurdskomu bratovi" (To my brother Kurd, 1963), which cites "Boritesia – poborete" in its epigraph. Symonenko was an early luminary of the *shistdesiatnyky* (the generation of the "Sixtiers"), a young poet whose lean and lucid anti-colonial verse was wildly popular in Soviet Ukrainian samvydav circles. Pliushch calls him the "poet of the birth of the Ukrainian resistance."[26] Months after the composition of "Kurdskomu bratovi," Symonenko died of cancer at the age of twenty-eight. After his death, Ivan Svitlychny circulated the poem in the underground and sent it to the West, an act that led to his arrest in an infamous 1965 roundup of Ukrainian intellectuals.[27] The poem was then published in the Munich-based Ukrainian émigré journal *Suchasnist* (Modernity) and broadcast on Radio Liberty soon thereafter.[28]

Employing the rhetoric of what Fanon calls a "literature of combat,"[29] "Kurdskomu bratovi" is an admonitory appeal to an anonymous Kurd addressee urging him to keep watch over his weapons and spare no mercy on his enemies. Although the poem's precise historical context is unclear – no individuals are named, no places cited, no dates given – Symonenko may be referring to clashes in Iraq in the early 1960s between Kurdish rebels led by Mustafa Barzani (who had studied political science in the Soviet Union in the mid-1950s) and Iraqi forces under the command of Prime Minister Abdul Karim Qassim. In "Kurdskomu bratovi" the lyrical persona passionately describes this distant struggle as one of Kurds defending their right of national self-determination against cruel, manipulative forces who "have come not only for your wealth / But to strip you of your language and your name."[30]

While the poem deals exclusively with the plight of the Kurds at the level of content, one word in the fourth stanza allows it to speak to the plight of Ukrainians: "*Our* most treacherous enemy is chauvinism" (*Nash* nailiutishyi voroh – shovinizm; emphasis mine). This use of the collective first-person in an echo of Lenin alludes to an interchangeability between the two peoples, presenting them as components of one metaphorical relation: *Kurds are Ukrainians*. One of Symonenko's readers, a teacher from Ternopil named Mykola Kots, made this interchangeability explicit, with dire consequences. He replaced the word *Kurd* with *Ukrainian* throughout the poem and distributed the amended text in cities across Ukraine. In 1967 a Soviet judge punished Kots for this creative editing by sentencing him to seven years of prison and five years in exile.[31]

A "dear brother" of Vasyl Symonenko, in the words of the journal *Ukraïnskyi visnyk* (*The Ukrainian Herald*), was a poet from Dnipropetrovsk in eastern Ukraine named Ivan Sokulsky, who employed national metaphorization in confronting the persecution of the Crimean Tatars. Sokulsky (1940–1992) is often remembered today as the primary author of the 1968 "Lyst tvorchoï molodi Dnipropetrovska" ("Letter of the Creative Youth of Dnipropetrovsk"), an indictment of Soviet authorities that was written in response to and under the influence of Ivan Dziuba's *Internatsionalizm chy russifikatsiia?* (*Internationalism or Russification?*, 1965) and Oles Honchar's *Sobor* (*The Cathedral*, 1968). Dziuba's treatise meticulously unpacks Soviet departures from Leninist nationalities policy; Honchar's novel inverts the genre of Socialist Realism in a defence of local Ukrainian history and memory. "Lyst tvorchoï molodi Dnipropetrovska" borrows from them both, but it stands out with a rhetorical ferocity inspired by Symonenko. "In the Party there is a place for murderers and tricksters – spiritual refuse[32] – but honest and principled Communists are thrown out from the Party and out of work?" the letter reads. "Monuments are built to Ivan the Terrible, Peter I, Catherine II, but no one will say that they seethed with hatred for Ukrainians, Tatars, Belarusians, Poles, Georgians, and others?"[33] Months later, Radio Svoboda broadcast the letter internationally, and the exposure placed "the creative youth of Dnipropetrovsk" in peril. In 1970 Sokulsky was arrested as he disembarked the Kyiv-Dnipropetrovsk steamship, where he worked on the crew.[34] He was sentenced to more than four years in the camps.

For all his outspoken courage, friends described Sokulsky as a "reserved" (zamknenyi), sensitive soul.[35] Much of his poetry bears an intimate, confessional tone, mourning a world descending slowly "into a vortex."[36] At a time of physical and moral disintegration, he sees poems as fortifications: "When catastrophe comes, / Place strophes of stone at the door."[37] Some of these "strophes of stone" were written concomitantly with "Lyst tvorchoï molodi Dnipropetrovska" in a poem entitled "Bakhchysarai (Tsykl)" (Bakhchysarai [a cycle], 1968).

"Bakhchysarai" made a considerable impression on writer and friend Viktor Savchenko, who distinctly remembers the first time he encountered the work. He recalls that, during a trip to Crimea, he and Sokulsky "were making our way down a winding road from Ai-Petri on the side of Bakhchysarai. It was raining, the asphalt was slippery [...] and behind me Ivan was reading ["Bakhchysarai"], a poem dedicated to the deported Crimean Tatars. The fate of the Crimean Tatars was as painful to him as the fate of Ukrainians."[38] Yet the identification of these two "fates," so evident to Savchenko, does not find any explicit expression in the poem. Like Vasyl Symonenko's "Kurds'komu bratovi," Sokulsky's text ventures into the realm of the coded and the implicit by way of national metaphorization.

For the Crimean Tatars, the mountains are a site of origin, a cradle of civilization and culture – a "zone of the spirit," in the words of Neal Ascherson.[39] Sokulsky begins "Bakhchysarai" in the mountains but transforms them into a site of loss, less a cradle than a grave. He visualizes the night of 18 May 1944 as an assault on vulnerable women and children:

Гори сиротіли, гори даленіли
Пеленали гори відчай і плачі.
І за ніч останню матері сивіли
І кричали діти - отоді вночі!
. . . .
Пусткою ці гори, тихі і чужі.
«Земле предків, що тебе не знаєм!» -
Голос дальній чується мені -
Кров татарська вдалині ридає ...
Серце в тузі - там, на чужині![40]

(The mountains were orphaned, the mountains were deserted,
They were enveloped in despair and in tears.
On that last night mothers turned grey,
And the cries of their children pierced the night air!
. . . .

Silent and strange, the mountains now stand empty.
"O ancestral land, we do not know you!"
I hear a distant voice –
The Tatar people weep from afar …
A heart in anguish in that foreign land!)

Sokulsky's lines remind Myroslav Marynovych of his own encounter with an emptied Crimea, "silent and strange." Visiting Feodosiia in the late 1960s, he wandered into the mountains and came upon what was clearly once a Crimean Tatar village. "I was stunned," he remembers. "It felt like I had walked into a massive cemetery where a whole culture was buried."[41]

Buried in Sokulsky's passage is a series of intertexts with the poetry of Taras Shevchenko. The peculiar evocation of a "heart in a foreign land" is a direct quotation from Shevchenko's "Do Osnov'ianenka" ("To Osnov'ianenko," 1839), for example, and the diacope of *hory* (mountains) in the line "Hory syrotily, hory dalenily" nods to the famous opening of Shevchenko's "Kavkaz": "Za horamy hory, khmaroiu povyti, / Zasiiani horem, kroviiu polyti" (Mountains upon mountains, covered in cloud, / sown with woe, soaked in blood). These clusters of allusions to Shevchenko are magnetic; they draw Ukrainian readers toward a lyrical "I" who speaks in a familiar, authoritative language denouncing injustice and empathizing with the victim.

This language is also Shevchenkian in its strategic hyperbole. When Sokulsky gives voice to the Crimean Tatars in his poem, these "distant voices" speak in a fatalistic language of nevers and nowheres. Sokulsky emulates Shevchenko in employing what the rhetoricians of antiquity called accismus, a device whereby what is sought is denied, refuted, or mourned as irrevocably lost: "We will never return. / We will never see this land again!"[42] Indeed, the refain of the Crimean Tatars in "Bakhchysarai (Tsykl)" is *ostannii* (the last). They lament "the last step on their ancestral land" and "the last night" of 18 May, which "spared neither young nor old." Voices of Soviet authorities also appear in the poem to taunt and torment them in a similarly defeatist language: "Now your land has been exchanged for another– / Now you will never recover!"

Sokulsky uses these repeated, gratuitous professions of finality and embarks on this rhetorical *via negativa* for a reason. As with Chichibabin's "Krymskie progulki" and Nekipelov's "Gurzuf," for example, they aim to foment the reader's refutation, to incite action. Hyperbole, after all, always tempts a response. At the conclusion of "Bakhchysarai (Tsykl)," Sokulsky's lyrical persona directly calls for action. He looks upon Bakhchysarai with cognitive dissonance and declares:

Я бачу Бахчисарай -
Я не бачу Бахчисарая!
Світ почує нехай
Про злочинство безкрає ...
Я бачу Бахчисарай –
Я не бачу Бахчисарая!

(I see Bakhchysarai –
I do not see Bakhchysarai!
Let the world hear
about this interminable crime ...
I see Bakhchysarai –
I do not see Bakhchysarai!)[43]

Sokulsky's lyrical persona sees the *space* of Bakhchysarai but not the *place* of Bakhchysarai. The poem concludes with this contradiction in order to gesture to a new beginning. Cognitive dissonance is, after all, an aversive drive state that spurs us to fix it or fight it, making the poem's ending a cry for resolution. "Let the world hear about this interminable crime," he implores the reader. "Bakhchysarai (Tsykl)" therefore does not document the suffering of the Crimean Tatars as in a human rights petition or an open letter; in fact, to a significant degree, it "resists demands for closure" and veils this suffering with intertextual codes and strategic inconsistencies.[44] Its defamiliarization or *ostranenie*, as Shklovsky called it, leans into the future, toward the prospect of the reader's solidary sense-making and action-taking. Meanwhile, the poem's "familiarization," as it were – its practice of national metaphorization, which posits a relation of familiarity and resemblance between the Ukrainians and Crimean Tatars – leans back into the past, toward Shevchenko's "Kavkaz," a work uniquely influential in the development of Ukraine's national identity.

3.

Ivan Sokulsky's "Bakhchysarai (Tsykl)" helped spark an epistolary exchange between two leaders of the Ukrainian and Crimean Tatar national movements. For over a decade Viacheslav Chornovil and Mustafa Dzhemilev knew each other by reputation, but it took a work of literature to help bring them into direct contact. In the 1970s Chornovil repeatedly wrote to friends asking for information about Dzhemilev's whereabouts.[45] News of Dzhemilev's most recent arrest and exile had travelled fast, and Chornovil wanted to reach out to Dzhemilev and ask about the itinerary or "staging" (etapirovanie) of his exile to Yakutiia in the Soviet Far East. When he composed his letter to Dzhemilev, he cited a passage from Sokulsky's "Bakhchysarai (Tsykl)," using the verse to express solidarity with his correspondent and the Crimean Tatar people.[46]

From Yakutiia, Dzhemilev replied to Chornovil with what he called probably his "longest letter in the last ten years." With characteristic wit, he explains that years earlier he had wanted to initiate correspondence with Chornovil but "managed to get myself arrested" instead. Dzhemilev then addresses Chornovil's questions about his *etapirovanie* at length.[47] He details the stages of his journey from Tashkent to Yakutiia, pausing to relay a darkly humorous story of his solitary confinement in Novosibirsk, where his prisoner classification as "anti-Soviet" in his file confused one of his guards, who mistook him as "non-Soviet," as a foreigner from Turkey. ("How's the meat there?" the guard asked.) At the end of the letter Dzhemilev returns to the question of the poem that helped spark Chornovil's contact. "If you can," he asks, "transcribe for me, even if only in parts, the poems from Sokulsky's Crimean cycle."[48]

Chornovil obliges. He also refers Dzhemilev to another Ukrainian literary work, Roman Ivanychuk's *Malvy* (The mallows, 1968), which he describes as an expression of "sympathy with your people."[49] Originally titled *Yanychary* (The janissaries), *Malvy* is an attempt to look at the history of Ukraine from a Crimean Tatar perspective.[50] Its publication – first in serialized form in the journal *Vitchyzna* (Fatherland) and then as a separate volume released in a run of over one hundred thousand copies – was a genuine event in Ukrainian culture. Politician Mykhailo Kosiv remembers it as an "explosion."[51] Part of the novel's combustibility was due to its genre, which could manipulate, revise, and upset fixed historiographic paradigms and nurture alternative sites of memory: the genre of historical fiction.

Another source of fuel was its time period: the seventeenth century. In the 1920s, as we saw in chapter 3, Soviet Ukrainian and Crimean Tatar writers and artists – people like Osman Akçokraklı and Ostap Vyshnia – seized upon a past of the Ukrainian and Crimean Tatar encounter that was not marked by slave raids and warfare against one another. They alluded to another history – one of friendship, alliance, and co-operation – which accompanied the emergence of a Ukrainian Cossack polity during the era of Bohdan Khmelnytsky, or the Khmelnychchyna, in the seventeenth century.[52] As Orest Subtelny remarks, at this time "when the Ukrainians sought to defend their political individuality, it was to the Tatars that they turned most often for support."[53] Shevchenko alludes to this past solidarity in his sketch *Khmelnytsky pered krymskym khanom* (Khmelnytsky before the Crimean khan, 1857), in which the composition's arched perimeter joins together a respectful Cossack hetman and a reclining Crimean Tatar khan in one harmonious visual field (fig. 7).[54]

7. Taras Shevchenko, *Khmelnytsky before the Crimean Khan* (1857)

In a similar vein, Ivanychuk's *Malvy* gathers Ukrainian, Crimean Tatar, and Ottoman characters from the period of the Khmelnychchyna and invites the reader to revisit their entangled relationships. By 1968, historical novels about the Khmelnytsky era were hardly a new phenomenon in Soviet Ukrainian literature, but Ivanychuk's text stood apart by making Khmelnytsky a marginal character and by upsetting the literary status quo with a biting allegory about national belonging in the Soviet Union.[55]

Soviet authorities were slow to pick up on the allegory, which likened the Soviet Union to a proselytizing and paranoid empire.[56] But they caught on eventually. Reading groups occasioned by the novel – such as one organized at Lviv's Ivan Franko University by Ihor Yukhnovsky, a theoretical physicist who would later become the head of the Institute of National Memory in independent Ukraine – were condemned and shut down.[57] Copies of *Malvy* were confiscated from bookstores and pulled from library shelves.[58] In the pages of *Pravda Ukrainy*, the official mouthpiece of the Communist Party of Ukraine, Ivanychuk (1929–2016) was severely criticized for writing a "historical novel without a history."[59] In official circles, as literary critic Taras Salyha explains, he was spared no "bitter word."[60] But in unofficial circles, Ivanychuk's supposed sins only provoked more readers to read the novel closely and to copy passages for circulation through samvydav networks.

At the heart of the novel's controversy is its intervention into the history of the Crimean Tatar "national question," which fundamentally challenges Soviet discursive cleansing after 1944. Beyond portraying the Crimean Tatars as complex, "round" characters whose actions defy easy categorization and caricature, *Malvy* establishes the Crimean Tatars as the indigenous inhabitants of the Black Sea peninsula. This claim to indigeneity was a corrective to a prevailing narrative in official post-war Soviet literature that appears in, for instance, Vasyl Kucher's novel of 1952, *Chornomortsi* (Black Sea sailors). The central protagonist of *Chornomortsi*, an Odesa-born, Second World War midshipman named Samiilo Vykhor, curses the Crimean Tatars for "treason" before reciting, predictably, a passage from Pushkin's *Bakhchisaraiskii fontan*. His ire erupts when he intercepts a German communiqué containing instructions "for all [Nazi] officers to support the Crimean Tatars":

Вихор сплюнув і гірко вилаявся:
— Пригріли гада за пазухою! Кращі виноградники *їм дано* в Криму, найбагатші сади і землі, випаси і курортні міста! Столицю в Сімферополі [...] Так ні ж! Гітлеру п'яти лизать кинулися![61]

(Vykhor spat and cursed [the Crimean Tatars] with scorn: "We warmed serpents in our bosom! *They were given* the best vineyards in Crimea, the most verdant gardens and tracts of land, the pastures, and the resorts! Even a capital in Simferopol [...] But no! They rushed to lick Hitler's boots!"; emphasis mine.)

This conceit of Crimea as a "gift" to the Tatars intersected with an ascendent campaign of discursive cleansing in the field of Soviet historiography in the early 1950s. It came to a head in June 1952, when leading Soviet Russian historian Boris Grekov published an essay entitled "O nekotorykh voprosakh istorii Kryma" (Concerning a few questions on Crimean history) in the pages of *Izvestiia*. It is a paean to historical revisionism.

"In shedding light on the history of Crimea, there have been many distortions," writes Grekov, because "Crimea has been the object of desire of many nations hostile to Russia for many centuries." He continues: "It is therefore not surprising that bourgeois scholars of various countries, in order to please the political agendas of their governments, have made every effort to falsify the history of Crimea."[62] The first "distortions" that Grekov targets in *Izvestia* pertain to the Crimean Tatars: "In the pre-war period, the role of the Crimean Khanate was exaggerated – unjustifiably and completely without proof – in some historical works in order to please Tatar bourgeois nationalists. The issue of the inclusion [*vkliuchenie*] of Crimea in Russia [in 1783] was completely misinterpreted. This historically progressive event was usually portrayed as a colonialist capture, as a terrible evil in the historical life of the population of the Crimean peninsula."[63] Grekov's critique of previous "bourgeois" works of Crimean history comes down to the issue of possession. He claims Crimea for "the Russian people" (russkii narod) who, he argues, have resided in Crimea since antiquity. Yet Crimea's Russian inheritance "did not interest prior researchers," writes Grekov, with incredulity. "Bourgeois archaeologists did not even look for traces of Slavdom there."[64]

Joining Grekov on a quest to make amends for these "distortions" was a former censor with little formal historical training named Pavel Nadinsky (Savely Posiagin). In 1952 Nadinsky published a work of popular history entitled *Ocherki po istorii Kryma* (Sketches of the history of Crimea). It was first intended as a brochure. Its title appropriated that of a prominent, highly successful precursor, Yevgeny Markov's *Ocherki Kryma* (Sketches of Crimea, 1872), whose condemnations of Russian colonial oppression were recycled in Ostap Vyshnia's feuilletons, as we saw in chapter 3. But Nadinsky brushed off Markov's work, vigorously asserting that Crimea was ancient *Russian* territory. "Crimea should never be characterized as a colony, because Crimean territory has been Russian territory since ancient times," he writes. "Crimea's economic development came at the hands of the Russian people, its towns were built by Russian workers, its fields were tilled by a huge majority of Russian peasants and farm labourers."[65] Today, when Vladimir Putin presents reasons for the 2014 annexation, his words echo those of Grekov and Nadinsky: "Crimea is native [*iskonno*] Russian land."[66]

This historical revisionism – weaponized in a broader campaign of discursive cleansing, promulgated by the Party across the Soviet Union, and perpetuated by the Kremlin – is the mottled backdrop to Ivanychuk's *Malvy*. Following in the footsteps of Kotsiubynsky in *Pid minaretamy*, Ivanychuk centres his novel on a Crimea dominated by the Crimean Tatars, who – pace Grekov and Nadinsky – are shown developing the economy of the peninsula, building towns, and tilling fields. The novel ascribes an innate Muslim alterity to the peninsula – it is a land most decidedly, to cite Chichibabin, "not Russia" – and portrays the Tatars as its autochthonous inhabitants to whom Polish, Muscovite, Cossack, and Ottoman dignitaries pay tribute. Ivanychuk's *Malvy* restores and projects, in other words, a tight bond between Crimean place and Tatar personality.

Malvy is the story of Mariia, the wife of a Cossack captain whose children are abducted and spirited off to Crimea and the Ottoman Empire, where they assume new lives, pursue divergent destinies, and largely forget their Ukrainian origins and common family past. Mariia's young son Semen, sold to the Tatars, takes the name Selim and joins the palace guards of the Crimean Tatar khan, whom he calls his only "father and family." Her other son, Andry, taken by the Tatars and dispatched to Istanbul, becomes a *çorbaci* or janissary colonel named Alim in the service of the sultan at the Sublime Porte. Her daughter, Solomiia, who is renamed Malva (mallow) after the small, resilient steppe flowers common to Ukraine and Crimea, enters the palace of İslâm Giray III at the age of twelve and eventually falls in love with the khan.

Mariia, meanwhile, converts to Islam in order to survive in Crimea, where she seeks to find her lost, scattered children and return home. She is the most morally virtuous and sympathetic character in *Malvy*, and she repeatedly speaks of guilt (*provyna*). To save her children's lives, she surrenders them. To recover her children, she commits apostasy. Political discord and military cruelty force her into untenable situations, and her choices burden her with guilt, for which she pledges to atone with "prayer, blood, and life itself."[67] Like Taras Shevchenko's eponymous biblical heroine in "Mariia" (1859), who courageously stewards her son's message after the crucifixion, she is indefatigable, long suffering, and self-sacrificing. There is another resemblance as well. "Am I not Ukraine," Ivanychuk's Mariia asks, "alienated and broken like my native land?"[68]

Ivanychuk did not conceal the fact that his characters are meant as symbols and his novel as a complex allegory for the psychological colonization of Ukrainian society in the Soviet period.[69] As one who eventually parts ways with his suzerain, Selim represents what we might term the *mazepinets*, a figure cut from the cloth of Ivan Mazepa who ultimately sides with his nation over the imperial sovereign to whom he once swore allegiance.[70] After he absorbs the truth about his identity and heritage as a Ukrainian, Selim joins the Cossacks and perishes in battle. Alim, meanwhile, represents an apostate *maloros*, a "Little Russian" who holds his Ukrainian origins in contempt and becomes a murderous servant of empire. In his hatred for Ukraine he resembles the spiteful Polonophile Masia in Anatoly Svydnytsky's *Liuboratski: Simeina khronika* (The Liuboratskys: A family chronicle, 1861–2). The character of the janissary that Alim embodies had particular figurative purchase in the Soviet period: Sviatoslav Karavansky, to cite one example, eviscerates members of the Soviet Ukrainian Union of Writers in 1968 as "Janissaries" who carry from prisons "the corpses of murdered brothers" in silence and in darkness.[71] Finally, Malva represents the Wallenrodist, a character cast in the vein of Adam Mickiewicz's Konrad Wallenod who walks the corridors of imperial power and, like the eponymous protagonist of the epic Ukrainian *duma* "Marusia Bohuslavka," uses this access to save her tormented compatriots.

Leading these compatriots against Polish rule in Ivanychuk's novel is the Cossack hetman Bohdan Khmelnytsky, comrade to Malva's deceased father and ally to Khan İslâm Giray. The alliance between the hetman and the khan is the same one that was chronicled by Canmuhammed in the seventeenth-century *destan* discussed in chapter 3. In Ivanychuk's novel the eventual breakdown of this alliance, provoked largely by external forces, is the narrative climax. Malva appeals to her husband, İslâm Giray – her "wise tsar, the light of [her] eyes" – to remain loyal to the Khmelnytsky and the Cossacks, speaking to him in a tone alternating between confidence and anxiety:

… подаруєш волю своєму і моєму народові.
— Якому твоєму, Мальво? [...] Ти ж мусульманка, як і я, і мій народ є твоїм народом.
— Я люблю тебе, хане, і Крим теж став моєю батьківщиною. Але ти зрозумій, що не байдужа журавлеві, коли він у теплих краях, холодна в'ялиця на півночі.

("...You will bestow freedom upon your people and upon mine." "Upon whose people, Malva? [...] You are Muslim, as I am, and my people are your people." "I love you, my khan, and Crimea has also become my homeland. But understand that the crane is not indifferent to the withering cold in the north, even when it resides in warm lands.")[72]

İslâm Giray ultimately does not heed Malva's entreaty. He aligns with the Poles against Khmelnytsky – and against the wishes of the Ottoman sultan – and orders his cavalry to abandon the Cossacks at the Battle of Berestechko of 1651. In *Malvy*, Ivanychuk employs artistic licence – by his own admission, his interest is less in historical accuracy than in the communication of the story's "psychological sense"[73] – and interprets the khan's betrayal of the Cossacks as a gesture of resistance against a demanding and presumptuous Istanbul, which considers him "putrescence and dust" (porokh i tlin) before the likes of the sultan.[74] This prideful act of self-assertion, however, is his undoing. The Poles forsake him, Khmelnytsky aligns with Muscovy, and his beloved Malva avenges the Cossacks and poisons him for "the blood [he has] spilled in vain."

For Ivanychuk, Crimean Tatar khan İslâm Giray stands as a "great politician and diplomat" for whom it is impossible not to feel sympathy.[75] The ambivalence of his nature and the complexity of his geopolitical position are continually highlighted in the novel. Although he betrays Khemlnytsky and Malva, he is "distinguished," in the words of Ivanychuk, "by his courage and, most importantly, by his audacious move to break free of the Porte forever."[76] Selim, then, is not the only *mazepinets* in *Malvy*. By foregrounding İslâm Giray's discontent with and "betrayal" of the Ottoman Empire – and thereby underscoring the agency and sovereignty of the Crimean Tatars in this period – Ivanychuk contradicts a post-war Soviet historiographical discourse that reduced the khans of the seventeenth century to puppets of the sultan.

In *Borba moskovskogo gosudarstva s Tatarami v pervoi polovine XVII veka* (The struggle of the Muscovite state against the Tatars in the first half of the seventeenth century, 1948) – which is considered "the most comprehensive work about Muscovite-Tatar relations of the period"[77] – Soviet historian Aleksei Novoselsky claims, for example, that the conduct of the khanate was essentially "a form of Turkish aggression."[78] "Behind Crimea always stood Turkey," he writes, even though Bakhchysarai and Istanbul conducted independent, and sometimes discordant, diplomatic relations with their neighbours in this period.[79] In Novoselsky's view, the khan was the sultan's subservient representative and nothing more, so any move toward "independence" for Crimea in this period could only have been a fanciful venture of Tatar princes.[80]

Ivanychuk advances a much different view. He gives us İslâm Giray as a guileful leader in the vein of Byron's "Mazeppa." Indeed, what unites all the narrative events and characters in *Malvy* is a theme of *duplicity* – not simply as double-dealing but as "double-being." This duplicity is both a quality of Ivanychuk's characters – Solomiia/Malva, Semen/Selim, and Andry/Alim, for example – and a quality of the text itself, which is meant as a synthetic allegory for Soviet Ukraine. Ivanychuk consistently invites us to read for the figural rather than the literal, and his early presentation of Istanbul as the seat of a lumbering, dogmatic power defended by janissaries welcomes associations with the Kremlin and its "apostate" Ukrainian functionaries.[81] The allegory does not end there, however. İslâm Giray's rebellion against Ottoman power, not to mention his relatively sympathetic portrayal, suggests that the Crimean Tatar khanate – struggling with sovereignty and dependency as a "periphery" bound by confessional and ethnic ties to an imperial "centre" – is a reflection of Soviet Ukraine itself. By extension, Maria and the displaced, suffering Ukrainians of the seventeenth century are reflections of the displaced, suffering Crimean Tatars of the twentieth.

Amid the allegory, in other words, we can discern another process of national metaphorization.

Ivanychuk hinted at this reading. "I was interested in [...] the problem of solidarity between peoples [*problema solidarnosti narodiv*] who struggle for their freedom," he writes, "as well as the problem of the enlightenment of a people compelled to subjugate others due to the force of historical conditions."[82] There is a constructive ambiguity in this remark. Is Ivanychuk referring to the seventeenth century or to the twentieth? His invitation to read *Malvy* allegorically – to tie the source context of the Crimean khanate to the target context of Soviet Ukraine – activates both periods in this exploration of the problem of solidarity between Ukrainians and Crimean Tatars, layering one century on top of the other. Across the centuries, despite their common aspirations to live in freedom, Crimean Tatars and Ukrainians were thus "compelled to subjugate" each other "due to the force of historical conditions." For Ivanychuk, Crimean Tatars and Ukrainians are bound by mutual guilt but absolved by mutual victimization. As we will see, this idea – a variant on Tvardovsky's "guiltless guilty" – occupies discussions of Ukrainian–Crimean Tatar relations after 1968.

4.

Shortly after *Malvy*'s release, the notion of oppressed nations pitted against each other becomes a theme that is advanced by self-professed Ukrainian nationalists, who return to the Crimean Tatar question in another public statement, in 1969. In the émigré journal *Suchasnist* the External Representation of the Ukrainian Supreme Liberation Council (Ukraïnska holova vyzvolna rada, UHVR), a political organization in exile formed from both the Organization of Ukrainian Nationalists and the Ukrainian Insurgent Army, declare the "contemporary struggle of the Crimean Tatars" as "one very important link in the wider struggle of the peoples of the Soviet Union."[83] This sentiment, which assigns a *pars pro toto* function to the Crimean Tatars, echoes the messages of the poems discussed in the previous chapter. Yet the authors of the UHVR appeal go further, supplementing a rhetoric of metonymical contiguity with one of metaphorical similarity: "The violent deportation of the Crimean Tatars from their homeland in 1944 must be qualified as a crime of genocide [*narodovbyvstvo*], *similar in character to the deliberate starvation of nearly four million Ukrainian villagers in 1933.*"[84]

The UHVR appeal foregrounds two national groups with a history of mass suffering under Stalinism and positions this suffering as the basis of solidarity between them: "We have no doubt that the

Ukrainian people sympathize [*spivchuvaie*] [with the Crimean Tatars] in their struggle [...] All Ukrainians, no matter where they may live, should support the lawful struggle of the Crimean Tatars."[85] This message had particular urgency in 1969. According to Crimean Tatar activists Rollan Kadyev and Zampira Asanova, KGB agents were spreading rumours among Crimean Tatars in Central Asia that "Ukrainian nationalists" stood between them and Crimea.[86] (Leonid Pliushch remembers laughing aloud at the idea.)[87] The UHVR appeal rails against this disinformation, condemning the Kremlin for attempts to divide and rule: "Forbidding the Crimean Tatars to return to Crimea, Russian chauvinists are spreading rumours that Ukrainians are agitating against the wishes of the Crimean Tatars. Such insidious manoeuvres on the part of Moscow must be judged and dismissed as provocations, as traditional tools in the politics of Russian imperialism to divide its enslaved peoples. Chauvinism of all kinds is foreign to the Ukrainian people, and [we are] bound to the Crimean Tatars by the ties of a common destiny, common interests, and friendship."[88] The image of the nation projected in this passage is of an organic, autonomous, discrete, and coherent unit with a homogeneity of viewpoint. The collective authorship of the appeal, which bears no individual names or signatures, simulates the voice of uniformity and consensus idealized in nationalist pedagogy. There is no diversity of opinion, no contestation of identity, no exception to the rule: each and every Ukrainian at least tacitly supports the Crimean Tatar cause and dismisses "chauvinism of all kinds." It is a laudable message. It is also an impossible one. "The danger is in the neatness of identifications," as Samuel Beckett once explained.[89] No national identity, not even one deeply sensitive to the injustices of "chauvinistic" state power, can shield individuals who ascribe to it from acts of complicity in crimes of their state, or from Jaspers's political guilt.

Prominent Ukrainian dissidents at this time – equally concerned with relationships between groups that were grounded in mutual suffering – surveyed this same terrain but dug much deeper. One of them was Ivan Dziuba, author of the sensational treatise *Internatsionalizm chy rusyfikatsiia? (Internationalism or Russification?*, 1965) that helped inspire Ivan Sokulsky's activism in Dnipropetrovsk. In 1966 Dziuba stood outside of Kyiv at Babyn Iar (Babii Iar), where Nazi Schutzstaffel squads had murdered nearly thirty-five thousand Jews in 1941. Borys Antonenko-Davydovych was next to him, waiting to address a crowd that had gathered to commemorate the massacre. Dziuba spoke first, reminding the assembled about the "tragic" histories of the Ukrainian and Jewish peoples: "The history of our peoples is so similar in its tragic nature that in his biblical-themed [poem] 'Moses' Ivan Franko recast the path of the Ukrainian people in the sacred vestments of Jewish legends, and Lesia Ukraïnka began one of her most powerful poems about the tragedy of Ukraine with the words, 'And you once struggled like Israel, [O my Ukraine].'"[90]

These tragedies, according to Dziuba, persist in the Thaw period because of a departure from the Leninist principles that were opposed to anti-Semitism and Great Russian chauvinism and because of a Stalinist tradition of manipulating the prejudices between Jews and Ukrainians.[91] To make his case, he offers examples of prominent Jewish and Ukrainian historical figures who supported Jewish-Ukrainian "brotherhood": Ze'ev Jabotinsky (1880–1940), the Zionist leader and ally of the Ukrainian national movement during the revolutionary period; and Taras Shevchenko, one of whose "last civic acts was a protest against the anti-Semitic policies of the tsarist regime."[92] These examples, among others, represent for Dziuba "a robust solidarity" between the groups in "a struggle for mutually held ideals of liberty and justice."[93]

Yet in highlighting this solidarity, Dziuba casts a glance at the other scene – at a history of discord and hostility between the Ukrainian and Jewish communities.[94] "In the past we have suffered from blind hostility and painful misunderstandings," he confesses. "As a Ukrainian, I feel ashamed that there is anti-Semitism among my own people."[95] Dziuba's recognition of the fraught, complex nature of the Ukrainian-Jewish historical encounter reflects a tension between the individual and the in-group in the process of what has been called "identity correspondence," the "linkage of individual and collective identities."[96] When the in-group is a nation, an imagined community offering a sense of belonging across time, the individual must weigh *nolens volens*, in the process of national self-ascription, a particular moral burden posed by the actions of the collective in both the past and the present. In identifying as a member of the nation, in claiming proprietary access to its constellation of symbols, traditions, and achievements, the individual abnegates the stance of the moral individualist and takes on obligations arising from national identification – including those related to historical wrongs committed against Others. As in Dziuba's case, this negotiation of an internal, in-group solidarity can come at the moment of an assertion of an external, intergroup solidarity.

The poet and human rights activist Mykola Rudenko (1920–2004) joined Dziuba in facing the fraught problem of guilt and national belonging. And he did so through the image of a Crimean Tatar Other. Rudenko was "the archetypical Ukrainian dissident," a Party loyalist betrayed by the system that he sought in good conscience to reform.[97]

Born the son of a coal miner in Donbas, he served as a political commissar in Leningrad in the Second World War. After being seriously wounded in October 1941, Rudenko convalesced in a hospital for nearly a year before leaving for the front once again. He returned from the war as a highly decorated veteran and became editor of the literary journal *Dnipro* and secretary of the Party Committee of the Union of Writers of Ukraine. Rudenko enjoyed success in the post-war period as both a poet and a prose writer whose novels, such as *Ostannia shablia* (The last sabre, 1959), became bestsellers.

The trajectory of Rudenko's life changed dramatically in the 1960s. After attending Khrushchev's "Secret Speech," he began to express doubts, both privately and publicly, that the crimes of Stalinism were nothing more than the consequence of one man's abuses and delusions. "When Khrushchev disclosed who Stalin really was, I was deeply shocked. I said to myself: something is not right here. The issue is not Stalin. How could a paranoid sadist assume such high office, wield such power, and shape the state? [...] I had to answer these questions for myself."[98] Myroslav Marynovych describes such Damascene conversions around the Twentieth Congress of the Communist Party as a "psychological breakdown" that elicited among some Soviet elites "a sense of collective guilt." Marynovych makes particular mention of Petro Grigorenko in this context as well. "Grigorenko, who was at first a stalwart Communist, was shocked by the sin the Communist regime had assumed. His decision to support the Crimean Tatars had not an ethnic impetus, but an ethical one."[99]

Grigorenko was the Ukrainian most prominently involved in the Crimean Tatar cause, but he was hardly alone. Between periods of lengthy incarceration, the poet and philologist Sviatoslav Karavansky proclaimed in a 1966 letter to the Soviet Council of Nationalities – notably, months before the 1967 decree – that the deportation of the Crimean Tatars was a "screaming injustice."[100] Party member Taras Franko and biologist Mariia Lysenko publicly criticized the Presidium of the Supreme Soviet in 1970 for preventing the Crimean Tatars from returning to their homeland, especially when the economy of Crimea was in such well-recognized need of a larger workforce.[101] Among Ukrainian academics the historian Mykhailo Kulychenko condemned the deportation of the Crimean Tatars and other nations as a "tangible blow to their national development" and "an offence" (narushenie) enabled by Stalin's "cult of personality," in his work of 1972, *Natsionalnye otnosheniia v SSSR* (National relations in the USSR).[102]

In 1975, while convalescing in a Moscow hospital, Grigorenko met Rudenko for the first time. It was a pivotal juncture in the lives of both men. Months before, Grigorenko had been released from his second sentence at a psychiatric hospital, which captured the world's attention. Rudenko, meanwhile, had recently been expelled from the Writer's Union, stripped of his privileges as a member of the Party, and forced to take up work as a night watchman in a sanatorium outside of Kyiv. He had also finished a lengthy analysis of Marx's *Kapital* entitled *Ekonomichni monolohy* (Economic monologues), which Andrei Sakharov helped distribute in samizdat and passed directly to Grigorenko, who read it with interest. *Ekonomichni monolohy*, as Ivan Lysiak-Rudnytsky puts it, "reads as if it were written by an intellectual Robinson Crusoe" who was unaware that Marx's theory of surplus value "had been [critiqued] by economists for the past hundred years."[103] Yet it also reveals a well-intentioned artist who was convinced that the system could still be reformed and that Soviet authorities might heed, or at least appreciate, his warnings.

Around the time of his first meeting with Grigorenko, Rudenko composed a poem entitled "Tataryn" (The [Crimean] Tatar), which was immediately distributed in samvydav and later published in a tamvydav (Ukrainian equivalent of tamizdat) collection of the poet's work in 1978. The poem stands out in Rudenko's oeuvre for a number of reasons, not least of which is its dark depiction of the villagers of the Donetsk basin before the war. On the whole, Rudenko tends to convey a strong fondness and nostalgia for Donetsk and the surrounding countryside in his verse. In "Donbas," for example, his lyrical persona professes an everlasting love for this "hearty" land in whose "silty streams" he swam as a child and on whose rocks he learned to write with pieces of coal.[104] Walking along village roads and across the shadows of trunks of pine trees, he addresses locals as trusted, longtime friends. These childhood memories of Donetsk often offer refuge and solace in trying times. In "V Donetsku" (In Donetsk, 1977), written after his second arrest, his lyrical persona travels "home, to my distant childhood," where "everything is full of hope, everything is as it should be."[105] While his hometown is not quite the unblemished idyll evoked by Taras Shevchenko under similarly trying circumstances in "Sadok vyshnevyi kolo khaty" ("The Cherry Orchard by the House," 1847) – herbs from the meadow stave off smells of dung and sweat in the Rudenko family home, for instance – it is still a place of innocence, bathed at night in the light of shining stars.

In stark contrast, the Donetsk of "Tataryn" is a site of savage violence against an innocent man. The poem is undated, but Rudenko's widow, Raïsa Kaplun Rudenko, believes that it was written around 1975, not long after his first encounter with Grigorenko in Moscow. She also makes clear that the "Tatar" referred to in the poem – and recalled in Rudenko's memories – was specifically a Crimean Tatar, despite the more prevalent number of Volga Tatars in cities in the Donbas region.[106] (According to KGB memoranda, there were nearly seven hundred Crimean Tatars in the Donetsk oblast around the time of the poem's composition.[107]) The poem, whose alternating twelve- and thirteen-syllable lines evoke the cadence of a lament, is a meditation on a haunting childhood memory:[108]

> Ніби душу лікую від давніх ошпарин —
> Років сорок це лихо забути велю:
> У багнюці конає побитий татарин,
> Його руки мотуззям зап'яті в петлю.[109]

> (Trying to heal my soul from old wounds,
> I have told myself to forget this evil for forty years:
> A beaten Tatar languishes in mud,
> His hands bound with rope in a slipknot.)

Oshparyn/tataryn, zeliu/ petliu – at the level of form, Rudenko plays it safe as a technician; throughout his poetic corpus, his strophes, metres, and rhymes have an almost militant regularity. The tightly ordered "Tataryn" does not surprise in this regard. At the level of content, his poems also tend to avoid inconsistency of mood or unpredictability of thought, keeping within a stable "ideological system" or "program," in the words of George Shevelov.[110] Here "Tataryn" decidedly breaks the mould, as the memory of the tortured Tatar provokes an "unprogrammatic" experience of confusion and despair:

> Я не знаю за віщо дядьки завелися —
> Дико люди жили у донецьких степах.
> Душу й досі пече голова його лиса
> І той камінь, що людською кров'ю пропах.
> Хто ж він був, цей татарин? … Не відаю досі.
> Били, мабуть, за те, що він череп голив.
> Чи за те, що у зайшлого очі розкосі.
> Чи за жменьку порічки, за пригорщу слив.

> (I do not know what drove the villagers to do this –
> Wildly did people live on the Donetsk steppe.
> The sight of that blood-soaked rock
> And his bald head still sears my soul.
> Who was he, this Tatar? I do not know to this day.
> Perhaps they beat him because he shaved his head.

Or because he was a stranger with oblique eyes.
Or because of his handfuls of red currants and plums.)

At play in "Tataryn" is a push and pull of two discourses, testimony and confession, and of two discursive temporalities, childhood and adulthood. Rudenko's lyrical persona "watches" his memory of the tormented Crimean Tatar from the point of view of a younger self – a boy approaching the world in largely spatial-visual terms – and reflects upon its deeper meaning from the point of view of an adult subject with particular conceptions of self and Other. When focused explicitly on the memory of the assault, the poem becomes a testimony, an externally directed discourse shuttling between chronicle and condemnation:

То не люди були — дикі звірі неначе.
Стала просто багном нежива голова.
І відтоді запала у серце дитяче
Недовіра до вашого, люди, єства.

(They were not human – they acted like wild animals.
His lifeless head became a swamp of gore.
And from that time, you people, my young heart was filled
With a distrust of your true nature.)

The same "kind and friendly" (dobri, i pryvitni) villagers who populate "Donbas" and "V Donetsku" are now "beasts" whom the young boy attempts to stop from murdering the Crimean Tatar in cold blood. This encounter with the disturbingly dual nature of his neighbours inspires not only his "distrust" but also a cognitive dissonance as profound as Sokulsky's in "Bakhchysarai (Tsykl)":

Я ненавиджу вас, дикуни-односельці.
Я люблю вас без міри, мої земляки.

(I hate you, savage fellow villagers.
I love you without measure, my countrymen.)

In denouncing his own people for violence against Others, Rudenko echoes Yevgeny Yevtushenko's "Babii Yar":

О, русский мой народ! –
        Я знаю –
                Ты

По сущности интернационален.
Но часто те, чьи руки нечисты,
Твоим чистейшим именем бряцали.[111]

(O, my Russian people! –
I know –
You
Are international by nature.
But often men with impure hands
Have disgraced your pure name.)

For all its power, "Babii Yar" exhibits a certain emotional distance that "Tataryn" lacks. Yevtushenko's lyrical persona stands in judgment over the anti-Semitic crimes of his own people; he is no danger of being implicated in them.

Rudenko's "I" speaks from a different subject position – one more immediate and personal. He struggles to reconcile individual innocence (his position as a child witness to the Crimean Tatar's murder) with collective responsibility (his national fellowship with the Crimean Tatar's murderers). In other words, he struggles with the moral claims of national *belonging*, and it is precisely the "question of belonging" that testimonial literature "puts into action."[112] The figure of the Crimean Tatar, the Other victimized at the hands of Ukrainian compatriots, impels the lyrical persona to interrogate the grounds for his identification with the collective. For Rudenko, this interrogation involves an inward turn. Here the poem shifts from testimony to confession, to an internally directed discourse of guilt, in the final lines:

Ніби душу лікую від давніх ошпарин,
Несучи у душі той донецький "рощот".
І приходить до мене забитий татарин,
І скривавленим ротом питає: за що?

(Trying to heal myself from old wounds,
I still bear in my soul that Donetsk beating.
The murdered Tatar comes to me,
And with a blood-stained mouth asks: why?)

In his memoirs Rudenko returned to this problem of the complex moral claims of the nation on the individual, again with reference to the Crimean Tatar question:

A Ukrainian writer once had the nerve to say this to me in conversation: "I don't understand Grigorenko. To suffer in the *psikhushki* [psychiatric hospitals] [...] And for whom, if not for [the Crimean Tatars] whose ancestors plundered Ukraine for centuries? It seems to me that something is just not right here. To give your life for your enemies – this is nonsense." This was not some ordinary writer, but one whose work was studied by Ukrainian schoolchildren. This man, crowned with laurels by state leaders, disturbed me. There is nothing more primitive or banal than sermonizing about the collective responsibility of descendants for the actions of their ancestors.[113]

In place of a sermon about "the collective responsibility of descendants for the actions of their ancestors" – sermons that would threaten to reduce internal solidarities and external solidarities to zero-sum propositions – Rudenko proposes testimony and (like Nekipelov in "Gurzuf") confession, modelling both for the reader in "Tataryn."

5.

In November 1976, not long after writing "Tataryn," Mykola Rudenko sat in central Moscow in the apartment of a physicist, dissident, and laureate of the Nobel Peace Prize, Andrei Sakharov. Before a clutch of foreign journalists, Rudenko declared the establishment of the Ukrainian Helsinki Group (UHG) – or the Ukrainian Civic Group for the Promotion of the Implementation of the Helsinki Accords (Ukraïnska Hromadska Hrupa spryiannia vykonanniu Helsinkskykh uhod) – which was committed to monitoring, on the territory of Soviet Ukraine, compliance with the 1975 Helsinki Final Act, which made human rights the crux of a fledgling détente between the Soviet Union and the West.[114] The setting of Rudenko's announcement in Moscow was not arbitrary: foreign journalists and dignitaries visited Kyiv only rarely.[115] They were very familiar with Sakharov's apartment, however, which had long become – in the words of KGB boss Yuri Andropov, his quotation marks dripping with condescension – "a place of pilgrimage for various kinds of 'victims' of 'arbitrary actions' by Soviet authorities."[116] Rudenko came to this place of pilgrimage by following in the footsteps of Yuri Orlov, who had announced the birth of the Moscow Helsinki Group (Moskovskaia Khelsinkskaia gruppa) earlier in May.

Rudenko's press conference may have appeared something of a sequel to Orlov's original, but, in the words of Liudmila Alekseeva, it was an "extremely significant event."[117] It demonstrated that the Helsinki phenomenon was not a flash in the pan confined to a cell of

Moscow intellectuals, but an organized, interconnected movement penetrating republics across the Soviet Union. Testament to this significance can be found in the fact that, notwithstanding the relative novelty of the UHG, Rudenko was arrested for his Helsinki-related activism *before* Orlov, in February 1977. The KGB in Kyiv – operating at a remove from the watchful gaze of Western journalists and international observers in Moscow – was widely viewed as the most "vicious" in the Soviet Union.[118] It moved quickly against Rudenko – arresting him alongside a compatriot from the Donbas, Oleksa Tykhy, who was a UHG founding member – and targeting in turn UHG founding members like Myroslav Marynovych. Rudenko was sentenced under Article 62 of the Soviet Criminal Code to seven years of hard labour and five years of exile. The verdict enraged Boris Chichibabin:

> Он чистое дитя, и вы его не троньте,
> Перед его костром мы все дерьмо и прах.
> Он жизни наши спас и кровь пролил на фронте,
> Он нашу честь спасёт в собачьих лагерях.[119]

> ([Rudenko] is a good man, and don't you dare touch him,
> Before his great fire, we are all shit and dust.
> He saved our lives and shed blood at the front,
> And in the wretched camps he will save our honour.)

By 1981, only four years after its inception, all members of the UHG – numbering roughly forty – had been imprisoned. According to Vasyl Ovsiienko, this group endured a total of 550 years in incarceration or exile. Four died in bondage: Tykhy, Yuri Lytvyn, Valery Marchenko, and Vasyl Stus, one of the most talented Ukrainian poets of the twentieth century. One, the historian Mykhailo Melnyk, committed suicide after years of harassment.[120]

The Kremlin swiftly and brutally cut back the growth of the UHG for a number of reasons. Not only was the UHG the first Soviet Ukrainian independent civil society organization to be founded on international legal principles, but it also united Ukrainian dissidents of various ideological persuasions, from Marxists like Pliushch to national democrats like Chornovil, into one coherent body.[121] Its announcement in Moscow was also an implicit recognition, particularly among Russian dissidents like Sakharov, that rights work could have different national valences. The Moscow and Ukrainian Helsinki Groups sought to hold Soviet authorities particularly accountable to Principle VII of the Helsinki Final Act, "Respect for human rights and fundamental freedoms, including freedom of thought, conscience, religion or belief," and to expose any violations of such principles before domestic and international audiences. Yet their respective adjectival descriptors – *Moskovskaia* and *Ukraïnska* – spoke to two different concepts of locality – city and nation – which in turn revealed different dispositions to the social order. For Orlov, Moscow was *where* the group was active; for Rudenko, Ukraine was *why* the group was active.

"[For the UHG] the national question is at issue above all," Rudenko writes in the first UHG memorandum in 1976.[122] Ukrainians and other non-Russian nations, in his view, are subject to persecution on the grounds of not only *doing* something "anti-Soviet" but also *being* something "anti-Soviet." His attention to the national question was not myopic or exclusivist, however. It was global, even cosmopolitan, and invested in the edification of the individual, because Rudenko saw the nation as an instrument in and a "context of choice" for individual self-identification. After his break with Marxism, Rudenko dabbled in eighteenth-century physiocracy in an attempt to articulate this political philosophy, animating early UHG advocacy documents with a poetic eccentricity that is often absent in political samvydav. "Civilization is united – this is seen well from the Cosmos," he writes. "There are no boundaries on the globe for the ray beaming down from the Sun. The human is formed from the rays of the Sun; he is a child of the Sun."[123] For Rudenko, the sun is the conduit of all living energy – material, intellectual, and moral – endowing each individual with worth, wisdom, and inherent rights upon which the state cannot infringe.[124]

For the UHG and the Ukrainian human rights movement, Petro Grigorenko was a luminary embodying this "radiated," rooted cosmopolitanism. He was seen as a Ukrainian who bridged two expanses. As a founding member of both the Moscow and the Ukrainian Helsinki Group, he dovetailed the struggle of ethical individualists in Moscow and the struggle of communitarians devoted to the problem of minority national discrimination in Ukraine and beyond. And as the "Ukrainian general" (tuğgeneral Ukraynalı, as the Turkish press referred to him) most visibly advocating the Crimean Tatar movement around the world, he represented a Ukrainian prepared to sacrifice not only for the rights of his own people but for the rights of Others displaced and dispossessed thousands of miles away.[125] Founding documents of the UHG punctuated his defence of the Crimean Tatars, while Chornovil and the editors of *Ukraïnskyi visnyk* (*The Ukrainian Herald*) – the Ukrainian counterpart to *Khronika tekushchykh sobytii* that served as an informational organ of the UHG in the 1980s – held him up as the preeminent example of Ukrainian–Crimean Tatar solidarity.[126]

These tributes understate the matter. "Grigorenko did much more for the Crimean Tatars than anyone among the Crimean Tatars themselves did," says Mustafa Dzhemilev, a man given the sobriquet Qırımoğlu (son of Crimea) who draws comparisons to Nelson Mandela today. In 1968 Dzhemilev lived for six months with Petro and Zinaida Grigorenko in Moscow, where he became a part of the family. He served as Petro's secretary; he called Zinaida "mama."[127] Their friendship – between a former Red Army general and a conscientious objector half his age, twice imprisoned for avoiding the draft – was unlikely, but Soviet dissent was a calling that could forge diverse bonds. "All the dissidents passed through the Grigorenko apartment," Dzhemilev remembers. "It is thanks to him that I joined the human rights dissident movement."[128] After leaving the Grigorenkos, Dzhemilev would be arrested, tried, and sentenced under all manner of "anti-Soviet" charges no less than five times. He would embark on what is considered the longest hunger strike in the history of human rights movements, surviving over 303 days only due to the torture of force-feeding. Across the Black Sea on Turkish television, the drama of Dzhemilev's protest triggered false news reports of his death.[129] Turkish newspapers repeated the rumours.[130] Days passed before the truth became known. On the front page of the leading Turkish daily *Milliyet*, a face of a Soviet dissident appeared to call on "all Muslims" to continue defending Dzhemilev, who was very much alive. It was the face of Leonid Pliushch, who was described in national terms as "a famous Ukrainian."[131]

Chapter Six

Incense and Drum

Long after his hunger strike, on the late morning of 10 February 1984, the sixth day of Mustafa Dzhemilev's sixth trial was underway in Tashkent. There was a skirmish outside his courtroom as police tried to wrangle Crimean Tatar protesters who were demonstrating their support for him. Dzhemilev by this point had spent most of his adult life incarcerated in the Soviet system, and his sixth trial had become both a local and an international cause célèbre. The charge against him was once again "anti-Soviet agitation." "The concept of 'anti-Soviet' is as vague as it is capacious," Lidiia Chukovskaia once wrote in a samizdat pamphlet defending Dzhemilev. "It is an insatiable chasm devouring human fates and human thoughts."[1]

Dzhemilev was not intimidated by any chasm, however. He approached the proceedings in Tashkent as farce, deploying his wit and hard-earned jurisprudential savvy to outmanoeuvre prosecutors and judges alike. As he put it, he was "long familiar with the Jesuitical thinking of such sedition hunters."[2] Transcripts reveal them to be ill equipped to handle his intellect and disarming humour, which could quickly turn the tables and put them in dock, vulnerable to his withering questions. At one point, after decrying the hypocrisy of the Soviet portrayal of the invasion of Afghanistan as a provision of "fraternal assistance" to a neighbouring country, he turned to the prosecutor and asked, "We live in a very interesting country, do we not?" The judge swiftly intervened: "The prosecutor is not to be questioned."[3]

One extended episode on the trial's sixth day centred on a poem. Written in Turkish by the Ankara-based scholar Şükrü Elçin (1912–2008), "Bahçesaray Çeşmesi" (The fountain of Bahçesaray) first appeared in print in 1981. In a manner similar to Hasan Çergeyev's Crimean Tatar–language precursor "Közyaş han çeşmesi" (1908), which we examined in chapter 2, the poem transforms Pushkin's Romantic fountain into a witness to centuries of dispossession, a vessel through which both tears and blood flow. A copy of Elçin's poem reached Dzhemilev from Turkey in an envelope tucked into the text of Atatürk's monumental *Nutuk* (*The Speech*) – material that was more palatable to Soviet epistolary gatekeepers at the time, presumably given the history of relatively warm relations between Lenin and Atatürk.[4] "Bahçesaray Çeşmesi" made a deep and immediate impression on Dzhemilev. After transcribing the poem by hand, he circulated it among a host of friends and colleagues, who then photocopied and distributed it further.

This simple act of propagating Elçin's "Bahçesaray Çeşmesi" became part of the criminal case against Dzhemilev. His prosecutors even solicited "forensic literary analysis" from "experts" at the nearby Pushkin Institute of Language and Literature in an effort to show that the poem was "thoroughly saturated with anti-Sovietism."[5] Their bumbling attempts at literary analysis took centre stage at the trial:

JUDGE: Why did you decide to propagate [Elçin's "Fountain of Bahçesaray"]?

DZHEMILEV: Because it is a beautifully written work, and good literary works should be read by as many people as possible. [...]

JUDGE: But don't you consider this "Fountain of Bahçesaray" a slanderous work?

DZHEMILEV: Of course not.

JUDGE: Have you been to Bahçesaray yourself? Have you seen this fountain?

DZHEMILEV: Yes, I have visited and seen the fountain.

JUDGE: So what, blood flows from the fountain, as the poem says?

DZHEMILEV: Well ... there is a difference between a poem and an accounting report. If we're going to think this way, I suppose I can give more evidence of "slander against the Soviet system" and "anti-historicism" in this work.

JUDGE: What evidence? Go on.

DZHEMILEV: For example, the poem says that, after the deportation of the Crimean Tatars, the birds stopped singing in Crimea. This is, of course, anti-historical, so the poet Şükrü Elçin is clearly slandering Soviet birds. They probably continued to sing their songs, regardless of who was deported from where. (Laughter, applause in the courtroom.)[6]

In disputing the absurd literalism of the prosecutors, Dzhemilev echoes Russian writer Andrei Siniavsky but with more irreverence. In 1966 Siniavsky and Yuly Daniel were on trial for "anti-Soviet agitation"; both were convicted and sentenced to terms in forced labour camps. In his

"Final Word," Siniavsky insisted that "a word is not a deed, but a word; the artistic image is a thing of convention" (khudozhestvennyi obraz usloven).[7] Dzhemilev may have mocked the authorities' argument with a deft *reductio ad absurdum*, but his point was the same. Literature does not advance a series of propositions and truth claims; unlike "accounting reports," as he reminds us (incidentally echoing Samuel Beckett, who once declared that "literary criticism is not book-keeping"), poems do not aspire to concrete, determinate meaning or full disclosure.[8] They are up to something else entirely.

In the Republic of Turkey, poems like Elçin's "Bahçesaray Çeşmesi," which we will examine more closely next, intersected with novels and pulp-fiction "penny dreadfuls" to engage in a poetics of solidarity with the Crimean Tatars throughout the latter half of the twentieth century. Like the dissident Soviet works of the previous two chapters, these literary texts invite the reader to visualize the suffering victim and to grapple with a language of guilt, but their we-relation conceives of the Crimean Tatars very differently, as "part of us," as ethnic Sunni brethren enslaved by Soviet communism. They are presented as *esir Türkler* (captive Turks). Especially in conservative pan-Turkist literature, poetry and prose are put to work in the cause of their "liberation": poetry as incense, summoning the oral traditions of folk poetry as well as the rhetoric of religious sermons and litany, and prose as a drum, pounding images of graphic victimization and heroism into the mind's eye.

The works of literature in this chapter, published under various censorship regimes, complicate the view that Turkey "ignored the plight" of the Crimean Tatars, as Alan Fisher posits, or failed to take "particular interest in the plight of the Crimean Tatars," as Isabelle Kreindler writes.[9] Such neglect may have been true of a "passive" elite in Ankara consumed by Cold War Realpolitik.[10] But on the level of culture, especially popular culture, we encounter a much different picture. As we will see, it is a picture of pan-Turkist journals like *Emel* publishing poetry about Crimean Tatars alongside digests of Soviet samizdat and tamizdat for a Turkish readership, which included a Crimean Tatar diaspora population numbering as many as five million.[11] It is a picture of millions of readers routinely entering into the perspective of dispossessed Crimean Tatars via the bestselling novels of Cengiz Dağcı, which are a staple in Turkish secondary-school curricula today. Through Crimean Tatar characters, also described as "Turks," tortured by both Stalinism and Nazism, Dağcı's novels offer readers "prosthetic memories" of the Second World War, false-but-felt memories of a conflict that Turkey had avoided by declaring neutrality. The success of these novels in turn inspired epigones in the realm of pulp fiction, which found particularly receptive audiences and enthusiastic distributors in the Turkish military. All of these texts – from high literature to low literature – contributed to a clear outcome: the installation of the Crimean Tatar Other as a paradigmatic Turkic victim of the twentieth century.

1.

To map the reverberations of Stalin's Crimean atrocity in Turkish literature is to navigate some of the most tempestuous currents of modern Turkish political thought. It is to feel an irratic push and pull between secularization and Islamicization, to move through a force field of growing tensions between right-wing and left-wing political forces after the introduction of multi-party politics in 1946. Literary activity in Turkey was far less regulated and far more heterogeneous than in the Soviet Union, but it could be just as dangerous, especially in the context of arrests, reprisals, and executions brought on by three military coups over three successive decades, in 1960, 1971, and 1980. Indeed, at the height of the Cold War, Turkish culture and society was afflicted by an often violent polarization between the right and the left, a contest of extremisms that turned academic life, for one, into a political gladiator sport. The Crimean Tatars – or at least their aesthetic representations – always seemed to figure in the arena.

Şükrü Elçin's "Bahçesaray Çeşmesi" – the poem that preoccupied Soviet prosecutors during Dzhemilev's trial in Tashkent, requiring "forensic literary analysis" – offers us a vivid example. Published in the Istanbul-based journal *Emel* in 1981, only months after the military coup led by General Kenan Evren, "Bahçesaray Çeşmesi" employs the figure of the Crimean Tatar Other to help translate an insurgent Turkish ideological project into a campaign of emotion and action.[12] It turns the emblematic fountain from Pushkin's "Bakhchisaraiskii fontan" and Çergeyev's "Közyaş han çeşmesi" into a makeshift monument to what is known as the Turkish-Islamic Synthesis (Türk-İslam Sentezi), a conservative political program adopted by the military leadership in one of the most radical changes to the Republic of Turkey since its inception. The Synthesis departed from Atatürk's strident secularism or laicism (laiklik) and accommodated Islam as a complementary force for national consolidation, placing Turkish culture on two pillars: "a 2,500-year-old Turkish element and a 1,000-year-old Islamic element."[13] The Synthesis was first articulated in the 1970s by a small group of scholars opposed to the growth of the political left, called Aydınlar Ocağı (Hearth of Intellectuals) – Elçin was a member – but after the

1980 coup it became "a popular ideological point of reference for power elites in Turkey, including the military."[14]

What are the Crimean Tatars doing in a poem advancing the Turkish-Islamic Synthesis? To an extent, they are performing a function ascribed to them from the time of Ziya Gökalp and Mehmet Emin Yurdakul: offsetting what might be called an unbearable lightness of national being with extranational relevance. For Elçin, and for so many of the writers in this chapter, the Crimean Tatars were broadly understood as *proxymate* – that is, both proximate and proxy, neighbour and surrogate, Turkic and Turkish. Chapter 1 revealed how poets like Gökalp and Yurdakul helped lay the foundations of this conceptualization in the early twentieth century, abstracting Tatar personality in the service of the ethnonym *Crimean Turk*. After 1944, as we will see, this peculiar standing – at once outside (*Crimean*) and inside (*Turk*) – offered thinkers and readers in Turkey a valued asset in nationalist politics: access to the position of the victim, without the direct experience of victimization. The dispossession of the Crimean Tatars outside of Turkey's borders could be used to raise the stakes of national agendas inside of them. It could turn what was, for right-wing Turkish activists, a domestic battle against Marxism, for instance, into a righteous struggle with global resonance not just against an enemy but against one's own oppressor.

In Elçin's "Bahçesaray Çeşmesi" the Crimean Tatars accordingly help inject a degree of extranational significance into the national design of the Turkish-Islamic Synthesis. Elçin was a prominent scholar and collector of folk culture, and his poem communicates this significance through an assortment of cultural references drawn from centuries past. In fact, his "Bahçesaray Çeşmesi" is less a fountain than a river brimming over with intertexts and allusions. In its flow are currents of both divan poetry and Turkic folklore, with eddies that mix quotations about mystical love from the classical verse of Fuzuli with references to the saz of folk poet Aşık Ömer (who, in Elçin's view, was of Crimean Tatar origin).[15] The language of the poem is often arcane, its metre loose and irregular:

Bahçesaray'da bir *Gözyaşı Çeşmesi* vardı Akyar mermerinden yapılmış,
Bu çeşme Kırım Giray'ın gönül ikliminde açan nilüferdi.[16]

(In Bahçesaray there is a "Fountain of Tears" made of Akyar [Sevastopol]
    marble,
The fountain was a water lily blossoming in the heart of Kırım Giray.)

As with Çergeyev's precursor, what distinguishes Elçin's fountain is its constancy, its enduring presence through periods of feast and famine and of suffering and renewal. It quenches the spiritual thirst of national awakeners across the eras, from Gasprinsky to Dzhemilev:

Gaspıralı İsmail bu çeşme başında duydu, sesini tarihin;
Bu çeşmede uyandırdı Cemiller'i, geçmiş zaman hüzniyle hatıralar.

(İsmail Gasprinsky [Gaspıralı] heard the sounds of history standing
  before this fountain;
At this fountain, the Dzhemilevs were roused by sorrowful memories of
  the past.)

Elçin does not confine the importance of this fountain to Crimea alone. He positions it as a point of crossing in the region of the Black Sea, a junction between the Anatolian and Crimean worlds. The fountain in Elçin's vision is not only a touching monument to Khan Kırım Giray's beloved, Dilara Bikeç, for instance; it also stands to honour Kerem and Aslı, the Anatolian "Romeo and Juliet" who were famous in Turkish folk poetry. In fact, for Elçin, it has significance for all of Islam, from the "ghazis" and the "warrior-saints" (erenler) to the "martyrs" of the faith.

Elçin's "Bahçesaray Çeşmesi," in other words, seeks to remind readers of the relevance of Crimea and the Crimean Tatars for Turkey *and* Islam, to wrench them away from Russian and Soviet historico-political space and stand them on pillars of Turkish culture as "part of us." To this end, Elçin provides an extended history lesson. His third and fourth quatrains delve into the story of the envelopment of Crimea within the Ottoman sphere of influence in the fifteenth century. He evokes the exploits of Mehmet II (Mehmet Fatih, Mehmet the Conquerer) and his grand vizier, Gedik Ahmed Paşa, against the Genoese, which placed Crimea under Ottoman protection. The message is a reminder of a long-standing Turkish stake in the fate of the Crimean Tatars, of a past of mutual connection and historical obligation.

Establishing this framework of identification – an intricate array of Turkish and Muslim affinities – is the concern of the poem's first section. The rest presents the effects of Stalin's Crimean atrocity. Here Elçin's lyrical persona turns to address the fountain in apostrophe, as in Çergeyev's poem from 1908: "You are the broken heart of tens of thousands, of hundreds of thousands exiled to Siberia." He then summons an army of apocalyptic metaphors, from "poisonous winds" blowing across the peninsula to bloody tears and silenced birds (which were raised as "evidence" in Dzhemilev's trial). Arid soil cracks from thirst; lead covers the sky; the dreams of abducted children sway to and fro in rotting trees. "No one can breathe," the lyrical persona intones, "in the darkness of night."

Amid these clusters of metaphor, Elçin highlights the most vulnerable victims of the deportation: children and their mothers, whose "eyes are seized by fear." He conjures an image of them on crowded cattle-cars in 1944, crawling eastward to destinations unknown. "On the way to Siberia, a girl from Sudak [in southeastern Crimea] holds tightly to a song," the lyrical persona observes. Upon hearing her singing, he says, "I was tortured by grief" (içimi kemirdi firâk; literally, "grief gnawed at me"). The moment marks the first use of the first-person in the poem. The little girl's song is "Soğuksu," a folk song written by Crimean Tatars fleeing Russian rule for the Ottoman Empire in the nineteenth century. Elçin included "Soğuksu" in a collection of Turkish folk poetry that he edited and published in 1981, the same year he wrote "Bahçesaray Çeşmesi." Here is a characteristic couplet:

Sana hasret gideriz güzel Kırım
Gurbet ellere düşüp ey yar eziliriz.[17]

(Beautiful Crimea, we die longing for you,
In faraway lands, O beloved, we are destroyed.)

This intertextual allusion to the hymns of Crimean Tatar refugees from an earlier era places Stalin's deportation in a wider chronological frame, communicating a perpetuity to their victimhood. For readers in the Crimean Tatar diaspora community, whose ancestors transplanted to Turkey in the nineteenth century, the allusion to "Soğuksu" also makes Soviet history personal – not distant or removed but present and familiar. Most importantly, the intertext marks a moment when the lyrical persona assumes a first-person pose to speak of his own grief at the sight of a vulnerable child, modelling guilt-processing for the reader.

This emotional pivot leads the lyrical persona to adopt an explicit language of solidarity at the conclusion of "Bahçesaray Çeşmesi." The "I" of the poem binds himself to the Crimean Tatar victim, generating a new "we." "*Our* saintly dead in Crimea are wrapped in white shrouds," the lyrical persona laments. "Together we lost *our* freedom [*kaybettik hürriyetimizi*]" (emphases mine). But not all is forsaken. After expressing grief and forging a "we" bound by loss and suffering, the lyrical persona promises action in defence of the Crimean Tatars. The action begins with prayer: "Tonight Fatih's [Mehmet II's] minarets pray for you."

Elçin's "Bahçesaray Çeşmesi" was first published in *Emel*, a journal of import in the post-war cultural history of the Black Sea. Inspired by

Gasprinsky's *Tercüman*, *Emel* (connoting both "hope" and "longing") has been a long-standing region maker, relaying from shore to shore news reports, historical essays, and literary texts from and about the Crimean Tatars and other Muslim Turkic peoples to thousands of readers in the Republic of Turkey and beyond.[18] *Emel* first emerged in 1930 under the leadership of the Crimean Tatar lawyer Müstecib Ülküsal. After a long hiatus prompted by the outbreak of the Second World War, it reappeared in 1960 to follow in the footsteps of Gökalp and Yurdakul and "realize pan-Turkism" (Türkçülük yapmaya çalışmak) by drawing attention to the suffering of the Crimean Tatars, among others, "in Siberia, Solovki, and Chekist prisons."[19]

Emel announced a pan-Turkist mission at its inception. Cultural journals in Turkey typically wore their ideology on their sleeves, avoiding political eclecticism and addressing readers as believers. After the Second World War, when the Kremlin began to encroach upon Turkey's eastern provinces and profess designs on the straits of the Bosporus and Dardanelles, a number of journals also emerged to agitate for the rights of Turkic-speaking peoples ensconced within the borders of the Soviet Union.[20] Invariably at the centre of these pan-Turkist publications were the Crimean Tatars, alongside Azerbaijanis, Kazakhs, Uzbeks, Kazan Tatars, and more – distinct peoples presented to the reader collectively as "outside Turks" (dış Türkler) or, more dramatically, "captive Turks" (esir Türkler).[21] In the campaign to free these "Turks" from captivity, lyric poems were the most widely solicited texts for publication.[22]

Everyday readers responded by sending in hundreds of poems to such journals as *Toprak* (The Land, 1954–76), a pan-Turkist monthly with a triadic orientation on "thought, art, and ideals." Their submissions were published alongside verse by more established poets like Refet Körüklü, whose lyrical persona decries the Soviet oppression of the esir Türkler and the Soviet dominion over the territory of Turan, the mythical Shangri-La of Turkic peoples extending from Anatolia into Asia: "In Turan my people are now oppressed, / While my heart overflows with hatred for Moscow."[23] Earlier in chapter 1, we saw how Turan became an object of desire for poets like Gökalp and Yurdakul, who mapped its vast borders with the posture of prophets. In journals like *Toprak*, poems are again put in the service of this imaginative cartography, tracing the vast expanse of Turan "from Karakorum [the thirteenth-century Mongol capital] to Crimea."[24] The guiding coordinates are first-person pronouns, an army of *we*, *us*, and *our* seeking to incorporate and assimilate Others into the "Turkic World." What we see in such pages is a pan-Turkist poetic worldview no longer confined to intellectuals but gradually embraced by everyday readers during the Cold War.

Two poems entitled "Gelsin" (Let them come) – one by an amateur poet named Halık Bikes Ulusoy, published in *Toprak* in 1954, and
another by a village teacher named Göktürk Mehmet Uytun, published
in *Toprak* in 1956 – provide an instructive example. They strike pan-
Turkist chords and employ the first person with constructive ambiguity, facilitating what could be both a call to liberate the esir Türkler and
an appeal to fellow Turks to join the pan-Turkist movement. Here is
Ulusoy:

Bayrak için, Vatan için,
Canı cana katan için,
Bu toprakta yatan için,
Bize *bizden* olan gelsin.[25]

(For the flag, for the homeland,
In order to join soul to soul,
In order to settle in this land,
Let those *who are part of us* come to us; emphasis mine.)

And here is Uytun:

Eli ele vermek için
Moskofu devirmek için
Bu murada ermek için
Bize *biziz*, deyen gelsin.[26]

(In order to join together hand in hand,
In order to overthrow Moscow,
In order to fulfil this dream,
Let those who say *"we are the ones"* come to us; emphasis mine.)

There is a tension in this verse between a Kemalist idiom and a
more aggressive, even mystical pan-Turkist message. Each in its own
way, these poems echo Atatürk's well-known remark, "Biz bize ben-
zeriz" (We resemble ourselves).[27] Atatürk's message is not only that
Turks are singular and unique, capable of doing what others cannot,
but also that the Turkish "we" has no other measure of itself than
itself.[28] Yet these poems also depart from Atatürk's politics by calling
to "overthrow Moscow," opposing the conciliatory Kemalist posture
toward the Soviet Union. They also enshroud this call in an aura of
the spiritual by deploying the syllabic metre, four-line strophe, and
internal rhyme common to religious folk poetry, particularly the *ilahi*

form. The appeal to the reader "to overthrow Moscow" and to free the Crimean Tatars and all the other esir Türkler is delivered in the cadence of a hymn.

The expansive, assimilatory impulse of this poetry aligned with the ethnonym that was assigned to the Crimean Tatars in these pan-Turkist periodicals: *Kırım Türkleri* (Crimean Turks).[29] For Ismail Gasprinsky at the fin de siècle, "Türk" was used to exorcise the negative Russian connotations of "Tatar"; for pan-Turkists in Turkey after the Second World War, it was used to efface ethnic and linguistic difference and extol a homogenous Turan. For Crimean Tatar emigrés in Turkey, meanwhile, the term was accepted as a way to petition the Turkish public for support, to communicate that "we are part of you."[30] By contrast, Crimean Tatar activists in the Soviet Union like Mustafa Dzhemilev – who, as we recall, had to contend with Decree 493, which labelled his people "the Tatars, formerly resident in Crimea" – employed *krymskie tatary* (and, if necessary, *Kırım Tatarları*) to appeal to the international community for the right to return to the homeland. As Aleksandr Nekrich suggests, in the Soviet period this mixed situational usage may have hindered the transnational coherence and outreach of the Crimean Tatar movement as a whole.[31] It remains contested to this day.[32]

In the Ankara-based journal *Türk Birliği* (Turkish Unity), the bounds between "Turks" and "Crimean Turks" were so porous that they seemed to produce a demographic explosion.[33] An article entitled "Türkleri nasıl parçaladılar?" (How have the Turks been scattered?) by Turkish journalist and civic activist Tekin Erer referred to "continuous deportations" that had flung over "six million" "Crimean Turks" across Soviet territory. The number was of course grossly inflated – the Crimean Tatars in the Soviet Union numbered in the hundreds of thousands at the time. But for Erer and the editors of *Türk Birliği*, *Kırım Türkleri* came to serve not as an ethnonym denoting a people with a specific territorialized history but as an ethnic *category* encompassing many Turkic peoples with histories on the Black Sea peninsula, from the Karachay to the Karaim.[34]

From 1969 such awkward attempts at historical and sociological editorializing became much more sophisticated and better informed. The distribution of Soviet documentary samizdat and tamizdat in Turkish circles was the primary reason. *Emel* in particular became a channel of Soviet underground literature in the 1970s and 1980s, regularly offering Turkish readers excerpts and digests of information from *Khronika tekushchikh sobytii* and Russian emigré journals like *Posev* (Sowing, based in Germany) and *Novoe russkoe slovo* (New Russian Word, based in New York). Edige Kırımal, a Munich-based Crimean Tatar scholar and activist, was an envoy of samizdat for Turkey. "Some samizdat materials are spirited into the hands of foreigners visiting the Soviet Union," Kırımal explained to Turkish readers, "who then relay it to journalists in countries in the free world [*dahil hür dünya memleketleri*] as well as to the Russian and Ukrainian emigré press."[35] Like Ukrainian dissidents, Kırımal and his colleagues paid particular attention to the Soviet persecution of "supporters of nationalism [*milliyetçilik taraftarları*] in the non-Russian republics of the Soviet Union, particularly in Crimea, Ukraine, and the Baltic states."[36] In *Emel*, specific accounts of the persecution of the "Crimean Turks" became mainstays in a segment entitled "News about the Crimeans in Exile," which was compiled from samizdat reports and international news clippings.

As we saw in chapter 4, Soviet samizdat journals like *Khronika tekushchikh sobytii* cordon off their clinical reports from imaginative literature with consistent discipline. By contrast, Turkish journals like *Emel* always muddle the line between the two, placing samizdat synopses above, below, and alongside lyric poems related to them in topic and tone. The effect of this mixed format – juxtaposing journalistic discourse about the injustices wrought by Soviet Communism with recitative poems calling upon the reader to defeat Communism – is to leverage imaginative literature as an agitational tool, as a means of rousing the reader to act on the information presented in the constative, documentary mode. When a taunt from Yurdakul's "Ey Türk Uyan" – "Tell me, what has happened to your all-conquering Golden Horde?" – prefaces an essay on the history of the Crimean Tatars, for instance, the reader is invited to trace a circuit between the history text and its poetic epigraph in which the events of the past become a question to be answered.[37] Poems lend these journals an expectant, even impatient air, communicating that action should be taken.

In *Emel* these texts invite the reader to speak from the position of the Crimean Tatar exile and model empathy and solidarity with him. Some poems express a topophila that resembles desire for a distant lover:[38]

Çatır göğe yaslanmış,
Salgır nazlı akarmış,
Her gün güller açarmış,
Ne güzel Vatan Kırım.[39]

(Çatır-Dağ [a moutainous massif] leans against the sky,
The Salgır River flows softly,
Every day roses bloom –
Crimea, what a beautiful homeland.)

Such passages echo one of the most popular songs among the Crimean Tatars in the Soviet Union at the time, "Ey Güzel Qırım" (O beautiful Crimea), but with an important difference. They openly use a word that is largely avoided or even forbidden among the displaced in Soviet Central Asia: *vatan*.[40]

Other poems in *Emel*, meanwhile, feature lyrical personae who observe, catalogue, and then deeply internalize Crimean Tatar suffering. In a text based on the *ağıt*, a verse of mourning derived from the popular *koşma* form, the Istanbul-based poet Azmi Güleç condemns the Soviet Union as an enemy "without a conscience" (vicdansız), detailing its abuses against the Crimean Tatars and other esir Türkler with an anaphora underscoring distant exile:

> Orda susturulmuş bütün ezanlar
> Orda boğdurulmuş dertli ozanlar
> Orda kurban olmuş kızlar, kızanlar
> İcimde bir büyük vatan ağlıyor.[41]

> (There [in the Soviet Union] the call to prayer is completely silenced
> There aggrieved poets are strangled
> There girls and boys become sacrifices
> And inside me the great homeland weeps.)

For poet Halil Abdülhakim Kırımman this internalization of suffering is a simulated journey of solidarity. In "Kırımlı Sürgünler" (Crimean exiles), published in *Emel* in 1969, he chronicles the deportation in detail, speaking initially from the first-person perspective of the Crimean Tatar victims:

> Bindokuzyüz kırkdört, bir sabah namazı
> İslamlar el açıp ederken niyazı
> Köyümüzde esti bir felaket rüzgarı.
> Her evden çıktı feryat, figan avazı.
> . . . .
> Azaba dayanamıyan hasta ihtiyar
> Öldüler, kaç yüzü de etti intihar.
> . . . .
> Bilemedik, aceb ne idi suçumuz
> Haykırıp, duyurmaya yetmez gücümüz.[42]

> (1944, during morning prayer
> As Muslims held out hands in supplication,

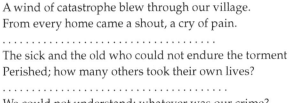

A wind of catastrophe blew through our village.
From every home came a shout, a cry of pain.
. . . .
The sick and the old who could not endure the torment
Perished; how many others took their own lives?
. . . .
We could not understand: whatever was our crime?
We have the strength neither to speak nor to scream.)

In "Kırımlı Sürgünler," these Crimean Tatar victims "search for joy" in the faintest of smiles; far removed from society, they "hang on every word of even the smallest news." They also search "in this deaf-blind world" for a bard (*ozan*) to represent "destitute Crimea and its people" and to render their experiences in poetry. Kırımman's lyrical persona, no longer speaking from the first-person perspective of the Crimean Tatar exiles, reveals himself as the poet for whom they are searching. "Halil Kırımman wrote you this *destan* [epic]," he explains:

Ben ozanım, ne sazım var, ne rübabım.
Bağrımı döğen yumruğumdur mızrabım.
Izdırabınız bana etti intikal,
Ben de sizler kadar perişan, harabım.[43]

(I am the bard, but I have no lyre, no instrument,
Only a fist pounding against my breast.
I have embraced your agony,
I suffer as much as you.)

Solidarity *unfolds* in Kırımman's "Kırımlı Sürgünler," emerging as the consequence of "hearing of the suffering of the Crimean people." The poem informs readers of the tragic details of Stalin's Crimean atrocity and, like Elçin's "Bahçesaray Çeşmesi" and the poems of chapters 4 and 5, visualizes its vulnerable victims, even assuming their voices. In pan-Turkist journals like *Emel*, such verse was actively solicited and regularly printed over the course of the twentieth century for its poetics of solidarity. It could not only sanctify ideology with sonic allusions to the prayerful and the mystical; it could also envelop documentary discourse in an air of anticipated future action.

The circle of readers of this poetry was not insignificant. *Emel* for one enjoyed a circulation in the thousands throughout the twentieth century. But in the 1970s, as the Crimean Tatar movement and its most visible leader, Mustafa Dzhemilev, garnered global attention, even the editors of *Emel* understood the need to reach larger audiences that were well beyond those attracted to cultural journals with scholarly aspirations. To help rally not thousands but millions in Turkey in response to Stalin's Crimean atrocity, the editors of *Emel* enthusiastically promoted the novels of one man: Cengiz Dağcı (1919–2011).[44]

2.

Happenstance first introduced the name Cengiz Dağcı to Mustafa Dzhemilev. At the Lenin Library in Moscow, Dzhemilev stole a look into the *spetskhran*, the "special holdings" department for sensitive material accessible only to party members with KGB clearance. (The network of these *spetskhrani* has been dubbed the "book Gulag."[45]) He remembers spying a file inside marked with the name "Cengiz Dağcı-Suvarsky" (Suvarsky was an early pseudonym) as well as a book title rendered in both Turkish and Russian: *Onlar da İnsandı, Oni tozhe byli liudmi* (They were people too).[46] When he returned to Uzbekistan, Dzhemilev raised Dağcı's name to Eşref Şemi-Zade, who was soon to leave for Kharkiv, where he would meet Chichibabin for the first time. Şemi-Zade had much to say. Not only did he reveal that he had known Dağcı personally before the war, but he also told Dzhemilev that he had engineered a way into the *spetskhran* to read Dağcı's quarantined book – by pretending to consult it in order "to counteract Western propaganda." With a KGB officer looking over his shoulder, Şemi-Zade perused the pages of *Onlar da İnsandı*. He was permitted only to take occasional notes about its "anti-Soviet" content, which Dzhemilev would later share in Crimean Tatar samizdat for years to come.[47]

This content made Dağcı one of the biggest names in Turkish popular fiction of the mid- to late-twentieth century. He remains a fixture of Turkish secondary-school curricula whose prolific output regularly enjoys new print runs in Turkey today. He helped install the Crimean Tatars as a major concern of Turkish culture, offering a blueprint for writers like Hasan Nail Canat, whose popular play *Moskof Sehpası* (The gallows of Moscow, 1968) cast the Stalinist persecution of the Crimean Tatars as a perfect storm of Soviet corruption, Islamophobia, and hypocrisy. In the 1950s, footballers on the Turkish national team read Dağcı's books in training camp; in the 1970s, newspapers advertised his novels alongside works by Flaubert, Hemingway, Dostoevsky, and Homer.[48]

Dağcı's sustained popularity, especially since the 1980s, is all the more remarkable for this fact: he never stepped foot in the Republic of Turkey. He was born in the long shadow of Aiu-Dag in the Crimean Tatar village of Kızıltaş, today's Krasnokamenka; he died not far from leafy

Wimbledon Common in London. Dağcı's life journey between Crimea and Great Britain – marked by an experience fighting on both sides of the Eastern Front, first in the Red Army and then in the Wehrmacht as part of the Turkestan Legion[49] – was fodder for eighteen Turkish-language novels, especially his two sets of twin semi-autobiographical sagas: *Korkunç Yıllar* (The terrible years, 1956) and *Yurdunu Kaybeden Adam* (The man who lost his home, 1957), which focus on the events of the Second World War; and *Onlar da İnsandı* (They were people too, 1958) and *O Topraklar Bizimdi* (That land was ours, 1966), which address more broadly the Soviet dispossession of the Crimean Tatars in the first half of the twentieth century.

Dağcı's sustained popularity – which led to a 2014 cinematic production of *Korkunç Yıllar*, distributed by Warner Bros. and entitled *Kırımlı* (The Crimean, directed by Burak Cem Arliel) – can be attributed to one key factor beyond his dynamic storytelling: his novels offer Turkish readers an ample store of prosthetic memories. Alison Landsberg develops the concept of prosthetic memories to account for artificial memories, often traumatic, that are consumed through media representations but *felt* as though they have been truly lived. This artificiality is not to be taken as superficiality. As Landsberg argues, prosthetic memories can exercise force, especially in the realm of prosocial political action: "two elements of prosthetic memory are particularly relevant: their indebtedness to commodification and mass culture on the one hand, and on the other, *their unique ability to generate empathy, a crucial step in the formation of political alliances and solidarities.*"[50]

In his most popular novels Dağcı facilitates such empathic solidarity by availing the Turkish reader of intimate access to two intersecting realms of traumatic memory. The first is the Second World War, which Turkey avoided by declaring neutrality. As Talat Halman notes, "Turkey miraculously escaped entry into World War II; consequently, Turkish authors did not experience the violence and devastation of that cataclysmic event, [except the] notably talented […] Cengiz Dağcı, who has written gripping novels and stories of war's brutality."[51] Dağcı's war-time sagas throw the Turkish reader into the chaos of the Second World War and position him as a unique stakeholder. As the journal *Emel* noted, "through Dağcı's pen, [Turkish] readers become one of the heroes of his novels."[52] These heroes are "Turks" who happen to be Crimean Tatars. "I am a Tatar," one of his protagonists declares, "a Turk, a Turk."[53] The prosthetic memories offered by these "Turks" are neither those of the victor nor those of the vanquished; they are the memories of the universal victim. Dağcı's novels confront the war by turning the condition of neutrality on its head. Instead of taking no side in the war,

Dağcı's heroes in *Korkunç Yıllar* and *Yurdunu Kaybeden Adam* take both sides. Instead of suffering at the hands of one totalitarian enemy, they suffer at the hands of two. They are tortured by both Stalinism and Nazism and enlisted to fight for Moscow and for Berlin in turn. Forced through borders and across fronts, in and out of enemy uniforms, they are consumed by only one abiding desire: vatan, Crimea.

The second realm of traumatic memory encompasses the Second World War but extends well beyond it. It is the past of a disposses-sion of territory and identity, of place and personality, at the hands of a Communist enemy. Dağcı once remarked that he felt Crimea like "an amputated arm,"[54] and in his prose he fashions this limb as a prosthesis for the Turkish reader, affixing the brutal past of a victimized group to the present of Turkish nationalist conservatism. "Thousands [in Tur-key] have come to know Crimea through him," writes Zafer Karatay.[55] This is a peculiar kind of knowledge, more universal than local, more symbolic than specific. With a persistent tone of melancholy and dread, his most prominent novels depict Crimea as a stage for an admoni-tory morality play comprising two acts. The first presents the assault on Tatar personality as an ontological war waged by Stalin's regime. In *Korkunc Yillar* the central protagonist Sadık Turan recalls his father's warnings about Soviet power during collectivization: "'They are afraid of us, Sadık! They are afraid of our very existence.' How right he was! [...] They want to Russify us shamelessly."[56] Sadık's lessons in the pre-war Soviet classroom are little more than attempts at organized mind control: "They want to get into our minds and occupy all our thoughts" (Bütün düşüncelerimizin sahibi olmak ister).[57] As a young boy he is scarred by Stalinist efforts to eviscerate his culture and religion. The demolition of the minaret of the town mosque is for him a destruc-tion of childhood innocence: "The minaret was demolished, and with it, something inside of me died as well."[58]

The second act of this morality play features Stalinist authorities violating the sacrality of Crimean place and violently transforming its physical landscape. For the Crimean Tatars of Kızıltaş, "there was no power that would part them from the land," remarks the narrator in *Onlar da İnsandı*, which has been listed among the Turkish Ministry of Education's top-one-hundred recommended books, alongside works by Atatürk, Cervantes, Dickens, and Faulkner.[59] "They would live on this land, the home of their ancestors for thousands of years; they would bury their tired, worn bodies in its soil, and only then would they surrender their souls to the sky, to the peace and silent repose of the sky."[60] The establishment of Soviet collective farms is therefore nothing less than a nightmare. Trucks and tractors encroach Kızıltaş like a "monster" (canavar), "uprooting hundreds of years of oak, pine, and cypress trees" and "sweeping away heavenly vineyards [...] and gutting the soil tilled by the dry, chapped hands of our ancestors."[61]

Dağcı's vivid portrayal of a Soviet assault on Crimean place and Tatar personality intersected with a pan-Turkist movement that was more assertive in the post-war world, particularly in its critique of left-ist intellectuals in Turkey. In June 1969, for instance, the Turkish daily newspaper *Milliyet* published an article entitled "Kırım Türkleri ile Niye İlgilenmiyoruz?" (Why are we indifferent to the Crimean Turks?), complaining that "[o]ur intellectuals, who follow closely the troubles of the Vietnamese and of black Americans [*Amerikan siyahları*], are to a surprising degree indifferent to the plight of the Crimean Turks. Only one or two touch upon the 'Tatar' situation ['*Tatarların' durumu*] with any interest in newspapers. By contrast, foreign outlets have published very compelling pieces about Soviet Russia's act of genocide against our Crimean countrymen [*Kırımlı soydaşlarımıza*] during the Second World War."[62] Turkish monthlies also joined in this chorus: "It is not championing liberty when our so-called intellectuals cry 'Vietnam-Vietnam' but *do not say a word* about the 100 million Muslim Turks who have fallen into Russian captivity [...] It is the duty of humanity, beyond the bonds of blood or religion, to support the righteous cause of the Crimean Turks by all possible means."[63]

Such opinion pieces seek to shame intellectuals – "so-called intellec-tuals," in their phrasing – for their indifference and silence in the face of the dispossession of the Crimean Turks. They cast these faults as a failure of recognition that amounts to a betrayal of one's own people. Dağcı's novels, meanwhile, have little interest in shame. They invite readers to process *guilt* over this presumed betrayal, by visualizing for the reader noble victims at their most vulnerable and modelling a com-missive language of confession that gestures to the possibility of pro-social action. Dağcı's deft manipulation of affect led Ahmet Tanpınar's protégé Mehmet Kaplan, director of the Turkish Studies Center in Istan-bul, to declare: "I am convinced that the power of art takes precedence today [...] Works of art inspire people by appealing to emotions. For these reasons I have great appreciation for Cengiz Dağcı."[64]

Characterization is Dağcı's most consistent source of such appeals to emotion. His heroes are consistently marked by a vulnerability that invites the reader's protective concern. Even those who wage war for the enemy or sacrifice themselves in brave, valiant gestures are rou-tinely portrayed as meek and sensitive at their core. Sadık Turan, the controversial semi-autobiographical protagonist of *Korkunç Yıllar* who joins the Turkestan Legion of the Wehrmacht after fighting in the Red

Army and languishing in a Nazi prisoner-of-war camp, appears early in the novel as a tender, devout child in an extended flashback. Here he recounts a memory of racing from school to his mother after witnessing the assault on his local mosque:

> Sınıftan nasıl çıkacağımı bilmiyorum, merdivenleri nasıl indiğimi hatırlamıyorum. En çok hatırlıyorım, şehrin sokaklarında, alnımdan, yanaklarımdan terler aka aka koşmamdır. Evimize girer girmez annemin ayaklarına sarıldım. Annem, zavallı annem, ne olduğunu bilmiyordu. Durmadan gözlerimden öperek:
> – Söyle yavrum, söyle, deye ağlıyordu.
> Ben hiçbir şey söyliyemiyordum, ağlıyamıyordum bile.[65]

(I don't know how I got out of class, I don't remember how I got down the stairs. All I remember was sprinting down the city streets, sweat pouring from my cheeks and my forehead. As soon as I entered the house, I threw my arms around my mother's legs. My mother, my poor mother, didn't know what had happened. Kissing my eyelids gently, she said through tears: "Tell me, darling, tell me." I couldn't say anything. I couldn't even cry.)

For the character of Sadık Turan, this is a flash-bulb memory, a vivid and emotionally resonant moment that lingers in his mind like photopsia in the eye. For the reader the passage has a flash-bulb effect as well: this poignant image of a boy at his gentle mother's feet, burdened with traumatic knowledge that he is unable to share with her, reverberates through the novel to inflect and soften the perception of his subsequent actions as an adult combatant in wartime. This originary vulnerability enlists the sympathetic reader to his side.

Children also take centre stage elsewhere in Dağcı's corpus, especially as first-person narrators who navigate with a mixture of whimsy and confusion a Crimea that has been overcome by death and despair.[66] The collision of cruel violence and childhood innocence unsettles the reader. "My friends, my kin, my loved ones have deserted me," a young boy named Haluk asks. "What will I say if the green uniforms [yeşil üniformalılar] come and find me?"[67] Women and the elderly also feature prominently among Dağcı's dramatis personae, with characters making dark, chilling reference to "the fate of women […] whose babies are lanced by enemy bayonets! The fate of old men dragged by their white beards!"[68]

One of these old men is the hard-working Bekir in *Onlar da İnsandı* (1958), who manifests such a love for Crimean place that he speaks to it. As he plants tobacco leaves, Bekir kisses the soil. He tells Selim, a fellow villager who reappears as the central protagonist in *Bu Toprak-lar Bizimdi*, that "I love my home, this land [...] I love everyone and everything, every place and every person on this land."[69] He and his wife, Esma, till the soil while singing *türkü* folk songs, acting as faithful stewards of the culture of their ancestors. Yet Bekir's warmth, hospitality, and open-heartedness are turned against him, as "Ruslar" (Russians) gradually overwhelm Crimea in the run-up to collectivization. The encroaching Russian-Bolshevik threat – Russians and Bolsheviks are conflated in Dağcı's prose – is personified in the treacherous Ivan, whom Bekir hires out of pity to help work the land and, despite warnings from neighbours, welcomes into his home. "They are people too," Bekir says, in a gesture to the novel's title.[70] Ivan proceeds to lead a reign of terror in the village and to assault Bekir's daughter, Ayşe, who gives up her young son, Alim, to Selim out of concern for his safety. She expresses the wish that Alim grow into another Alim Aidamak, the Crimean Tatar Robin Hood whom we see as a hero of Soviet film in chapter 3. At the climax of the novel, Bekir dies defending the land, martyring himself as it is ravaged by dynamite: "Even if the entire Russian army comes, runs me over, breaks my bones, and shatters my body and my mind into pieces, I will not leave my land!"[71]

In a didactic gesture amid the novel's last pages, Dağcı's own voice enters to address the reader and discuss his hero's motivations. "When he first saw Ivan," he says, "Bekir did not flee from him or drive him off his land. He said, 'Whoever he is, whatever his appearance, he is a person.' I halted for hours on Bekir's words and repeatedly thought to myself, 'Who knows, maybe Bekir is right.'" But something interrupts Dağcı as he tries to come to terms with his own story. "At this moment there is a magazine on my desk, a Russian magazine [...] My eyes spy a picture on one of its pages, and I see clearly: [my hometown] Kızıltaş."[72] Accompanying the picture in the magazine is the text of Petr Pavlenko's "Rassvet," the short story examined in chapter 3 about Ukrainians and Russians claiming Crimean Tatar property as if it were manna from the sky. Dağcı translates the entire story into Turkish, giving an unaware Pavlenko an audience of millions in Turkey. Working through rage, his eyes darkening, Dağcı then resolves to pray. "Pavlenko has the right to be happy, to be delighted in the dawn, to gaze at the warm sun rising into sky beyond Aiu-Dag [...] Why not write about it? Isn't he a person too? [...] My God, they are people too. Pity them. Make them believe that others, just like them, are people too. Others, who were driven out of Crimea like animals. They were people too."[73]

Dağcı's prayer of empathic understanding, even forgiveness, offers the reader yet another exemplar of quiet, noble vulnerability. It is a voice to admire and emulate. For a Turkish reader silent or indifferent to the plight of the Crimean Tatars, it can also be a voice through which to process guilt. In the sequel, *O Topraklar Bizimdi* (1966), set in the fateful period of 1941–4, Dağcı enriches this guilt-processing by modelling for his readers an act of redemption as well as a rhetoric of confession. The novel's protagonist is Selim, who leaves Kızıltaş at the end of *Onlar da İnsandı* and comes to terms with Soviet power. In suffering from false consciousness and self-alienation, he resembles Roman Ivanychuk's own Selim in *Malvy* (introduced in chapter 5), a character who first clashes with his people, only to realize his transgressions, confront his guilt, and redeem himself by the end of the novel. Yet unlike Ivanychuk's Selim, who has no memory of his Crimean Tatar origins, Dağcı's duplicitous Selim is fully aware of his background. He simply chooses to sacrifice it on the altar of Communist ideology.

For most of *O Topraklar Bizimdi*, Selim is indifferent to the suffering of his fellow Crimean Tatars. He is a man so seduced by authority and status that he becomes split in two, between a "human" and "genuine" Selim and a "demonic spirit" (şeytanca bir ruhu) known by the Russified version of his surname, Çilingirov.[74] "Sometimes Çilingirov wanted to take Selim in his hands and strangle him," observes the narrator, while at other times "Selim wanted to crush Çilingirov's head with the heel of his boot."[75] As head of a collective farm in the village of Çukurca near Simferopol, Dağcı's Selim "cannot part" from his despotic alter ego. Instead he succumbs to it and systematically dismantles Crimean Tatar culture and society to satisfy Stalin's five-year plan. His friend Hasan tries to break the hold of Soviet ideology on Selim, demanding with sarcastic taunts that he face up to his behaviour: "Don't be a coward! Don't say, 'I'm doing this all for the people' […] Tell the truth! Say clearly, 'I am working with my enemies to decimate my own people!'"[76] His voice trembling, Hasan tells Selim that his actions are an assault on the bond between Crimean place and Tatar personality, using the metaphor of the nation as a tree planted in the soil: "You are not pruning the tree, Selim. You are ripping it out of the ground, cutting it from its roots. You don't see it. Don't you understand? This tree has grown in this soil for thousands of years […] and you are cutting it to pieces! Don't you see it, Selim?"[77]

In these desperate questions Hasan implies that Selim's betrayal is a failure to understand, to recognize, to see. War brings him clarity. Selim loses his arm as a soldier in the Red Army. While convalescing in Novorossiisk, he learns of the violent persecution of Crimean Tatars at the hands of the NKVD in Çukurca. The scales begin to fall from his eyes. He becomes a penitent man, returning to Crimea on a quest to find Alim, the son Ayşe had entrusted to him in *O Topraklar Bizimdi*. Along the way he confesses his sins: "I forgot myself. I turned my back on my own home, my own people; I was contemptuous of my kin. I became a traitor to my own people. I spurned their very existence, blood of my blood, bone of my bone."[78] In a sense Dağcı offers a script for the Turkish reader who had been previously indifferent to the plight of the Crimean Tatars, a rhetoric of confession that acknowledges guilt while offering resurrection as a fearless hero. At the end of the novel, against all odds, Selim finds young Alim amid the post-deportation landscape of Crimea. Alim wants to run for safety to the mountains, but Selim pledges to return with him to Çukurca, where they may be killed. "Do not be afraid," Selim tells Alim. "Sometimes dying is better than living."[79]

3.

Dağcı's novels of Crimean Tatars in the vice between Stalinism and Nazism – novels that offered readers prosthetic memories and invited guilt-processing – were so popular that they spawned a host of pulp-fiction imitations. One was a purported "memoir" of a Crimean Tatar spy who wreaked havoc in a war-torn Soviet Union, entitled *Kırım Kurbanları* (Crimean sacrifices, 1969) by Mehmet Pişkin and Mehmet Coşar. What makes this work particularly notable was its active promotion by the Turkish Armed Forces. In March 1969, Major-General Hayri Yalçıner, who would later become a member of the so-called 9 March junta associated with the 1971 military coup, declared *Kırım Kurbanları* "useful" (yayarlı) and recommended it to the Gendarmerie General Command in his capacity as head of the military's Education Department.[80]

In October 1969 the novel made its way to the gendarmerie, where Major-General Zeki Erbay announced that "it is clear from committee reports [...] that the book *Kırım Kurbanları* is useful for our units."[81] Erbay assigned a preferential price of six lira to the work, which sold well enough to appear in three editions (1969, 1972, and 1976). The back cover of the third edition bears this quatrain:

Minareler ezansiz
Camiler bomboş
Yurtlarından sürulenler
Kim bilir şimdi nerde?

(Silent minarets
Deserted mosques
A people driven from their homes
Who knows where they are now?)

Why did the Turkish military consider *Kırım Kurbanları* useful? In the late 1960s, after a period of rapprochement with the Soviet Union, the Republic of Turkey became troubled by an increased Soviet naval presence in the Mediterranean and by a domestic leftist movement that was taking to the streets in growing numbers.[82] The military appeared especially concerned about this leftist ascendency and, upon taking power in 1971, immediately outlawed the socialist Turkish Workers' Party, which was sympathetic to Soviet ideological positions. The strong anti-Communist tenor of *Kırım Kurbanları* provided something of a propitious response to the advance of the Turkish left. The authors Pişkin and Coşar proclaim in their preface that "as long as the Communist world is not confined to its own borders, the rest of the free world will never know peace." They make explicit the intended instrumental nature of their work, exhorting the reader "to make this realization [about the evils of Soviet Communism] and *to work accordingly [buna göre çalışmalıdır]*."[83]

Pişkin and Coşar contextualize the anti-Soviet message of *Kırım Kurbanları* with little of Dağcı's complexity. They see a perpetual struggle of Turkish good versus Russian evil, citing the "Muscovite infidel's hostility to Turks" from time immemorial. In twentieth-century Crimea this hostility manifests itself as a betrayal of the political aspirations of Crimean Turks after 1917 and as a "cowardly rape" of the people through the Stalinist purges, deportation, and exile.[84] As one character declares, "the Crimean Turks endured the most pain during Stalin's reign."[85] Despite the singularity of this experience, the Crimean Turks are meant to stand for all esir Türkler, who collectively have fewer rights than "cannibals in Africa" (Afrika'da yamyamlar), as the authors argue with racist overtones in the preface.[86] Once again, this attention to an in-group victim who suffers subhuman treatment at the hands of the foreign enemy is meant as a reposte to pro-Communist and anti-American Turkish leftist groups protesting the war in Vietnam: "We hope that some of the breath being expended on Vietnam [...] will be directed toward the captive Turks after this book is read."[87]

Like Dağcı's prose, the novel is also designed to be entertaining in a way that the often sermonizing poems of the journals *Emel*, *Toprak*, and *Türk Birliği* are not. *Kırım Kurbanları* is a work for young male soldiers, a tale of espionage, sabotage, double agents, and beautiful Russian defectors to the Turkish cause.[88] Its hero and narrator is Ahmet Hamdi, a "Crimean Turk" from Sudak who becomes a Communist in the 1920s, during the Crimean "Golden Age" presided over by the popular local administration of Veli İbraimov. After İbraimov's execution Ahmet joins the "Crimean Turk" anti-Soviet underground, determined not to become "a servant to the Russians" (Rus uşağı). He infiltrates the NKVD and "begins an adventure" which leads to an assignment at a bomb factory in an unnamed city. Ironically his NKVD superiors want him to "follow and study" anyone he may find "with a bad intention – like committing sabotage."[89] The mole becomes the mole-hunter. After numerous fits and starts that build narrative suspense, he and a team of conspirators succeed in blowing up the bomb factory. Along the way Ahmet kills a number of "cowards" and "dogs" and dispatches "their foul souls to hell" (pis ruhlarını cehenneme).

For authors Pişkin and Coşar, Ahmet is not a Crimean Tatar; he is simply a Turk from Crimea who frequently and enthusiastically attests to his Turkish identity throughout the novel.[90] He represents one of the scattered children, the esir Türkler, separated from the bosom of the mother: "Turkey is the motherland [anayurdu] of all the world's Turks, isn't it?"[91] The novel's narrative works to resolve this separation and division, albeit not by envisioning a defeat of the Soviet Union that would lead to an establishment of a pan-Turkist state from Anatolia to Central Asia. These overtly irredentist designs are put aside in Kırım Kurbanları. Instead, Ahmet ends up only escaping to Anatolia, a "captive Turk" in captivity no longer.

In addition to being an exuberantly anti-Communist, pro-Turkish dime novel, Kırım Kurbanları also offers a revisionist historical account of the Second World War and its aftermath for the Turkish reader. In one of the novel's more striking moments Pişkin and Coşar give us a member of the Soviet elite – a boss at the bomb factory, no less – who knows before the war of Stalin's plan to deport the entire Crimean Tatar population. He confesses to Ahmet, who is still under his NKVD cover: "They will deport all of you from Crimea to Central Asia at the first opportunity, using any reason or pretext to do so."[92] The scene invites the reader to conclude that collaboration with German occupiers, who are treated with kid gloves in Kırım Kurbanları, amounted to a practical necessity.

Issues of content and characterization aside, the utility of Kırım Kurbanları resides to a significant degree in its exploitation of a seam between the genres of the first-person novel and autobiography to allow the reader to experience the world of Ahmet's "I" and to persuade him of its verisimilitude. In the foreword Pişkin and Coşar claim that *Kırım Kurbanları* is "not a novel, but a hair-raising account of a life lived."[93] This is a convenient conceit, fiction forswearing its fictionality. Verifiable extradiegetic biographical information about Ahmet Hamdi is not presented to the reader, nor is the relationship of the protagonist to the authors explained. The novel's flat narrative style – devoid, for instance, of Dağcı's swift pacing and descriptive colour or the allusory and allegorical flourishes of Hüseyin Nihal Atsız's pseudo-autobiographical *Ruh Adam* (The man of the soul, 1977) – manifests little of what Michał Głowiński calls "formal mimetics," the imitation of a particular style or form of discourse.[94] Ahmet's "I" speaks with no phonic, syntactic, or dialectical individuality. *Kırım Kurbanları* is a third-person novel poorly dressed in first-person costume.

The reasons for such literary accoutrement are clear. This narrative first-personalization invites the reader to stage himself as an esir Türk and to view the world from his perspective. The novel's autobiographical pretence, meanwhile, seeks to persuade the reader of the verifiability of the world invoked in its pages – a world in which factory functionaries have pre-war intelligence of the 1944 deportation. For the young male soldier in training, *Kırım Kurbanları* offers what purports to be both a primer in anti-Communist ideology based on empirical, "lived" reality and a passage to an experience of the self as hero – and victim.

For the inculcation and promulgation of ultra-nationalist politics, this last point is crucial. Ultra-nationalism, after all, "needs its victims."[95] When Ahmet returns to Crimea after sabotaging the bomb factory and enduring his five-year term in Solovki, he is reunited with his distraught mother and enquires after the rest of his family. In a reversal of Dağcı's scene from *Korkunç Yıllar*, in which young Sadık runs to his mother, Ahmet's mother is the one burdened with traumatic knowledge:

> Sorma yavrum, dedi annem; başımıza gelenleri sorma. Babanı, albanı, enişten, kardeşini beş yıl önce öldürdüler. Küçük kardeşin Osman'ı da alip götürdüler. Hala dönmedi yavrum. Sağ mı, ölü mü bilmiyorum. [...] Evimizi soyup sovana çevirdiler, tamtakır bıraktılar. Bağımızı, bahçemizi, tarlalarımızı da elimizden aldılar.

> ("Don't ask, my dear," my mother said. "Don't ask what befell us. They killed your father, sister, brother-in-law, and brother five years ago. They took your little brother Osman as well. He still hasn't returned, my dear. I don't know if he's alive or dead [...] They ransacked our house and left it completely empty. They took our vineyards, gardens, and fields right from our hands.")

Ultra-nationalism has the propensity "to create and perserve reservoirs of pain," and Pişkin and Coşar allow the reader to tap these reservoirs from a distance. The Crimean Tatars "captive" in the Soviet Union become proxy victims for Turkish soldiers (among other readers) who are safely ensconced within the borders of an independent, sovereign state. They offer proprietary access to national victimhood where it might be considered otherwise unavailable.

Pişkin and Coşar underscore Ahmet's assumption of responsibility for his family's suffering: "I brought this disaster upon my family. *Yes; I was guilty [Evet; suçlu ben idim]*. The bloodthirsty, cruel, pitiless enemy – out for me – took revenge upon my family instead."[96] *Kırım Kurbanları* frames Ahmet's actions, as well as the accepted consequences of those actions, as a *kurban* or sacrifice, a ritual generative of communal solidarity. "Common sacrifice is a sign of common interests, and an act which asserts and promotes them," notes the anthropologist Godfrey Lienhardt. "It represents a common life, and not only on an ideal or metaphorical plane, but in the day-to-day practical affairs of human cooperation."[97]

This solidarity becomes an objective of other pulp-fiction novels that are consumed by the problem of the dispossession of the Crimean Tatars, including *Kırım: Türk'ün dramı* (Crimea: The drama of a Turk), which appeared in serialized form in 1980 in Yozgat's *Sabah* newspaper. Written by a young author from Nevşehir named Ali Gündüz, *Kırım* swells with scenes of violence and sensationalized tragedy. At times the violence is so gratuitous that it prompts the narrator to address the reader with passionate hortatory, as at the novel's conclusion:

> Sovyet Rusya'nın bu insanlık dışı tutumunu birlikte protesto edelim. Kırım Türkleri bu acı işkencenin içindeyse [...] Yarın komünizm yumruğu seni de böyle ezecektir. Onun için uyanalım [...] Komünizme karşı omuz omuza duralım [...] Mücadele verelim.[98]

> (Let us join together in protest against Soviet Russia's inhumane attitude. If the Crimean Turks are enduring bitter torture today, the fist of Communism will crush you too in the same way tomorrow [...] So let us wake up [...] Let us stand shoulder to shoulder against Communism [...] Let us fight.)

Again the Crimean Tatars are presented as emblematic of "100 million captive Turks," a stirring symbol of Turkish victimhood. In the hands of writers like Gündüz, this symbolization tends to efface their individuality and their historical, cultural, and linguistic differences. Indeed, in *Kırım*, the tragedy of their deportation in 1944 is not a Tatar drama (Tatar dramasɪ), much less a Turkish or Turkic drama (Türk dramasɪ). It is, as the novel's subtitle insists, a drama of the Turk (Türk'ün dramɪ).

4.

In 1991 the man who helped inspire this school of Turkish pulp fiction about Stalin's Crimean atrocity received an unexpected invitation. The Soviet Union had not yet collapsed, but Cengiz Dağcı was in London, gripped by the drama of unfolding events, by an enduring dream becoming reality. Perestroika had quickened the Crimean Tatar movement, and its momentum had become unstoppable. Thousands of Crimean Tatars were finally returning to their ancestral homeland, and their leaders had sent Dağcı a letter.

What had sparked the dramatic return of the Crimean Tatars was, in part, the concerted intervention of writers and cultural figures in a barrage of appeals to the Presidium of the Supreme Soviet. Following a mass demonstration of Crimean Tatars in Red Square in the summer of 1987, writers like Yevgeny Yevtushenko and Anatoly Pristavkin had written to Soviet authorities and declared that "it was finally time to speak out loud" about the "unjust" deportation and dispossession of the Crimean Tatars.[99] Their advocacy was highlighted in a segment devoted to the "complex" Crimean Tatar problem on the news program *Vremia*. What had been solely the domain of samizdat was now material for Soviet broadcast television.[100]

Meanwhile, in Kyiv, Ukrainian national activists were demanding the organized, state-subsidized return of the Crimean Tatars to Crimea. At the founding congress (Ustanovyi z'izd) of the political party Narodnyi rukh Ukraïny (People's Movement of Ukraine) – a party populated by dissidents like Ivan Sokulsky and led by Viacheslav Chornovil and Mykhailo Horyn – the assembled made a series of proclamations from a dais at the Kyiv Polytechnical Institute in March 1989. Among them was this pledge: "Let us help our brothers, the Crimean Tatars [...] Let us help them revive their autonomy, their culture, their educational system, their sovereignty! Let us stop those Ukrainians or Russians without a conscience who repeat Stalin's and Beriia's lies about the Crimean Tatars [...] Long live the revival of our fraternal Crimean Tatar people!"[101]

The Kremlin could no longer ignore the writing on the wall. In November 1989 the Supreme Soviet of the USSR condemned the 1944 deportation as "barbaric" and finally announced the "unconditional restoration" of the rights of the Crimean Tatars, on the front pages of

Izvestiia and *Pravda*.[102] It was the dramatic culmination of decades of tireless work and sacrifice among Crimean Tatar activists and Soviet dissidents, galvanized by brewing political crises in the Soviet metropole under perestroika. Yet as we will see, there was a "cunning of recognition" behind this announcement, an unspoken conditionality that sacrificed a deeper restitution of the rights of the Crimean Tatars *in* Crimea in exchange for a public acknowledgment of their right to return *to* Crimea.[103]

Dağcı had been following these developments closely. The invitation from the Crimean Tatars that he held in his hands in 1991 was to Simferopol, where he was to participate as a guest of honour in a historic event billed as the successor to the first Qurultay led by Noman Çelebicihan in 1917. This invitation to the "second Qurultay," Dağcı remembers, was "an invitation like any other" – a simple piece of paper nestled inside two envelopes. "But for a moment, I held it in shock. I trembled." Would he accept it? He had waited for this moment for nearly fifty years. "You were born out of this tragedy," he told himself, "but you cannot remain trapped in it."[104]

Dağcı struggled with the decision. It was a lot to ask of himself at the age of seventy-two. He debated with himself late into the night: "Can you even make it up the stairs easily anymore? Don't you have to rest against walls when walking down the street?" His mind could go to Crimea, but his body was a different story. "If you go back," he told himself, "your heart will not stand it." As he lay in bed on the edge of sleep, Dağcı began to see his old haunts in Aqmescit (Simferopol), his mind's eye flooding with memories. "The streets are filled with people […] But they are not the people of Aqmescit; they are the people of Simferopol." He asked himself, "Do you really know them?"[105] Dağcı declined the invitation, and he would die without ever returning to the homeland that he remembered but no longer knew.

PART THREE

Repossession

Chapter Seven

Selective Affinities

After the collapse of the Soviet Union, Mustafa Dzhemilev finally had occasion to meet Boris Chichibabin and Liliia Karas-Chichibabina in person. Their encounter defied his expectations. The tall, slender Chichibabin had shyly approached Dzhemilev. "I am Chichibabin," he said, quietly. Dzhemilev was incredulous; Chichibabin's soft-spoken manner threw him. "It was amazing," he remembers, "because there were few Crimean Tatars who did not know of him." Dzhemilev shook his hand. "To us you are a legend," he told Chichibabin.[1]

To understand how a modest poet from eastern Ukraine became a legend to a dispossessed Sunni Muslim nation, we embarked in part 2 on a journey with two destinations. At the first destination we find compelling evidence of a faith in literature to change the world. We are conditioned to recoil at such cliché, but to speak otherwise is to misrepresent the clarity of purpose with which artists like Boris Chichibabin, Ivan Sokulsky, or Cengiz Dağcı approached their responses to Stalin's Crimean atrocity. It is also to misrepresent the clarity of purpose with which their readers endeavoured to compile, transcribe, and share these texts – often at risk of arrest and imprisonment. All of them sensed that imaginative literature could be not only artistically satisfying but also morally educative and politically effective in remedying what they saw as a grave injustice. In the Soviet Union a testament to this efficacy was the pre-emptive role of the literary aesthetic in confronting the deportation and its aftermath. Before journalistic reports, open letters, and other documentary texts began to inform Soviet samizdat readers about the fate of the Crimean Tatars, literary texts had already made a mark. Poetry in particular led the way.

This faith in literature was not misplaced. Stalin had condemned the Crimean Tatars to distant exile; literature helped keep them close. The reception of these texts among Crimean Tatar activists alone – who led the largest, most organized, and most sustained dissident movement in the Soviet Union – is demonstrable proof of literature's moral traction in the empirical world. Slipped into envelopes, concealed in notebooks, these texts travelled thousands of miles to a persecuted community who drew regular consolation and inspiration from them. They were read through tears alongside national hymns. In the end, these works of literature contributed to a movement that led to state reparations for a state crime.

In arriving at this first destination, we bump up against a number of the debates that have been occasioned by ethical criticism over recent decades, arguments over whether or to what extent literature can be said to make readers "better people." These debates can betray an Anglo-American centrism and a lack of historico-cultural contextualization that this book seeks to avoid. And at times these debates risk missing the point entirely. The issue is less that literary texts have some kind of ethical upper hand or an inside track to moral enrichment. It is that, when seeking to *invite* prosocial action, they do so by telling it slant. What fascinates us is their insistent rebellion. They run in a different direction from documentary, constative, propositional discourse. They choose circuitous, complicated routes to communciation, but in doing so, they can expedite understanding. As we have seen, no matter their point of origin – Kharkiv, Moscow, Dnipropetrovsk, Kyiv, Ankara, Istanbul – the texts in this study employ generic strategies and conventions (e.g., lyric address), figures of speech (metaphor), rhetorical devices (accismus), and figurative modes (allegory) that feed off textual gaps and discontinuities instead of papering over them. And for the most part, rather than engaging in banal or moralizing uplift, they seek to stimulate, model, and process feelings of guilt.

The second destination, meanwhile, offers a view of the abiding importance of the Crimean Tatars to the entire Black Sea region. For a small, displaced nation whose very mention could bring controversy, the investment of Russian, Ukrainian, and Turkish writers in their representation was steady during the height of the Cold War, in the 1960s, 1970s, and 1980s. This significance stems from their standing not only as an indigenous people of Crimea but also as a people through whom Ukrainians and Turks especially have engaged in collective self-reflection. For Ukrainian readers, Crimean Tatars were counterparts in processes of metaphorization that cultivated national identity, while for Turkish readers, the representation of the plight of the Crimean Tatars in the Second World War, for instance, served as a font of prosthetic memory of a formative event of twentieth-century world history. The Crimean Tatars have been, in other words, a constitutive presence in the Black Sea, a consequential region maker.

As we have seen, the literary texts in part 2 moved among diverse audiences in Moscow, Kharkiv, Kyiv, Istanbul, and Ankara, capturing the attention of readers and activists and helping contribute to the sea-change in Soviet policy that led to the repatriation of the Crimean Tatars after 1989. These itineraries through sites of political and cultural power were practical and strategic, but they mapped an orbit *around* Crimea. They did not permeate it. Archival searches and records of literary readings in cities like Simferopol, for instance, offer only faint traces of the presence of texts like Chichibabin's "Krymskie progulki" or Nekipelov's "Gurzuf." The poetry and prose at the centre of this study thus succeeded in advancing the cause of the Crimean Tatar return *to* Crimea, but appeared to have had less of a role before 1989 in prompting guilt-processing among readers *in* Crimea.

The event of the collapse of the Soviet Union, moreover, sent deep shock waves throughout the Black Sea region, reconfiguring bonds of attachment and structures of feeling. Crimea once again became a nodal point in a dense, unsettled web of shifting interrelationships. With the loss of the frame of Soviet identity, the civic we-denomination behind, say, Nekipelov's advocacy of the Crimean Tatars as "one of us" was suddenly less salient in places like Moscow. After 1991, Russian literature accordingly registers little concern for the fate of the Crimean Tatars, which becomes more of a consistent preoccupation in Ukrainian culture, as we will see. Guilt, meanwhile, recedes from this literary discourse. With only a few exceptions, it disappears along with the Soviet Union, the state bearing responsibility for the Sürgün and ensnaring citizens in a co-responsibility that Karl Jaspers terms political guilt. Moreover, the long-standing rhetorical focus on the Crimean Tatars' right of *return* (avdet, in Crimean Tatar; vozvrashenie, in Russian; povernennia, in Ukrainian) invited a widespread impression that the 1989 Presidium decree had finally satisfied their demands, that the wrongdoing had been addressed. But the Crimean Tatar return to Crimea marked a beginning as well as an end. Repatriating in waves from Central Asia, the Crimean Tatars had to embark on a new struggle and confront a structure of local injustice that, despite dramatically changing political fortunes, had not gone away.

After the dissolution of the Soviet Union, Crimea thus becomes widely understood as a land of three alienations. It is seen as home to returning Crimean Tatars who endure discrimination at the hands of local authorities; to ethnic Ukrainians who struggle to come to grips with their position as the titular group of a newly independent state; and to politically and culturally dominant ethnic Russians who express an insecure nationalism aligned less with Kyiv than with a collapsed imperium and its legal successor.[2] This symmetrical triadic conceptualization of Crimean society – a generalization that can flatten variations and subcategories and elide other national minorities (Belarusians, Armenians) and new emergent identities ("Crimeans") from the picture – has tended to predominate in analyses of the politics and society of post-Soviet Crimea. But it almost completely ignores the hierarchies and nested post-colonialisms that determine the interrelationships of all sides. In fact, it rarely makes reference to a colonial framework at all.[3]

This is a troubling silence. After 1991, like much of former Soviet territory, Crimea was a site of decolonization, a place of transition where the scaffolding of imperialism was being dismantled and remade with a view to the construction of a liberal democratic state. Much has been made of the term *empire* vis-à-vis the Soviet Union,[4] but the question of the wholesale application of such a complex and contested term is too often a distraction. What Crimea experienced especially after 1944 was a paradigmatic *project* of settler colonialism. Stalin ethnically cleansed an entire indigenous population from the peninsula – roughly 20 per cent of the population at the time – and presided over an erasure of their material and symbolic traces and a rewriting of their history. He then replaced this population with tens of thousands of Russians and Ukrainians who were transplanted from outside the peninsula: a program of ethnic cloning.

These Slavic settlers appear in Aleksei Adzhubei's memories of Crimea shortly after Stalin's death. Adzhubei was Khrushchev's son-in-law – and arguably the most prominent figure in Soviet journalism, who rose to the post of editor-in-chief of both *Komsomolskaya pravda* and *Izvestiia*. He recalls travelling to Crimea in 1953 with an anxious Khrushchev, who, not knowing how to swim, "dangled" in the Black Sea in an inflatable inner tube when he was not working.[5] Crimea at this time was a "desolate" region still struggling to emerge from the crucible of war. The fountain in the hansaray, Adzhubei notes, had "no strength even to cry."[6] Transferring Crimea to Ukraine in 1954 was therefore, according to Adzhubei, a "business transaction" (delovaia tekuchka) directed toward its economic development, a response to the decay and stagnation under Russian SFSR administration that Khrushchev had witnessed personally. At one point, Adzhubei remembers how desperate "settlers" confronted Khrushchev about the need for more material assistance. "The settlers for the most part came from Russia," writes Adzhubei, before making a critical clarification. "I write 'came from' now, but they shouted, 'We were sent here' [*nas prignali*]."[7] Unlike the North Caucasus, which saw Chechen and Ingush deportation survivors return in 1957, the settler colonialist project in Crimea was left to harden for nearly half a century, offering the light of myth of a Soviet "paradise" to a Slavic majority but obscuring clear view of its nature like translucent stone.

When the return of the Crimean Tatars began to upset this myth, Crimea became a paradox: a site of decolonization active in the reinscription of patterns of colonial dominance. On the one hand, there was state support for programs aiding the Crimean Tatars in their return. Struggling with poverty and hyperinflation, Kyiv allocated in the first decade of Ukrainian independence the equivalent of over USD 140 million from the state budget for Crimean Tatar resettlement, and Turkey pledged in 1994, for instance, to build one thousand new homes for Crimean Tatar returnees.[8] (By contrast, the legal successor of the Soviet state responsible for the original crime – Russia – paid nothing at all.) On the other hand, there was a rebirth of settler colonial practices on the peninsula that diminished such attempts at historical redress. Local elites consistently stymied efforts to secure proportionate political representation for the Crimean Tatar returnees, who endured inadequate housing, high unemployment, and police harassment. The fates of these families were determined, as Constantine Pleshakov puts it, "arbitrarily and meanly."[9] In 2007, after hundreds of Ukraine's Interior Ministry forces had been used to destroy Crimean Tatar cafés on Ai-Petri peak, President Viktor Yushchenko's Our Ukraine party openly accused Crimean authorities of a "discriminatory attitude toward repatriated Crimean Tatars" and a "selective application of the law."[10]

Chauvinistic rhetoric was not uncommon. In a widely publicized diatribe in the Russian nationalist newspaper *Krymskaia pravda*, Russian science fiction writer Natalia Astakhova mocked the Crimean Tatars for their activism, for their indigenous resistance: "Since their return, they have done nothing but protest – as if it were their national profession,[11] their very way of life – picking at wounds, inciting resentment and hatred, rocking the boat we are all in." She turns to address the Crimean Tatars directly, ridiculing them for their "greasy *cheburek*, sticky baklava, and stale kebabs": "Really, what has been taken from you? What did you leave behind? And what remains of you here: pitiful shacks? [...] The land, the sea, the wine, the mountains, the orchards, the vineyards, the cities, the villages – nothing escapes the web of your claims, everything is either ruined, plundered, or contaminated by the impurity of your thoughts. Only the sky remains. But then the cry of the muezzin penetrates it, blocking all the other sounds of a previously peaceful life."[12] Such taunting, Islamophobic screeds call to mind Albert Memmi's observation in *The Colonizer and the Colonized* that "the colonialist [...] devotes himself to a systematic devaluation of the colonized. He is fed up with his subject, who tortures his conscience and his life. He tries to dismiss him from his mind, to imagine the colony without the colonized."[13]

For Memmi, this aggressive attempt to erase the colonized native from view – to condemn him for his grievance and then "dismiss him from the mind" – is a function of a *system* indiscriminate in its corrosive effect. "Colonization distorts relationships, destroys or petrifies institutions, and corrupts [...] *both colonizers and colonized*."[14] Our prevailing reading of post-Soviet Crimean politics and society according to a regional interethnic paradigm consumed by a negotiation of interests – rather than according to a decolonization paradigm concerned with transitional justice and intergroup reconciliation – has neglected to account adequately for the structural echoes of the colonial system. More importantly, this conventional wisdom has impeded our ability to make historical parallels and learn from other cases of settler colonialism around the globe – from the United States to Australia – and to foreground the use of tested mechanisms of restorative policy: official apology, truth commissions, and electoral quotas. In other words, Ukraine never had a coherent strategy for Crimea, and a blindness to the history and legacy of settler colonialism is part of the reason. This blindness also prevented us from noting that in 2014 the Russian Federation became not only the first European country since the Second World World to annex another European country's territory by force, but also the first successor of a modern empire to take back a former colonial possession.

Crimea therefore has not had a "Crimean Tatar problem," as the unfortunate turn of phrase goes. It has had a festering post-colonial problem. Devoid of a conscious, structured approach to decolonization, politics in Crimea in the post-Soviet period was highly inconsistent and haphazard, an exercise in putting out fires through elite bargaining and "multi-vector" negotiation.[15] Kyiv juggled balls in an earthquake, developing state institutions amid severe economic crises across the country while contending with repeated threats of Crimea's secession between 1991 and 1995. Often Kyiv aligned with the Crimean Tatars, who were frequently referred to as "the greatest Ukrainians in Crimea."[16] Sometimes, as in 1998, when roughly eighty thousand Crimean Tatars were made ineligible to vote in parliamentary elections, Kyiv abandoned them in order to appease the dominant majority.

A silence on the matter of decolonization similarly overshadowed Crimea's post-Soviet cultural landscape. As a consequence, it became a forest of bilateralisms or, to mix metaphors, a room of two-legged stools. Ground-breaking Russian novels like Vasily Aksenov's *Ostrov Krym* (*The Island of Crimea*), published abroad in the 1980s but widely circulated in Crimea the 1990s, reimagined relations with the Crimean Tatars but effaced Ukrainians from view. A utopian project called "geopoetics," meanwhile, revelled in Russian and Ukrainian interliterary connections but rarely integrated Crimean Tatar writers into the process, taking the elevation of Crimean place over Tatar personality to new theoretical heights instead. Ukrainian and Crimean Tatar writers, for their part, engaged in a concerted search for a "practical past" and for resilient narratives of solidarity outside the chronological frame of empire. As we will see, this renewed Ukrainian–Crimean Tatar encounter is one of the most fascinating, and potentially transformative, cultural developments in the region of the Black Sea.

On the other shore, Turkish writers in the post-Soviet period saw not selective affinities on the peninsula but a disturbing stasis of alienation and oppression, with Crimean Turks caught in a perpetual loop of victimization. In the pulp-fiction novel *Kırım Kan Ağlıyor* (Crimea in agony, 1994), for instance, Crimean Tatar patients at a Simferopol hospital languish at the hands of NKVD "vampires," one of whom bears the moniker "The Executioner" (Cellat) owing to his thirst for blood.[17] Plot lines are recycled and stereotypes perpetuated in a never-ending Cold War. Indeed, for pan-Turkist poets like Yücel İpek, the dissolution of the Soviet Union brought nothing new to Crimea and the Crimean Tatars. "Russians have gone, Ukrainians have come," he writes in 1998, "but what has changed?" (Rus gitti, Ukraynalı geldi, değişen nedir?)[18]

1.

In the world of Vasily Aksenov's *Ostrov Krym* (*The Island of Crimea*), everything has changed. Originally published by Ardis publishing house in tamizdat in 1981, the novel was serialized in the journal *Yunost* (Youth) as the Soviet Union collapsed. It became a literary sensation in the 1990s, especially in Crimea itself, where it seemed that everyone had a well-worn copy. *Ostrov Krym* is a work of "allohistorical" fiction – an imaginative exercise in alternative history – which envisions the peninsula as an island and dramatizes the end of the engagement between the White Army and Red Army in 1920 as a kind of Jonbar hinge, marking a point where time moves along a new diachronic trajectory.[19] Secured and fortified by the White Army, Crimea breaks free from history to become a thriving capitalist and cosmopolitan Taiwan off the shore of a Communist giant. Aksenov's main protagonist, the hedonist and ultimately naive media magnate Andrei Luchnikov, seeks to join Crimea to the Soviet Union in a movement called the "Union of Common Fate." His success ends with a Soviet invasion – and with a loss of a grip on his own sanity.

Aksenov's Crimea, of course, is a place where Stalin's ethnic cleansing and discursive cleansing of the Crimean Tatars have not occurred. The Crimean Tatars populate the island alongside Russians, Italians, Bulgarians, Greeks, Turks, and even descendants from officers of the British navy. Crimean Tatar personality is very much alive in Aksenov's kaleidoscopic Crimean place: their language pushes Coca-Cola products on billboards, while their words pop up in a creole dialect unique to the island.[20] *Atats* – a portmanteau of *ata* (Crimean Tatar) and *otets* (Russian) – means "father," for example.[21] A television broadcaster shoots the breeze in Crimean Tatar alongside counterparts who use Russian and English, "interrupting each other with smiles."[22] The smell of Crimean Tatar food wafts through bazaars in Bakhchisarai and, notably, in "Karasubazar," which has not been ascribed the post-1944 toponym Belogorsk.[23] Even Soviet authorities hatching post-annexation plans refer to Crimean Tatars as Crimea's "indigenous people" (korennoe naselenie).[24] It is a surreal, heart-breaking fantasy.

When the fantasy turns to tragedy – as Crimean residents look on in horror as Soviet forces mount an aggressive invasion of a peninsula that is ready to welcome them without one – it is a Crimean Tatar character named Mustafa who gives the feckless Luchnikov his comeuppance toward the end of the novel. "To hell with the Russians," Mustafa shouts at him. "You are all bastards! I am a Tatar! [...] Know that I am not spitting in your face, only out of respect for your age. I respect in you nothing else."[25] Aksenov's counterfactual flight of fancy ends on a decidedly ominous note, in a "union" between Crimea and the Soviet mainland that spells a kind of spiritual doom. In 2014, Sergei Aksenov – the once marginal, ironically named Russian nationalist who manoeuvred to the centre of the Kremlin's annexation drama – clearly had not understood the book's conclusion when he boasted that he was trying to realize the "second part of the novel."[26]

Like Roman Ivanychuk (chapter 5) and Cengiz Dağcı (chapter 6), Vasily Aksenov (1932–2009) mines the past to reassert a bond between Crimean place and Tatar personality, but his allohistory makes a plaything out of our logic of cause and effect and even linear time itself. In this way it feels peculiarly present and alive, only slightly beyond our reach. With the collapse of the Soviet Union prompting a rethinking of the very concept of the end of history, the wild popularity of Aksenov's novel was therefore no accident. But a curious erasure also haunts the book. For all its linguistic eclecticism and carnivalesque displays of ethnic diversity, there are no Ukrainians in the novel at all. They are not included in its parade of national groups, nor are they among its dramatis personae. It is a curious exclusion. In Liudmila Ulitskaia's *Medeia i ee deti* (*Medea and Her Children*, 1996) – an intricate novel set in Crimea and alive to its rich, complex ethnic inheritance and to the tragic consequences of Stalin's Crimean atrocity – Ukrainian characters may also be out of sight, but they only seem off stage.[27] Ulitskaia peppers the margins of her family novel with signs of Ukrainian life: items of clothing are "Ukrainian"; summer homes are "cosy in a Ukrainian way"; the namesake of the popular Soviet Charcot water therapy is humorously mistaken for a Ukrainian ("Sharko").[28] But in *Ostov Krym*, the absence of Ukrainians is conspicuous and total, suggesting that the cosmopolitanism of Aksenov's alternate vision of the peninsula had its limits.[29]

In the 1990s, Aksenov was invited to become honorary president of an ambitious Bohemian collective called the Crimean Club. Led by avant-garde Dzhankoi-born Russian poet Igor Sid (a contraction of the Ukrainian surname Sidorenko), the Crimean Club professed an intention to depoliticize Crimea and turn it into nothing less than a "world cultural training ground," a nerve centre of cultural exchange and collaboration.[30] Its seemingly self-serious motto – axis aestheticus mundi Tauricum transit (the axis of art passes through Crimea) – is actually a manufactured Latin axiom passed off as wisdom from "Biberius Caldius Mero," a mocking nickname given to Emperor Tiberius Claudius Nero for his devotion to wine.[31] Sid (b. 1963) is a prodigious impresario, and soon Aksenov found himself participating in his literary happenings on the islet of Tuzla, which is suspended like a filament of sand amid the Strait of Kerch separating the Crimean peninsula from the Russian Federation.

With the Crimean Club, Sid sought to remake the peninsula in the form of Maksimilian Voloshin's home in Koktebel, as a waystation for artists and intellectuals of diverse modes and genres. He vigorously promoted Ukrainian-Russian literary socialization and interaction, translating, for instance, the work of Yuri Andrukhovych and Serhiy Zhadan. (Zhadan describes Sid as "a man of the nineteenth century, for whom there is no clear division between poetics and, say, botany."[32]) For over two decades Sid's Crimean Club hosted countless performances, installations, conferences, and readings in Moscow, Crimea, and even Madagascar. These events manifested a "certain insanity of discussion" and even proudly insisted that participants agree to one simple idea – namely, that Crimea was the centre of the world.[33]

Yet there is barely a whisper of a presence in this world of Crimean Tatar poets or prose stylists. For Crimea's most active and audacious international artistic initiative, Igor Sid's Crimean Club has placed relatively little emphasis on the culture of Crimea's indigenous peoples. Crimean Tatar writers feature almost nowhere in its program. A driving factor behind this absence is a notion called "geopoetics," which Sid prominently positions as a vague guiding principle. Geopoetics is, in his words, the "management of [...] a topographical-territorial myth" (upravlenie [...] landshaftno-territorialnim mifom).[34] Its conceptual opponent is geopolitics. "The age of politicians is over," proclaims literary scholar Mikhail Gasparov in one of Sid's emblematic epigraphs, "and in the place of geopolitics comes geopoetics."[35]

Geopoetics is the apogee of a process that we began to trace in the Russian literary tradition in chapter 1: the elevation of Crimean place over Tatar personality. It turns its back on the idea of territorial-based sovereignty, of a bond of a particular people to a particular space. It responds to imperial colonialism and to the claims of the colonized by overlooking them in the sway of utopian alternatives. "The Crimean version [of geopoetics]," writes Sid, "affirms the transition of humankind from the era of power ambitions to the era of creative ambitions."[36] But an era of creative ambitions can be poor refuge for those with little secure political power. Holding fast to the concept of an ancestral homeland was precisely what powered the Crimean Tatar movement in the Soviet Union and informed its campaign for a restitution of rights, land, and respect after the Soviet collapse. Abandoning geopolitics for projects like geopoetics, in other words, was a luxury they could not afford.

2.

Both Igor Sid and Serhiy Zhadan participated in a Kyiv roundtable discussion on the cultural dynamics of Crimea in May 2008. Zhadan (b. 1974) is one of the most fascinating phenomena of contemporary Ukrainian culture – a Ukrainian-language poet, novelist, and rock performer from eastern Ukraine who defies easy categorization. "When Sid told me about the idea of this roundtable," Zhadan said, "he asked me to suggest Ukrainian writers who write about Crimea." Zhadan explained that it was not a straightforward task. "Ukrainian writers, like the majority of the population of Ukraine, still consider Crimea not as a part of Ukraine but as a kind of tourist zone from which one comes and goes." The problem, he said, was "an unspokenness, an unwrittenness of Ukrainian literature" vis-à-vis Crimea (neozvuchenist, nepropysanist ukraïnskoï literatury). Zhadan concluded, "I do not know what to do with it."[37]

But Sid had an idea. Reflecting on Zhadan's remarks, he writes, "One of the central reasons why Crimea is often perceived as something alien [*nechto chuzherodnoe*] in the Ukrainian imaginary is the connection of the peninsula with Russian history and culture over two centuries."[38] Sid therefore counsels Ukrainian writers to generate more literary texts about Crimea and its inhabitants. "Writers build better bridges than politicians," he declares. It is sage advice. But unwittingly or not, Sid also presumes something about literary representations and their role in geopoetics: they are seen as agents of possession. To make Crimea one's own – not something alien – is to write about it. Two centuries of Russian poetry and prose about Crimea, he suggests, had the benefit of making it understandable to Russian readers as uniquely *theirs*.

While enlightening, the roundtable contributions by Zhadan and Sid also betray a "reverse hallucination," a failure to see what is there.[39] It is not only a failure to recognize a sustained tradition of Ukrainian writing about Crimea since the nineteenth century, as we have seen in chapters 2 and 5, or a failure to consider the question of Crimean Tatar literature alongside or within the Ukrainian tradition itself. It is also a blindness to Ukrainian writing *in* Crimea – poetry and prose by Ukrainians for whom Crimea is not a tourist zone but home. The community of artists who wrote from this perspective was a self-described "minority within a minority," but it was an active one.[40] Only a few years before the Kyiv roundtable, in fact, the Simferopol-based poet and translator Danylo Kononenko compiled a three-hundred-page anthology of works by contemporary Ukrainian writers in Crimea.[41] It was subsidized by the Ukrainian state; three thousand copies were printed. The texts in the compilation are largely averse to formal experimentation and preoccupied with the celebration of national tradition, but they nonetheless testify to committed activity on the part of a Ukrainian literary community in Crimea that is often counted out or overlooked, even by intellectual circles in Kyiv.

In 1992 Kononenko had challenged the passivity of his "Crimean brothers" and called on them to make the realization that "you are home" in the first issue of Crimea's Ukrainian-language newspaper, *Krymska svitlytsia*.[42] Assuming a full-throated Shevchenkian posture, he implores them: "Why do you shrink away as if there are none of you on this land?" His rallying cry helped spark creative expression that has been especially steadfast in its devotion to the cause of Ukrainian–Crimean Tatar solidarity. In "Povernennia" (The return), for example, Kononenko's lyrical persona wanders through makeshift Crimean Tatar settlements made up of "temporary shelters" (tymchasivky) and welcomes them back to the peninsula. "How much suffering, humiliation, and hardship must these people endure," he laments:

…Перетерплять все, перебідують,
Лиш би жити на землі батьків![43]

(They bear everything and suffer all over again,
Just to live in the land of their ancestors!)

Orest Korsovetsky, a veteran of the Second World War whose early work was recommended to the editor of the journal *Dnipro* by Maksym Rylsky, likens the Crimean Tatar return to a victory of truth and justice over lie and illusion:

Міражі розпливаються,
І йдуть татари, йдуть.
Верта-а-ються! Верта-а-ються!
Легка-хай-буде-пу-у-ть![44]

(The mirages are lifting,
And the Tatars are coming, they are coming at last.
"They are re-turn-ing! They are re-turn-ing!
May the journey be not burdensome!")

Such Ukrainian poetic expressions of solidarity with the Crimean Tatars were reciprocated. A striking example is "İqrarlıq" (Declaration), written by Samad Şukur in 1993:

Ukraina – qardaşım, soyum!
Sensiñ doğmuşım.
Eger maña rastkelgen
Duşman
Saña apansızdan
Intılsa,
Meni çağır,
Men sağım
. . . .
Seniñ serbest
Olmañ içün
Men ölümge de azırım![45]

(Ukraine – my brother, my kin!
I am your family.

If facing me
The enemy
Suddenly sets
Upon you,
Call on me,
I am by your side
. . . .
For your freedom
I am prepared to die.)

These works of literature were only a small part of a much broader cultural and academic campaign to fortify a post-Soviet Ukrainian–Crimean Tatar alliance. Translation projects proved an especially resilient mortar, with the team of Yunus Kandym and Mykola Miroshnychenko publishing a series of massive bilingual collections of Crimean Tatar poetry and prose. They helped build on practices of national metaphorization and deepen a solidary bond that has defied socio-cultural gravity, surmounting centuries of mutual stereotyping and historical antagonism. Even today, in some currents of Ukrainian cultural memory, stories of Crimean Tatars raiding Ukrainian homes for slaves in the sixteenth and seventeenth centuries have had lasting currency.[46] In some currents of Crimean Tatar cultural memory, meanwhile, stories of Ukrainians participating in the dismantling of the Crimean Tatar khanate in the eighteenth century and in the dispossession of Crimean Tatar families in the nineteenth and twentieth centuries have left a deep scar. Yet the modern Ukrainian–Crimean Tatar alliance has succeeded in overcoming such stories by excavating and promoting, inter alia, a "practical past" of solidarity in their stead.

Hayden White adapts Michael Oakeshott's concept of practical past to refer not to history ensconced in the archive but to history offering "guidelines for acting in the present and foreseeing the future."[47] For the project of post-Soviet Ukrainian–Crimean Tatar solidarity, this practical past is seen at first to exist entirely outside the Russian colonial frame, in the seventeenth century of alliance and co-operation between the khanate and the Zaporozhian Cossacks. This is the period of the poetry of Canmuhammed (chapter 3) and the period at the centre of the prose of Roman Ivanychuk in *Malvy* (chapter 5). It has become the subject of novels, films, and even comic books written by authors who see Ukrainians and Crimean Tatars as bound so tightly in metaphorical relation that even their national symbols – the trident and the tamğa – are noted for mirroring each other.[48]

After 1991 this Ukrainian–Crimean Tatar discourse of *encounter* also evolves into a discourse of *entanglement*, of hybridity, interpenetration, and even transfiguration. As we will see in the next chapter, it evolves further into a discourse of *enclosure* after the 2014 annexation. One of the agents of this entanglement is Şamıl Alâdin, whom we met in chapter 3. Alâdin adapts Canmuhammed's seventeenth-century poem about the Ukrainian–Crimean Tatar campaigns against Poland, into a novel entitled *Tuğay-Bey*, which he worked on until his death in 1996. Published posthumously in an incomplete form in 1999, the work stages a cultural and even spiritual intermingling of his Ukrainian and Crimean Tatar heroes.

Alâdin's *Tuğay-Bey* seeks to transport the reader to a period when a Ukrainian–Crimean Tatar alliance was actively changing the very map of Europe. Guided by a first-person narrator named Sahib, who identifies himself as an aide to Tuğay-Bey, the novel begins as a journey through a vibrant, diverse Crimean Tatar society under the Giray khans. Rendering snapshots of such diversity in prose was one of Alâdin's literary passions, evident in a companion historical novel entitled *İblisniñ ziyafetine davet* (The devil's invitation to the feast, 1979), which finds inspiration in the life of Üsein Şamil Toktargazy, whose work was featured in chapter 2. Alâdin's Toktargazy travels across Crimea against the backdrop of bustling markets and ivy-covered minarets, from the capital, Bağçasaray, to the cosmopolitan Qarasuvbazar (Karasuvbazar, so cosmopolitan that Ismail Gasprinsky called it "Karasu-Paris").[49] His itinerary plots the coordinates of a diverse, contested, but fully coherent Crimean Tatar society at the twilight of the Russian Empire.[50]

In *Tuğay-Bey* we encounter this robust society in the seventeenth century under threat from abroad. The novel's centrepiece, at least in its incomplete form, is an elaboration on Canmuhammed's depiction of the Ukrainian entreaty to Khan İslâm Giray for military assistance. In his version of the entreaty, Alâdin attends to the warm relationship between Khmelnytsky and the khan himself, who briefly focalizes the narrative and welcomes "Bogdan" [Bohdan] to this inner sanctum: "[The khan] had great respect for Bohdan's military command and mastery. After twenty-five minutes, [Khmelnytsky] entered the khan's sacred reception quarters, and İslâm Giray greeted him warmly. The hetman respectfully responded to him in the Turkish and Crimean Tatar languages [*türk ve tatar tillerinde cevap berdi*]."[51]

Alâdin casts such linguistic exchanges not only as evidence of mutual respect but also as testament to a deeper mutual intelligibility and intersection. Between the leaders of the Crimean Tatar and Ukrainian peoples, no translation is needed.[52] Here, for instance, is Khmelnytsky's direct plea to the khan for military aid:

İzzetli ve saadetli İslâm Girey han! Ukraina halqı Polonya esareti altında
iñlemekte. Adamlar pek ezildi […] aç, çıplaq qaldılar, — dedi tatar tilinde,
soñra ukraincege keçti. Han getmannı tercimesiz diñledi.[53]

("Venerable and blessed Khan İslâm Giray! The Ukrainian people are gro-
aning from the oppression of Poland. The people are crushed […] hungry,
naked," he said in the Tatar language, before moving into Ukrainian. The
khan listened to the hetman without translation.)

Here Alâdin echoes Canmuhammed's source text and frames the
Ukrainian *casus belli* as the self-defence of a "crushed," "hungry,"
"naked" victim against a foreign aggressor. He foregrounds a Crimean
Tatar khan and a Ukrainian hetman who understand fluently the language of the other. Their mutual comprehension extends beyond Realpolitik into the realm of speech and identity. In fact, at one pivotal
moment, it produces an almost spiritual confusion of their languages
and cultures. To underscore the purity of his intentions, Alâdin has
Khmelnytsky swear before the khan in the name of Allah *in the Ukrainian language* before kissing the Qur'an three times. From this moment,
a solidary bond between Ukrainians and Crimean Tatars is forged. "At
a time of such tense circumstances, Ukrainians and Crimeans Tatars
should be united [*qırımtatarları ve ukrainalılar birlik olmaq*]," remarks
Alâdin's narrator. "The two peoples […] should desire to be always at
the ready to help each other."[54]

This theme of cultural and spiritual intermingling is taken in novel
directions by the Ukrainian filmmaker Oles Sanin (b. 1972), whose
first feature film, *Mamai* (2003), counterposes the very foundations of
national identity with what Ernesto Laclau calls an "empty locus," "a
formation without foundation."[55] Laclau likens the empty locus to a
horizon, a field of possibility and potentiality that can orient forms of
human organization without binding them to the same points in space.
For Sanin, this empty locus is incarnate in the mysterious figure of the
Cossack Mamai.

Ubiquitous in Ukrainian art from the seventeenth to the nineteenth
century, the image of the Cossack Mamai is at once familiar and
strange. With a horse and sword by his side attesting to freedom and
martial prowess, he wears a *zhupan* (Cossack overcoat) and displays the
trademark *oseledets*, the long lock of hair on an otherwise shaved head
(figure 8).

Yet this is not Gogol's belligerent Taras Bulba, Kulish's Byronic
Kyrylo Tur, or one of Repin's rakish Zaporizhians. The Cossack Mamai
sits in the Turkish *bağdaş* (cross-legged) position, projecting a serenity

8. The Cossack Mamai (c. early nineteenth century, artist unknown)

like Buddha under the bodhi tree, and bears the name of a fourteenth-century khan of the Golden Horde. He strums a lute or a bandura in solitude, his eyes passive and capacious, a site of memory of an era somehow both distant and close at hand.[56]

For Sanin – who considers Sergei Paradzhanov, Yuri Illienko, and Leonid Osyka his artistic forebears – an image like the Cossack Mamai bears revelatory poetic potential when translated into film. *Mamai* is accordingly a feast for the eyes, a constellation of images rife with ethnographic detail in which the cinematic frame becomes a startlingly fresh and vivid still-life tableau: incandescent lovers shimmering in the moonlight, a woman's haunting eyes emerging from niqab, and men caked in a white dust scaling a pale cliff. Yet the privileging of these images and sequences – which are "more juxtaposed than connected"[57] – confuses an ambitious triadic narrative that, according to Sanin, is meant as an act of recovery of an oft-forgotten history of entanglement between the Ukrainian and Crimean Tatar communities.[58]

Sanin weaves together three distinct yet interrelated plot lines, the first adapted from the Ukrainian epic tradition, the second derived from Crimean Tatar folklore, and the third conceived by the filmmaker himself.[59] The first plot is based on "Duma pro trokh brativ azovskykh"

(A duma [a Cossack lyrico-epic folk poem] about three brothers from Azov) in which two brothers, fleeing from Crimean Tatar captivity on horseback, abandon their youngest brother who is on foot.[60] According to Sanin, the second is inspired by a Turkic legend about the search for the Golden Cradle of Genghis Khan, a talismanic object whose disappearance, like that of the Roman aquila, portends death and destruction.[61] In *Mamai* these two tales are conflated into a story that pits the three Crimean Tatar brothers, seemingly empowered by the Golden Cradle, against the two escaped Cossacks, who become increasingly regretful of the abandonment of their brother. A pursuit across the steppe ensues. Sanin supplements this chase narrative with a romance between the two protagonists who have been deserted by these warring sides – the Cossack brother left for dead and Amai, the sister of the Crimean Tatar brothers, who discovers and revives him.

As in Ivanychuk's *Malvy*, the Crimean Tatars and Ukrainian Cossacks are largely at odds with one another in the film. One side hunts the other. There is ample dramatic irony in the presentation of this antagonism, however, because the spectator observes a strong symmetry between those who hunt and those who flee, a symmetry that neither side can see. Sanin ensures that the actions of the Cossacks are mirrored in those of the Crimean Tatars: when the former ride, pray, emote, or fight, so do the latter. To underscore their similarities, visual and aural features of the film simulate a slippage between the Ukrainian and Crimean Tatar worlds from its very outset. The breve of the *iot* in the film's title heading is rendered with a cross and then, subtly, with a crescent. Interspersed among the opening credits are stills of Cossack Mamai genre paintings and Crimean Tatar calligraphy, of abstract Crimean Tatar *tamğalar* (insignias) and aging manuscripts of Ukrainian *dumy*. The film's score, meanwhile, incorporates elements of both the Ukrainian and Crimean Tatar musical traditions, building to a scene featuring asynchronous sound in which the two styles of music replace the words exchanged in a passionate argument between Amai and the abandoned Cossack brother, who speak in a language the other does not understand.

Mamai was shot on location on the Crimean steppe, and the historically porous region is a critical character in the film, a vast and open land where no man-made enclosed space can be found. There are no towns or villages, no farms or fortresses, no churches or mosques; there is only Amai's barren, roofless homestead covered by a loose patchwork of tattered tarps and Kilims. Her home evokes the so-called *samozakhvaty* ("self-seized" shanties) occupied by many Crimean Tatars in the post-Soviet period. The film's elaborate plot lines and pregnant

9. *Mamai*, directed by Oles Sanin (2003)

images build to a moment when the abandoned Cossack brother literally becomes the open, "empty" figure of the Cossack Mamai. After Amai rescues him and cleanses his face of hardened white dust, naming him "Mamai," the spectator watches as the young Cossack crafts a lute while enveloped in a nocturnal haze. Sounds of distant voices, alternately diegetic and extradiegetic, give him pause, and he looks up with curiosity and trepidation before sitting *bağdaş* with his instrument. He becomes the Cossack Mamai, and in the best traditions of Ukrainian poetic cinema, the film becomes a genre painting (fig. 9).

To emphasize the profundity of his protagonist's transformation, Sanin splices into the scene images of painting inscriptions, one of which reads: "Though you endeavour to look upon me, you cannot divine my origins; of my name you know nothing at all." This "mamaification" is brief and devoid of elaboration, a moment in which a Ukrainian Cossack becomes a vague emblem, an "empty locus." Sanin offers us a provocative filmic meditation on the position of Mamai as a marker of an identity formed by interethnic, cross-cultural encounter and the vast openness of the steppe. As the director himself observes, "in Turkic languages, 'Mamai' means 'no one,' 'the impossible,' 'he who is without a name, without the word.' This is emptiness itself."[62]

3.

Mamai marked the silver screen debut of Akhtem Seitablaiev (b. 1972), an actor and director who plays one of the wayfaring Crimean Tatar brothers in Sanin's film. Born in exile in Tashkent to parents who survived the deportation, Seitablaiev settled in Crimea after 1989. He has become one of contemporary Ukraine's foremost actors and celebrities since his appearance in *Mamai*. In recent years he has also won renown as a director with a rare touch for the Hollywood-style blockbuster. One of them is *Khaitarma* (2013), which centres on a week in the life of legendary Second World War pilot Amethan (Amet-Khan) Sultan, whose standing as a two-time Hero of the Soviet Union hangs in the air of the film as damning refutation of the accusation of mass treason behind Stalin's Crimean atrocity. The film's sequence of events culminates in the night of 18 May 1944, when Seitablaiev's Sultan, on leave from his military base to visit his family in Alupka, witnesses the deportation operation in horror. What begins as an encomium to his heroism ends as a nightmare of his heroism, as he must flee from agents of a state that he has not only defended but monumentalized with his bravery. Not unlike Andrzej Wajda's *Katyń* (2007), Seitablaiev's *Khaitarma* concludes with an extended representation of the atrocity in all its senseless cruelty.

Khaitarma had its Turkish premiere in Eskişehir, the 2013 "Cultural Capital of the Turkic World." The event was attended by a group of Turkish politicians and dignitaries, testifying to the significant standing of the transnational Crimean Tatar community in Turkey after 1991.[63] No longer are the Crimean Tatars considered objects of "passivity" or "indifference" in Ankara's corridors of political power. They have been subjects of often intense domestic political discussion and a lead agenda item in Turkey's evolving strategic relations with independent Ukraine. In 1998, for instance, former Turkish president Süleyman Demirel visited Crimea and gave a stirring speech on the grounds of the hansaray, declaring, "We have come to support you – our neighbours and good friends – in the new historical role placed on your shoulders as loyal citizens of Ukraine, both in the strengthening of the independence, territorial integrity, and stability of this young state and in the rooting of your people, once again, in the ancestral homeland." He added, with a note of reassurance that seems naive today: "The past is past. Put your fears aside."[64]

High-level visits of Turkish officials to Crimea have been frequent over the past decade. In 2011, for instance, Foreign Minister Ahmet Davutoğlu helped bring the remains of Cengiz Dağcı back to the peninsula for burial. Dağcı had died in England, having never returned to his homeland, even for the second Qurultay to which he was invited in 1991. "When the news of Cengiz Dağcı's death reached me," Davutoğlu said, "suddenly I thought of all the novels I had read in middle school and high school: *Onlar da İnsandı, O Topraklar Bizimdi, Yurdunu Kaybeden Adam, Korkunç Yıllar.*" Dağcı's memorial was a uniquely regional event. As Davutoğlu declared, it marked "the meeting of two sides of the Black Sea [*Karadeniz'in iki yakasının buluşmasıdır*], the meeting of Ukraine and Turkey, which will always remain friends."[65]

Like his erstwhile foreign minister, Recep Tayyip Erdoğan has repeatedly spoken of the Crimean Tatars as a "bridge" joining Turkey and Ukraine.[66] In May 2013 he counselled Mustafa Dzhemilev to strengthen this bridge by working more closely with (disgraced former) Ukrainian president Viktor Yanukovych. It made good political sense, Erdoğan advised, to have the Mejlis represented in Yanukovych's administration before the 2015 Ukrainian presidential election. Dzhemilev's response to the Turkish prime minister was a blend of principle and prophecy. He explained that the democratic structure of the Mejlis – and the Qurultay, which elected its members – was not conducive to such political volte-face. In any case, he seemed to imply, the potential price of such co-operation would be too high. Dzhemilev then offered Erdoğan something of a political forecast. "As far as the 2015 elections bothering Yanukovych so much," he said, "he had better hope to God he remains president until then."[67] Yanukovych would flee from office within a year.

Chapter Eight

Losing Home, Finding Home

Before Viktor Yanukovych abandoned his role as president of Ukraine, he held the occasional press conference at Ukraïnskyi dim (Ukrainian House) on the northern end of Khreshchatyk, Kyiv's central thoroughfare. The late-Soviet brutalist building, an uneasy marriage of dark glass and white marble and granite, overlooks a square that has gone by many names over the past century. During the Nazi occupation of Soviet Ukraine, it was Adolf Hitler Platz; after 1944, it became Stalinskaia ploshchad (Stalin Square). It has been called Yevropeiska ploshcha (European Square) since 1996, a nod to the old Hotel Europe that dominated the site for generations.

In January 2014, where the Hotel Europe once stood, a movement called Euromaidan secured a home. As if shrugging off the enforced designations of the past, Yevropeiska ploshcha embraced its name. Ukrainians calling for European democracy and transparency and fighting the corruption of the Yanukovych regime occupied Ukraïnskyi dim, expelling forces of the Interior Ministry who had made it a base. Almost overnight, it became a community centre providing shelter, medical care, and even a library for the protestors. It also served as the headquarters of an initiative called AutoMaidan, which mobilized cars and vans to ferry demonstrators and supplies to Euromaidan encampments and take the protests beyond the city centre, to the dachas of Ukraine's political elite.

Among the AutoMaidan volunteers was an award-winning filmmaker from Simferopol named Oleg Sentsov. On 26 February 2014, with scores of protestors dead and Yanukovych spirited off to Rostov-on-Don with the help of the Russian military,[1] Sentsov was handed the telephone at AutoMaidan headquarters inside Ukraïnskyi dim. A Crimean Tatar activist – Sentsov could not remember the name – was on the line. In Simferopol thousands of demonstrators, organized and led by the

Crimean Tatars, had gathered outside Crimea's parliament building to voice support for Ukraine's territorial integrity. They chanted "Ukraïna!" in what would become the most visible mass defence of Ukraine's sovereignty in Crimea, an event now commemorated as the Day of Crimean Resistance against Russian Aggression. Confronting them were activists affiliated with what had long been a very marginal Russian nationalist political party called Russkoe edinstvo (Russian Unity), which had won only three seats in the one-hundred-seat Crimean parliament in 2010. Sentsov's advice on the phone was succinct and to the point. He told his Crimean Tatar counterpart to "get some tires." The caller asked, "And then?" Sentsov replied, "Burn them."[2]

In Kyiv, burning tires had become a ubiquitous means of defence and fortification for Euromaidan protesters. Nearly impossible to extinguish, they burned for hours, producing a wall of thick, overpowering, impenetrable smoke. In Simferopol they were ultimately not used, but the sky was no clearer. What few could see was an unfolding operation by Russian regular troops and Spetsnaz units to seize Ukraine's Crimean peninsula by force of arms. On 27 February 2014, the day after the confrontation outside Crimea's parliament, Russian soldiers surrounded Ukraine's Belbek Air Base, their lack of insignia an implicit admission of the illegality of the operation. On 28 February they took Simferopol airport and began to airlift reinforcements into Crimea.[3] Crimean Tatars, meanwhile, slid food and supplies through the gates of the bases housing encircled Ukrainian soldiers, grasping their hands through the threshold with exclamations of "Slava Ukraïni" (Glory to Ukraine).[4] An NGO called KrymSOS scrambled to mobilize volunteers to provide food and supplies to the Ukrainian military and offer foreign journalists access to independent, real-time information on the ground.

Weeks later, Russian tanks stormed Belbek's walls. Under cover of darkness, tanks and Mi-8 helicopters fired on a base of Ukrainian navy personnel in Feodosiia, dragging servicemen out of their barracks, handcuffing and humiliating them.[5] It was a carefully orchestrated, violent takeover – the first time since the end of the Second World War that one European country seized another European country's territory by force. More than that, it was Europe's largest country seizing the territory of Europe's second-largest country by force. And if history is any guide, the de facto Russian-Ukrainian border on the Black Sea that emerged from this seizure – which runs along the Isthmus of Perekop, a stretch of territory less than five miles wide – is very fragile. In the period of the khanate the Crimean Tatars used to call the strategic steppeland north of Perekop "Özü qırları" or "Özü çölleri" (the Dnipro fields). The name is telling. The Crimean peninsula is warm and arid, historically in need of the Dnipro's fresh water from the Ukrainian mainland. In fact, over the past five hundred years the Crimean peninsula and the adjacent steppeland to its north have never been completely divided between competing states for more than eight months. Until now.

1.

For the region of the Black Sea, 2014 was a threshold year – or, in the words of one Crimean Tatar activist in Turkey, a "disaster year" (felaket yılı).[6] The Kremlin's aggression against Ukraine – not only its annexation of Crimea but also its subsequent orchestration of the war in the industrial region of eastern Ukraine known as Donbas, which has claimed over thirteen thousand lives to date and displaced over two million people – seemed to take the concepts of "before" and "after" hostage, demanding new chronologies and periodizations. As Erdoğan remarked, "in recent years the Crimean Tatars experienced the hope and joy of returning to their ancestral homeland, but now, exactly seventy years after the deportation, *they have entered a new era [yeni bir döneme girmişlerdir]* reminiscent of past traumas."[7] Suddenly, a term like *interwar* could be applied to the quarter century between 1989 and 2014 – between the end of the Cold War and the beginning of both a frozen conflict in Crimea and an undeclared war in Donbas between Ukraine and Russia.

The danger of such historical periodization is, of course, its coaxing of teleology, the way it can prime us to conceive of events in retrospect as "bound to happen." But there was precious little in Crimea in the run-up to 2014 that suggested conditions for anything like secession at all. To be sure, for over two decades Ukraine's Autonomous Republic of Crimea had been a locus of interethnic contestation beset by unacknowledged colonialist trauma and, in the 1990s, by separatist rhetoric from some politicians and members of the public alike. But this history was progressively receding into the rear view. By 2014 Crimea had become "well integrated into Ukrainian political structures," as James Hughes and Gwendolyn Sasse make clear.[8] In a survey of twelve hundred Crimean residents in May 2013, the large majority of respondents expressed the view that Crimea should be a part of Ukraine.[9] Eleanor Knott's in-depth, one-on-one interviews reveal that "in the period immediately prior to the annexation (2012–13), separatism was framed as impossible and undesirable, even by the minority who were most vociferously and actively pro-Russian."[10] That Crimea was stony ground for active separatism was precisely why the Kremlin's annexation operation required a barrage of obfuscation, denial, and disinformation, not to mention a rushed Potemkin plebiscite at the barrel of a gun.[11] On 16 March, Moscow reported that 96.7 per cent of Crimean voters cast ballots for union with Russia, with a total turnout of 83.1 per cent. As Andrew Wilson writes, "Russia was used to such dictator-majorities, but this one wasn't even ethnically plausible – 24% of the population were Ukrainian and 13% Crimean Tatar."[12]

In mainstream Russian political discourse, March 2014 marked not an "annexation" but a "reunification" (vossoedinenie) of Crimea with Russia, a well-worn terminological fig leaf that has concealed acts of imperial expansion in Russian and Soviet history for centuries.[13] Its destructive nature became evident in mass displacement flows from 2014, when at least twenty thousand residents began to leave Crimea for mainland Ukraine.[14] The discovery, on the day before the rushed 16 March vote, of the body of Reshat Ametov, a Crimean Tatar man abducted in broad daylight while he was protesting Moscow's armed intervention, was an ominous harbinger for those disputing the annexation.[15] Since Ametov, there have been over twenty other political disappearances, with six men found dead, all of them Crimean Tatars.[16] Hundreds more professing views sympathetic to Kyiv have been arrested and incarcerated. The sheer number and nature of these attacks on civil liberties and human rights have compelled Krym SOS to compile a multivolume "encyclopedia" of repressions in Crimea since 2014.[17]

Oleg Sentsov was one of these prisoners of conscience. Russian by ethnicity, he stridently opposed the annexation of Crimea in the face of a twenty-year sentence on charges widely decried as politically motivated. His 145-day prison hunger strike in 2018, calling for the release of all the Kremlin's political prisoners, garnered international attention. In the words of Mustafa Dzhemilev, "Oleg Sentsov's principled position, courage, and resilience have earned him a special place."[18] During his incarceration the Crimean Tatar community honoured this place by supporting Sentsov's mother and children with regular material assistance.[19] Dzhemilev also appealed to Erdoğan in the hope of securing his help with Sentsov's release. "'Name three people,' Erdoğan said, 'because getting everyone released at once will be difficult,'" remembers Dzhemilev. "Without hesitation, I named Sentsov first."[20] Sentsov was finally released in a prisoner swap arranged between Putin and Ukrainian president Volodymyr Zelensky in 2019.

As a young man in 1989, Sentsov had a negative view of the Crimean Tatars. "But when they arrived, when it turned out that they were just people too, that this was their land, that they were illegally deported and persecuted," he recalls, "of course my attitude changed."[21] Today he takes the gravity of the Crimean Tatar deportation personally. "When I too was expelled from my homeland," he said, "I truly came to understand the Crimean Tatars."[22] Sentsov met with Dzhemilev and the Mejlis leadership shortly after his release. "Oleg is a real fighter who […] changed the frontiers of Ukraine's defence," said Refat Chubarov following the encounter. "Together we will liberate Crimea from Russian occupiers, and together we will return to Crimea."[23]

Oleg Sentsov calls the Crimean Tatars "the biggest threat to the stability of [Putin's] regime in Crimea."[24] He does so for good reason. In accordance with international law, Crimea remains sovereign Ukrainian territory under Russian military and political occupation. In 2016 the International Criminal Court made this point clear, referring to an "ongoing state of occupation" and to "a situation within the territory of Crimea [amounting] to an international armed conflict between Ukraine and the Russian Federation."[25] The Crimean Tatar Mejlis is the most vocal and organized non-state actor enunciating the terms *annexation* and *occupation* and contesting them in word and deed both inside and outside the peninsula. Its "primary aim is the return of Crimea to the Ukrainian state," according to its chair, Refat Chubarov, who like Dzhemilev is forbidden to set foot in Crimea by de facto Russian authorities.[26]

Beyond the Mejlis in exile, there are thousands of Crimean Tatars on the ground in Crimea whose mere exercise of agency appears to challenge the Russian occupation. They describe being placed in one of two boxes. Secular Crimean Tatars professing political views at odds with Russian power are labelled "extremists"; religious Crimean Tatars professing an adherence to conservative Islam are labelled "terrorists."[27] In June 2019 a young father named Riza Omerov was assigned the second label. He was arrested in a round-up of suspected members of Hizb ut-Tahrir, a fundamentalist pan-Islamist group that is legal in Ukraine (and in the United Kingdom and United States) but banned in Russia. When agents of the Russian Federal Security Service (FSB) took him from his home, a camera captured an intimate moment in which he locked eyes with his pregnant wife through the window of a prison transport vehicle (avtozak). The image inspired poet Emine Üseyin to write "Saqın mennen vedalaşma" (Take care not to say goodbye), published in Crimean Tatar in the journal *Emel* in 2020:

Ah, canım
. . . .
ne bu avtozaknıñ camı, ne bu yol,
ne bu zaman, ne bu asret bizni ayıramaz

közleriñ közlerime aşıqıp baqa
asret tolu baqışıñ, vedalaşmaq istey
amma menim közlerim saña baqıp ayta,
Ah, canım, saqın mennen vedalaşma.
. . . .
Oğlumız qorqudan soray:
– Qayda alıp keteler sizni, baba?[28]

(O, my love,
. . . .
Neither the glass of this *avtozak*, nor this road,
Nor this jail sentence, nor this longing can keep us apart
Your eyes rush to meet mine,
In the deep longing of your gaze, you try to bid farewell,
But my eyes look at you and say,
O my love, take care not to say goodbye.
. . . .
Our son asks in fear:
– Where are they taking you, daddy?)

For Omerov's sister Fatma, "the deportation of the Crimean Tatar people is taking place once again, only this time to prisons."[29] This is a deportation by instalments, an exile through the backdoor that seeks to discipline the Crimean Tatar community and enforce conformity with the Russian occupation.

This "hybrid deportation"[30] has exiled mass commemoration of Stalin's atrocity from Crimea's most pronounced public square. Before 2014 the Crimean Tatars held large public commemoration events every 18 May on Lenin Square in Simferopol, a space where memory and citizenship had intersected for years.[31] Rituals and displays of communal remembrance featuring legions of blue-and-yellow Crimean Tatar flags took place there in full view of Crimea's Council of Ministers, injecting testimonials of trauma into the public sphere to protest disenfranchisement at the hands of local authorities. The prominent Russian-language Crimean Tatar poet Lilia Budzhurova speaks of the importance of such testimony in working through painful traumatic emotions and warding off a return of the repressed, in "Govori, otets, govori" (Speak, father, speak):

Память крови нельзя задушить,
Боль народа нельзя приглушить,
Говори, отец, о том дне,
Это нужно и важно мне.

Не щади меня, не щади,
Вновь из дома родного иди,
Вновь теряй по вагонам родных,
Вновь считай, кто остался в живых.[32]

(The memory of blood cannot be silenced,
The people's pain cannot be stifled,
Speak, father, about that day,
It is necessary and important to me.
Do not spare me, do not hold back,
Relive the way you left your family home,
Relive the way you were separated from loved ones on different train cars,
Relive the way you counted who was still alive.)

In May 2014, in the immediate wake of the Russian annexation, the people's pain was indeed stifled. The Crimean Tatars were forbidden by decree to gather in public and commemorate the deportation across the peninsula. To speak and mourn their dead together, they had to break what posed as law. Today public commemoration of the deportation in Crimea – in much less conspicuous sites of memory, always at a remove from loci of political power like Lenin Square – is tightly controlled and monitored by Russian authorities. What was once protest memory, as it were, is now policed memory.

In Turkey the journal *Emel* describes such restrictions on Crimean Tatar testimony and civil society as the actions of an "expansionist, invasive, and *colonialist*" (yayılmacı, işgalci ve sömürgeci; emphasis mine) Russian state that has "attacked Ukraine and annexed Crimea for a third time," after 1783 and 1917.[33] The editors' reaction is representative of a Turkish political and cultural class more keenly aware of Ukraine's geopolitical importance. As state leaders in Ankara pressed to support the Mejlis and affirm Ukraine's territorial integrity after 2014, Turkish cultural activists began to rediscover Ukraine and express a new-found solidarity with their neighbour across the Black Sea. In 2017, for example, an issue of the prominent cultural journal *Ihlamur* (Lime Blossom) featured a series of articles about and reflections on Taras Shevchenko, "the foundation of Ukrainian literature" whose humanism was a "committed stance against imperialism."[34] With war and conflict looming in the background, poet Hüsamettin Olgun travels to Kyiv and bows before the monument to the "great master" (büyük Usta):

Gökyüzünde kara kara
Bulutlar dolaşmasın,

Dinyeper'in suları,
Bır daha asla
Kızıla boyanmasın,
Şevçenko'nun mezarında
Kan gülleri açmasın,
Ne Ukrayna, ne dünya acıya uyanmasın![35]

(Pitch black in the sky,
May the clouds disappear;
May the waters of the Dnipro
Never again
Be the colour of blood;
On Shevchenko's grave
May red roses bloom;
And may Ukraine and the entire world never again awake to pain!)

A driving force behind the renewed Ukrainian-Turkish solidarity in the wake of Russian aggression is the Crimean Tatar diaspora in Turkey itself, whose size, activity, and domestic political influence are formidable. Organizations like the Kırım Türkleri Kültür ve Yardımlaşma Derneği (Crimean Turk [sic] Culture and Solidarity Association, or "Kırım Derneği") routinely host Ukrainian dignitaries and organize Ukrainian cultural events, public demonstrations of solidarity, and even commemorations of Holodomor, Stalin's 1932–3 terror-famine in Ukraine.[36] The reach of Kırım Derneği is vast, with over twenty physical branches across Turkey; it is highly organized, well funded, and steadfast in its support of the Crimean Tatar Mejlis, a commitment enshrined in its mission statement.[37] Understanding this regional network of loyalties and alliances is key to assessing the long-term viability of unelected "alternatives" to the Mejlis promoted today by the Kremlin, such as Qırım Birliği (Crimean Unity).[38] Such institutional analogues may have local sway on the peninsula, but they have none of the transnational reach and influence enjoyed by the Crimean Tatar Mejlis across both shores of the Black Sea.

The intense activism of the Crimean Tatar emigré community in Turkey has coincided with a return of the Crimean Tatar protagonist in contemporary Turkish literature since 2014, particularly across an array of genres of prose. Like Şamil Alâdin and Oles Sanin, Turkish prose stylists are notably delving into the pre-colonial past in particular. The eponymous hero at the heart of *Yedikuleli Mansur*, for instance – a fantasy novel set at the height of Ottoman power – is an itinerant Crimean Tatar at war with a menagerie of vampires, ghouls, and monsters let loose in the dark streets of early seventeeth-century Istanbul.[39] In *Gözyaşı Çeşmesi: Kırım'da Son Düğün* (Fountain of tears: The last wedding in Crimea, 2017), meanwhile, novelist Sevinç Çokum wrests the fountain of the hansaray back from Pushkin and returns us to the heyday of the khanate. She transforms Pushkin's love triangle into a sweeping epic of historical fiction that explicitly seeks to "bring us 'closer' to Crimea and the past."[40] Whereas Pushkin's fearsome khan is steely and silent, Çokum's Khan Kırım Giray is thoughtful, benevolent, and erudite, an enlightened leader of a proud people at the centre of the narrative. Peppered with Crimean Tatar idioms and folk songs, the novel restores the bond between Crimean place and Tatar personality, transporting the Turkish reader to an eighteenth century when the Crimean Tatars exercised political and cultural dominion over the Black Sea littoral. The Crimean khan tussles with the Sublime Porte; he is not subservient to it. With Muscovy in mind, he declares that "no invader will ever enter my lands."[41]

By contrast, in Russian literature after 2014 there is little to be found of the past of Crimean Tatar sovereignty, even in the work of writers with little patience for the *vossoedinenie* or "reunification" euphemism. The Yevpatoriia-born, New York-based poet and journalist Gennady Katsov, for example, makes a point of emphasizing *anneksiia* in interviews and condemning the Russian operation for its breaches of international law.[42] In 2014, Katsov joined forces with Igor Sid to flip the triumphalist meme *KrymNash* (Crimea Is Ours) on its head with a Russian-language poetry anthology entitled *NashKrym* (Our Crimea).[43] Published in 2015, the collection is a diverse selection of texts about Crimea from 120 contemporary Russian-language poets from nine different countries. It is a self-styled "peace-keeping mission," an attempt to return Crimea "from a space of discord to a space of literature and intellectual dialogue."[44] As we saw in the previous chapter, Sid conceived of "geopoetics," the intellectual touchstone of his Crimean Club, as an antipode and even antidote to geopolitics. In the midst of a geopolitical crisis, he and Katsov could put this antidote to the test.

It turns out to be a placebo. The geopoetics of *NashKrym* is simply an ideology of possession convinced of its own apoliticism. Poets who love Crimea, Katsov and Sid write, find meaning in it; "on this basis, and on this basis only, Crimea is ours." As presented in the anthology, Crimea is above all a canvas of rugged mountains, roaring waves, and fragrant orchards – a territorial object of desire to which the elect are entitled. This elevation of place, which skirts the legacy of Crimea's settler colonialism entirely, only serves to affirm the geopolitical status quo, a point which Sid virtually concedes elsewhere.[45] There are no Crimean Tatar voices featured in the anthology, and no languages other than Russian. *NashKrym* marks yet another stage in the elevation of Crimean place over Tatar personality, whereby the latter is expunged even as the geopolitical designs of a former imperium are called into question.

For all its hopes of inspiring concord, the *NashKrym* anthology sparked controversy upon its publication. The title of the collection was particularly polarizing, causing figures like Russian poet German Lukomnikov and Ukrainian poet Boris Khersonsky to back out of the project. Lukomnikov called the title "odious," too similar to the meme it sought to subvert. *KrymNash* or *NashKrym* – "this is six of one and half a dozen of the other" (chto v lob, chto po lbu), he said.[46] Lukomnikov also rejected the framing of Crimea and the war in Donbas as two separate events; the relationship between the two was, for him, simultaneous and interconnected. "The seizure of Crimea has started a war, and the war is ongoing. Many thousands of people killed, wounded, crippled on both sides. Hundreds of thousands of refugees."[47]

2.

War has a track record of dividing national communities into competing tribes and uniting them around orthodox, monolithic ideologies. "War makes the world understandable, a black and white tableau of them and us," writes Chris Hedges. "It suspends thought, especially self-critical thought."[48] The intuitive truth of this observation makes the work of a number of prominent writers, artists, and filmmakers in today's Ukraine all the more remarkable. On the whole, they do not circumscribe and enforce boundaries of a national "we"; in the wake of the annexation of Crimea and the war in Donbas, they explicitly probe and question them.

This introspection takes place as war-time Ukraine sees an entrenchment of what may be the most dynamic civic national identity in Europe. It is an identity for which figures like Oleg Sentsov and Mustafa Dzhemilev have sacrificed – a voluntarist, inclusive Ukrainian identity grounded not in language or ethnicity but in an anti-colonial ethos, in the values of democracy and the rule of law. Sentsov calls it being "Ukrainian in spirit," and a clear majority of Ukrainians embrace it as the primary mode of national belonging today.[49] The Ukrainian–Crimean Tatar solidary relationship is at the vanguard of this expanding identity project, advancing its boundaries in the realms of culture and social communion. Since the 2014 annexation, Ukrainians have received Crimean Tatar IDPs in their local communities,[50] while Crimean Tatars IDPs have embraced the Ukrainian language, for instance, as "a political language associated with liberty and freedom."[51]

To be sure, at times of demonstration and display, the introspection at the heart of this relationship can give way to declarations. In the US House of Representatives, for example, former president Petro Poroshenko channelled John F. Kennedy by proclaiming, "I am a Crimean Tatar," in 2014.[52] Demonstrators in marches and processions in Ankara, Kyiv, and cities across the world display signs with similar nominal metaphors and solidary proclamations: *Je suis l'Ukraine, Ukraina – Krym, Qırım – Ukraina*. Speaking in a visual idiom, the protest art of graphic designer Andry Yermolenko reappropriates the Russian meme *KrymNash* and transvalues it with typographical play, rendering the *m* of *Krym* as the Crimean Tatar tamğa and the *sh* of *Nash* as the Ukrainian trident.

Aider Rustamov, mufti of the Crimean Tatars in mainland Ukraine, is one of the tens of thousands of IDPs who left Crimea after 2014. Born in exile in Uzbekistan, Rustamov says, "Crimea is Ukraine. We feel free here. People who flee to mainland Ukraine say it even feels different to breathe here."[53] The most prominent representative of this Crimean Tatar–Ukrainian solidarity in popular culture is the singer Jamala, who won the Eurovision Song Contest in 2016 with the song "1944." In the words of Mustafa Dzhemilev, citing an American diplomat, "Jamala did in three minutes what we have been trying to do to bring the Crimean Tatar issue to the world's attention for decades."[54] Her efficiency is active in shaping Ukrainian national identity as well. "Crimea is Ukraine," says Jamala. "And I believe for me it's my motherland. It's where I gave birth to my first son, where I make music inspired by Ukrainian melodies, by Crimean Tatar melodies."[55]

If this solidarity has quickened since the annexation, it has also matured in Ukraine's cultural sphere, which is so often a bellwether of deeper social changes. In the long-standing meditation on the Ukrainian–Crimean Tatar relation, discourses of *encounter* and *entanglement* have made way for a discourse of *enclosure*. This is a discourse concerned with questions of mutual ontological security, of home as both body and shelter, which for Ukrainians begin with a reckoning – the loss, temporary or not, of Crimea itself. "In the Ukrainian collective consciousness," writes Kateryna Mishchenko, "Crimea is a wound, a trauma of the outbreak of war, a lost home."[56] Or in the words of V'iacheslav Huk, "like an incurable wound, Crimea bleeds in the distance."[57] For Mar'iana Savka, the bond between Ukrainians and Crimean Tatars can help suture it:

Хоч різні ми, брате, лінія долі спільна -
Як нитка, якою зшито пекучу рану.[58]

(Although we are different, brother, the line of our destiny is joined,
Like a thread stitching a burning wound.)

Kateryna Kalytko amplifies the metaphor. She likens the loss of Crimea to an amputation. Her prize-winning collection of stories, *Zemlia zahublenykh, abo malenki strashni kazky* (Land of the lost, or Little terrible tales, 2017), is set in a nameless no man's land exhausted by the spectre of war where water is in short supply. It is an eerie, otherwordly vision of a Crimea suspended perpetually "in-between."[59]

Elsewhere, in her essayistic prose, Kalytko reflects on the treatment of this amputated Crimea in contemporary Ukrainian literature, characterizing reductive and even Orientalist representations of the peninsula as constituting a "flimsy plastic prosthesis."[60] Like Savka, she sees the project of Ukrainian–Crimean Tatar solidarity as offering something much more organic, palliative, and "alive." She also returns us to the question of the role of culture in guilt-processing:

> We all bear so much guilt [*my vsi duzhe zavynyly*] before the Crimean Tatars. Before those whose homes, with bread still warm on the table, were seized in 1944 by "liberators," whose children and grandchildren now walk the same streets as we do [...] Before those who stood next to us on Maidan. Before those who came out on 26 Feburary [2014] to the Crimean parliament with Ukrainian flags and on 27 February woke up in a completely different Crimea [...] Before those who are now being persecuted, thrown in jail on trumped-up charges, and killed. [...] No, now it is not in the power of every single citizen [...] to clean the long-standing Augean stables of Ukrainian politics [...] and regain control over state borders [...] But it is in the power of each individual citizen to try, for example, to learn the basics of the Crimean Tatar language – and at least in this way to offer them something of home.[61]

Awareness, much less acknowledgment, of the role of Ukrainians as unwitting accomplices in the history of Crimea's settler colonialism remains rare. Kalytko addresses it directly and explicitly, seeking to cultivate empathy and establish a framework of identification in which Ukrainians and Crimean Tatars can offer each other "something of home."

Nariman Aliev's debut feature film *Evge* (*Homeward*, 2019) is both a product and a proponent of such home work. Awarded the distinction of "Un Certain Regard" at Cannes Film Festival in 2019, *Evge* is a predominantly Crimean Tatar–language film funded by the Ukrainian Ministry of Culture. It was selected as Ukraine's entry for competition in the ninety-second Academy Awards, following in the footsteps of Tasin's *Alim* of 1926 as a Crimean Tatar film that is also a milestone of Ukrainian cinema. A resounding success on the international festival circuit, *Evge* presents Ukraine in all its complexity as a multi-ethnic, multiconfessional, and multilingual country exploring itself as a homeland of homelands.

In *Evge* the concept of home is plural and mobile. It is also a source of intense devotion to which one sacrifices his life. At the centre of the film is a Crimean Tatar named Mustafa who journeys across Ukraine to return the body of his estranged son Nazim to Crimea for burial. Years before, Nazim had left Crimea for mainland Ukraine, where a sense of duty to his country led him to fight and die in the war against Russian and Russian-backed forces in Donbas. Reluctantly travelling with Mustafa is his younger son, Alim, who like his brother has also found a home in Ukraine beyond Crimea. At one point he announces to his father that he has no desire to return and live under Russian occupation. Instead he sees his future in Kyiv, where he is a university student. Mustafa demands that Alim give up his plans. Mustafa exclaims: "There is nothing for you back there [in Kyiv]. Can you even imagine what we went through to return to Crimea?" Alim replies: "Who gives a damn about this Crimea?! There is no life there, and there never will be."

The argument between father and son is visceral and revelatory, laying bare the divergent conceptions of home and tradition between two different generations.[62] Mustafa's home is Crimea; Alim's and Nazim's home is Crimea in Ukraine. There is another divergence as well: in the previous exchange, Mustafa speaks in Crimean Tatar, Alim in Ukrainian. At a moment of bracing honesty, director Nariman Aliev (b. 1992) has his characters test their bonds of intimacy while speaking different languages. In fact, he crafts a cinematic moment in which monolingual accommodation gives way to bilingual non-accommodation, as Alim first converses with his father in Crimean Tatar before switching to Ukrainian. Aliev presents this multilingualism casually, as a simple fact of Ukrainian life; neither Mustafa nor Alim remarks upon their language use or requires any translation. There are no misunderstandings, only outbursts of fear, anger, and desperation. Their confrontation is only one of a number of scenes in *Evge* in which citizens of Ukraine dialogue with one another about matters of life and death, war and peace, and past and future across the Crimean Tatar, Ukrainian, and Russian languages. No matter their viewpoint, ethnicity, or linguistic profile, they exercise a bond, however tenuous, with one another. As Mustafa's brother asks, "Biz, ozumizge kerek olmasak, kimge kerekmiz?" (Who will need us if we do not need each other?)

In *Evge*, Crimea is, in effect, an island. Due to a violent confrontation at the de facto border checkpoint at Chonhar, Mustafa and Alim cannot reach Crimea by car. Instead they row to the peninsula in a boat across the shallow lagoons of the Azov Sea's western shore. Transporting Nazim's body, they turn the Syvash under cover of night into a river Styx. It is unclear whether they ever really reach their final destination. As Alim drags Nazim's enshrouded body along the shore – repeating the *basmala* refrain recited before each sura of the Qu'ran, "*bismillah Rahmani Rahim*" (in the name of Allah the most gracious, the most merciful) – an infirm Mustafa collapses behind him (fig. 10). Just as the son Nazim dies for Ukraine, so the father Mustafa dies for Crimea. Alim survives them both, moving along the border between Crimea and mainland Ukraine. In this way, his character promises a suture of the wound, but a suture that comes at great cost – through loss, sacrifice, and trauma. As Roger Luckhurst observes, trauma is "a breach of the border that puts inside and outside into a strange communication."[63] For Alim, this strange communication is the prayer from Sura 112 that he learns and desperately recites at the end of the film, a prayer whose plaintive hope he must embrace to find his way home.

The character of Mustafa in *Evge* is played with depth and sensitivity by Akhtem Seitablaiev, the director of *Khaitarma* who has been called Ukraine's Spielberg after the success of *Kiborhy* (*Cyborgs*, 2017), a feature film dramatizing a defence of the Donetsk airport by Ukrainian military forces in the autumn and winter of 2014–15.[64] Like Jamala, Seitablaiev is helping nurture civic nationalism in contemporary Ukrainian culture and society, not only through his art but also through his activism. His work as the director of Krymsky dim (Crimean House) – together with colleague Alim Aliev, a tireless and creative Crimean Tatar activist who settled in mainland Ukraine after the annexation – has been less glamorous but no less consequential. Established in Kyiv in 2015 "to protect the rights and freedoms of citizens of Ukraine, most especially the national minorities and the indigenous peoples on its temporarily occupied territory," Krymsky dim has become a flagship of Ukrainian–Crimean Tatar cultural exchange and interaction, a hub of concerts, film screenings, and Crimean Tatar language teaching. It positions Crimea as a constitutive force for all of Ukraine, as if inspired by Pierre-Jean Jouve's maxim "Car nous sommes où nous ne sommes

10. *Evge*, directed by Nariman Aliev (2019)

pas" (We are where we are not).[65] One of its most impactful initiatives is the literary festival Qırım inciri (Crimean Fig), which celebrates the best contemporary Ukrainian and Crimean Tatar writing about Crimea, including translations between the Ukrainian and Crimean Tatar languages. It builds on the legacy of the late Yunus Kandym and Mykola Miroshnychenko, whose prodigious bilingual collections of Crimean Tatar poetry and prose have contributed to a rebirth of *krymskotataroznavstvo* (Crimean Tatar Studies) in Ukraine. Such projects of translation used to be seen as tools for cross-cultural understanding; now they are understood more as forms of nation-building.

Among the most resonant contributions to the 2019 *Qırım inciri* anthology are works by women writers and translators working in the Ukrainian and Crimean Tatar languages. In a cycle entitled "Toponimy" (Toponyms), for instance, Ilona Chervotkina mourns the discursive cleansing of Crimea that has effaced ancient Crimean Tatar towns from the consciousness of residents and visitors. One of these towns is Solkhat, known instead by its Russian toponym Stary Krym. In an extended apostrophe Chervotkina's lyrical persona pleads with Solkhat to forgive a local bus driver who has turned a blind eye to its heritage, turning to his passengers to ask instead, "Who got on at Stary Krym?":

о, Солхате, він нічого не розуміє -
пробач йому.
він не бачив

середньовічний святковий базар
і тополі мінаретів,
він не дихав твоим повітрям.[66]

(O, Solkhat, [the bus driver] doesn't understand a thing –
Forgive him.
He didn't see
The medieval holiday bazaar
And the minarets like poplars,
He didn't breathe in your air.)

A short story in the *Qırım inciri* anthology entitled "Pro shcho lysty Nasymy" (The messages of Nasyma's letters) by Yevheniia Svitoch centres on an epistolary exchange between a Crimean Tatar woman named Nasyma and an aspiring Ukrainian journalist named Olesia. They form an intimate connection, with Olesia sending Nasyma poems by Lesia Ukraïnka and with Nasyma sharing lessons from her life as "a woman who has succeeded in uniting the roles of a mother, a wife, and a leader in business and culture."[67] Nasyma's letters become reflections on events and movements in Crimean Tatar history and on the role of women in driving them – such as Ismail Gasprinsky's daughter Sefika, who helmed the first magazine for women in the Muslim world. Nasyma fashions these letters for Olesia as ethnographic introductions to Crimean Tatar mores and traditions, which are meant "to promote the strengthening of peace and love between our peoples."[68]

One of the most prominent contemporary Crimean Tatar–language poets and translators is Seyare Kökçe (b. 1971), who is based in Simferopol. Her deft rendering of Serhiy Zhadan's "Yak my buduvaly svoï domy" (How we built our homes) from Ukrainian into Crimean Tatar won the 2019 Qırım inciri Prize for Best Translation. Zhadan is an artist who is unafraid of painting in dark hues on canvases of urban peripheries and barren steppelands. At the same time, he is unafraid of uplifting and inspiring the reader – a "black Romantic," as Ivan Dziuba dubs him.[69] In "Yak my buduvaly svoï domy," published in the 2015 collection *Tampliiery* (The Knights Templar), Zhadan explores home work as an engagement with the land by way of spirit as well as shovel and spade, an act of building in an environment of risk and threat. As he has made clear in public readings, the poem is inspired by the Crimean Tatars,[70] but he makes no reference to them in the text, which instead positions Crimea as an ellipsis, a halting silence on the tip of the tongue. In her translation "Bizim evlerimiz nasıl qurula?" Kökçe maintains

Zhadan's elusive tone and explores a similarly unspecified space of both sacred attachment and violent intimidation, but with an intertextual allusiveness that positions Stalin's Crimean atrocity as an event with present-day urgency. Read together, the poems present Ukrainians and Crimean Tatars grappling with the stakes of belonging and attachment at a time of crisis and insecurity, each through the other's defence of home.

"Yak my buduvaly svoï domy" offers a corrective to a quip by Zhadan's fellow writer and performer Yuri Andrukhovych that there are two types of places in life: those you escape from, and those you escape to.[71] Zhadan gives us something else in the poem – a place escaping from us. His lyrical persona is stationary; it is the sky that pivots and floats away:

Як ми будували свої доми?
Коли стоїш під небесами зими,
і небеса розвертаються й відпливають геть,
розумієш, що жити потрібно там, де тебе не лякає смерть.[72]

(How did we build our homes?
When you stand beneath winter's skies
And the heavens turn and float away,
You understand you need to live where you are not afraid of death.)

Zhadan is a writer with a penchant for aphorisms, and the poem has its share. Yet it never loses sight of its abiding thematic orientation, which is how the intimate bond between place and personality, between culture and territory, subtends our appreciation of home. Assaults on this bond lead not only to forced expulsion and exile, Zhadan reminds us. Under the shifting skies of occupation, your home can be taken from you even when you do not leave it at all.

Kökçe's translation underscores the tragedy of these shifting skies, likening them to an abandonment. Whereas Zhadan uses the past tense in his first line, she refers to the present. And whereas Zhadan's lyrical persona "stands" beneath winter's skies, Kökçe's lyrical persona is "left" deserted beneath them:

Bizim evlerimiz nasıl qurula?
Qışnıñ kökleri altında qalğanda,
em olar aylanıp ketseler avlaqqa,
sen añdaysıñ: tek ölüm qorquzmağan
    mekân lâyıq ayatqa.

(How do we build our homes?
When you are left beneath the winter's skies,
And they turn and move into the distance,
You understand: the right place for life is one without fear of death.)

In the face of this threat of a loss of home, Zhadan calls for digging, for nicking and slicing the "hard black earth":

Будуй стіни з водоростей і трави,
рий вовчі ями й рови.
Звикай жити разом з усіма день при дні.
Батьківщина — це там, де тебе розуміють, коли ти говориш вві сні.

(Go and build walls from reeds and grass,
Dig wolf pits and trenches.
Get used to living together with neighbours day after day.
Homeland is where they understand you when you talk in your sleep.)

In Kökçe's translation, Zhadan's reeds become *saman* (adobe), the material used in the makeshift huts built by Crimean Tatars upon their return after 1989:

Divarlarnı köter ottan, samandan,
Çuqkur arıqlar qaz topraqta.
Kuñ küñden yaşap ögren er kesnen birlikte.
Tüşüñdeki aytqan sözlerni añlasalar – Vatanıñ o yerde.[73]

(Build walls from grass and *saman*,
Dig deep pits in the land.
Live day to day and learn with everyone.
Your homeland is the place where they understand the words you speak
    in dreams.)

Zhadan's poem abounds in directives like a dog-eared omnibus, a guide to ontological security that urges the addressee to "place stone against stone" and "pick coal and salt from the pockets of land." Here he channels the naturalist mysticism of Bohdan Ihor Antonych (1909–37):

Поближче до сонця, подалі від пустоти.
Дерева будуть рости, діти будуть рости.
На тютюновому листі виступає роса.

Ми будували так, ніби вивершували небеса.
Мов упорядковували висоту.
Ніби словами наповнювали мову пусту.
Ніби повертали речам імена.
До брили брила, до цвяха цвях, до стіни стіна.

(Closer to the sun, farther from the void.
Trees will grow, children will grow.
On the tobacco leaf, dew gathers.
We built our homes as if we were completing the heavens.
As if we were fixing their height.
As if filling empty language with words.
As if returning names to things:
Brick for brick, nail for nail, wall for wall.)

For Zhadan, such home work bears cosmic significance. It brings purpose to human experience as well as meaningful contact with the natural world. "Water is worth something," he writes, "when it is water for drinking." Kökçe holds tightly to these lines, translating them faithfully.

At the poem's conclusion, however, Zhadan and Kökçe part ways. They diverge in their presentation of what is for Zhadan a mysterious, empowering image:

Ночі не мають сенсу без темноти.
Світи наді мною, чорне сонце, світи.

(Nights have no sense without darkness.
Shine over me, black sun, shine on.)

As Ivan Dziuba points out, black is the most popular "colour" in Zhadan's palette and, moreover, an "aggressively life-affirming" force in his verse.[74] Zhadan's "black sun" is akin to Camus's "sun with shadow," an interdependence of light and dark from which each draws its significance and power.[75] Kökçe turns this peculiar image into a coded reference to 18 May 1944:

Qara gecenin maiyeti qaranlıqta,
Qara kün töpemde parılday, töpemde yana.

(The black night finds its essence in darkness,
Black Day, shine over me, burn over me.)

It is a poignant, deliberate mistranslation. Where we expect *Qara kuneş* (black sun), we find *Qara kün* (The Black Day), a name by which the deportation is remembered by Crimean Tatars today. Kökçe alludes to its enduring, even searing legacy in the present – using the verb *yanmaq*, meaning "to burn" and "to ignite" – in a defiant enjoinder against forgetting. Like Budzhurova, she presents memory of the deportation as a kind of spiritual fire, a weapon of resilience in a time of insecurity.

3.

"The occupation of Crimea is no distant thing," says Zhadan. Poems like "Yak my buduvaly svoï domy" pull it closer. *"We built our homes [...] as if returning names to things: brick for brick, nail for nail, wall for wall."* In 2018, his words – alluding to the sacred meaning of even mundane material traces of our presence at home – began to take on a troubling poignancy in a scandal over a "restoration" of the hansaray, the palace of the Crimean Tatar khans. Undertaken by a Moscow firm with no experience in historical preservation, this "Potemkin renovation," as Crimean Tatar activists have called it, shows at best an aggressive indifference to the call to "respect original material" at the heart of the 1964 Venice Charter (the International Charter for the Conservation and Restoration of Monuments and Sites).[76] Lilia Budzhurova worries that the hansaray "is being literally destroyed before our eyes."[77] Photographs and videos taken by citizen journalists reveal ancient wooden beams ripped from the interior of the palace and discarded outside, exposed to the elements; they show workers tossing ceramic artefacts from deep within the khan's old stables into a heap, as if harvesting potatoes.[78] In the almost mystical world of "Yak my buduvaly svoï domy," such a localized material assault on the vestiges of Crimean Tatar personality – on the bricks, nails, walls of its past – becomes an event of universal spiritual import, a tear in the fabric of a common human heritage.

It has urgent relevance for Ukrainians. "The plight of Crimean Tatars is the plight of Ukrainians," Zhadan continues. "Our future path with the Crimean Tatars is narrow and long – because they are our compatriots."[79] Reading "Yak my buduvaly svoï domy" alongside "Bizim evlerimiz nasıl qurula?" offers a view of Ukrainians and Crimean Tatars searching for what it means to be at home through the experience of the other – and exploring what it means to be at home together, as "compatriots."

As a cultural and political matter, the Crimean question for Ukrainians and Crimean Tatars after 2014 is therefore about restoring home. It is about restoring Ukraine's territorial integrity as well as the rights of Crimea's indigenous people to exercise political and cultural agency without fear of arbitrary arrests, disappearances, or backdoor deportations. One proposed mechanism for this joint restoration is an amendment to Ukraine's constitution that would recognize the "national-territorial autonomy" of the Crimean Tatars and, in effect, vest Crimean sovereignty in them. It would be a powerful rebuke to *KrymNash* chauvinism. A majority of Ukrainians support the idea, but fears of precedent-setting and a creeping federalization of Ukraine have prompted politicians in Kyiv to kick the can down the road, despite repeated promises of action.[80] Recently the administration of President Volodymyr Zelensky claimed that the proposal needed wider debate in Ukrainian society, pulling it back from the constitutional amendment process.[81] "We are working on it," insisted Zelensky's spokesperson.

Where politics often stalls, culture forges ahead. As we have seen, prominent works of literature and film have enmeshed the Ukrainian and Crimean Tatar quests for home, for ontological security, so deeply as to blur the lines between them. In this cultural discourse the national-territorial autonomy of the Crimean Tatars is nearly a fait accompli. As Myroslav Marynovych argues, it is "the key to restoring justice on the peninsula." After all, he says, "the Crimean Tatars are the only truly organizing force in Crimea."[82] In recent years they have become an organizing force in mainland Ukraine as well, a driver of civic nationalism at a time of war. Our glimpse into the evolving cultural reflections of the solidary relation between Ukrainians and Crimean Tatars – from discourses of metaphorical encounter and entanglement to a discourse of enclosure – therefore reveals a startling picture, with potential lessons for European liberalism and even global Islam. It is a model of interethnic fellowship in the region of the Black Sea, a portrait of Crimea's Sunni Muslim indigenous people helping shape the national identity of a country that Karl Schlögel calls "Europe in miniature."[83] Ukraine may have lost control of Crimea for the foreseeable future. But at least in one sense, Crimea has not lost control of Ukraine.

Coda

At the centre of a region of occupied and disputed territories, Crimea juts into the map of the Black Sea like a trigger. We forget its significance at our peril. Yet since the dramatic events of 2014, media outlets have largely consigned Crimea to afterthoughts and back pages. Prominent international relations pundits in the West have declared it "surely lost for good," making little effort to connect geostrategic dots between its annexation and the war in Donbas, two sites of armed conflict – one "frozen," the other "hot" – only three hundred miles away from each other.[1] Such throes of "Crimnesia" do not change the fact that the peninsula remains a global flashpoint whose "structural predisposition" to conflict has only worsened under Russian occupation. According to the United Nations General Assembly, the Kremlin has overseen a "gravely concerning" "transfer of nuclear-capable aircraft and missles, weapons, ammunition, and military personnel" to Crimea.[2] This militarization of infrastructure has coincided with a militarization of consciousness, which today normalizes draconian crackdowns on independent civil society, most especially among the Crimean Tatars.

In the words of Crimean Tatar activist and Amnesty International prisoner of conscience Emir-Usein Kuku, this militarization of consciousness has done swift work to turn Crimea into a space of Orwellian "thoughtcrime." "Doesn't it seem strange," he asked in his "Final Word" while on trial in Rostov-on-Don in 2019, "that in the twenty-three years under Ukrainian authority there were no 'extremists,' no 'terrorists,' and no 'acts of terror' for that matter? But then Russia arrived with its FSB, and suddenly all of these things appeared together?"[3] This book has traced the anxieties of possession behind this militarization to Stalin's Crimean atrocity, which was a culmination of a project of settler colonialism that sought to expunge Crimea's indigenous people from the territory that helped define them. As a cultural study of the Black

Sea, it has cast the Crimean Tatars not as "intermittent presences" in the history of the region but as key determinants of its past, present, and future trajectories.[4]

At the same time, *Blood of Others* has also sought to combat a different "Crimnesia" – a forgetting of acts of transnational literary solidarity in the aftermath of this atrocity. "Solidarity wavers," writes Avishai Margalit, "when the memory of a strong feeling of solidarity fades away."[5] The book has traced the disruptive vibrations of Stalin's deportation of the Crimean Tatars across the cultural spaces of Russia, Turkey, and Ukraine to renew memory of this solidarity and to consider how literary texts can inspire its strong feeling. Myroslav Marynovych calls this corpus of poetry and prose "invaluable" today. It exposed audiences to the brutal realities of the Sürgün, often well before news reports or other documentary sources, and aimed to elicit a prosocial response in the empirical world. "It is a testament from the past," Marynovych continues, "that we, as heirs to these writers, must fulfil."[6] From the Soviet underground to the realm of Turkish popular culture, these texts invited readers to process an emotion with quiet motivational utility – guilt – and engaged them in a poetics of solidarity that ultimately played a role in achieving something many thought impossible: the return of the Crimean Tatars to their ancestral homeland after nearly half a century in exile.

Today, in an era of disconnected connectivity, when social networks spawn thought-silos based more on the putative threat of enemies than on the comfort of friends, solidarity can seem a rare commodity. In a region of the world beset by contestation and conflict, where a persecuted indigenous people is targeted once more, it can even appear naive. But the literary works at the heart of this book – texts of poetry and prose composed under similarly challenging historical conditions – see little point in cynicism. They speak instead to the way culture can empower us to envision new alternatives to the political status quo and to foster empathic human connection in the face of difference and distance. With uncanny foresight, Carol Weaver wrote in 2013 that "the Black Sea region is still an area where some people are afraid of invasion, ethnic cleansing, or general oppression."[7] *Blood of Others* has sought to show how the Black Sea region is also an area where people have succeeded in comforting Stalin's victims with verse and in spurring people to activism with stories. It is an area where people embraced imaginative artistic expression in a fight against invasion, ethnic cleansing, and oppression – and secured a victory whose remembrance today is not indifferent to tomorrow.

Acknowledgments

I am finishing this book under COVID-19 lockdown in Cambridge, at a humbling time when giving regular thanks has never had more urgency.

The pandemic has placed stories of solidarity – or of its absence – at the forefront of our attention. Through the noise, I find myself regularly returning to one story in particular. It is a story about the Native American indigenous Choctaw people, who in 1847 sent precious relief aid to Irish families in the grip of famine, and about the people of Ireland, who in 2020 responded in kind with a flood of grassroots donations to Choctaw families hit hard by COVID-19. For nearly two centuries, poetry and song have helped keep this bond of solidarity alive.

I remember learning of the "Choctaw gift" as a child. My parents, Farrell and Paul Finnin, filled our home with music and with stories of acts of empathy and friendship across borders. I am grateful to them for their love and care and to my sister Anni for her laughter and for the example of her strength. Mary and John Lally have staggered me with their kindness and generosity for more than twenty years, and I am proud to be their second son. With David and Sheila Lally, midnight has always been a glimmer, and noon a purple glow. I also have brothers and sisters in Karl and Megan Kleinert; John and Jill McCormac; Chris Long and Kathleen Lapenta Long; Erik Ekroth and Leslie Rubisch; Ihor and Yulia Potapchuk; Tania and Yura Kovalchuk; Mary Brendler Zouaoui and Slim Zouaoui; and Christina Fanelli and Mick Daly. I am grateful to them and to all my friends and family – Finnins, Lallys, DeVitoes, McLaughlins, Walshes, Thomes, Freckmanns, Pallases – for their support and encouragement. My nieces and nephews and godchildren – Adare, Aidan, Jane, Liam, Patrick, Nicholas, and Cate – are an inexhaustible source of pride.

In a sense, this book began in a village in central Ukraine, where Tetiana Mykolaïvna and Ivan Opanasovych Kaplun changed my life with the gift of their friendship and with a slim volume of poetry. My fascination with the cultures of Ukraine and the Black Sea region later matured at Columbia University, where I had the privilege of working, sometimes in a suit and tie, with the wonderful Vitaly Chernetsky, Frank Sysyn, Cathy Popkin, Valentina Izmirlieva, Irina Reyfman, Yaroslav Hrytsak, Volodymyr Kulyk, Valerii Kuchynskyi, Rebecca Stanton, Etem Erol, Antonina Berezovenko, Yuri Shevchuk, Alla Smyslova, David Goldfarb, Mark Andryczyk, Maria Rewakowicz, Colleen McQuillen, Christopher Harwood, Elazar Barkan, Nader Sohrabi, Bohdan Rubchak, and Alexander Motyl. Two visionary, intellectually adventurous mentors at Columbia who helped shape this project – Catharine Theimer Nepomnyashchy and Mark von Hagen – passed away before its publication. Theirs are the voices I hear most often as I look over the final manuscript.

My academic home at the University of Cambridge has spoiled me with giving colleagues, some of whom have read and workshopped chapters in this book: Simon Franklin, Emma Widdis, Stanley Bill, Rebecca Reich, Hubertus Jahn, Harald Wydra, Ivan Kozachenko, Marta Jenkala, Natasha Franklin, Susan Larsen, Mel Bach, Olesya Khromeychuk, Uilleam Blacker, Rachel Polonsky, Jana Howlett, Olenka Pevny, Elena Filimonova, Brendan Simms, Olga Płócienniczak, Sander van der Linden, John Barber, Aleksandr Etkind, Julie Fedor, Dominic Keown, Diane Oenning Thompson, Chris Ward, Wendy Bennett, Andrii Smytsniuk, Brad Epps, Rhiannon McGlade, Dominic Lieven, Tony Cross, and many others. I am also very grateful to the officers of the Ukrainian Studies Endowment Fund at the University of Cambridge for their support of the publication of this book. Robinson College has been a warm, welcoming community of scholars at Cambridge, and I thank all of my colleagues in the Fellowship and on staff for their help and input, especially Joanna Page, Liz Guild, Mary Stewart, Emily Price, Scott Annett, Robin Kirkpatrick, Glenys Denton, Dzintra Kilbloka, David Woodman, Elizabeth Pettit, Bill Nolan, David Yates, and Susanna West Yates.

I have been very fortunate to work with many talented undergraduate and postgraduate students who inspire and motivate me with their creativity and enthusiasm. Special thanks go to my brilliant doctoral students, who have taught me so much and whose searching questions, kindness, and good humour have always invigorated me: Daria Mattingly, Mariia Molodyk (Terentieva), Jon Roozenbeek, Iryna Shuvalova, and Bohdan Tokarskyi.

Writing this book has involved meeting some of my heroes: Mustafa Dzhemilev, Liliia Karas-Chichibabina, Myroslav Marynovych, and Raïsa Rudenko. I am deeply indebted to them for their time and for our fascinating exchanges. Throughout the Black Sea region, from Kharkiv to Ankara, colleagues and friends in libraries, archives, universities, and non-governmental organizations have assisted me in more ways than I can count, especially Alim Aliev, Stas Menzelevskyi, Sait Ocaklı, Oleh Kotsarev, Zenife Seydametova, Balkız Öztürk Başaran, Mubeyyin Batu Altan, Tony Greenwood, and Hakan Kırımlı. For their comments, conversations, and collaborations, I am also very grateful to Andrii Portnov, Serhii Plokhii, Vsevolod Samokhvalov, Timothy Snyder, Michael Flier, Idil Izmirli, George Grabowicz, Hiroaki Kuromiya, Victor Ostapchuk, Volodymyr Dibrova, Maria Sonevytsky, Anne Applebaum, Oleksandr Halenko, Nataliya Gumeniuk, Maria Montague, Eleanor Knott, Sophie Pinkham, Taras Koznarsky, Gwendolyn Sasse, Charles King, Serhy Yekelchyk, Simon Lewis, Sabra Ayres, Kateryna Stetsevych, Volodymyr Dubovyk, Mikhail Minakov, Yohanan Petrovsky-Shtern, David Marples, Volodymyr Yermolenko, Sasha Dovzhyk, Maxim Tarnawsky, Marta Dyczok, Peter Pomerantsev, Michael Moser, Kevin M.F. Platt, Andrew Wilson, Molly Brennan, Bill Brennan, Tanya Zaharchenko, Halyna Hryn, Olga Zeveleva, Jack Rathschmidt, Mila Rosenthal, Jonathan Birchall, Elektra Birchall, Ivy Birchall, Linda Fisher, Stanley Rabinowitz, Mícheál Ó Mainnín, Janice Carruthers, Andrew Fedynsky, Peter Fedynsky, Justin DeKoszmovszky, Tatiana Thieme, Paul Robert Magocsi, Phil Bautista, Jeff Gamble, Mike Graf, Thom Yorke, Andy Heil, Larry LoPresti, Tom Kelley, Daniel Cleary, Doug Latham, Chris Hunkins, and all the Returned Peace Corps Volunteers of Group V (Ukraine). Filmmakers Oles Sanin and Nariman Aliev and Ivan Kozlenko of the Dovzhenko Centre in Kyiv generously allowed me to reprint images in this book. Three anonymous reviewers read the manuscript with thoughtful circumspection and helped me to improve it. The enthusiasm, critical rigour, and steady hand of my editor at University of Toronto Press, Stephen Shapiro, polished it into a finished product. My copy editor, Angela Wingfield, brought a very keen, meticulous eye to the manuscript. Of course, any unintended errors or shortcomings in the book are mine alone.

Public lectures based on material in *Blood of Others* were given at Harvard University, the University of Oxford, the University of Amsterdam, the University of Alberta, and New Europe College, Bucharest. I am grateful to my colleagues at these institutions for the honour of their invitations and to the audiences in attendance for their curiosity and their feedback. Parts of chapter 1 first appeared in "The Poetics of Home: Crimean Tatars in Nineteenth-Century Russian and Turkish Literatures," *Comparative Literature Studies* 49, no. 1 (January 2012): 84–118. Parts of chapters 2, 3, and 7 first appeared in "'A Bridge between Us': Literature in the Ukrainian–Crimean Tatar Encounter," *Comparative Literature Studies* 56, no. 2 (Spring 2019): 289–319. Parts of chapters 3 and 4 first appeared in "'Forgetting Nothing, Forgetting No One': Boris Chichibabin, Viktor Nekipelov, and the Deportation of the Crimean Tatars," *Modern Language Review* 106, no. 4 (September 2011): 1091–124. Parts of chapter 6 first appeared in "Captive Turks: Crimean Tatars in Pan-Turkist Literature," *Middle Eastern Studies* 50, no. 2 (Spring 2014): 291–308. I thank all of these journals for granting me permission to adapt this material here.

Finally, I dedicate this book to my partner, Anne Lally, and our son, Shane, who lift me every day.

Notes

Introduction

1 "Liliia saved my life," Chichibabin observed in a 1993 interview. "We met when I was living through a very terrible, very catastrophic time ... I was close to going mad – or to killing myself. And at that moment Liliia appeared in my life." Chichibabin, "Ia siuda stremilsia vsiu zhizn'," 91.

2 Mukha, "O pervom vystuplenii Borisa Chichibabina," 44.

3 Mukha, 45.

4 The precise date of the poem is unclear. Chichibabin recalls its composition in 1959 or 1960. See Chichibabin, "Pis'mo Aideru Emirovu," 77.

5 "O priznanii nezakonnymi i prestupymi repressivnykh aktov protiv narodov, podvergshikhsia nasil'stvennomu pereseleniiu, i obespechenii ikh prav (14 noiabria 1989 g)," 570.

6 "Doklad N.S. Khrushcheva XX s"ezdu Kommunisticheskoi partii Sovetskogo Soiuza, 25 fevralia 1956g," 372.

7 Burlatsky is quoted in Lur'e and Maliarova, *1956: Seredina veka*, 107.

8 Orwell, *Nineteen Eighty Four*, 46. As Aleksandr Nekrich observes with solemnity, the Crimean Tatars "might just as well have not existed" (*The Punished Peoples*, 136). In the superb *Black Sea* (1995), Neal Ascherson incorrectly states that Khrushchev "had specifically named and denounced the Tatar deportation" at the Twentieth Congress of the Communist Party (32).

9 Liliia Karas'-Chichibabina, interview with the author, 16 May 2013.

10 Liliia Karas'-Chichibabina, interview with the author, 23 May 2013.

11 Reddaway, "The Crimean Tatars," 252.

12 In an emblematic example, prominent Ukrainian civic activist Yevhen Zakharov, director of the Kharkiv Human Rights Protection Group, ended a widely circulated Facebook post commemorating the anniversary of the Crimean Tatar deportation in May 2016 with Chichibabin's poem,

which – as Zakharov attests – "has been imprinted in the memory since childhood." See "S'ohodni – 72 roky, iak deportuvaly kryms'kykh tatar." The poem has its own page on the website of Kharkiv Human Rights Protection Group. See also, for example, Bekirova, "Boris Chichibabin."

13 On the campaign trail, Democratic hopeful for the US presidency Pete Buttigieg spoke of the "gift" of literature, which helps us "better understand what it is like to be alive." See "Pete Buttigieg: 'Shortest Way Home.'"

14 Nazar, "Mystetstvo pro viinu: Mizh tvorchistiu ta ahitkoiu."

15 I take the term *nets of kinship* from Benedict Anderson, *Imagined Communities*, 6. As Richard Rorty explains, "the goal of this manipulation of sentiment is to expand the reference of the terms 'our kind of people' and 'people like us.'" Rorty, "Human Rights, Rationality and Sentimentality," 74.

16 Steven Pinker uses the term *empathy circle* in *The Better Angels of Our Nature*, 210.

17 Pinker, 210–13.

18 Hunt, *Inventing Human Rights*, 38.

19 C.P. Snow, *The Two Cultures*, 70.

20 Nussbaum, *Love's Knowledge*, 171.

21 Nussbaum, *Poetic Justice*, 72–7.

22 Charles Altieri goes so far as to liken some of Nussbaum's work to "imperialist philosophizing," in Davis and Womack, *Mapping the Ethical Turn*, 44.

23 Nussbaum, *Poetic Justice*, 12. Richard A. Posner contests Nussbaum's strident instrumentalization of this literary capacity in public life; in his view, it tethers the aesthetic to the ideological and "enlists literature … in the service of therapeutic and political goals." Posner also says of Nussbaum: "She does not cite a single case of a nation, a group, a community, or even a single person edified by the novels of Dickens or James or of Wright or Forster, or any other works of literature." Posner, "Against Ethical Literature, Part Two," 398–400. The case of Liliia Karas'-Chichibabina alone is a riposte to Posner's "aestheticist" critique.

24 Nussbaum, *Love's Knowledge*, 51. James's original use of the term can be found in *Art of the Novel*, 45.

25 Take, for instance, a much-publicized 2013 study in *Science* by psychologists David Comer Kidd and Emanuele Castano. Drawing from a series of experiments on human subjects, they conclude that reading literary fiction enriches our facility to anticipate and understand the mental states of others. Lyric poetry does not figure anywhere in the analysis. Kidd and Castano, "Reading Literary Fiction Improves Theory of Mind," 377–80. See also Zunshine, *Why We Read Fiction*, and Keen, *Empathy and the Novel*.

26 "Lyric poetry seems to me to raise different issues," Nussbaum writes. "They are important to the continuation of the larger project; I leave them for those who are more involved than I am in the analysis of poems." Nussbaum, *Love's Knowledge*, 46.
27 Smith, *The Theory of Moral Sentiments*, 286.
28 Among those stars are often constructive group discussions about literary works and their influence on our "moral self-exploration," as Larry P. Nucci argues. See Nucci, *Education in the Moral Domain*, 177 and 212.
29 Steven Pinker refers to literature as "moral technology" in "The Seed Salon: Steven Pinker and Rebecca Goldstein," 48.
30 Rorty, *Contingency, Irony, Solidarity*, 146.
31 See, for example, Tsur, *Toward a Theory of Cognitive Poetics*.
32 The Swiss scientist and physician Hans Jenny (1904–72) is widely considered the pioneer of cymatics. See Jenny, *Cymatics*.
33 Hayden White, *The Practical Past*, 49 and 59.
34 Paul Ricoeur uses a different metaphor to impart a similar message: in his view, historical events drive narratives about the past as plot points, influencing the stakes of the story and the significance of its characters, determining who matters and who matters more. See *Time and Narrative*, 1:208.
35 Rilke, "Brief an Witold Hulewicz, 13.11.1925," 899.
36 Apter, *The Translation Zone*, 243.
37 Wellek, *Concepts of Criticism*, 262.
38 Shafak, "The Silencing of Writers in Turkey."
39 *The Geography of Strabo*, vol. 3, bk. 7.3.6, 189.
40 *The Geography of Strabo*, vol. 1, bk. 2.5.22, 478–80.
41 Sezer, "Balance of Power in the Black Sea," 159. A more expansive cultural study of this kind would ideally include the other Black Sea countries of Georgia, Bulgaria, and especially Romania, which has had a particularly sizeable Crimean Tatar emigré community since 1783.
42 King, *The Black Sea*, 4. Constantine Pleshakov similarly regrets the neglect of Crimea's Ottoman inheritance in contemporary Western discussions of the region. The impact of Istanbul "was no less significant and lasting than Kiev's or Moscow's." Pleshakov, *The Crimean Nexus*, 71.
43 Ivanova, *The Black Sea*, 268. For an innovative interdisciplinary study of the Black Sea in the field of international relations, see Samokhvalov, *Russian-European Relations*.
44 The Office of the Prosecutor of the International Criminal Court, *Report on Preliminary Examination Activities, 2016*, 35.
45 See, for instance, "Ukraine Seeks Closure of Turkish Straits after Russian Aggression"; "Genshtab: ChF Rossii mozhet unichtozhit' protivnika eshche pri vydvizhenii s bas"; Urcosta, "Prospects for a Strategic Military Partnership."

46 Ascherson, *Black Sea*, rev. ed., xi.
47 During the Second World War, Bratianu, a Romanian historian who was instrumental in promoting the Black Sea as an object of knowledge, taught a course entitled "The Black Sea Question" at the University of Bucharest. His default metaphor for the Black Sea was a "plaque tournant," a "turntable" around which societies and cultures rotated and coalesced. See Bratianu, *La mer Noire*, 43.
48 In 1914 Ahmad Cavad (1892–1937) wrote a poem during a journey from Istanbul to his native Azerbaijan entitled "Çırpınırdın Karadeniz" ("Çırpınırdı Qaradəniz" in Azerbaijani; "The Black Sea Convulsed"), which became the lyrical foundation for a very popular Turkish march and a beloved song in both Turkey and Azerbaijan. Cavad was murdered in the Stalinist purges of 1937. See Zeyrek, "Şehit Ahmed Cevad," 27.
49 Hrushevs'kyi, "Na porozi Novoï Ukraïny," 236.
50 Belinskii, "Russkaia literatura v 1840 godu," 427.
51 Kulish, "Kazky i baiky z susidovoï khatky, perelyts'ovani i skomponovani prydnipriantsem," 305.
52 Quoted in Kaplan, *Kültür ve Dil*, 117.
53 Lenin, "O rabote Narkomprosa," 331.
54 Mykola Skrypnyk, *Statti i promovy z natsional'noho pytannia*, 163–4.
55 Cited in Borak, *Atatürk ve Edebiyat*, 61–2. See also Karpat, *Çağdaş Türk Edebiyatında Sosyal Konular*, 43–4.
56 Atatürk, *Atatürk'ün Fikir ve Düşünceleri*, 147; emphasis mine.
57 Halman et al., *Türk Edebiyatı Tarihi*, 4:31.
58 Nazım Hikmet, "Şevçenko'nun kalemi," 58.
59 Sontag, "The Erdogan Experiment."
60 Şakir Selim, "Vatan ve şiiriyet," in *Küneşten bir parça / Okrushyna sontsia*, ed. Miroshnychenko and Kandym, 664. Throughout this book I translate the polysemous terms *vatan* (Crimean Tatar and Turkish), *batkivshchyna* (Ukrainian, motherland), *rodyna* (Russian, motherland), and *otechestvo* (fatherland) as "homeland."
61 Williams, *The Crimean Tatars*, 10–11 and 29.
62 Lazzerini, "The Crimea under Russian Rule," 124. For more on the Crimean Tatar emigrations to the Ottoman Empire, see Karpat, *Ottoman Population, 1830–1914*.
63 Rossiiskii gosudarstvennyi istoricheskii arkhiv (RGIA), f. 384, op. 8, d. 434, l. 23; cited in Vozgrin, *Istoriia krymskikh tatar*, 2:616.
64 As Williams argues, "the Crimean ASSR was, from 1921–1945, established as an unofficial Crimean Tatar republic," a fact that poses a "conundrum for many Crimean Tatar nationalists" who are unwilling to acknowledge the role of the Soviet state in consolidating a Crimean Tatar national identity. Williams, *The Crimean Tatars*, 337.

65 Williams, 360. Fisher, *The Crimean Tatars*, 138–40.

66 Williams, *The Crimean Tatars*, 360.

67 Most of the Crimean Tatar deportees were sent to the Uzbek Soviet Socialist Republic (SSR) and the Ural Mountains region. Other destinations included the Kazakh SSR and various oblasts of the eastern Russian Soviet Federative Socialist Republic (RSFSR). Chubarov, "Peredmova," 7. See also Vozgrin, *Istoriia krymskikh tatar*, 4:180.

68 Vozgrin, *Istoriia krymskikh tatar*, 4:181–2.

69 Vozgrin, 4:181–2.

70 "Tovarishchu Stalinu, 10 maia 1944g," in *Deportatsiia narodov Kryma*, ed. Bugai, 85; and "Postanovlenie GOKO No. 5859ss, 11 maia 1944g," in *Deportatsiia narodov Kryma*, ed. Bugai, 70–3.

71 Williams, *The Crimean Tatars*, 383.

72 Bugai, *L. Beriia–I. Stalinu,* 146. Fisher, *The Crimean Tatars*, 155.

73 Williams, *The Crimean Tatars*, 378–9. For more on the provocations of Russian partisans, see Statiev, "The Nature of Anti-Soviet Armed Resistance," 310–11. To this list of "betrayals," an internal Soviet memorandum of December 1941 adds "perfidious demagoguery" (*kovarnoi demagogii*), which allowed the Germans to win over "*a certain part* of the Crimean Tatars" (*nekotoruiu chast'* krymskikh tatar; emphasis mine) to their side. See "Iz doklada Sekretaria Krymskogo OK VKP(b) V. S. Bulatova v Politbiuro TsK VKP(b), 20 dekabria 1941g" in *Deportatsiia narodov Kryma*, ed. Bugai, 56.

74 Broshevan and Tygliiants, *Izganie i vozvrashchenie*, 34.

75 Uehling, *Beyond Memory*, 53. Fisher, *The Crimean Tatars*, 161–2.

76 Bugai, *L. Beriia–I. Stalinu*, 146.

77 Williams, *The Crimean Tatars,* 382.

78 Fisher, *The Crimean Tatars*, 169.

79 Williams, *The Crimean Tatars*, 385.

80 Uehling, *Beyond Memory*, 38 and 79.

81 Documents 59, 61, and 66 in *Deportatsiia narodov Kryma*, ed. Bugai, 86–9. On the NKVD soldiers' lack of advance knowledge of the deportation, see Uehling, *Beyond Memory*, 38 and 79. Kobulov and Serov's "efficiency" was due to their experience coordinating the deportations of the Karachay, Kalmyk, Chechen, Ingush, and Balkar peoples from the Caucasus months before. See Williams, *The Crimean Tatars*, 387, and Nekrich, *The Punished Peoples*, 108n.

82 Vozgrin, *Istoriia krymskikh tatar*, 4:192.

83 Vozgrin, 4:193.

84 Crimean Tatars sometimes refer to the deportation as the *ikinci sürgün* or "second exile" – the first being the mass emigration to Ottoman Turkey following the Russian annexation of Crimea in 1783. Williams, *The Crimean*

Tatars, 109 and 374. As we will see in chapter 8, the displacement of Crimean Tatars and the crackdown on Crimean Tatar civil society on the peninsula after 2014 have invoked cries of a "third exile" and a "hybrid deportation."

85 "Reizova, Shadie Dzhaferovna," 90.

86 Vozgrin, *Istoriia krymskikh tatar*, 4:197.

87 According to Michael Rywkin, nearly eight thousand Crimean Tatars perished during the deportation itself. See Rywkin, *Moscow's Lost Empire*, 67.

88 Williams, *The Crimean Tatars*, 237. The special settlement regime was lifted in April 1956, two months after Khrushchev's "Secret Speech."

89 Gul'nara Bekirova, *Krymskotatarskaia problema v SSSR, 1944–1991*, 108. According to Williams, the total percentage of those killed in the first five years was likely lower, "probably thirty percent of the deported population." Williams, *The Crimean Tatars*, 401.

90 Ol'ga Glezer et al., "Krym v fevrale 1954," 10.

91 Pleshakov, *The Crimean Nexus*, 90.

92 Glezer et al., "Krym v fevrale 1954," 10.

93 "Stenogramma zasedaniia Prezidiuma Verkhovnogo Soveta SSSR," 48.

94 "Gorbanevskaia ob osnovanii 'Khroniki tekushchikh sobytii,'" 46. See also Raskina, "Natal'ia Gorbanevskaia," 523. On the Initiative Group for the Defense of Human Rights in the USSR and its standing as the "first Soviet human rights NGO," see Horvath, "Breaking the Totalitarian Ice," 148.

95 Chervonnaia, "Krymskotatarskoe natsional'noe dvizhenie (1994–1996)," 16.

96 "Crimean Tatar Activist Confined in Psychiatric Hospital," and "'Povtoriu na dopyti shche raz." The Mejlis has pushed back against such measures, and not without controversy. In late 2015, for instance, Crimean Tatar activists launched an economic and energy blockade of Crimea, which caused power outages across the peninsula and prompted a state of emergency. The Mejlis was subsequently banned as an "extremist" organization by the Russian Supreme Court. See Cooper, "Crimean Tatar Elected Body Banned in Russia."

97 Since the Ottoman period, writes Hakan Kırımlı, Crimea has been the "cardinal issue in determining Turko-Ukrainian relations." See Kırımlı, "The Ottoman Empire and Ukraine, 1918–21," 205.

98 Sonevytsky, "Radio Meydan," 110.

99 Gessen, "Russia Declares War on Eurovision"; "President Erdoğan Congratulates Jamala on Her Eurovision Victory." In response to a popular video clip of Jamala's performance modified with Turkish-language subtitles, a YouTube commenter remarked that "we rejoiced as if Turkey had won." The comment was liked over 315 times. See "Ukrayna Eurovision 2016."

100 Sasse, *The Crimea Question*, 4.
101 Arkanov, *Ot Il'icha do lampochki*, 171.
102 Said, *Culture and Imperialism*, 160.
103 Charron, "Whose Is Crimea?," 225.
104 Snyder, "The Causes of the Holocaust," 153.

1 Imperial Objects

 1 Ségur, *Mémoires; ou, Souvenirs et anecdotes*, 179.
 2 "Sadrâzamın Başkanlığında yapılan toplantıda Kırım ve Rusya
    Konularında alınan kararlar (15 Haziran 1783)," in *Osmanlı belgelerinde
    Kırım Hanlığı*, ed. Ünal and Gurulkan, 310.
 3 Ünal and Gurulkan, 310–12.
 4 Miranda, *Puteshestvie po Rossiiskoi Imperii*, 135.
 5 Ségur, *Mémoires; ou, Souvenirs et anecdotes*, 175.
 6 Ségur, 190.
 7 Ségur, 191–2.
 8 Ségur, 192.
 9 Potemkin, "Rasporiazheniia svetleishago kniazia Grigoriia
    Aleksandrovicha Potemkina-Tavricheskago," 287.
10 "Ekaterina II – G. A. Potemkinu (20–21 maia 1787)," in *Ekaterina II i G. A.
    Potemkin*, ed. Lopatin, 216.
11 For more on the "Greek project" for Crimea, see Zorin, *By Fables Alone*,
    92–120.
12 "G. A. Potemkin – Ekaterine II (5 Avgusta 1783)," in *Ekaterina II i G. A.
    Potemkin*, ed. Lopatin, 180. As David Schimmelpenninck van der Oye
    observes, "[d]espite its Hellenic associations, or partly because of them,
    it was the Orient that the Crimea most often evoked in Catherine's day,
    both in Russia and abroad." Schimmelpenninck van der Oye, *Russian
    Orientalism*, 47. As Susan Layton notes, "the Crimea would indeed
    acquire an aura of eastern exoticism in Russian literature." See Layton,
    Russian Literature and Empire, 1.
13 Said, *Culture and Imperialism*, 69.
14 Cambrensis, *The Topography of Ireland*, 68–70.
15 Pope, *An Essay on Man*, 14.
16 Tuan, *Space and Place*, 4.
17 Vozgrin, *Istoriia krymskikh tatar*, 2:418.
18 Holderness, *Notes Relating to the Manners and Customs of the Crim Tatars*,
    49–50.
19 Sasse, *The Crimea Question*, 4.
20 Said, *Culture and Imperialism*, 225.

21 "Önsöz," in *Osmanlı belgelerinde Kırım Hanlığı*, ed. Ünal and Gurulkan, 3. Koca Yusuf Paşa's report, for instance, refers to Peter I as "Mad Peter" in "Sadrâzamın Başkanlığında yapılan toplantıda Kırım ve Rusya Konularında alınan kararlar (15 Haziran 1783)," in *Osmanlı belgelerinde Kırım Hanlığı*, ed. Ünal and Gurulkan, 313.
22 Çağman, "III. Selim'e sunulan bir ıslahat raporu," 225.
23 "Rus işgalinden sonra Kırım'ın genel durumu (21 Aralık 1787)," in *Osmanlı belgelerinde Kırım Hanlığı*, ed. Ünal and Gurulkan, 335.
24 Vozgrin, *Istoriia krymskikh tatar*, 2:420.
25 Chepurin, "Orientir," 47–61. Agnia Grigas argues that a "reimperialization policy trajectory" is at the heart of contemporary Russian foreign policy. See Grigas, *Beyond Crimea*, 10.
26 Arendt, *The Life of the Mind*, 203.
27 Mostafa, "The Cairene Sabil," 34.
28 Sinyavsky, *Strolls with Pushkin*, 46.
29 Brodsky, "A Guide to a Renamed City," 93. In reference to literature of and about Saint Petersburg, Brodsky writes of a "second Petersburg – the one made of verse and of [...] prose."
30 Schönle, "Catherine's Appropriation of the Crimea," 10–11.
31 Lotman, "Mezhdu veshch'iu i pustotoi," 305.
32 Liusyi, *Krymskii tekst v russkoi literature*, 32.
33 Liusyi, 66.
34 Bobrov, *Tavrida*, 27.
35 Bobrov, 86.
36 Al'tshuller and Lotman, "Primechaniia," 819; Bayley, *Pushkin*, 85.
37 Pushkin, *Bakhchisaraiskii fontan*, 177. Hereafter cited by page number.
38 Bobrov, *Tavrida*, 235.
39 Bobrov, 237.
40 For an example of a view on the khan's putative marginality, see Bayley, *Pushkin*, 83.
41 Belinskii, "Sochineniia Aleksandra Pushkina," 318.
42 Baudelaire, *Petits poèmes en prose*, 39.
43 Sandler, *Distant Pleasures*, 77.
44 Shakespeare, *Macbeth*, 1062 (3.1.60–4), emphasis added.
45 Boym, *The Future of Nostalgia*, 50.
46 Boym, 50.
47 Voloshin, "Dom poeta," 80.
48 Voloshin, "Kul'tura, iskusstvo, pamiatniki Kryma," 341.
49 "Dyskusiia 'Krym v ukraïns'kii literaturi.'"
50 Nabokov, "Commentary," in Pushkin, *Eugene Onegin*, 256.
51 Pushkin, "Otryvki iz puteshestviia Onegina," in *Polnoe sobranie sochinenii*, 5:28.

52 Tumanskii, "Elegiia," 135–6.
53 Benediktov, "Oreanda." 130–1.
54 Nekrich, *The Punished Peoples*, 105.
55 Voloshin, "Kul'tura, iskusstvo, pamiatniki Kryma," 340–1.
56 Herzen [Gertsen], "Gonenie na krymskikh tatar," 966–7.
57 "Muhacir Türküleri," 27.
58 Tanpınar, *19uncu asır Türk edebiyatı tarihi*, 441. If one prominent source is
    to be believed, the emotionality of Kemal's plays prevailed in his personal
    life as well. Sultan Abdülhamid remembers Kemal, whom he banished to
    Lesbos in 1876 and counted "among his victims" (mağdurlarım arasında),
    as a "fickle and complicated" (karışık ve çapraşık) but nonetheless sincere
    man with a tendency to wear his heart on his sleeve. See İsmet Bozdağ,
    Abdülhamid'in Hatıra Defteri, 47–51. Decades later, Mustafa Kemal Atatürk
    would reportedly declare Namık Kemal "the father of his emotions." See
    Parla, *The Social and Political Thought of Ziya Gökalp, 1876–1924*, 93.
59 Greenleaf, *Pushkin and Romantic Fashion*, 2. Responding to his critics in
    1830, for instance, Pushkin likened *Bakhchisaraiskii fontan* to the product
    of a young, naive poet prone to an exaggeration of feeling. See Pushkin,
    Pushkin on Literature, 253.
60 Bernard Lewis, *The Emergence of Modern Turkey*, 358.
61 Tanpınar, *19uncu asır Türk edebiyatı tarihi*, 407.
62 Fisher, *The Crimean Tatars*, 14. See also Fisher, *The Russian Annexation of the
    Crimea*, 15; and Fisher, *Between Russians, Ottomans, and Turks*, 79.
63 Tanpınar, *19uncu asır Türk edebiyatı tarihi*, 400. See also Evin, *Origins and
    Development of the Turkish Novel*, 11.
64 Zürcher, *Turkey*, 74.
65 Tanpınar, *19uncu asır Türk edebiyatı tarihi*, 410.
66 I am very grateful to Etem Erol for our discussions about this poem.
67 Kemal, *Cezmi*, 123.
68 Kemal, 125.
69 Kemal, 125.
70 Kemal, 125.
71 Akçura, *Üç Tarz-ı Siyaset*, 28–30.
72 Akçura, 31.
73 Akçura, 33.
74 Akçura, 40. Ali Kemal is also remembered today as the paternal great-
    grandfather of British prime minister Boris Johnson.
75 In *Türkçülüğün esasları*, Gökalp dismisses those who conceive of the
    nation primarily according to territory as "geographic nationalists."
    See Parla, 36.
76 Öztürkmen, "Folklore on Trial," 203, 211n13; Landau, *Pan-Turkism*, 38.

77 Gökalp, "Altın Destan," 135.
78 Landau, *Pan-Turkism*, 1; emphasis mine.
79 Yurdakul is referred to as the "first nationalist poet of Turkey" in Schamiloglu's "Tatar or Turk?," 240. For the sake of clarity and consistency I refer to him by his pen name "Yurdakul" (which can be translated as "slave to the homeland"), although "Mehmet Emin" or "Emin Bey" is preferred in Turkish sources.
80 Yurdakul, "Nifâk," 106.
81 Yurdakul, "Ey Türk Uyan," 136.
82 Yurdakul, 136.
83 Yurdakul, 138.
84 Lazzerini, "Ismail Bey Gasprinskii (Gapirali)," 50.
85 Yurdakul, "İsmail Gaspirinski'ye," 123–4.
86 Quoted in Kırımer, *Gaspıralı İsmail Bey*, 98.
87 Yurdakul, "Petersburg'a," 251; Yurdakul, "Çar'a," 250–1. For more on Gasprinskii, see also Fisher, "A Model Leader for Asia," 29–47.
88 Schamiloglu, "Tatar or Turk?," 238.

2 Colonial Eyes

1 Vozgrin, *Istoriia krymskikh tatar*, 2:796.
2 Gasprinskii, *Polnoe sobranie sochinenii*, 2:8; and Gasprinskii, *Polnoe sobranie sochinenii*, 1:8.
3 Abduramanova, "Gazeta 'Terdzhiman' kak istochnik po izucheniiu sotsial'no-bytovoi zhizni Kryma v kontse XIX v.," 74–5.
4 *Perevodchik (Tercüman)* 40 (26 November 1893): 25–8.
5 See, for instance, *Perevodchik (Tercüman)* 32 (26 September 1893): 4; and *Perevodchik (Tercüman)* 33 (4 October 1893): 8.
6 Gasprinskii, "Russkoe musul'manstvo," 57.
7 Gasprinsky's views on Pushkin, which were originally published in *Tercüman* in 1899, are quoted in İsmail Asanoğlu Kerim, *Gasprinskiyniñ "Canlı" tarihi 1883–1914*, 87. For more on Gasprinsky's views of Sultan Abdülhamid, see Ortaylı, *Ottoman Studies*, 204–7.
8 İsmail Gaspıralı, "Yine lisan bahsi," *Tercüman*, 21 November 1905; cited in Kırımlı, *National Movements and National Identity*, 41.
9 Vozgrin, *Istoriia krymskikh tatar*, 2:805.
10 "Cumhurbaşkanı Erdoğan."
11 "Prem'ernyi pokaz dokumental'noho fil'ma E.M. Kozhokina «Ismail i ego liudi»."
12 Sergei Aksenov, "Pozdravliaiu krymskikh tatar …"
13 Foucault, "What Is an Author?" 114.

14 Quoted in Hakan Kirimli, "The Young 'Tatar' Movement in the Crimea, 1905–1909," 538.
15 Kirimli, "The Young 'Tatar' Movement in the Crimea," 541.
16 Çergeyev, "Közyaş han çeşmesi," 392.
17 Szymborska, "The Three Oddest Words," in *Monologue of a Dog*, 28–9.
18 Ukraïnka, "Do sestry Ol'hy (11 veresnia 1897)," 380.
19 Ukraïnka, "Do M. P. Drahomanova (3 veresnia 1891)," 113.
20 In a letter to Ahatanhel Krymsky, Ukraïnka explains that there is something "diabolical" about the Don Juan legend that has "tortured people for 300 years," prompting successive revisions and interpretations across cultures. Ukraïnka, "Do A. Iu. Kryms'koho (6 travnia 1912 r)," 395–7.
21 Ukraïnka, "Bakhchysarais'kyi dvorets'," 107.
22 Derzhavnyi arkhiv Avtonomnoi Respubliky Krym (DAARK) / Gosudarstvennyi arkhiv Respubliki Krym (GARK), f. 706, op. 2, d. 35, l. 519; quoted in Kerim, "Poeticheskii genii Asana Chergeeva (1879–1946)."
23 Çergeyev, "Eşit, mevta ne söyleyür!" 390.
24 "Tatarskaia lopatka" (literally, Tatar shovel) is a slur equivalent to "Tatar dog" or, here, "Tatar scum."
25 Decades after Çergeyev, the Ukrainian poet Vasyl Stus would ask, "Who are you? Living or dead? Is it possible / To be both dead and alive?" See Stus, "Sto dzerkal spriamovano na mene," 74.
26 Derrida, *Specters of Marx*, 99.
27 Ukraïnka, "Nad morem," 160.
28 Ukraïnka wrote "Nad morem" in 1898, a year before Chekhov's "Dama s sobachkoi" ("Lady with a Lapdog").
29 Ukraïnka, "Nad morem," 169.
30 Fanon, *Peau noire, masques blancs*, 108.
31 Bhabha, "The Other Question," 116.
32 Ukraïnka, "Nad morem," 169.
33 Bhabha, "The Other Question," 115.
34 Ukraïnka, "Nad morem," 169.
35 Ukraïnka, 187.
36 Fanon, *L'an V de la révolution algérienne*, 29.
37 Fanon, *Peau noire, masques blancs*, 113.
38 Toktargazi, "Nale-i Kırım adlı eserin önsösü," 395.
39 Kryms'kyi, "Literatura kryms'kykh tatar," 179.
40 Toktargazi, "Fi-medkh-i-Qırım," 396.
41 Toktargazi, 396.
42 Toktargazi, "Satma saqın," 396.
43 Toktargazi, "Para," 182.

44 Toktargazi, *Mollalar proyekti*, 398.
45 For more on this debate see Pavlychko, "Modernism vs. Populism," 83–103.
46 I take the text of *Pid minaretamy* from Kotsiubyns'kyi's *Tvory v dvokh tomakh*, 1:192–234.
47 On the struggle of Ismail Gasprinsky with traditional mullahs or "qadimists," see Lazzerini, "Ismail Bey Gasprinskii (Gapirali)," 52–4.
48 Crews, *For Prophet and Tsar*, 326.
49 Iefremov, "U poiskakh novoi krasoty," 110.
50 Nechui-Levyts'kyi, "Ukraïns'ka dekadentshchyna," 177–8.
51 Kotsiubyns'kyi, "Lyst do Ol'hy Kobylians'koï" (25.10.02), 317.
52 Kotsiubyns'kyi, "Lyst do Ol'hy Kobylians'koï" (2.7.03), 318; emphasis mine.
53 Kotsiubyns'kyi, "Lyst do Ivana Franka" (16.2.03), 271; emphasis mine.
54 Krymsky explains his Crimean Tatar heritage in a letter of 1901 to Borys Hrinchenko. See Kryms'kyi, *Tvory v p'iaty tomakh*, 5:360.
55 Bahalii, Kryms'kyi, et al., "Poiasniuiucha zapyska do proektu orhanizatsiï Istorychno-Filolohichnoho Viddilu Ukraïns'koï Akademiï Nauk," ix.
56 Pavlychko, *Natsionalizm, seksual'nist', oriientalizm: Skladnyi svit Ahatanhela Kryms'koho*, 177.
57 *Ukrayna, Rusya ve Türkiye*, 30. For more on the Union of the Liberation of Ukraine, which published *Ukrayna, Rusya ve Türkiye*, see Hakan Kırımlı's excellent study, "The Activities of the Union for the Liberation of Ukraine in the Ottoman Empire during the First World War," 194–6.
58 Otar, "İstanbul Gazetelerinde Kırım," 15–16.
59 Kırımer, *Bazı hatıralar*, 187.
60 "Ukraina i Krym," *Golos Tatar* 2 (29 July 1917), 2.
61 Kırımer, *Bazı hatıralar*, 188–9.
62 Ivanets', *Pershyi Kurultai*, 47.
63 Kırımer, *Bazı hatıralar*, 201.
64 "Dokument No. 121 (9 veresnia 1917)," 291.
65 "Doklad," *Golos Tatar* 9 (23 September 1917), 3.
66 "Doklad," 3.
67 Kermençikli, "Tatarym," 85–6.
68 Fazıl and Nagayev, *Qırımtatar edebiyatınıñ tarihı*, 300–1.
69 Bektöre, "Tatarlığım," 301.
70 Kyrymohlu [Dzhemilev], "Noman Chelebidzhikhan z namy," 11.
71 Bunegin, *Revoliutsiia i grazhdanskaia voina v Krymu*, 326.
72 Kırımer, *Bazı hatıralar*, 213.
73 On Çelebicihan, Namık Kemal, and martyrdom (*şahadet*), see Kırımlı, *National Movements and National Identity among the Crimean Tatars, 1905–1916*, 155–6.

74 Çelebicihan, "Ant etkenmen," 103–4.
75 Pulatov, "Ölümge 'Yoq' dep ayt," 68.
76 Ivanets', *Pershyi Kurultai*, 106.

3 Ethnic Cleansing, Discursive Cleansing

1 Bektöre, "Dalgalara," 45–6. See also Şahin, "Kırım Mecmuasında Neşredilen Kırım Konulu Şiirler Üzerine Bir İnceleme," 178.
2 Kırımlı, "The Activities of the Union," 194–6.
3 Attila Bektore, *A Nomad's Journey*, 38.
4 "Mustafa Kemal Paşanın Lenin'e Mektubu (4 ocak 1922)," 261.
5 *Kırım Mecmuası* 1, no. 13 (October 1918): 241.
6 Stalin, "Marksizm i natsional'nyi vopros," 363.
7 Stalin, 361.
8 RTsKhIDNI (Russian Center for the Preservation and Study of Documents of Most Recent History) 558/1/4490 (1929): 9; quoted in Martin, *The Affirmative Action Empire*, 5.
9 "Soviet legislation […] directly connected nationality with territory." Khazanov, *After the USSR*, 18.
10 Trotskii, *Predannaia revoliutsiia*, 75.
11 Finnin, "Forgetting Nothing, Forgetting No One," 1093.
12 See, for instance, Sharma, "Scholars Targeted as Uighur Purge Engulfs Universities"; Wong et al., "Facebook Bans Rohingya Group's Posts as Minority Faces 'Ethnic Cleansing'"; and Stevenson, "Facebook Admits It Was Used to Incite Violence in Myanmar."
13 Aleksandr Solzhenitsyn, *Sobranie sochinenii v deviaty tomakh*, 6:298.
14 Vozgrin, *Istoriia krymskikh tatar*, 3:426.
15 Vozgrin, 3:494.
16 Vozgrin, 3:498–9.
17 Martin, *The Affirmative Action Empire*, 274.
18 Martin, 274.
19 Martin, 342.
20 Ubiria, *Soviet Nation-Building in Central Asia*, 161.
21 Buzuk, "Ab belaruska-ukrainskim literaturnym pabratsimstve," 77.
22 Buzuk, 82.
23 Buzuk, 79.
24 Suny, "The Contradictions of Identity," 22–3.
25 Fazıl and Nagayev, *Qırımtatar edebiyatınıñ tarihı*, 273–4.
26 The influence of Toktargazy on İpci was recognized in an article of 1936, which celebrated İpci's twenty years of literary activity. A year later, İpci was arrested on charges of "bourgeois nationalism." See "Dvadtsatiletnii iubilei literaturnoi deiatel'nosti t. Umera Ipchi," 131.

27 For insight into the extraordinary success of VUFKU, see Hoseiko, *Istoriia ukraïns'koho kinematohrafa*, esp. 25.

28 "Novi viddili VUFKU," *Kino* 10, August 1926, 19.

29 Mandelshtam eviscerated Leo Mur's film *Pesn na kamne* (Song on the rock, 1926) for such an offence in "Tatarskie kovboi," 432–4.

30 Ursu, *Ocherki istorii kul'tury krymskotatarskogo naroda*, 22.

31 "Liudy ekranu: H. Tasin," *Kino* 3 (February 1927): 6. The critics also highlighted Tasin's achievement in bucking a "distasteful" trend: "At the heart of *Alim* lay a great peril [*velyka nebezpeka*]: the peril of exoticism, of a thoughtless approach to 'eastern peoples,' which has become established among our directors as a rule. Everyone agrees that Tasin has skirted the peril of this distasteful and mendacious cliché." Russian colleagues tended to agree, with one noting that "defying expectations, the director was not carried away by the horse chases so typical of 'eastern' films." Vilenskii, "Novye fil'my," 16.

32 O. Akçokraklı (Akchokrakly), "Tatars'ka poema Dzan-mukhammedova pro pokhid Isliam-Hireia II spil'no z Bohdanom Khmel'nyts'kym na Polshchu 1648–49rr," 163–71.

33 A. E. Kryms'kyi, "Literatura kryms'kykh tatar," 168.

34 Akçokraklı, "Tatars'ka poema Dzan-mukhammedova," 163–71.

35 Hrushevs'kyi, *Istoriia Ukraïny-Rusy*, vol. 8, pt. 3, sec. 13, 171.

36 Akçokraklı, "Tatars'ka poema Dzan-mukhammedova," 165.

37 Canmuhammed, "Tuğaybey," 108. See also "Canmuhammed" in Fazıl and Nagayev, *Qırımtatar edebiyatınıñ tarihı*, 125–6.

38 Deny, "Redīf," in *Encyclopaedia of Islam*.

39 Semeniuk, *Nikoly ne smiiavsia bez liubovi*, 6.

40 For more on the "hybrid tongues of the colonial space," see especially Bhabha, "Of Mimicry and Man," 121–31, and "Sly Civility," 132–45.

41 Khvyl'ovyi, "Ostap Vyshnia v svitli livoï balabaiky," 309.

42 Vyshnia, "Tatarynove zhyttia," 76. The work was originally published as "Zhyttia Tatarynove," *Visti VUTsVK i KhHVK* 25 (29 June 1924): 2–3.

43 See Iefremov, *Korotka istoriia ukraïns'koho pys'menstva*, 105–6.

44 I take this example from "Pobeh trekh brat'ev iz Azova," in Mikhail Maksimovich, *Sbornik ukrainskikh pesen*, 24.

45 Vyshnia, "Tatarynove zhyttia," 76–7.

46 See Markov, *Ocherki Kryma*, 314–31.

47 Markov, 314.

48 Nadinskii, *Ocherki po istorii Kryma*, vol. 1. As Greta Uehling notes, many politicians in the Crimean parliament continue to toe Nadinsky's historical line. See Uehling, *Beyond Memory*, 35.

49 Markov, 314.

50 Vyshnia, "Tatarynove zhyttia," 77. Markov, *Ocherki Kryma*, 315. Markov confuses the origins of Minikh and Lacey (Lassi) here; Minikh was ethnically German, Lacey an Irishman.
51 Vyshnia, "Tatarynove zhyttia," 80. Markov, *Ocherki Kryma*, 317.
52 *Vyshnevi usmishky kryms'ki* was repeatedly reprinted on its own (1961 and 1969); sampled in general usmishky compilations (1965, 1967, 1969, 1974, 1978, 1979, 1983, and 1985); or included in Vyshnia's multivolume collected works (1963, 1974, and 1988) – but always without "Tatarynove zhyttia."
53 Vyshnia, *Vyshnevi usmishky: Zaboroneni tvory* (2011).
54 Glavnoe upravlenie po kontroliu za zrelishchami i repertuarom (GURK), "Rasporiazhenie 700/r (17 April 1937)."
55 See, for example, Rollberg, *Historical Dictionary of Russian and Soviet Cinema*, 733.
56 "Ipchi, Dzhevair Umerovna," 58–9.
57 Khabarova, *Dnevnik* [19 May 1944]. Weeks later, Red Army soldiers arrested Zoia's parents for refusing to surrender their apartment to a party apparatchik, leaving her orphaned and homeless.
58 Khabarova, *Dnevnik.*
59 Vasil' Sokil, "Nichto ne zabyto, nikto ne zabyt!" 353–4.
60 Solzhenitsyn, *Arkhipelag GULag 1918–1956*, vol. 1, 95.
61 Sokil, "Nichto ne zabyto, nikto ne zabyt," 354. As Solzhenitsyn remarks, after the deportation "[t]obacco vanished from Crimea for many years to come." Solzhenitsyn, *Arkhipelag GULag 1918–1956*, vol. 3, part 6, 407.
62 "V krymskom nebe," *Pravda*, 12 May 1944, 3.
63 Muzafarov, *Krymskotatarskaia entsiklopediia*, 690. Years after the deportation Sultan wrote to the Central Committee of the Communist Party that "my people have been humiliated" and "deported from their native land needlessly and without foundation [*bez nuzhdy i osnovaniia*]. Return them to their native land – Crimea." Quoted in Broshevan and Tygliiants, *Izganie i vozvrashchenie*, 45.
64 Shkadov and Babakov, *Geroi Sovetskogo Soiuza*, 1:51.
65 Aliadin [Alâdin], "Ia – vash tsar i boh," 231.
66 Asanin, "Menim antım," 397.
67 Kalaycı, "Interview with Professor Jay Winter," 34.
68 Umerov, *Chornye poezda*. In the short story "Odinochestvo" (Loneliness), the Nazi occupation of Crimea and its aftermath, including the deportation, are focalized through the perspective of a dog named Sabyrly. "Chernye poezda" (Black trains), meanwhile, recounts the deportation operation in an elliptical, almost cinematic fashion.
69 Temirkaya, "Taras Şevçenkoğa," 3.
70 Caruth, *Unclaimed Experience.*

71 Laub, "Truth and Testimony," 66.
72 Quoted in Pulatov, "Vsem mirom – pomoch bratiam," 127.
73 Conquest, *The Nation Killers*, 67. Conquest states that "nothing was said about the [Crimean Tatars and other deported peoples] for a period of about ten years" after 1944. The silence was in fact broken in Soviet literature as early as 1948, when prominent works of historical fiction began to brand the entire Crimean Tatar nation as traitors to the Soviet motherland, as we will see.
74 Muzafarov, *Krymskotatarskaia entsiklopediia*, 653–7.
75 Polian, *Against Their Will*, 152.
76 For very likely saving the hansaray, Leonid Pliushch sardonically exclaimed, "Thank you, Comrade Pushkin!" Pliushch, *Na karnavale istorii*, 250.
77 Subbotin, "Bor'ba s istoriei," 10.
78 See Bushakov, "Svits'ki ta religiini tytuly i nazvy profesiinykh zaniat'," 135–9.
79 Vul', *Nemetskie varvary v Krymu*, 63–4.
80 Russian State Archive of Socio-political History (RGASPI), f. 14, op. 44, d. 759, l. 103, cited in Bekirova, *Krymskotatarskaia problema v SSSR, 1944–1991*, 44; emphasis mine.
81 Jones, "'A Symptom of the Times,'" 163.
82 Shentalinsky, *The KGB's Literary Archive*, 176.
83 Pavlenko, "Rassvet," 450.
84 Pavlenko, 453.
85 Pavlenko, 455.
86 Kotyhorenko, *Kryms'kotatars'ki repatrianti*, 14.
87 Kotyhorenko, 14.
88 Wolfe, *Settler Colonialism*, 1. Wolfe cites Rose, *Hidden Histories*, 46.
89 "Ob uprazdnenii Checheno-Ingushskoi ASSR i preobrazovanii Krymskoi ASSR v Krymskuiu oblast'," *Izvestiia*, 26 June 1946, 3.
90 Fisher, *The Crimean Tatars*, 167.
91 "O zhurnalakh 'Zvezda' i 'Leningrad' iz postanovlenie TsK VKP(b) ot 14 avgusta 1946g," *Pravda*, 21 August 1946, 1.
92 "Obrashchenie krymskikh tatar k K. Val'dkhaimu," 2.
93 Ivan Kozlov, *V krymskom podpol'e*, 76.
94 Kozlov, 81–2.
95 Nekrich, *The Punished Peoples*, 32.
96 Ivan Kozlov, *V krymskom podpol'e*, 159 and 279. I was guided to these particular passages by Refik Muzafarov in *Krymskotatarskaia entsiklopediia*, no pages given. Born in 1928 in Simferopol, Muzafarov was fifteen years old when his family was deported to the Urals. He became an active leader in the Crimean Tatar movement in 1957. See Nekrich, *The Punished Peoples*, 198–9.

97 Muzafarov, *Krymskotatarskaia entsiklopediia*, no pages given. "Kogda russkii ukradet, govoriat: 'Ukral vor,' a kogda ukradet evrei, govoriat, 'Ukral evrei'"; Maksim Gorkii, *Zhizn' Klima Samgina*, 431–2.

98 Perventsev, *Chest' smolodu*, 370. Italics reflect text taken directly from the 1946 Presidium decree.

99 The passage quoted was removed from the 1979 edition of Perventsev's collected works. See Perventsev, *Sobranie sochinenii*, 4:329. Perventsev also wrote a screenplay called *Tretii udar* (The third strike) with many anti-Tatar passages, which he removed in later versions. In 1976 Perventsev published a book called *Navstrechu zhyzni* (Meet life) in which he expressed a positive sentiment toward the Crimean Tatars. See Muzafarov, *Krymskotatarskaia entsiklopediia*, 380–1.

4 The Guiltless Guilty

1 Berdinskikh, *Istoriia odnogo lageria (Viatlag)*, 18.

2 Medvedev and Chiesa, *Time of Change*, 217. Evtushenko, "Krotost' i moshch'," 149.

3 Mazus, *Istoriia odnogo podpol'ia*, 319.

4 Rakhlin, *O Borise Chichibabine i ego vremeni*, 30 and 54.

5 Karas'-Chichibabina, "Predislovie," 5.

6 Karas'-Chichibabina, 5.

7 "In every epoch," writes Mikhail Epstein, "poetry is the battleground between convention and freedom." Epstein, "Theses on Metarealism and Conceptualism," 105–12.

8 Tvardovskii, "Po pravu pamiati," 108.

9 "Iosif Brodskii v zashchitu Maramzina," 11.

10 Aslan, *Tablet and Pen*, 275.

11 In 1921, for instance, Atatürk petitioned Nazım Hikmet, arguably Turkey's greatest poet of the twentieth century, to write verse "committed" to the independence movement. See Gologlu, *Milli Mücadele Tarihi IV*, 53.

12 Bezirci, *Orhan Veli ve seçme şiirleri*, 194.

13 Ayhan, *Şiirin bir altın çağı*.

14 The Ukrainian poet Lina Kostenko warns against the creep of the internal censor in the Soviet-era poem "Shukaite tsenzora v sobi" (Find the censor in yourself), who "quietly takes the 'you' out of 'you,'" leaving behind only a shell. See Kostenko, *Vybrane*, 12.

15 Anna Akhmatova aptly described samizdat technology as "pre-Gutenberg." See Komaromi, "The Material Existence of Soviet Samizdat," 598.

16 Cited in Alekseeva, *Istoriia inakomysliia v SSSR*, 211.

17 Svitlychna, "Interv'iu z Nadiieiu Svitlychnoiu," 29; Alekseeva, *Soviet Dissent*, 284.

18 Daniel', "Istoki i smysl sovetskogo samizdata," 20.
19 Daniel', 20.
20 Aronov, "Ia b ne vzial tebia, konechno," 97.
21 Grigorenko used scare quotes in referring to "our 'dissidents'" (nashkikh "dissidentov") in a letter to Leonid Pliushch of 3 March 1976. See Petro and Zinaida Grigorenko Family Papers (hereafter PGFP), series II, box 3, folder 2. For his part, Boris Chichibabin forcefully refused any association with the term. See Chichibabin, *Pered zemleiu krymskoi sovest' moia chista*, 90.
22 Amal'rik, *Zapiski dissidenta*, 35. As Ann Komaromi argues, the blanket use of the term *dissident* can obscure a highly diverse and differentiated group of writers and readers, a patchwork of publics that "cannot be unified comfortably [...] under a single discourse." See Komaromi, "Samizdat and Soviet Dissident Publics," 87. Or, as Michael Meerson-Aksenov and Boris Shragin put it, the term *dissident* "creates an illusion of clarity which does not exist in reality." See their preface to *The Political, Social and Religious Thought of Russian "Samizdat,"* 13.
23 Daniel', "Istoki i smysl sovetskogo samizdata," 26. Andrei Siniavsky makes a similar point in Terts [Siniavskii], "Iskusstvo i deistvitelnost'," 113.
24 Chornovil and the editors at *Ukraïnskyi visnyk* identify three phases in the development of Ukrainian samvydav: first, a seminal literary phase; second, a phase (1963–5) marked by political articles and anonymous letters; and third, a phase (from 1965 to the time of the publication of *Ukraïnskyi visnyk* in January 1970) marked by more public petitions, alerts, and open letters. Chornovil, "Pro ukraïns'kyi samvydav," 153. See also Obertas, *Ukraïns'kyi samvydav*, 56; and Kas'ianov, *Nezhodni*, 89.
25 Zhylenko, "Homo Feriens" (part II), 16.
26 See, for instance, Meerson-Aksenov, "The Dissident Movement and *Samizdat*," 28.
27 Even fresh studies of samizdat culture over the past two decades make this move. Sergei Oushakine, for instance, hops over the literary origins of samizdat to offer insightful critical assessments of "political samizdat," which he argues manifests a "discursive dependency" on the Soviet state. What starts out as a study of "political samizdat," however, soon leads to generalizations about "samizdat" and "dissident discourse" *tout court*. See Oushakine, "The Terrifying Mimicry of Samizdat," 191–214. Aleksei Yurchak perpetuates this generalization – this unqualified conflation of "samizdat" with "political samizdat" – while critically engaging with Oushakine's work. See Yurchak, *Everything Was Forever Until It Was No More*, 106, 130.
28 Gorbanevskaia is quoted in Reddaway, *Uncensored Russia*, 35.
29 For more on the transformation of Gorbanevskaia's Olympia typewriter, see Hopkins, *Russia's Underground Press*, 16.

30 The term *cultural opposition* is Andrei Amalrik's. See Amalrik, *Will the Soviet Union Survive until 1984?*, 16–18.
31 Giritli, "Modern çağda bilim ve ideolojiler," 2.
32 See Komaromi, "Samizdat and Soviet Dissident Publics," 81.
33 Alekseeva and Goldberg, *The Thaw Generation*, 4.
34 Solzhenitsyn, *Zhit' ne po lzhi*.
35 Amal'rik, *Zapiski dissidenta*, 40.
36 Grossman, *Vse techet...*, 71.
37 Chukovskaia, *Sof'ia Petrovna*.
38 Alekseeva, *Istoriia inakomysliia v SSR*, 210.
39 For an intriguing discussion of the importance of memorization of unofficial poetry in the Soviet Union, see Gronas, *Cognitive Poetics and Cultural Memory*, 7–8, 71–96.
40 Mukorovský, "Standard Language and Poetic Language," 19.
41 Jakobson, *O cheshkom stikhe preimushchestvenno v sopostavlenii s russkim*, 16.
42 Shklovsky, "Art as Technique," 12.
43 Raskina, "Natal'ia Gorbanevskaia," 523. Gobanevskaia's remarks are cited in Hopkins, *Russia's Underground Press*, 23.
44 "The dry, factual tone of *Chronicle* has led to the conclusion that its authors and producers were primarily scientists rather than literary intellectuals." Gayle Durham Hollander, "Political Communication and Dissent in the Soviet Union," 264.
45 "Kratkie soobshcheniia," 45.
46 Hörmann, *Meinen und Verstehen*, 187 and 192–6; quoted in Iser, *The Fictive and the Imaginary*, 18.
47 Kant, *Critique of Pure Reason*, 70.
48 Chichibabin, "Rodnoi iazyk," 43. Chichibabin self-identified as Russian but lived most of his life in Kharkiv and professed love for Ukraine and Ukrainian culture.
49 Rakhlin, *O Borise Chichibabine i ego vremeni*, 23.
50 Rakhlin, 97.
51 Selim, "Ev," 123.
52 Rakhlin, *O Borise Chichibabine i ego vremeni*, 97; emphasis mine.
53 Leonovich, "Mezh rozovykh barkhanov," 228.
54 Leonovich, 228.
55 Correspondence between Viktor Sokirko and the author, August 2009.
56 Andrew Wachtel, *Remaining Relevant after Communism*, 40.
57 For an excellent study of reader letters to Tvardovsky's *Novyi Mir*, which tended to focus more on the Stalinist crimes of 1937, see Denis Kozlov, *The Readers of "Novyi Mir."*
58 Mustafa Dzhemilev, interview with the author, December 2019.

59 For a fascinating discussion of Khrushchev's "Secret Speech" and its hasty composition, see Polly Jones, *Myth, Memory, Trauma*, 17–53.
60 Quoted in Paradzhanov, *Dremliushchii dvorets*, 89; emphasis mine.
61 Wilder, *The Bridge of San Luis Rey*, 16.
62 Mustafa Dzhemilev, interview with the author, December 2019.
63 Myroslav Marynovych, interview with the author, November 2019.
64 Chichibabin, "Genrikhu Altunianu," 163.
65 Myroslav Marynovych, interview with the author, November 2019.
66 Chichibabin, *Pered zemleiu krymskoi sovest' moia chista*, 79.
67 Ginzburg, "I zaodno s pravoporiadkom," 292.
68 Jaspers, *The Question of German Guilt*, 25.
69 Boobbyer, *Conscience, Dissent and Reform in Soviet Russia*, 3.
70 Aşkın, "Tatar Türklerini savunan subayın hatıra defteri Paris'e kaçırıldı," 3. Aşkın's use of *tımarhane* echoes Grigorenko's own use of *durdom* (madhouse) a year before in his samizdat pamphlet of 1969, "O spetsial'nykh psikhiatricheskikh bol'nitsakh ('durdomakh')" [Regarding special psychiatric hospitals ('madhouses')]." See Grigorenko, *Mysli sumasshedshego*, 232–42.
71 Grigorenko, "Vystuplenie P. Grigorenko na pokhoronakh A.E. Kosterina (14 noiabria 1968 g.)," 159; emphasis mine.
72 Jaspers, *The Question of German Guilt*, 29.
73 Helen Lewis, *Shame and Guilt in Neurosis*, 30.
74 Gilbert, *Human Nature and Suffering*, 241 and 239. See too Darwin's observation that "under a keen sense of shame there is a strong desire for concealment." Charles Darwin, *The Expression of the Emotions in Man and Animal*, 320.
75 Tangney, "Recent Advances in the Empirical Study of Shame and Guilt," 1137.
76 O'Connor and Berry, "Interpersonal Guilt," 77.
77 Tangney, "Recent Advances," 1137.
78 Thomas, "*The Fictive and the Imaginary*," 624; Iser, *Prospecting*, 39.
79 Iser, *The Implied Reader*, 281.
80 Frye, *Anatomy of Criticism*, 73.
81 Iser, *Prospecting*, 239; Iser, "*The Fictive and the Imaginary*," 5.
82 Taylor, *Sources of the Self*, 36.
83 Goodhart's opposition of solidarity and diversity has become notorious as a harbinger of pro-Brexit politics among moderate political circles in Great Britain. See Goodhart, "Too Diverse?"
84 Heise, "Conditions for Empathic Solidarity," 197.
85 Smith, *The Theory of Moral Sentiments*, 2.
86 Schwarz, "A Humanistic Ethics of Reading," 5.
87 Iser, *Prospecting*, 29; emphasis mine. Luc Boltanski views the faculty of the imagination as key to overcoming an essential distance between what he

calls the "spectator" and the "unfortunate" in cases of suffering. See Boltanski, *Distant Suffering*, 38.
88 McGinn, *Ethics, Evil, and Fiction*, 176.
89 Frank, "Layers of the Visual," 84.
90 Okudzhava, "Ia rad by byl pokoem voskhitit'sia," 60.
91 Brysk, *Speaking Rights to Power*, 18.
92 I take the text of "Krymskie progulki" from Chichibabin, *I vse-taki ia byl poetom*, 73–6.
93 Waters, *Poetry's Touch*, 8.
94 Seven years after the composition of "Krymskie progulki," Grigorenko turned Chichibabin's lyrical persona's declaration into a question: "Est li u tebia sovest, Rossiia?" (Do you have a conscience, Russia?). See Grigorenko, "Rech' Gen. P.G. Grigorenko," 196.
95 Lotman, *Struktura khudozhestvennogo teksta*, 66.
96 Eliot, "The Three Voices of Poetry," 96.
97 Vendler, *The Given and the Made*, xi.
98 Grigorenko, "Pis'mo Iu. V. Andropovu," 143.
99 As quoted in Lazzerini, "Local Accommodation and Resistance," 174.
100 Emphasis mine.
101 Hosking, "The State and Russian National Identity," 201.
102 Chichibabin, "Pis'mo Aideru Emirovu," 78–83.
103 I take the text of "Chernoe piatno" from Chichibabin, *Pered zemleiu krymskoi sovest' moia chista*, 81–2.
104 Furmanov, "Zametki o literature," 393.
105 Emirov, "Istoriia odnogo stikhotvoreniia," 1.
106 See Kirimca, "Symbols," 71–83.
107 *Boris Chichibabin: Zamist' spovidi*, directed by Rafail Nakhmanovich, 1993 (part of the Narody Ukraïny documentary film cycle produced by the Ukrainian Studio of Documentary-Chronicle Films).
108 Pliushch, *Na karnavale istorii*, 252.
109 Sheehy, *The Crimean Tatars and Volga Germans*, 14. Petro Grigorenko recalls Crimean Tatar activists collecting over two thousand signatures in only one hour. See Grigorenko, *Memoirs*, 362.
110 Bekirova, *Piv stolittia oporu*, 195.
111 See, for example, "Arest i golodovka Mustafy Dzemileva"; "Delo Mustafy Dzemileva," 207–10; or "Sud nad Mustafoi Dzhemilevym."
112 Reddaway, "The Crimean Tatar Drive for Repatriation," 227. The excerpts from the 1967 decree are taken from Russkie druz'ia krymskikh tatar, "Sudiat krymskikh tatar," 174.
113 Grigorenko, "Kto zhe prestupniki?" 224.
114 Grigorenko, "Pamiati soratnika i druga," 156.
115 Grigorenko, 156.

116 Grigorenko, "Pis'mo Iu. V. Andropovu," 145.
117 Hablemitoğlu, *Yüzbinlerin Sürgünü Kırımda Türk Soykırımı*, 170.
118 Grigorenko, "Zapis' rechi proiznesennoi 17 marta 1968 goda," 150.
    See also Grigorenko, "Rech' Gen. P.G. Grigorenko," 198. Alekseeva,
    "Krymskotatarskoe dvizhenie za vozvrashchenie v Krym," 9.
119 Pliushch, *Na karnavale istorii*, 321.
120 Sarıkamış, "Sana Hasret Gideriz Güzel Kırım," 23.
121 "Kırım Türkleri hala insanca yaşayamıyor," 8.
122 Haluzevyi derzhavnyi arkhiv Sluzhby bespeky Ukraïny [State Archive of
    the Security Service of Ukraine], Kyiv [hereafter HDA SBU], f. 16, op. 1,
    spr. 963, ark. 163.
123 Roditi, "Review of *A Last Lullaby*," 763.
124 Halman, "Sovyet Cennetinde İzzet ile İdris," 2.
125 Selim, "Ev," 123.
126 Tvardovskii, *Za dal'iu – dal'*, 131–40.
127 Ognev et al, *Akhmatovskie chteniia*, 37.
128 The poem was published in *Znamia* 2 (1987) and *Novyi Mir* 3 (1987).
129 Alexander Tvardovskii, "Po pravu pamiati," 111. For a helpful
    contextualization of the poem's controversial reception, see Denis Kozlov,
    The Readers of "Novyi Mir," esp. 317–20.
130 Emphasis mine.
131 Here is Pushkin: "Slukh obo mne proidet po vsei Rusi velikoi, / I nazovet
    menia vsiak sushchii v nei iazyk, / I gordyi vnuk slavian, i finn, i nyne
    dikii / Tungus, i drug stepei kalmyk." (Word of me will pass through
    all of great Rus' / And her every single tongue will call my name, /
    The proud descendant of the Slavs, and the Finn, and today's savage /
    Tungus, as well as the Kalmyk, friend of the steppe.)
132 Nekipelov wrote the manuscript in 1976 and arranged for its passage to
    the West, where it appeared in English in an edition published by Farrar
    Straus and Giroux in 1980. Along with selections of Nekipelov's poetry,
    Institut durakov was finally published in Russia in 2005 by an organization
    called Aid to the Victims of Psychiatry (Pomoshch postradavshim ot
    psikhiatrii).
133 Grigorenko, "O spetsial'nykh psikhiatricheskikh bol'nitsakh
    ('durdomakh')," 234.
134 Sakharov, *Vospominaniia*, 2:434.
135 Petrenko-Pod"iapol'skaia, "Biografiia Viktora Nekipelova," 2–3. See also
    Komarova-Nekipelova, *Kniga liubvi i gneva*.
136 Petrenko-Pod"iaiapol'skaia, "Biografiia Viktora Nekipelova," 1.
137 Nekipelov, "Chufut-Kale," 37.
138 I take the text of "Gurzuf" from Nekipelov, *Stikhi*, 38–9.

139 With Tatiana Khodorovich and Tatiana Osipova, Nekipelov released the *ekspress-zhurnaly* "Oprichnina 76," "Oprichnina 77," and "Oprichnina 78," three of the most influential compilations of documents from the Moscow Helsinki Group. See Petrenko-Pod"iapol'skaia, "Biografiia Viktora Nekipelova," 6.

140 Vendler, *The Given and the Made*, xi.

141 I take the text of "Ballada ob otchem dome" from Nekipelov, *Stikhi*, 40.

142 Michael Wachtel, *The Development of Russian Verse*, 23.

143 Russkie druz'ia krymskikh tatar, "Sudiat krymskikh tatar," 176; emphasis mine. According to Dzhemilev, Yakobson was the primary author. Dzhemilev, interview with the author, December 2019. Documents in *Khronika tekushchikh sobytii* detail that in 1968, at the time "Ballada ob otchem dome" was written, over ten thousand Tatars who had returned to Crimea after the discreet promulgation of Decree 493 were forcibly exiled from their homeland once again. See Chubarov, "Peredmova," x.

144 *Khronika tekushchikh sobytii* 2 (June 1968). See also "'Delo' krymskikh tatar,'" 178–91.

145 PGFP, series II, subseries 1–2, boxes 3–5.

146 PGFP, series IV, subseries 3, box 14, folder 2.

147 Parts of "Sudakskie elegii" were published in the first issue of the Moscow-based samizdat journal *Poiski* (Quest) in 1979. Chichibabin, "Sudakskie elegii," *Poiski*, 76–7. The poem was also reprinted in 1986 in *Antologiia noveishei russkoi poezii u goluboi laguny*, 75–6.

148 Kul'chyts'kyi and Iakubova, *Kryms'kyi vuzol*, 256.

149 Chichibabin, "Otvet redaktoru zhurnala *Novyi mir*," 74–5.

150 Myroslav Marynovych, interview with the author, November 2019.

5 Trident and Tamğa

1 HDA SBU, f. 16, op. 1, spr. 960, ark. 326.

2 Antonenko-Davydovych, *Smert'*, 32. In 1929 Antonenko-Davydovych was also a part of an infamous meeting of Ukrainian writers with Stalin in Moscow. His account of the meeting circulated in samvydav for decades. At one point, when approaching the headquarters of the Communist Party Central Committee, he calls to mind Dostoevsky's *House of the Dead*. "If this isn't 'the house of the dead,' what is?" Antonenko-Davydovych, "Spohad pro pryiom Stalinom ukraïns'koï delegatsiï 1929 roku," 6–7. For more on the meeting, see Maximenkov and Heretz, "Stalin's Meeting with a Delegation of Ukrainian Writers on 12 February 1929," 361–431.

3 HDA SBU, f. 16, op. 1, spr. 960, ark. 326.

4 HDA SBU, f. 16, op. 1, spr. 960, ark. 326; emphases mine.

5 As Kul'chyts'kyi and Iakubova point out, "the Crimean Tatar movement already had Soviet authorities seriously concerned." See Kul'chyts'kyi and Iakubova, *Kryms'kyi vuzol*, 270.

6 Pliushch, *Na karnavale istorii*, 250.

7 Jakobson, "The Metaphoric and Metonymic Poles," 93.

8 Central Intelligence Agency, *The Spectrum of Soviet Dissent*, 3.

9 References to *non-Russian* in Sheila Fitzpatrick's introduction to an important study of everyday resistance in the Soviet Union are followed by the word *nationalist*, for instance. See Edel'man, Fitzpatrick, Kozlov, et al., *Sedition*, 3 and 14.

10 Horyn', "Ostannie slovo Mykhaila Horynia (16 kvitnia 1966 r)," 40.

11 Horyn', 39.

12 Kuzio, "Ukraine," 342.

13 Brubaker, *Nationalism Reframed*, 8.

14 Pliushch, *Na karnavale istorii*, 282.

15 Pliushch, 283; emphasis mine.

16 Olgun, "Şevçenko'nun ülkesinde," 29.

17 Conquest, *The Nation Killers*, 206.

18 Kul'chyts'kyi and Iakubova, *Kryms'kyi vuzol*, 252.

19 Arkhiv Tsentru doslidzhen' vyzvol'noho rukhu [Archive of the Centre for the Study of the Liberation Movement] (hereafter ATsDVR), f. 23, t. 6, ark. 1032, 1.

20 ATsDVR, f. 23, t. 6, ark. 1032, 1–2.

21 ATsDVR, f. 23, t. 6, ark. 1032, 2–3.

22 Jameson, "Third World Literature," 69.

23 *Aristotle's Poetics*, 150.

24 Hikmet, "Nash Shevchenko," 4.

25 Finnin, "Mountains, Masks, Metre, Meaning," 426.

26 Pliushch, *Na karnavale istorii*, 134.

27 Tarnawsky, "Dissident Poets in Ukraine," 24.

28 Browne, *Ferment in the Ukraine*, 2.

29 Fanon, "National Culture," 155.

30 I take the text of "Kurds'komu bratovi" from Symonenko, *Bereh Chekan'*, 162.

31 Chornovil, *Tvory v desiaty tomakh*, vol. 4, bk. 2, 969.

32 Sokulsky takes the term *dukhovni pokydky* (spiritual refuse, or even moral scum) from Vasyl Symonenko's poem "Odynoka matir" (Single mother, 1962). See Symonenko, "Odynoka matir," 181.

33 "Lyst tvorchoï molodi m. Dnipropetrovs'ka," 93, 96.

34 Savchenko, "Khronika odnoho kryminal'noho protsesu," 154.

35 Savchenko, 154.

36 Sokul's'kyi, "Planovanyi – tut," 125.

37 Sokul's'kyi, "Kredo," 124.

38 Savchenko, "Khronika odnoho kryminal'noho protsesu," 159.
39 Eric Kudusov, "Ethnogenez korenogo naseleniia Kryma," 16. Neal Ascherson, *Black Sea*, 21. In Ascherson's eloquent framework the Crimean coast is the "zone of the mind" and the inland steppe the "zone of the body" (*Black Sea*, 17–18).
40 I take the text of "Bakhchysarai (Tsykl)" from Sokul's'kyi, *Oznachennia voli*, 48–50.
41 Myroslav Marynovych, interview with the author, November 2019.
42 See Rory Finnin, "Nationalism and the Lyric, Or How Taras Shevchenko Speaks to Compatriots Dead, Living, and Unborn," 47–8.
43 Sokulsky's lines call to mind a Ukrainian *duma* about the Cossack Holota in which a Crimean Tatar mountaineer addresses a young Tatar women with the question, "Do you see what I see?" (Chy ty bachysh, shcho ia bachu?). She responds, "I do not see what you see" (Ia ne bachu, shcho ty bachysh). Gatsak, *Ukrainskie narodnye dumy*, 77.
44 Iser, *Prospecting*, 134.
45 See Chornovil's letters to Heorhii Davydov (16 June 1979), Iosyp Behun (21 July 1979), and Oleksandr Podrabinek (25 July 1979), in Chornovil, *Tvory v desiaty tomakh*, vol. 4, bk. 2, 728, 742, and 749.
46 Chornovil, "Do Mustafy Dzhemilieva (26.7.1979)," 752.
47 Dzhemilev, "Pis'mo M. Dzhemileva Viacheslavu Chernovilu ot 11 avgusta 1979g," 152–3.
48 Dzhemilev, 157.
49 Chornovil, *Tvory v desiaty tomakh*, 777. Pliushch also describes Ivanychuk's novel as a work of literature intended to support the Crimean Tatar cause. See Pliushch, *Na karnavale istorii*, 249.
50 Ivanychuk, "Iak ia shukav svoï «Mal'vy»," 194. Serhii Plokhy considers *Malvy* "a new approach to the dramatic history of Ukrainian-Tatar relations in the sixteenth and seventeenth centuries." Plokhy, *Ukraine and Russia*, 177.
51 Kosiv, "Zhyttia korotke, mystetstvo – vichne."
52 As Plokhy notes, Ukrainian politicians in the post-Soviet era have highlighted this history to legitimize "the Ukrainian–Crimean Tatar political alliance of the 1990s." Plokhy, *Ukraine and Russia*, 11.
53 Subtelny, "The Ukrainian-Crimean Treaty of 1711," 809.
54 Shevchenko, "Khmel'nyts'kyi pered kryms'kym khanom," 90.
55 In connection with the three-hundredth anniversary of the Pereiaslav Treaty of 1654, there appeared historical novels by Natan Rybak (*Pereiaslavs'ka rada* [The Pereiaslav council], 1948, 1954), Petro Panch (*Homonila Ukraina* [Ukraine stirred], 1954), and Ivan Le (*Khmel'nyts'kyi*, 1957–65). See Marko Pavlyshyn, "*Ia Bohdan (spovid' u slavi) Pavla Zahrebel'noho*," 62.

56 See, for example, Humesky, "Text and Subtext in Roman Ivanychuk's *Mal'vy*," 284–5.
57 Zaitsev, "Bezzbroinyi opir totalitarnomu rezhymovi," 339.
58 Plokhy, *Ukraine and Russia*, 177.
59 Ravliuk, "Istoricheskii roman bez istorii," 4.
60 Salyha, *Vidlytyi u strofy chas*, 101.
61 Kucher, *Chornomortsi*, 302–3.
62 Grekov, "O nekotorykh voprosakh istorii Kryma," 3.
63 Grekov, 3.
64 Grekov, 3.
65 Nadinskii, *Ocherki po istorii Kryma*, 168. See also Fisher, *Between Russians, Ottomans, and Turks*, 182; and Williams, *The Crimean Tatars*, 74.
66 Putin, "Obrashchenie Prezidenta Rossiiskoi Federatsii (18 marta 2014 goda)."
67 See Ivanychuk, *Mal'vy (Ianychary)*, 17.
68 Ivanychuk, *Mal'vy (Ianychary)*, 17. Moreover, in his reflections on the origins and composition of *Mal'vy*, Ivanychuk refers to Mariia as "Mariia-Ukraina." See Ivanychuk, "Iak ia shukav svoï «Mal'vy»," 197.
69 Ivanychuk, "Iak ia shukav svoï «Mal'vy»," 194 and 198.
70 For an insightful analysis of the perceptions of Ukrainians (as "mazepintsy" and "malorossy") in the Russian imperial hierarchy, see Kappeler, "Mazepintsy, malorossy, khokhly," 125–44.
71 Karavans'kyi, "Pisnia ianychariv," 70.
72 Ivanychuk, *Mal'vy (Ianychary)*, 194.
73 Ivanychuk, "Iak ia shukav svoï «Mal'vy»," 195.
74 Ivanychuk, *Mal'vy (Ianychary)*, 229.
75 Ivanychuk, "Iak ia shukav svoï «Mal'vy»," 198.
76 Ivanychuk, 198.
77 Sysyn, *Between Poland and the Ukraine*, 308n88.
78 Novosel'skii, *Bor'ba moskovskogo gosudarstva s Tatarami v pervoi polovine XVII veka*, 6. Novoselsky denies a correspondence between Crimean place and Tatar personality, referring only to *tatary*, not *krymskie tatary*, in his work.
79 Novosel'skii, 422. Historians like Valerii Vozgrin and Alan Fisher counter Novoselsky, making clear that the khans maintained a great degree of independence in this period. See Vozgrin, *Istoriia krymskikh tatar*, 1:558; and Fisher, *Between Russians, Ottomans, and Turks*, 86–7.
80 Novosel'skii, 420. Khmelnytsky himself noted the desire of İslâm Giray to seek complete independence from the Ottoman Empire. See Smolii and Stepankov, *Bohdan Khmel'nyts'kyi*, 174.
81 Humesky, "Text and Subtext in Roman Ivanychuk's *Mal'vy*," 284.

82 Ivanychuk, "Iak ia shukav svoï «Mal'vy»," 194.
83 Prezydiia zakordonnoho predstavnytstva ukraïns'koï holovoï vyzvol'noï rady, "U spravi povernennia tatar na Krym," 91.
84 Prezydiia zakordonnoho predstavnytstva ukraïns'koï holovoï vyzvol'noï rady, 92; emphasis mine.
85 Prezydiia zakordonnoho predstavnytstva ukraïns'koï holovoï vyzvol'noï rady, 92.
86 Pliushch, *Na karnavale istorii*, 248.
87 Pliushch, 248.
88 Prezydiia zakordonnoho predstavnytstva ukraïns'koï holovoï vyzvol'noï rady, 92.
89 Beckett, "Dante ... Bruno ... Vico ... Joyce," 19.
90 Ivan Dziuba, "Vystup u babynomy iaru 29 veresnia 1966r," 306.
91 Dziuba, 305.
92 Dziuba refers here to Shevchenko's public protest against Vladimir Zotov's anti-Semitic tirades in the Saint Petersburg journal *Illiustratsiia* in 1858.
93 Dziuba, "Vystup u babynomy iaru 29 veresnia 1966r," 306–7.
94 For more on Ukrainian-Jewish relations, see Magocsi and Petrovsky-Shtern's outstanding volume *Jews and Ukrainians*.
95 Dziuba, "Vystup u babynomy iaru 29 veresnia 1966r," 305–6.
96 David A. Snow and Doug McAdam, "Identity Work Processes," 42.
97 Rudnytsky, "Political Thought of Soviet Ukrainian Dissidents," 485–6.
98 As quoted in Vlasenko, "Formula sontsia Mykoly Rudenka," 12.
99 Myroslav Marynovych, interview with the author, November 2019.
100 For more on Karavansky, see Etkind, Finnin, et al., *Remembering Katyn*, 63–8.
101 See "Novosti samizdata: T. Franko, M. Lysenko."
102 Kulichenko, *Natsional'nye otnosheniia v SSSR i tendentsii ikh razvitiia*, 325.
103 Rudnytsky, "Political Thought of Soviet Ukrainian Dissidents," 486.
104 Mykola Rudenko, "Donbas," 81–2.
105 Mykola Rudenko, "V Donets'ku," 169–70.
106 Raisa Rudenko, interview with the author, December 2007.
107 According to a letter from Vitaly Fedorchuk to Volodymyr Shcherbytsky in 1975, there were an estimated 693 Crimean Tatars in Donetsk around the time of the composition of Rudenko's "Tataryn." See "Z dopovidnoï zapysky holovy KDB pry PR URSR (8 travnia 1975r)," 23. Relevant census data from 1926, when Rudenko was a young child, give statistics only for "Tatars" in Donbas (over nine thousand), making no distinction between different nations with "Tatar" in the ethnonym.
108 Roman Jakobson, "Studies in Comparative Slavic Metrics," 33–9, 55–7.
109 I take the text of the poem from Rudenko, "Tataryn," in *Poezii*, 158–9.

110 Shevelov cites Rudenko as a talented but "programmatic poet," in contradistinction to the "unprogrammatic" Stus, whose variable and diverse emotions constantly surprise. Shevel'ov, "Trunok i trutyzna," 371–2.
111 Evtushenko, "Babii Iar," 421.
112 Felman and Laub, *Testimony*, 116.
113 Mykola Rudenko, *Naibil'she dyvo – zhyttia*, 412.
114 Morgan, *The Final Act*, 6.
115 See Bilocerkowycz, *Soviet Ukrainian Dissent*, 82.
116 Rubenstein and Gribanov, *The KGB File of Andrei Sakharov*, 120.
117 Alekseeva, *Soviet Dissent*, 48.
118 Subtelny, *Ukraine*, 521. The KGB in Ukraine became particularly vicious with the appointment of director Vitaly Fedorchuk in 1970. At its height the members of the Ukrainian Helsinki Group numbered forty, including seven women; the Moscow Helsinki Group numbered twenty-two. Bilocerkowycz, *Soviet Ukrainian Dissent*, 35 and 81.
119 Boris Chichibabin, "Ia plachu o dushe …," 190. Rudenko received this poem from Chichibabin in 1977 and relied on it as an important source of moral support. "At the time I did not believe that I would see this poem published someday," he recalled in 1997, "but I understood one thing: even if I did not survive to be remembered as a poet, Chichibabin had already immortalized me with his heavenly word." Mykola Rudenko, "Slovo pro druha," 210.
120 See Zakharov, "History of Dissent in Ukraine." See also Zwarun, preface to *The Human Rights Movement in Ukraine*, 10.
121 Kas'ianov, *Nezhodni*, 175.
122 Ukraïns'ka hromads'ka hrupa spryiannia vykonanniu hel'sinks'kykh uhod, *Ukraïns'kyi pravozakhysnyi rukh*, 72. As Ivan Lysiak Rudnytsky points out, this prevailing attention to the "national factor" contributed to a greater cohesion among Ukrainian dissidents relative to their Russian counterparts, whose ideological views tended to vary widely. See Rudnytsky, "Political Thought of Soviet Ukrainian Dissidents," 485.
123 Ukraïns'ka hromads'ka hrupa spryiannia vykonanniu hel'sinks'kykh uhod, *Ukraïns'kyi pravozakhysnyi rukh*, 97. Rudenko wrote the first three UHG memoranda before his arrest. His successor, Oles Berdnyk, a writer of science fiction, would perpetuate this poetic style.
124 Swoboda, "The Evolution of Mykola Rudenko's Philosophy in His Poetry," 78–9; Pavlyshyn, "'Sobor' Olesia Honchara ta 'Orlova Balka' Mykoly Rudenka," 55.
125 Kırımal, "Kırım Türkleri," 21.
126 "Z redaktsiinoï poshty," 375. See also Verba and Yasen, *The Human Rights Movement in Ukraine*, 31 and 252.

127 Mustafa Dzhemilev, interview with the author, December 2019. Dzhemilev calls Zinaida Grigorenko "mama" in a letter of 19 May 1970. See PGFP, series II, subseries 2, box 3, folder 27.
128 Mustafa Dzhemilev, interview with the author, December 2019. After Grigorenko protested the 1968 Soviet and Warsaw Pact invasion of Czechoslovakia, an act that led to his expulsion from the Party, the KGB searched his home. Dzhemilev, staying in his apartment and fearing arrest, jumped out of the window and broke his leg. Soviet authorities apparently regretted that "it was not his neck." Gorbanevskaia, *Polden'*, 284.
129 The TRT television channel broadcast an announcement that Dzhemilev had died on 5 February 1976. See Özcan, *Kırım Dramı*, 197.
130 See for instance "Sürgünü açlık greviyle protesto eden Kırım Türkü Cemiloğlu öldü," 7.
131 Perlman, "Bütun Müslümanlar Mustafa Cemiloğlu'nu savunmali," 1 and 10. Anatolii Levitin-Krasnov issued a similar appeal in "Müslüman Dünyasına Çağrı," 22.

6 Incense and Drum

1 Chukovskaia, "Litso beschelovech'ia," 49.
2 Dzhemilev, "Poema 'Bakhchisaraiskii fontan' Shiukriu El'china," 436.
3 Dzhemilev, "Den' shestoi," 403.
4 Mustafa Dzhemilev, interview with the author, December 2019.
5 Dzhemilev, "Poema 'Bakhchisaraiskii fontan' Shiukriu El'china," 437.
6 Dzhemilev, "Den' shestoi," 405.
7 "Poslednee slovo Andreia Siniavskogo," 155.
8 Beckett, "Dante... Bruno... Vico... Joyce," 19.
9 Fisher, *The Crimean Tatars*, 181; Kreindler, "The Soviet Departed Nationalities," 396.
10 Reddaway, "The Crimean Tatar Drive for Repatriation,'" 233.
11 Eren, "Crimean Tatar Communities Abroad," 328.
12 Elçin, "Bahçesaray Çeşmesi," 13–15. The poem was republished in *Türk Kültürü* 314 (June 1989): 328–9.
13 Zürcher, *Turkey*, 288. In privileging both an ancient concept of Turkishness and a devout Muslim way of life, the Synthesis bears the influence of Ziya Gökalp. See Eligür, *The Mobilization of Political Islam in Turkey*, 97.
14 Paul J. White and Joost Jongerden, *Turkey's Alevi Enigma*, 79; Zürcher, *Turkey*, 288.
15 Elçin, *Aşık Ömer*, 1.
16 Elçin, "Bahçesaray Çeşmesi," 13.
17 Elçin, *Halk edebiyatına giriş*, 209.

18 Lowell Bezanis estimates the circulation of *Emel* at roughly two thousand. See Bezanis, "Soviet Muslim Emigrés in the Republic of Turkey," 107.
19 "Yeniden Çıkarken," 1.
20 Aydin, "Turkish Foreign Policy," 107–8. In 1945 the Soviet Union declared that it would not renew the Turkish-Soviet non-aggression pact. As Fisher notes, this declaration came soon after the deportation of the Crimean Tatars, which lends credence to the thesis that they represented for Stalin a potential fifth column in a war with Turkey. Fisher, *The Crimean Tatars*, 169.
21 These journals on the whole prefer *esir Türkler* to the more neutral *dış Türkler* (outside Turks), a term also in circulation in pan-Turkist circles. Unlike *esir*, *dış* explicitly introduces concepts of inside/outside that are irrelevant for the ardent pan-Turkist. In any case, as Lowell Bezanis notes, the term *dış Türkler* still "betrays a subtle irrendentism suggesting that these groups await deliverance and that Turkey is the natural protector of their interests." Bezanis, "Soviet Muslim Emigrés in the Republic of Turkey," 61.
22 See, for instance, the appeals of the editors of *Türk Birliği*, who wrote in 1966: "We await your poems too! Our magazine will have a large space for the poems of its readers." *Türk Birliği* 1, no. 1: 36.
23 Körüklü, "Bırakın a dağlar," 12.
24 Bolulu, "Bu Toprağa ve İnsanına Dair Destan'dan," 43. This description of Turan is reminiscent of one found in the pan-Turkist canon: "[F]rom wherever the sun rises to wherever the sun sets" (güneşin doğduğu yerden battığı yere kadar). See Güzel et al., *Genel Türk Tarihi*, 9:398.
25 Ulusoy, "Gelsin," 14.
26 Uytun, "Gelsin," 12.
27 Belge, *Kemalizm*, 34.
28 Atatürk's memorable tautology was made to help claim more power for the Grand National Assembly. See Rustow, "Political Parties in Turkey," 12.
29 Less often used is the composite ethonym Kırım Türk-Tatarları (Crimean Turk-Tatars).
30 The Turkish state, which sought to assimilate its national minorities to the extent possible, also promoted the use of *Türk* at the expense of other ethnonyms, even citing on at least one occasion the use of *Tatar* as evidence of *kabilecilik* (tribalism). Bezanis, "Soviet Muslim Emigrés in the Republic of Turkey," 81. See also Williams, *The Crimean Tatars*, 252.
31 Nekrich, *The Punished Peoples*, 19. Nekrich also believes that the term *Crimean Turks*, as employed by Crimean Tatar emigrés like Edige Kırımal advocating their cause in Germany during the war, "did much to harm the Crimean Tatars in the fateful year of 1944." Nekrich, 19.
32 Eren, "Crimean Tatar Communities Abroad," 337.

33 See especially Erer, "Kırım Türkleri ve Esir Türkler!" 25. *Türk Birliği* appeared in Ankara in 1966 and saw a print run of five years.

34 *Türk Birliği* 33 (December 1968): 22.

35 Kırımal, "Sürgündeki Kırımlılara dair," 40. Many of Kırımal's essays and articles in *Dergi*, the German-based Turkish-language journal under his editorship, were also carried in *Emel*.

36 Kırımal, 43.

37 See *Türk Birliği* 14–15 (1967): 5–6.

38 Yi-Fu Tuan coined the term *topophilia* to describe "all of the human being's affective ties with the material environment," in *Topophilia*, 93.

39 Giray, "Can Kırım," 25.

40 Aliev, *Antologiia krymskoi narodnoi muzyki*, 84.

41 Güleç, "İçimde Bir Büyük Vatan Ağlıyor," 19.

42 Halil Kırımman, "Kırımlı Sürgünler," 23–4.

43 Kırımman, 24.

44 See *Emel* 63 (Mart-Nisan 1971), 47.

45 Dzhimbinov, "Epitafiia spetskhranu?" 243.

46 Mustafa Dzhemilev, interview with the author, December 2019.

47 Mustafa Dzhemilev, interview with the author, December 2019.

48 Kıvanç, "Kampta," 6. An example of such advertisements can be found in *Milliyet*, 6 June 1973, 8.

49 Dağcı, *Hatıralarda Cengiz Dağcı*, 121–8.

50 Landsberg, "Prosthetic Memory," 149–50; emphasis mine.

51 Halman, *The Turkish Muse*, 151.

52 Karatay, "Yansılar, Cengiz Dağcı ve Kırım," 9.

53 Dağcı, *Korkunç Yıllar*, 113.

54 Dağcı, *Hatıralarda Cengiz Dağcı*, 258.

55 Karatay, "Yansılar, Cengiz Dağcı ve Kırım," 9.

56 Dağcı, *Korkunç Yıllar*, 48.

57 Dağcı, 43.

58 Dağcı, 26.

59 Dağcı, *Onlar da İnsandı*, 21. For an example of a full list of the Ministry of Education's top one hundred recommended books, see Doğan Hızlan, "'1000 Temel Eser'den '100 Temel Eser'e."

60 Dağcı, *Onlar da İnsandı*, 21.

61 Dağcı, 147.

62 Kılıç, "Kırım Türkleri ile niye ilgilenmiyoruz?" 3.

63 Sarıkamış, "Sana Hasret Gideriz Güzel Kırım," 24; emphasis mine. The historian Necip Hablemitoğlu (also known as Necip Abdulhamitoğlu) uses the Crimean Tatars to take this "double standard" argument to another level. In the preface to the third edition of an influential work originally titled *Türksüz Kırım: Yüzbinlerin Sürgünü* (A Crimea without

Turks: The deportation of hundreds of thousands, 1974), which emerged
from a series of articles titled "Kırım Faciasının İçyüzü" (The inside story
of the Crimean tragedy) in the newspaper *Son Havadis* (The Latest News)
in the early 1970s, Hablemitoğlu complains that "Turkey has been sitting
in the dock accused of genocide [against the Armenians] since 1915"
while few pay attention to the "genocide of the Crimean Turks." See
Hablemitoğlu, *Yüzbinlerin Sürgünü Kırımda Türk Soykırımı*, 21.

64 Quoted in Dağcı, *Yansılar 1*, 96.

65 Dağcı, *Korkunç Yıllar*, 26.

66 A young boy named Halûk navigates a Crimea that is stricken with death
and despair in the darkly titled *Badem Dalına Asılı Bebekler* (Babies hanging
on the almond branch, 1970). See Dağcı, *Badem Dalına Asılı Bebekler*.

67 Dağcı, *Badem Dalına Asılı Bebekler*, 265.

68 Dağcı, *Korkunç Yıllar*, 252.

69 Dağcı, *Onlar da İnsandı*, 393.

70 Dağcı, 488.

71 Dağcı, 405.

72 Dağcı, 488.

73 Dağcı, 494.

74 Dağcı, *O Topraklar Bizimdi*, 128.

75 Dağcı, 128.

76 Dağcı, 138.

77 Dağcı, 140.

78 Dağcı, 384.

79 Dağcı, 510.

80 Yalçıner's wife is believed to have secretly informed the national
intelligence service about the junta's activities. Kirişçioğlu, *12 Mart
(İnönü—Ecevit) ve 1960 Tahkikat Encümeni raporum*, 227.

81 This letter is given as an appendix to the novel *Kırım Kurbanları*. Pişkin and
Coşar, *Kırım Kurbanları*, n.p.

82 Aydin, "Turkish Foreign Policy," 125.

83 Pişkin and Coşar, "Sunuş," in *Kırım Kurbanları*, 7; emphasis mine.

84 Pişkin and Coşar, 9 and 15.

85 Pişkin and Coşar, 218.

86 Pişkin and Coşar, 10.

87 Pişkin and Coşar, 12.

88 In this regard, Pişkin and Coşar follow in the footsteps of Hüseyin Nihal
Atsız, whose ultra-nationalist novels (e.g. *Bozkurtlar Ölümü* [The death
of the grey wolves, 1946] and *Ruh Adam* [Soul man, 1972]) appealed to a
young audience. Jacob M. Landau, "Ultra-Nationalist Literature in the
Turkish Republic," 206.

89 Pişkin and Coşar, *Kırım Kurbanları*, 19.

90 Pişkin and Coşar, 115 and 142, for example.
91 Pişkin and Coşar, 47.
92 Pişkin and Coşar, 38.
93 Pişkin and Coşar, 9.
94 Atsız has been called the "subconsciousness of the ultra-nationalist movement" in Turkey. See Cenk Saraçoğlu, "Ülkücü Hareketin Biliçaltı Olarak Atsız," 100–24. On "formal mimetics," see Michał Głowiński, "On the First-Person Novel," 103–14.
95 Anastasiou, *The Broken Olive Branch*, 1:148.
96 Anastasiou, 1:145; emphasis mine.
97 Lienhardt, *Social Anthropology*, 144–5.
98 Gündüz, *Kırım*, 119.
99 "Obrashchenie pisatelia A. I. Pristavkina v Prezidium Verkhovnoho Soveta SSSR," 15 July 1987, 218.
100 "Soobshchenie TASS," 23 July 1987, 219.
101 "Zaiava z'ïzdu na pidtrymku prahnen' kryms'ko-tatars'koho narodu," 216–17. See also Burakovs'kyi, *Istoriia rady natsional'nostei Narodnoho Rukhu Ukraïny 1989–1993*, 45. The Crimean Tatars were represented at Rukh's founding congress, which ultimately produced an open letter in support of their right of return, and were considered one of the most active groups in attendance. Burakovs'kyi, 57. See also Drach, *Polityka*, 175.
102 "O priznanii nezakonnymi i prestupymi repressivnykh aktov protiv narodov," 570.
103 In an allusion to Hegel's "cunning of reason," Elizabeth A. Povinelli employs the term "cunning of recognition" to refer to darker motives behind acts of the legal recognition of indigenous peoples subjected to settler colonialism. See Povinelli, "The Cunning of Recognition," 635.
104 Dağcı, *Yansılar 4*, 65.
105 Dağcı, 67.

7 Selective Affinities

1 Mustafa Dzhemilev, interview with the author, December 2019.
2 See, for instance, Dawson, "Ethnicity, Ideology and Geopolitics in Crimea," 427–44.
3 Even clear-eyed scholarship on the crime of the deportation can neglect the colonial frame. See, for instance, Williams, "Hidden Ethnocide in the Soviet Muslim Borderlands," 357–73.
4 David Chioni Moore's essay "Is the Post- in Postcolonial the Post- in Post-Soviet? Toward a Global Postcolonial Critique" remains one of the most trenchant interventions into this problematic.
5 Adzhubei, "Kak Khrushchev Krym Ukraine otdal," 20.

6 Adzhubei, 20–1.
7 Adzhubei, 21.
8 Hal'chyns'kyi et al, "Intehratsiia kryms'kykh tatar v ukraïns'ke suspil'stvo," 209. The number cited in Ukrainian currency is UAH 776 million. In 1999 alone, for instance, Kyiv allocated UAH 20 million – approximately USD 5 million– for such purposes. See "Document 8655," 5. According to this report, however, only a quarter of the budgeted total in 1999 was dispersed. For Turkish aid in the 1990s, see Karatay, "Demirel'in Tarihî Ziyaretinin Kırım İçin Önemi," 1–6.
9 Pleshakov, *The Crimean Nexus*, 115.
10 V'iacheslav Kyrylenko, "Zaiava 'Nashoï Ukraïny' z pryvodu provokuvannia kryms'koiu vladoiu ta militsiieiu mizhnatsional'nykh konfliktiv (7 lystopada 2007 r)."
11 Vladimir Putin makes a similar quip about Crimean Tatar activism as a "profession" in the propaganda film chronicle *Krym: Put' na rodinu* (Crimea: The way home), dir. Sergei Kraus, 2015.
12 Astakhova, "Prinesennye vetrom."
13 Albert Memmi, *The Colonizer and the Colonized*, 110.
14 Memmi, 195; emphasis mine.
15 Hughes and Sasse, "Power Ideas and Conflict," 318.
16 Shevel', "Kryms'ki tatary ta ukraïns'ka derzhava," 22.
17 Bahadıroğlu, *Kırım Kan Ağlıyor*, 17.
18 İpek, "Vatanda Gurbet," 17.
19 I take the term *allohistory* from Gavriel Rosenfeld, "Why Do We Ask 'What If?,'" 90.
20 Vasilii Aksenov, *Ostrov Krym*, 168.
21 Vasilii Aksenov, 22.
22 Vasilii Aksenov, 176.
23 Vasilii Aksenov, 202.
24 Vasilii Aksenov, 230.
25 Vasilii Aksenov, 307.
26 "Sergei Aksenov: Referendum nikto ne otmenit."
27 Ulitskaia was a prominent critic of the Russian annexation of Crimea in 2014, describing it as a "revolting seizure" (otvratitel'nyi zakhvat). See, for instance, "Liudmila Ulitskaia pro 'krymnash'."
28 Ulitskaia, *Medeia i ee deti*, 188, 215.
29 In 2006 a Russian nationalist youth group called Proryv (Breakthrough) took up shovels and tried to separate Crimea from mainland Ukraine by digging across Perekop, citing Aksenov's book as inspiration. See "19.01.2006, Chongar."
30 Sid, *Geopoetika*, 72.
31 Sid, 11. The nickname stems from "bibo," to drink, "calidus," warm, and "merum," potent wine. See Smet, *Menippean Satire*, 128.

32 Zhadan, "Pivostriv svobody."

33 Saburov, "Sviatye Kirill i Mefodii kak ideologi avangarda," 7.

34 Sid, *Geopoetika*, 61.

35 Sid, 69.

36 Sid, 72.

37 Quoted in Starozhyts'ka, "Nashe korinnia v Krymu."

38 Sid, *Geopoetika*, 51.

39 I take the term *reverse hallucination* – "not seeing what is there" – from Abbas, *Hong Kong*, 6.

40 See especially the remarks of Leonid Pilunskii and Volodymyr Pritula in Ol'ga Dukhnich and Nataliia Belitser, *Pliuralism identichnostei*, 63–4.

41 *Sontsia i moria na mezhi.*

42 Kononenko, "Slovo do kryms'kykh ukraïntsiv." This passivity is discussed in Dukhnich and Belitser, *Pliuralism identichnostei*, 62.

43 Kononenko, "Povernennia," 232.

44 Korsovets'kyi, "Chokrak," 93.

45 Şukur, "İqrarlıq," 659–60.

46 Plokhy, *The Gates of Europe*, 75.

47 Hayden White, *The Practical Past*, 9.

48 The twin brothers Vitaly and Dmytro Kapranov, who have produced a history of Ukraine employing comic-book illustrations for narrative effect, emphasize the importance of the Ukrainian–Crimean Tatar encounter, in Braty Kapranovy, *Mal'ovana istoriia Nezalezhnosti Ukraïny*. For more on their interpretation of the Ukrainian and Crimean Tatar national symbols as mutually "inverted," see "Krymskie tatary stali geroiami komiksov."

49 Kryms'kyi, "Literatura kryms'kykh tatar," 173.

50 Alâdin, *İblisniñ ziyafetine davet.*

51 Alâdin, "Toğaybey," 364.

52 Historical evidence of the khan's knowledge of Ukrainian and the hetman's knowledge of Crimean Tatar can be found in the works of Cossack chronicler Samiilo Velychko. See Velichko, *Letopis' sobytii v Iugo-zapadnoi Rossii v XVII veke*, 44.

53 Alâdin, "Toğaybey," 360.

54 Alâdin, 354.

55 Laclau, "Politics and the Limits of Modernity," 81. Parts of this section first appeared in Rory Finnin, "Oles' Sanin, *Mamai*."

56 For more on the "conceptual enigma" of the Cossack Mamai, see the visually arresting collection *Kozak Mamai*, ed. Bushak et al.

57 This comment is made by Frank Curot ("les plans sont plus juxtaposés qu'enchaînés") in reference to the filmmaking of Sergei Paradzhanov. See Curot, "Singularité et liberté," 231.

58 Sanin, "Khto boïtsia Mamaia."

59 Sanin.

60 Excerpts from "Duma pro samars'kykh brativ" ("Usi polia samars'ki pochornily, / Ta ne iasnymy pozharamy pohorily, / Til'ky ne zhorily/ U richtsi Samartsi, / V krynytsi Saltantsi") are also read in an extradiegetic voiceover at the beginning of the film.
61 Sanin, "Khto boïtsia Mamaia." For more about the legend of the Golden Cradle, see Zarubin and Zarubin, *Skazky i legendy krymskikh tatar*, 77–89.
62 Sanin, "Khto boïtsia Mamaia."
63 "'Haytarma' Filminin Türkiye Galası Eskişehir'de Yapıldı."
64 Karatay, "Demirel'in Tarihî Ziyaretinin Kırım İçin Önemi," 3.
65 "Cengiz Dağcı'nın Cenazesinde Dış İşleri Bakanı Ahmet Davutoğlu'nun Konuşması," 11.
66 Volodymyr Prytula, "Krym vidviduie turets'kyi prem'ier." After one of these meetings in October 2012, Turkish state television broadcast a nine-part documentary film based on Dzhemilev's life and on the collective struggle of the Crimean Tatar people after the 1944 deportation. Among the prominent figures interviewed for the series were Demirel, Davutoğlu, and Erdoğan. See "V Turechchyni znialy fil'm pro istoriiu kryms'kykh tatar."
67 Samar, "Mustafa Dzhemilev."

8 Losing Home, Finding Home

1 It has become commonplace to refer to Yanukovych's flight from office as an "ouster," which – in the standard narrative, if left unqualified – implies that he was forced out of office by Euromaidan protesters. There is no direct proof of such a claim. In fact, there is as much circumstantial evidence that he was "ousted" by the Kremlin and told to leave office in order to facilitate rhetoric of Ukraine's "illegitimacy" and feed justifications for intervention in Crimea. As Andrew Wilson points out, "video footage at Mezhyhirya [Yanukovych's lavish mansion] shows Yanukovych packing [...] over the course of three days before he fled Kiev, starting on 19 February." (See Wilson, *Ukraine Crisis*, 88. See also Berezovets', *Aneksiia*, 38–45.) Putin's directive to seize Crimea reportedly took place the next day – on 20 Feburary 2014, two days before Yanukovych fled from Ukraine. (See Galeotti, *Armies of Russia's War in Ukraine*, 7.) In the information space, the Kremlin quickly proceeded to leverage Yanukovych's sudden flight to allege a "coup" and to claim, as Dmitrii Medvedev did on 24 February 2014, that "there are major doubts about the legitimacy of the entire structure of organs of power in Ukraine." (See "Dmitrii Medvedev.")
2 Musaeva, "Oleg Sentsov."
3 See the chronology in Kofman, Migacheva, et al, *Lessons from Russia's Operations*, 8–9.

4 "Crimean Tatars Take Food to Ukraine Soldiers Blocked on Their Bases by Russian Troops."

5 "Rossiiskie voennye shturmom vziali bazu morpekhov v Feodosii."

6 Kalkay, "2014 'ün bıraktıkları!" 4.

7 Erdoğan, "Cumhurbaşkanımız mesajları," 19; emphasis mine.

8 Hughes and Sasse, "Power Ideas and Conflict," 320.

9 "Public Opinion Survey," 17.

10 Knott, "Identity in Crimea before Annexation," 283.

11 See, for example, Nakashima, "Inside a Russian Disinformation Campaign."

12 Wilson, *Ukraine Crisis*, 113.

13 *Vossoedinenie* is used to describe, for instance, the formalization of the Ukrainian Hetmanate as a protectorate of Muscovy in 1654 and the annexation of Polish territory to Soviet Belarus and Soviet Ukraine in 1939.

14 This number is difficult to specify in total, but in 2017 Ukraine's State Emergency Service announced that there were 22,822 IDPs from Crimea resident in mainland Ukraine. See "Rehional'nymy shtabamy DSNS zareiestrovano ponad 1 mln. 70 tysiach vnutrishn'o peremishchenykh osib."

15 "15 marta 2014 goda v pole u sela Zemlianichnoe Belogorskogo raiona obnaruzhen trup muzhchiny."

16 "Infografika po nasyl'nyts'kym znyknenniam v okupovanomu RF Krymu."

17 See Andreiuk et al, *Entsyklopediia represiï v Krymu z momentu okupatsiï Rosiieiu*, vols. 1 and 2.

18 Rudenko and Sardalova, "Pro Putina, svobodu i Tsemakha."

19 Gumeniuk, *Poteriannyi ostrov*, 129 and 290. See also "Krymskie tatary pomogaiut sem'e Sentsova."

20 Rudenko and Sardalova, "Pro Putina, svobodu i Tsemakha."

21 Musaeva, "Oleg Sentsov."

22 "Sentsov: 'Stal namnogo luchshe ponimat' krymskikh tatar posle togo, kak menia vygnali s Rodiny.'"

23 Chubarov, "S'ohodni vidbulasia tepla druzhnia zustrich z Olehom Sentsovym."

24 Sentsov, "Odniieiu z velykykh hrup."

25 The Office of the Prosecutor of the International Criminal Court, *Report on Preliminary Examination Activities, 2016*, 35.

26 Taraniuk, "Lider Medzhlisu."

27 This distinction is made by Crimean Tatar lawyer Emil Kurbedinov in Gumeniuk, *Poteriannyi ostrov*, 302.

28 Üseyin, "Saqın mennen vedalaşma," 32.

29 Savchuk, "Semeinoe delo."

30 See, for instance, Uehling, "A Hybrid Deportation," 62–77.

31 "Molytvy i povitriani kuli."
32 "'Govori, otets, govori…' Chitaet Lilia Budzhurova."
33 Karatay, "Başyazı," 3–5.
34 Olgun, "Şevçenko'nun ülkesinde," 27.
35 Olgun, 29.
36 See, for instance, "Holodomor Soykırımı Kurbanları İstanbul'da Anıldı."
37 See "Hakkımızda," *KirimDernegi.org.tr*, http://www.kirimdernegi.org.tr/dernek/hakk-m-zda.
38 "SMI."
39 Yaltirik, *Yedikuleli Mansur.*
40 Çokum, *Gözyaşı Çeşmesi*, back cover.
41 Çokum, 241.
42 See, for instance, an interview with Gennady Katsov on the RTN WMNB (Russian Television Network of America) program "Chto noven'kogo?" *YouTube* (5 April 2015).
43 Krymskii klub, *Nashkrym*. All the poems of the anthology can be read at https://nkpoetry.com.
44 Krymskii klub.
45 Sid, *Geopoetika*, 349. Sid is guided toward this realization by Serhiy Zhadan.
46 Lukomnikov, "Moe uchastie v sbornike stikhov o Kryme…"
47 Lukomnikov.
48 Hedges, *War Is a Force That Gives Us Meaning*, 11.
49 Higgins, "Oleg Sentsov"; Tsentr Razumkova, *Identychnist' hromadian Ukraïny v novykh umovakh.*
50 Sereda, "'Social Distancing' and Hierarchies of Belonging," 417.
51 Zubkovych, "Language Use among Crimean Tatars in Ukraine," 173.
52 "Joint Meeting to Hear an Address by His Excellency Petro Poroshenko, President of Ukraine," 15032.
53 "Crimean Tatars: Who Are They?"
54 Mustafa Dzhemilev, interview with the author, December 2019.
55 "Crimean Tatars: Who Are They?"
56 Ekaterina Mishchenko, "Predislovie. Golosa ostrovitian," in Gumeniuk, *Poteriannyi ostrov*, 8.
57 Huk, "Liuds'ke zhyttia …," 135.
58 Savka, "Khoch rizni my, brate, liniia doli spil'na."
59 Kalytko, *Zemlia zahublenykh, abo malen'ki strashni kazky.*
60 Kalytko, "Nastupnoho roku v Bakhchysaraï."
61 Kalytko, "Nastupnoho roku v Bakhchysaraï."
62 Parts of this discussion of *Evge* also appear in Finnin and Kozachenko, "Beyond 'Narrating the Nation.'"
63 Luckhurst, *The Trauma Question*, 3.

64 Seitablaiev fights off the comparisons with Spielberg. See, for instance, "U studiï Snidanku rezhyser fil'mu 'Dodomu' Nariman Aliiev ta aktor Akhtem Seitablaiev," *Snidanok z 1+1* (7 November 2019), https://www.youtube.com/watch?v=X4Ilhrrsav4

65 Jouve, *Lyrique*, 59.

66 Chervotkina, "Toponimy (Tsykl)," 143.

67 Svitoch, "Pro shcho lysty Nasymy," 237.

68 Svitoch, 243.

69 Dziuba, *Chornyi romantyk*.

70 "Serhii Zhadan v hostiakh u 503 OBMP, Chastyna 2."

71 Andrukhovych, "Mistse zustrichi Germanschka," 266.

72 I take the text of the poem from Serhiy Zhadan, *Tampliiery*, 8–9.

73 Kökçe, "Bizim evlerimiz nasıl qurula?" 285–6.

74 Dziuba, *Chornyi romantyk*, p. 4.

75 "There is no sun without shadow," writes Camus, "and it is essential to know the night." Camus, *The Myth of Sisyphus, and Other Essays*, 123.

76 Crimean Tatar activist Edem Dudakov calls the project "Potemkin repair" and "vandalism," in "Khanskii dvorets v Krymu." For more on the Venice Charter, see International Council on Monuments and Sites (ICOMOS), "International Charter for the Conservation and Restoration of Monuments and Sites."

77 Budzhurova, "Pochemu my molchim?"

78 Dudakov, "Tot ne znaiet ..."

79 Rodichkina, "Dyvyshsia na suchasnu Ukraïnu ..."

80 For more on Ukrainian public opinion on the issue of Crimean Tatar national-territorial autonomy, see "Povernennia Krymu." Former president Petro Poroshenko condemned the longstanding failure of the Ukrainian state to "secure Crimean Tatar autonomy," only to fail himself. See, for example, "Poroshenko zaiavyv pro hotovnist' vnesty zminy do Konstytutsiï shchodo kryms'kotatars'koï avtonomiï."

81 See "U Zelens'koho khochut' obhovoryty kryms'kotatars'ku avtonomiiu z narodom."

82 Marynovych, "Kryms'ka kryza i tsyvilizatsiini shansy Ukraïny."

83 Schlögel, *Ukraine: A Nation on the Borderland*, 61.

Coda

1 See, for instance, Mearsheimer, "Don't Arm Ukraine." As Marci Shore observes, "Europeans preferred to put Crimea out of their minds." Shore, *The Ukrainian Night*, 150.

2 "A/RES/74/17," 2.

3 Kuku, "Poslednee slovo v sude."

4 Edward Said critiques what he sees as a predominant representation of Palestinians as "interruptions" and "intermittent presences" in historical scholarship. See Said, *After the Last Sky*, 26.
5 Margalit, *The Ethics of Memory*, 144.
6 Myroslav Marynovych, interview with the author, November 2019.
7 Weaver, *The Politics of the Black Sea Region*, 135.

Bibliography

All websites were last accessed on 1 June 2020.

"15 marta 2014 goda v pole u sela Zemlianichnoe Belogorskogo raiona obnaruzhen trup muzhchiny." *Medzhlis krymskotatarskogo naroda*, 16 March 2014. http://qtmm.org.

"19.01.2006, Chongar: Otsoedinenie Kryma ot Ukrainy." YouTube, 18 March 2014. https://www.youtube.com.

Abbas, Ackbar. *Hong Kong: Culture and the Politics of Disappearance.* Minneapolis: University of Minnesota Press, 1998.

Abduramanova, S.N. "Gazeta 'Terdzhiman' kak istochnik po izucheniiu sotsial'no-bytovoi zhizni Kryma v kontse XIX v." *Voprosy krymskotatarskoi filologii, istorii i kul'turi* 1 (2015): 71–6.

Adzhubei, Aleksei. "Kak Khrushchev Krym Ukraine otdal." *Novoe vremia* 6 (February 1992): 20–1.

Akçokraklı (Akchokrakly), O. "Tatars'ka poema Dzan-mukhammedova pro pokhid Isliam-Hireia II spil'no z Bohdanom Khmel'nyts'kym na Polshchu 1648–49rr." *Skhidnyi svit* 12, no. 3 (1930): 163–70.

Akçura, Yusuf. *Üç Tarz-ı Siyaset.* Ankara: Türk Tarih Kurumu Basımevi, 1976.

Aksenov, Sergei. "Pozdravlaiu krymskikh tatar ..." Facebook, 5 May 2018. https://www.facebook.com.

Aksenov, Vasilii. *Ostrov Krym.* Ann Arbor, MI: Ardis, 1981.

Alâdin, Şamil [Shamil Aliadin]. "Ia – vash tsar i boh." In *Merdyven*, 227–312. Kyiv: Maister Knyh, 2019.

– *İblisniñ ziyafetine davet.* Simferopol': Sputnik, 2004.

– *Toğaybey.* In *Sailama eserler.* Simferopol': Kyrym devlet okuv-pedagogika neshriiaty, 1999.

Alekseeva, Liudmila. *Istoriia inakomysliia v SSSR.* Benson, VT: Khronika Press, 1984.

– "Krymskotatarskoe dvizhenie za vozvrashchenie v Krym." *Kryms'ki studiï* 5–6 (2000): 4–16.

– *Soviet Dissent: Contemporary Movements for National, Religious, and Human Rights.* Translated by Carol Pearce and John Glad. Middletown, CT: Wesleyan University Press, 1987.

Alekseeva, Liudmila, and Paul Goldberg. *The Thaw Generation: Coming of Age in the Post-Stalin Era.* Pittsburgh, PA: University of Pittsburgh Press, 1993.

Aliev, Fevzi. *Antologiia krymskoi narodnoi muzyki.* Simferopol': Krymuchpedgiz, 2001.

Al'tshuller, Mark G., and Iuri M. Lotman. "Primechaniia." In *Poety 1790–1810x godov,* edited by Mark Al'tshuller and Iu. M. Lotman, 807–87. Leningrad: Sovetskii pisatel', 1971.

Amalrik, Andrei. *Will the Soviet Union Survive until 1984?* London: Penguin, 1980.

– *Zapiski dissidenta.* Ann Arbor, MI: Ardis, 1982.

Anastasiou, Harry. *The Broken Olive Branch: Nationalism, Ethnic Conflict, and the Quest for Peace in Cyprus.* Vol. 1, *The Impasse of Ethnonationalism.* Syracuse, NY: Syracuse University Press, 2008.

Anderson, Benedict. *Imagined Communities: Reflections on the Origin and Spread of Nationalism.* Rev. ed. London: Verso, 1991.

Andreiuk, Ievheniia, Anastasiia Moïseieva, Mariia Kvityns'ka, Dmytro Koval', and Anastasiia Donets'. *Entsyklopediia represiï v Krymu z momentu okupatsiï Rosiieiu.* Vols. 1 and 2. Kyiv: KrymSOS, 2019.

Andrukhovych, Yuri. "Mistse zustrichi Germanschka." In *Dyiavol khovaiet'sia v syri: Vybrani sproby 1999–2005 rokiv,* 258–75. Kyiv: Krytyka, 2007.

Antonenko-Davydovych, Borys. *Smert'.* London: Ukrainian Publishers, 1954.

– "Spohad pro pryiom Stalinom ukraïns'koï delegatsiï 1929 roku." *Suchasnist'* 7–8 (July–August 1984): 4–12.

Apter, Emily. *The Translation Zone: A New Comparative Literature.* Princeton, NJ: Princeton University Press, 2006.

Arendt, Hannah. *The Life of the Mind.* London: Harcourt, 1978.

"A/RES/74/17: Problem of the Militarization of the Autonomous Republic of Crimea and the City of Sevastopol, Ukraine." United Nations General Assembly. New York: United Nations, 2019.

"Arest i golodovka Mustafy Dzemileva." *Khronika tekushchikh sobytii* 32 (17 July 1974). http://www.memo.ru.

Aristotle's Poetics. Translated by George Whalley. Montreal, QC: McGill-Queen's University Press, 1997.

Arkanov, Arkadii. *Ot Il'icha do lampochki: Uchebnik istorii sovetskoi i antisovetskoi vlasti dlia slaborazvitykh detei.* Saint Petersburg: Blints, 1997.

Arkhiv Tsentru doslidzhen' vyzvol'noho rukhu (ATsDVR) [Archive of the Centre for the Study of the Liberation Movement]. Fond 23. L'viv, Ukraine.

Aronov, Aleksandr. "Ia b ne vzial tebia, konechno," *Sintaksis* 1 (1959): 97. In *Grani* 58 (1965): 95–31.

Asanin, İdris. "Menim antım." In *Qırımtatar edebiyatınıñ tarihı*, edited by Riza Fazıl and Safter Nagayev, 397. Aqmescit: Qırım devlet oquv-pedagogika neşriyatı, 2001.

Ascherson, Neal. *Black Sea*. New York: Hill & Wang, 1995.

– *Black Sea*. Rev. ed. London: Vintage, 2015.

Aşkın, Engin. "Tatar Türklerini savunan subayın hatıra defteri Paris'e kaçırıldı." *Milliyet*, 26 April 1970.

Aslan, Reza. *Tablet and Pen: Literary Landscapes from the Modern Middle East*. New York: W.W. Norton, 2011.

Astakhova, Natal'ia. "Prinesennye vetrom." *Krymskaia Pravda* no. 53 (24396), 22 March 2008. https://web.archive.org.

Atatürk, Kemal. *Atatürk'ün Fikir ve Düşünceleri*. Edited by Utkan Kocatürk. Ankara: Edebiyat Yayınevi, 1971.

Aydin, Mustafa. "Turkish Foreign Policy: Changing Patterns and Conjunctures during the Cold War." *Middle Eastern Studies* 36, no. 1 (January 2000): 103–39.

Ayhan, Ece. *Şiirin bir altın çağı: Yazılar, söyleşiler, dipyazıları*. İstanbul: Yapı Kredi Yayınları, 1993.

Bahadıroğlu, Yavuz. *Kırım Kan Ağlıyor*. İstanbul: Yeni Asya Yayınları, 1994.

Bahalii, D.I., A. Iu. Kryms'kyi, H.H. Pavluts'kyi, and Ie. K. Tymchenko. "Poiasniuiucha zapyska do proektu orhanizatsii Istorychno-Filolohichnoho Viddilu Ukraïns'koi Akademiï Nauk." In *Zapysky istorychno-filolohichnoho viddilu Ukraïns'koi Akademiï Nauk*, bk. 1, i–xviii. Kyiv: Drukar', 1919.

Baudelaire, Charles. *Petits poèmes en prose*. Edited by Melvin Zimmerman. Manchester, UK: Manchester University Press, 1968.

Bayley, John. *Pushkin: A Comparative Commentary*. Cambridge: Cambridge University Press, 1971.

Beckett, Samuel. "Dante ... Bruno ... Vico ... Joyce." In *Disjecta*, edited by Ruby Cohn, 19–34. London: John Calder, 1983.

Bekirova, Gul'nara. "Boris Chichibabin: 'Bez kapli nenavisti k drugim.'" *Krym.Realii*, 9 January 2018. https://ru.krymr.com.

– *Krymskotatarskaia problema v SSSR, 1944–1991*. Simferopol': Odzhak", 2004.

– *Piv stolittia oporu: Kryms'ki tatary vid vyhnannia do povernennia (1941–1991 roky)*. Translated by Kateryna Demchuk. Kyiv: Krytyka, 2017.

Bektore [Bektöre], Attila. *A Nomad's Journey: A Memoir*. New York: iUniverse, 2007.

Bektöre, Şevki. "Dalgalara." *Kırım Mecmuası* 1, no. 3 (May 1918): 45–6.

– "Tatarlığım." In *Qırımtatar edebiyatınıñ tarihı*, edited by Riza Fazıl and Safter Nagayev, 301–2. Aqmescit: Qırım devlet oquv-pedagogika neşriyatı, 2001.

Belge, Murat. *Kemalizm*. 3rd ed. İstanbul: İletişim, 2001.

Belinskii, Vissarion. "Russkaia literatura v 1840 godu." In *Stati i retsenzii 1840–1841 godov*, edited by N.F. Bel'chikov, 408–47. Vol. 4 of *Polnoe sobranie sochinenii v 13 tomakh,* edited by N.F. Bel'chikov. Moscow: Izd-vo Akademii nauk SSSR, 1954.

– "Sochineniia Aleksandra Pushkina: Stat'ia shestaia." In *Sobranie sochinenii v deviati tomakh,* vol. 6, edited by Iu. S. Sorokin, 298–321. Moscow: Khudozhestvennaia literatura, 1981.

Benediktov, Vladimir. "Oreanda." In *Sochineniia V. G. Benediktova,* vol. 1, edited by Ia. P. Polonskii, 130–1. Saint Petersburg: M.O. Vol'f, 1902.

Berdinskikh, Viktor. *Istoriia odnogo lageria (Viatlag).* Moscow: Izd-vo "Agraf", 2001.

Berezovets', Taras. *Aneksiia: Ostriv Krym; Khroniky "hibrydnoï viiny."* Kyiv: Brait Star Pablishynh, 2015.

Bezanis, Lowell. "Soviet Muslim Emigrés in the Republic of Turkey." *Central Asian Survey* 13, no. 1 (1994): 59–180.

Bezirci, Asım. *Orhan Veli ve seçme şiirleri: İnceleme, antoloji.* İstanbul: Cem Yayınevi, 1976.

Bhabha, Homi. "Of Mimicry and Man." In *The Location of Culture,* 121–31. New York: Routledge, 1994.

– "The Other Question: Stereotype, Discrimination, and the Discourse of Colonialism." In *The Location of Culture,* 94–120. New York: Routledge, 1994.

– "Sly Civility." In *The Location of Culture,* 132–45. New York: Routledge, 1994.

Bilocerkowycz, Jaroslaw. *Soviet Ukrainian Dissent: A Study of Political Alienation.* Boulder, CO: Westview Press, 1988.

Bobrov, Semen. *Tavrida.* In *Rassvet polnochi/Khersonida v dvukh tomakh,* vol. 2, edited by V.L. Korovin. Moscow: Nauka, 2008.

Boltanski, Luc. *Distant Suffering: Morality, Media and Politics.* Translated by Graham Burchell. Cambridge: Cambridge University Press, 1999.

Bolulu, Osman. "Bu Toprağa ve İnsanına Dair Destan'dan." *Toprak* 1 (December 1954): 43.

Boobbyer, Philip. *Conscience, Dissent and Reform in Soviet Russia.* New York: Routledge, 2005.

Borak, Sadi. *Atatürk ve Edebiyat.* İstanbul: Kaynak Yayınları, 1998.

Boris Chichibabin: Zamist' spovidi. Directed by Rafail Nakhmanovich. Ukrainian Studio of Documentary-Chronicle Films, 1993.

Boym, Svetlana. *The Future of Nostalgia.* New York: Basic Books, 2001.

Bozdağ, İsmet, ed. *Abdülhamid'in Hatıra Defteri.* İstanbul: Pınar Yayınları, 2002.

Bratianu, Georges. *La mer Noire: Des origines à la conquête ottoman.* Munich: Societas Academica Dacoromana, 1969.

Braty Kapranovy. *Mal'ovana istoriia Nezalezhnosti Ukraïny.* Kyiv: Zelenyi pes, 2013.

Brodsky, Joseph. "A Guide to a Renamed City." In *Less than One: Selected Essays,* 69–94. New York: Farrar, Straus, Giroux, 1986.

Broshevan, V., and P. Tygliiants. *Izganie i vozvrashchenie*. Simferopol': Tavrida, 1994.

Browne, Michael, ed. *Ferment in the Ukraine*. Woodhaven, NY: Crisis Press, 1973.

Brubaker, Rogers. *Nationalism Reframed: Nationhood and the National Question in the New Europe*. Cambridge: Cambridge University Press, 1996.

Brysk, Alison. *Speaking Rights to Power: Constructing Political Will*. Oxford: Oxford University Press, 2013.

Budzhurova, Lilia. "Pochemu my molchim?" *Krym. Realii*, 22 February 2018. https://ru.krymr.com.

Bugai, N.F., ed. *Deportatsiia narodov Kryma: Dokumenty, fakty, kommentarii*. Moscow: Insan, 2002.

– *L. Beriia–I. Stalinu: "Soglasno Vashemu ukazaniiu."* Moscow: Airo-XX, 1995.

Bunegin, Maksim. *Revoliutsiia i grazhdanskaia voina v Krymu (1917–1920 gg.)*. Simferopol': Krymgosizdat, 1927.

Burakovs'kyi, Oleksandr. *Istoriia rady natsional'nostei Narodnoho Rukhu Ukraïny 1989–1993*. New York: IRSA, 2001.

Bushakov, V.A. "Svits'ki ta religiini tytuly i nazvy profesiinykh zaniat', vidobrazheni v istorychnii toponimiï Krymu." *Skhidnyi svit* 1 (2004): 135–9.

Buzuk, P. "Ab belaruska-ukrainskim literaturnym pabratsimstve." *Maladniak* 7 (1928): 77–82.

Çağman, Ergin. "III. Selim'e sunulan bir ıslahat raporu: Mehmet Şerif Efendi Layihası." *Divan* 2 (1999): 217–33.

Cambrensis, Giraldus. *The Topography of Ireland*. Translated by Thomas Forester and edited by Thomas Wright. Cambridge, ON: In Parentheses Publications, 2000.

Camus, Albert. *The Myth of Sisyphus, and Other Essays*. London: Vintage International, 1991.

Canmuhammed. "Tuğaybey." In *Küneşten bir parça / Okrushyna sontsia: Antolohiia kryms'kotatars'koï poeziï XIII–XX st*, edited by M. Miroshnychenko and Iu. Kandym, 106–13. Kyiv: Holovna spetsializovana redaktsiia literatury movamy natsional'nykh menshyn Ukraïny, 2003.

Caruth, Cathy. *Unclaimed Experience: Trauma, Narrative, and History*. Baltimore, MD: Johns Hopkins University Press, 1996.

Çelebicihan, Noman. "Ant etkenmen." In *Qırımtatar halq yırları*, edited by Il'ias Bakhshysh and Edem Nalbandov, 103–4. Simferopol': Tavriia, 1996.

"Cengiz Dağcı'nın Cenazesinde Dış İşleri Bakanı Ahmet Davutoğlu'nun Konuşması." *Kırım Bülteni* 70 (July–December 2011): 10–11.

Central Intelligence Agency. *The Spectrum of Soviet Dissent*. N.p.: Directorate of Intelligence, May 1977.

Çergeyev, Hasan. "Eşit, mevta ne söyleyür!" In Kösoğlu, *Türkiye dışındaki Türk edebiyatları antolojisi*, 389–92.

– "Közyaş han çeşmesi." In Kösoğlu, *Türkiye dışındaki Türk edebiyatları antolojisi*, 392.

Charron, Austin. "Whose Is Crimea? Contested Sovereignty and Regional Identity." *REGION: Regional Studies of Russia, Eastern Europe, and Central Asia* 5, no. 2 (2016): 225–56.

Chepurin, Aleksandr. "Orientir: Kongress sootechestvennikov." *Mezhdunarodnaia zhizn'* 6 (2009): 47–61.

Chervonnaia, Svetlana. "Krymskotatarskoe natsional'noe dvizhenie (1994–1996)." *Issledovaniia po prikladnoi i neotlozhnoi etnologii* 101 (1997): 3–28.

Chervotkina, Ilona. "Toponimy (Tsykl)." In *Qırım inciri*, edited by Mar'iana Savka, 143–6. L'viv: Vydavnytstvo Staroho Leva, 2017.

Chichibabin, Boris. "Chernoe piatno." In Chichibabin, *Pered zemleiu krymskoi sovest' moia chista*, 81–2.

– "Genrikhu Altunianu." In *Konchus', ostanus' zhiv li …: Boris Chichibabin rannee i pozdnee*, 163–4. Khar'kov: Folio, 2002.

– "Ia plachu o dushe …" In *V stikhakh i proze*, 190. Moscow: Nauka, 2013.

– "Ia siuda stremilsia vsiu zhizn'." In Chichibabin, *Pered zemleiu krymskoi sovest' moia chista*, 84–93.

– "Krymskie progulki." In *I vse-taki ia byl poetom…: Boris Chichibabin v stikhakh i proze*, 73–6. Khar'kov: Folio, 1998.

– "Otvet redaktoru zhurnala *Novyi mir*." In Chichibabin, *Pered zemleiu krymskoi sovest' moia chista*, 74–5.

– *Pered zemleiu krymskoi sovest' moia chista*. Simferopol': Arial, 2013.

– "Pis'mo Aideru Emirovu." In Chichibabin, *Pered zemleiu krymskoi sovest' moia chista*, 77–9.

– "Rodnoi iazyk." In *I vse-taki ia byl poetom …: Boris Chichibabin v stikhakh i proze*, 43–5. Khar'kov: Folio, 1998.

– "Sudakskie elegii." In *Antologiia noveishei russkoi poezii u goluboi laguny*, vol 3A, edited by Konstantin Kuzminskii and Gregorii Kovalev, 75–6. Newtonville, MA: Oriental Research Partners, 1986.

– "Sudakskie elegii." In *I vse-taki ia byl poetom …: Boris Chichibabin v stikhakh i proze*, 226–30. Khar'kov: Folio, 1998.

– "Sudakskie elegii." In *Poiski: Svobodnyi moskovskii zhurnal* 1 (1979): 76–7.

Chornovil, Viacheslav. "Do Mustafy Dzhemilieva (26.7.1979)." In *Tvory v desiaty tomakh*, vol. 4, bk. 2, edited by A. Pashko, 752. Kyiv: Smoloskyp, 2005.

– "Pro ukraïns'kyi samvydav." In *Tvory v desiaty tomakh*, vol. 3, edited by A. Pashko, 153–68. Kyiv: Smoloskyp, 2006.

– *Tvory v desiaty tomakh*. Vol. 4, bk. 2, edited by A. Pashko Kyiv: Smoloskyp, 2005.

Chubarov, Refat. "Peredmova." *Kryms'ki studiï: Informatsiinyi biuleten'* 5–6 (September–November 2000): v–xii.

– "S'ohodni vidbulasia tepla druzhnia zustrich z Olehom Sentsovym."
Facebook, 20 September 2019. https://www.facebook.com.
Chukovskaia, Lidiia. "Litso beschelovech'ia." *Khronika tekushchikh sobytii* 40
(20 May 1976): 47–51.
– *Sof'ia Petrovna.* In *Sochineniia v 2 tomakh*, vol. 1. Moscow: Gudial Press, 1999.
Çokum, Sevinç. *Gözyaşı Çeşmesi: Kırım'da Son Düğün.* İstanbul: Kapı
Yayınları, 2016.
Conquest, Robert. *The Nation Killers.* New York: Macmillan, 1970.
Cooper, Tanya. "Crimean Tatar Elected Body Banned in Russia." Human
Rights Watch, 29 September 2016. https://www.hrw.org.
Crews, Robert D. *For Prophet and Tsar.* Cambridge, MA: Harvard University
Press, 2006.
"Crimean Tatar Activist Confined in Psychiatric Hospital." Human Rights
Watch, 26 August 2016. https://www.hrw.org.
"Crimean Tatars Take Food to Ukraine Soldiers Blocked on Their Bases by
Russian Troops." YouTube, 4 March 2014. https://www.youtube.com.
"Crimean Tatars: Who Are They?" *Ukraïner,* 27 September 2019. https://
ukrainer.net.
"Cumhurbaşkanı Erdoğan: 'Harekatımızı sonuna kadar götürmekte
kararlıyız. Başladığımız işi bitireceğiz. Bir kere yükselen bayrak bir daha
inmez.'" Türkiye Cumhuriyeti Cumhurbaşkanlığı, 14 October 2019. https://
www.iletisim.gov.tr.
Curot, Frank. "Singularité et liberté: Serguei Paradjanov ou les risques du
style." *Études cinématographiques* 65 (2000): 221–37.
Dağcı, Cengiz. *Badem Dalına Asılı Bebekler.* İstanbul: Ötüken, 2018.
– *Hatıralarda Cengiz Dağcı.* İstanbul: Ötüken, 1998.
– *Korkunç Yıllar.* İstanbul: Ötüken, 2019.
– *Onlar da İnsandı.* İstanbul: Ötüken, 2019.
– *O Topraklar Bizimdi.* İstanbul: Ötüken, 2018.
– *Yansılar 1.* İstanbul: Ötüken, 2012.
– *Yansılar 4.* İstanbul: Ötüken, 1993.
Daniel', Aleksandr. "Istoki i smysl sovetskogo samizdata." In *Antologiia
samizdata: Nepodtsenzurnaia literatura v SSSR, 1950-e-1980-e*, vol. 1, bk. 1,
edited by V.V. Igrunov, 17–33. Moscow: Mezhdunarodnyi institut
gumanitarno-politicheskih issledovanii, 2005.
Darwin, Charles. *The Expression of the Emotions in Man and Animal.* Chicago:
University of Chicago Press, 1965. First published in 1872.
Davis, Todd F., and Kenneth Womack. *Mapping the Ethical Turn: A Reader in
Ethics, Culture, and Literary Theory.* Charlotteville: University of Virginia
Press, 2001.
Dawson, Jane I. "Ethnicity, Ideology and Geopolitics in Crimea." *Communist
and Post-Communist Studies* 30, no. 4 (1997): 427–44.

"'Delo' krymskikh tatar." *Novyi Zhurnal* 97 (1969): 178–91.

"Delo Mustafy Dzhemileva." *Novyi zhurnal* 97 (1969): 207–10.

Deny, J. "Redīf." In *Encyclopaedia of Islam, First Edition (1913–1936)*, edited by M.Th. Houtsma et al. http://dx.doi.org/10.1163/2214-871X_ei1_COM_0106.

Derrida, Jacques. *Specters of Marx*. Translated by Peggy Kamuf. London: Routledge, 1994.

"Dmitrii Medvedev: Legitimnost' rada organov vlasti na Ukraine ..." *RT na russkom*, 24 February 2014. https://russian.rt.com.

"Document 8655: Repatriation and Integration of the Tatars of Crimea." In *Documents (Working Papers) of the Parliamentary Assembly of the Council of Europe*, vol. 3, 1–7. Strasbourg: Council of Europe Publishing, 2000.

"Doklad." *Golos Tatar* 9, 23 September 1917.

"Doklad N.S. Khrushcheva XX s"ezdu Kommunisticheskoi partii Sovetskogo Soiuza, 25 fevralia 1956g." In *Antologiia samizdata: Nepodtsenzurnaia literatura v SSSR, 1950-e–1980-e*, vol. 1, bk. 1, edited by V.V. Igrunov, 360–74. Moscow: Mezhdunarodnyi institut gumanitarno-politicheskikh issledovanii, 2005.

"Dokument No. 121 (9 veresnia 1917)." In *Ukraïns'ka Tsentral'na Rada: Dokumenty u dvokh tomakh*, vol. 1, edited by V.A. Smolii, 290–3. Kyiv: Naukova dumka, 1996.

Drach, Ivan. *Polityka: Statti, dopovidi, vystupy, inter'viu*. Kyiv: Ukraïns'ka vsesvitnia koordynatsiina rada, 1997.

Dudakov, Edem. "Tot ne znaiet ..." Facebook, 4 March 2019. https://www .facebook.com.

Dukhnich, Ol'ga, and Nataliia Belitser. *Pliuralism identichnostei: Ugroza ili blago? Issledovanie osobennostei sokhrannosti i retransliatsii identichnosti predstavitelei osnovykh etnokul'turnykh grupp AP Krym (Ukraina)*. Cluj-Napoca, Romania: Patrir, 2013.

"Dvadtsatiletnii iubilei literaturnoi deiatel'nosti t. Umera Ipchi." *Literatura i iskusstvo Kryma* 2 (1936): 129–32.

"Dyskusiia 'Krym v ukraïns'kii literaturi.'" Facebook, 1 December 2018. https://www.facebook.com.

Dzhemilev, Mustafa. "Den' shestoi." In *Shestoi protsess Mustafy Dzhemileva*, 401–15. Simferopol': Fond "Krym", 2001.

– "Pis'mo M. Dzhemileva Viacheslavu Chernovilu ot 11 avgusta 1979g." In *Shestoi protsess Mustafy Dzhemileva*, 152–6. Simferopol': Fond "Krym", 2001.

– "Poema 'Bakhchisaraiskii fontan' Shiukriu El'china." In *Shestoi protsess Mustafy Dzhemileva*, 436–8. Simferopol': Fond "Krym", 2001.

Dzhimbinov, S. "Epitafiia spetskhranu?" *Novyi mir* 5 (1990): 243–52.

Dziuba, Ivan. *Chornyi romantyk: Serhii Zhadan*. Kyiv: Lybid', 2017.

– "Vystup u babynomy iaru 29 veresnia 1966r." In *Lykho z rozumu*, edited by Viacheslav Chornovil, 303–8. Paris: Persha ukraïns'ka drukarnia u Frantsiï, 1968.

Edel'man, O.V., Sheila Fitzpatrick, V.A. Kozlov, Sergei V. Mironenko, eds. *Sedition: Everyday Resistance in the Soviet Union under Khrushchev and Brezhnev*. New Haven, CT: Yale University Press, 2013.

Elçin, Şükrü. *Aşık Ömer*. Ankara: Kültür ve Turizm Bakanlığı, 1987.

– "Bahçesaray Çeşmesi." *Emel* 126 (1981).

– *Halk edebiyatına giriş*. Ankara: Kültür Bakanlığı, 1981.

Eligür, Banu. *The Mobilization of Political Islam in Turkey*. Cambridge: Cambridge University Press, 2010.

Eliot, T.S. "The Three Voices of Poetry." In *On Poetry and Poets*. New York: Farrar, Straus, & Cudahy, 1957.

Emel 63 (Mart–Nisan 1971).

Emirov, Aider. "Istoriia odnogo stikhotvoreniia." *Meraba* 2 (1993). In Chichibabin, *Pered zemleiu krymskoi sovest' moia chista*, 80–3.

Epstein, Mikhail. "Theses on Metarealism and Conceptualism." In Mikhail Epstein, Alexander A. Genis, and Slobodanka M. Vladiv-Glover, *Russian Postmodernism: New Perspectives on Post-Soviet Culture*, 169–76. Translated by Slobodanka Vladiv-Glover. New York: Berghahn Books, 1999.

Erdoğan, Recep Tayyip. "Cumhurbaşkanımız mesajları." In *Kırım Bülteni* 78 (January–June 2015): 19.

Eren, Nermin. "Crimean Tatar Communities Abroad." In *The Tatars of Crimea: Return to the Homeland*, 2nd. ed., edited by Edward Allworth, 323–51. Durham, NC: Duke University Press, 1998.

Erer, Tekin. "Kırım Türkleri ve Esir Türkler!" *Türk Birliği* 19 (October 1967).

Etkind, Alexander, Rory Finnin, Uilleam Blacker, Julie Fedor, Simon Lewis, Maria Mälksoo, and Matilda Mroz. *Remembering Katyn*. Cambridge: Polity Press, 2012.

Evge. Directed by Nariman Aliev. Ukraine: Limelite, 2019.

Evin, Ahmet Ö. *Origins and Development of the Turkish Novel*. Minneapolis, MN: Bibliotheca Islamica, 1983.

Evtushenko, Evgenii. "Babii Iar." In *Grazhdane, poslushaite menia: Stikhotvoreniia i poemy*, 421–2. Moscow: Khudozhestvennaia literatura, 1989.

– "Krotost' i moshch'." In *Vsemu zhivomu ne chuzhoi: Boris Chichibabin v stat'iakh i vospominaniiakh*, 149–50. Khar'kov: Folio, 1998.

Fanon, Frantz. *L'an V de la révolution algérienne*. Paris: La Découverte & Syros, 2001.

– "National Culture." In *The Post-Colonial Studies Reader*, edited by Bill Ashcroft, Gareth Griffiths, and Helen Tiffin, 153–7. London: Routledge, 1995.

– *Peau noire, masques blancs*. Paris: Seuil, 1965.

Fazıl, Riza, and Safter Nagayev. *Qırımtatar edebiyatınıñ tarihı*. Aqmescit: Qırım devlet oquv-pedagogika neşriyatı, 2001.

Felman, Shoshana, and Dori Laub. *Testimony: Crises of Witnessing in Literature, Psychoanalysis, and History*. New York: Routledge, 1992.

Finnin, Rory. "'A Bridge between Us': Literature in the Ukrainian-Crimean Tatar Encounter." *Comparative Literature Studies* 56, no. 2 (2019): 289–319.
– "Captive Turks: Crimean Tatars in Pan-Turkist Literature." *Middle Eastern Studies* 50, no. 2 (2014): 291–308.
– "Forgetting Nothing, Forgetting No One: Boris Chichibabin, Viktor Nekipelov, and the Deportation of the Crimean Tatars." *Modern Language Review* 106, no. 4 (October 2011): 1091–1124.
– "Mountains, Masks, Metre, Meaning: Taras Shevchenko's 'Kavkaz.'" *Slavonic and East European Review* 83, no. 3 (July 2005): 396–439.
– "The Poetics of Home: Crimean Tatars in Nineteenth-Century Russian and Turkish Literatures." *Comparative Literature Studies* 49, no. 1 (2012): 84–118.
– "Nationalism and the Lyric, Or How Taras Shevchenko Speaks to Compatriots Dead, Living, and Unborn." *Slavonic and East European Review* 89, no. 1 (January 2011): 29–55.
– "Oles' Sanin, *Mamai.*" *KinoKultura* 9 (December 2009). http://www .kinokultura.com.
Finnin, Rory, and Ivan Kozachenko. "Beyond 'Narrating the Nation': Cultural Producers and Multilingualism in Wartime Ukraine." In *Multilingualism and Identity: Interdisciplinary Perspectives*, edited by Wendy Ayres-Bennett and Linda Fisher. Cambridge: Cambridge University Press, forthcoming.
Fisher, Alan W. *Between Russians, Ottomans, and Turks: Crimea and Crimean Tatars*. Istanbul: Isis Press, 1998.
– ed. *The Crimean Tatars*. Stanford, CA: Hoover Institution Press, 1978.
– "A Model Leader for Asia, Ismail Gaspirali." In *The Tatars of Crimea: Return to the Homeland*, 2nd ed., edited by Edward Allworth, 29–47. Durham, NC: Duke University Press, 1998.
– *The Russian Annexation of the Crimea: 1772–1783*. Cambridge: Cambridge University Press, 1970.
Foucault, Michel. "What Is an Author?" Translated by Josué Harari. In *The Foucault Reader*, edited by Paul Rabinow, 101–20. New York: Pantheon Books, 1984.
Frank, Gustav. "Layers of the Visual: Towards a Literary History of Visual Culture." In *Seeing Perception*, edited by Silke Horstkotte and Karin Leonhard, 76–97. Newcastle, UK: Cambridge Scholars, 2007.
Frye, Northrup. *Anatomy of Criticism*. New ed. Princeton, NJ: Princeton University Press, 1971.
Furmanov, Dmitrii. "Zametki o literature." In *Sobranie sochinenii*, edited by A.G. Dement'ev, E.I. Naumov, and L.I. Tymofeev, vol. 4, 392–4. Moscow: Gosudarstvennoe izdatel'stvo khudozhestvennoi literatury, 1961.
Galeotti, Mark. *Armies of Russia's War in Ukraine*. London: Bloomsbury, 2019.
Gasprinskii, Ismail. *Polnoe sobranie sochinenii*. Vol. 1, edited by R.S. Khakimov. Simferopol': Kazan', 2016.

– *Polnoe sobranie sochinenii*. Vol. 2, edited by R.S. Khakimov. Simferopol':
   Kazan', 2017.
– "Russkoe musul'manstvo." In *Rossiia i vostok*, 17–58. Kazan': Fond Zhien,
   1993.
Gatsak, Viktor. *Ukrainskie narodnye dumy*. Moscow: Nauka, 1972.
"Genshtab: ChF Rossii mozhet unichtozhit' protivnika eshche pri
   vydvizhenii s bas." *RIA Novosti*, 14 September 2016. https://ria.ru/20160914
   /1476907926.html.
The Geography of Strabo. Vol. 1, bk. 2.5.22. Translated by Horace Leonard Jones.
   Cambridge, MA: Harvard University Press, 1917.
The Geography of Strabo. Vol. 3, bk. 7.3.6. Translated by Horace Leonard Jones.
   Cambridge, MA: Harvard University Press, 1924.
Gessen, Masha. "Russia Declares War on Eurovision." *New Yorker*, 17 May
   2016. https://www.newyorker.com.
Gilbert, Paul. *Human Nature and Suffering*. Hove, UK: Lawrence Erlbaum
   Associates, 1989.
Ginzburg, Lidiia. "I zaodno s pravoporiadkom." In *Zapisnye knizhki,
   vospominaniia, esse*, 285–96. Saint Petersburg: Iskusstvo–SPB, 2002.
Giray, Raif. "Can Kırım." *Emel* 54 (September–October 1969).
Giritli, İzmet. "Modern cağda bilim ve ideolojiler." *Milliyet*, 15 September 1971.
Glavnoe upravlenie po kontroliu za zrelishchami i repertuarom (GURK).
   "Rasporiazhenie 700/r (17 April 1937)." VUFKU.org. https://vufku.org.
Glezer, Ol'ga, Nikita Khrushchev, and Vladimir Shevelev. "Krym v fevrale
   1954." *Moskovskie novosti* 5 (600), 2 February 1992.
Głowiński, Michał. "On the First-Person Novel." *New Literary History* 1
   (Autumn 1977): 103–14.
Gökalp, Ziya. "Altın Destan." In *Kızıl Elma*. Istanbul: Bilgeoğuz Yayinlari,
   2017.
– *The Principles of Turkism*. Translated by Robert Devereaux. Leiden: E.J. Brill,
   1968.
Goloğlu, Mahmut. *Milli Mücadele Tarihi IV: Cumhuriyete Doğru 1921–1922*.
   İstanbul: Türkiye İş Bankası Kültür, 2010.
Goodhart, David. "Too Diverse?" *Prospect*, 20 February 2004. https://www
   .prospectmagazine.co.uk.
Gorbanevskaia, Natal'ia. *Polden': Delo o demonstratsii 25 avgusta 1968 goda na
   Krasnoi proshchadi*. Moscow: Novoe izdatel'stvo, 2007.
"Gorbanevskaia ob osnovanii 'Khroniki tekushchikh sobytii.'" *Khronika
   zashchity prav v SSSR* 29 (January–March 1978): 45–8.
Gorkii, Maksim. *Zhizn' Klima Samgina*. In *Sobraniie sochinenii v 30 tomakh*,
   vol. 22. Moscow: Khudozhestvennaia literatura, 1953.
"'Govori, otets, govori …' Chitaet Lilia Budzhurova." YouTube, 18 May 2016.
   https://www.youtube.com.

Greenleaf, Monika. *Pushkin and Romantic Fashion: Fragment, Elegy, Orient, Irony*. Stanford, CA: Stanford University Press, 1994.

Grekov, Boris. "O nekotorykh voprosakh istorii Kryma." *Izvestiia* 131, no. 4 (June 1952).

Grigas, Agnia. *Beyond Crimea: The New Russian Empire*. New Haven, CT: Yale University Press, 2016.

Grigorenko, Petr. (Petro Hryhorenko.) "Kto zhe prestupniki?" In Grigorenko, *Mysli sumasshedshego*, 218–31.

– *Memoirs*. New York: Norton, 1982.

– *Mysli sumasshedshego: Izbrannye pis'ma i vystupleniia*. Amsterdam: Fond imeni Gertsena, 1973.

– "O spetsial'nykh psikhiatricheskikh bol'nitsakh ('durdomakh')." In Grigorenko, *Mysli sumasshedshego*, 232–42.

– "Pamiati soratnika i druga." In Grigorenko, *Mysli sumasshedshego*, 154–60.

– "Pis'mo Iu. V. Andropovu." In Grigorenko, *Mysli sumasshedshego*, 127–46.

– "Rech' Gen. P. G. Grigorenko." In "'Delo' krymskikh tatar." *Novyi Zhurnal* 97 (1969): 195–201.

– "Vystuplenie P. Grigorenko na pokhoronakh A. E. Kosterina (14 noiabria 1968 g.)." In Grigorenko, *Mysli sumasshedshego*, 154–60.

– "Zapis' rechi proiznesennoi 17 marta 1968 goda." In Grigorenko, *Mysli sumasshedshego*, 147–53.

Gronas, Mikhail. *Cognitive Poetics and Cultural Memory: Russian Literary Mnemonics*. London: Routledge, 2011.

Grossman, Vasilii. *Vse techet…* Frankfurt: Posev, 1970.

Güleç, Azmi. "İçimde Bir Büyük Vatan Ağlıyor." *Emel* 5 (July–August 1961).

Gumeniuk, Natal'ia. *Poteriannyi ostrov*. L'viv: Vydavnytstvo Staroho Leva, 2020.

Gündüz, Ali. *Kırım: Türk'ün Drami*. İstanbul: Gündüz Yayınevi, 1982.

Güzel, Hasan Celal, and Ali Birinci, eds. *Genel Türk Tarihi*. Vol. 9. İstanbul: Yeni Türkiye, 2002.

Hablemitoğlu, Necip. *Yüzbinlerin Sürgünü Kırımda Türk Soykırımı*. İstanbul: Toplumsal Dönüşüm Yayınları, 2004.

Hal'chyns'kyi, A., O. Vlasiuk, and S. Zdioruk. "Intehratsiia kryms'kykh tatar v ukraïns'ke suspil'stvo: Problemy i perspektyvy." *Ukraïns'ke relihiieznavtsvo* 3–4 (2004): 203–23.

Halman, Talat. "Sovyet Cennetinde İzzet ile İdris." *Milliyet*, 11 May 1969.

– *The Turkish Muse: Views and Reviews, 1960s–1990s*. Syracuse, NY: Syracuse University Press, 2006.

Halman, Talat Sait, Osman Horata, Yakup Çelik, Ramazan Korkmaz, Nurettin Demir, Mehmet Kalpaklı, and M. Öcal Oğuz. *Türk Edebiyatı Tarihi*. Vol. 4. İstanbul: TC Kültür ve Turizm Bakanlığı Yayınları, 2006.

Haluzevyi derzhavnyi arkhiv Sluzhby bespeky Ukraïny [HDA SBU, State Archive of the Security Service of Ukraine]. Fond 16. Kyiv, Ukraine.

"'Haytarma' Filminin Türkiye Galası Eskişehir'de Yapıldı." Haberler.com, 19 November 2013. https://www.haberler.com.

Hedges, Chris. *War Is a Force That Gives Us Meaning*. New York: Random House, 2003.

Heise, David. "Conditions for Empathic Solidarity." In *The Problem of Solidarity: Theories and Models*, edited by Patrick Doreian and Thomas Fararo, 197–211. Amsterdam: Gordon & Breach, 1998.

Herzen [Gertsen], Aleksandr. "Gonenie na krymskikh tatar." *Kolokol* 117, 22 December 1861. [Faksimil'noe izdanie]. Moscow, 1962.

Higgins, Andrew. "Oleg Sentsov: Russian by Blood and Language, Ukrainian in Spirit." *New York Times*, 27 September 2019. https://www.nytimes.com.

Hikmet, Nazım. "Nash Shevchenko." *Literaturnaia gazeta* 30, no. 8, 9 March 1961.

– "Şevçenko'nun kalemi." In *Yeni şiirler*. Ankara: Dost Yayınları, 1970.

Hızlan, Doğan. "'1000 Temel Eser'den '100 Temel Eser'e." *Hürriyet*, 27 December 2018. https://www.hurriyet.com.tr.

Holderness, Mary. *Notes Relating to the Manners and Customs of the Crim Tatars*. London: J. Warren, 1821.

Hollander, Gayle Durham. "Political Communication and Dissent in the Soviet Union." In *Dissent in the USSR: Politics, Ideology, and People*, edited by Rudolf L. Tökes, 233–75. Baltimore, MD: Johns Hopkins University Press, 1975.

"Holodomor Soykırımı Kurbanları İstanbul'da Anıldı." KirimDernegi.org.tr. 24 November 2019. http://www.kirimdernegi.org.tr.

Hopkins, Mark. *Russia's Underground Press: The Chronicle of Current Events*. New York: Praeger, 1983.

Hörmann, Hans. *Meinen und Verstehen: Grundzüge einer psychologischen Semantik*. Frankfurt am Main: Suhrkamp Verlag, 1976.

Horvath, Robert. "Breaking the Totalitarian Ice: The Initiative Group for the Defense of Human Rights in the USSR." *Human Rights Quarterly* 36, no. 1 (February 2014): 147–75.

Horyn', Mykhailo. "Ostannie slovo Mykhaila Horynia (16 kvitnia 1966 r)." In *Lykho z rozumu (portrety dvadtsiaty "zlochyntsiv")*, edited by Viacheslav Chornovil, 37–44. Paris: Persha ukraïns'ka drukarnia u Frantsiï, 1967.

Hoseiko, Lubomyr. *Istoriia ukraïns'koho kinematohrafa: 1896–1995*. Kyiv: Kino-kolo, 2005.

Hosking, Geoffrey A. "The State and Russian National Identity." In *Power and the Nation in European History*, edited by Len Scales and Oliver Zimmer, 195–211. Cambridge: Cambridge University Press, 2005.

Hrushevs'kyi, Mykhailo. *Istoriia Ukraïny-Rusy.* Vol. 8, *Roky 1626–1650.* Kyiv: Naukova dumka, 1995.
– "Na porozi Novoï Ukraïny." In *Tvory u 50 tomakh,* edited by Pavlo Sokhan' and Iaroslav Dashkevych. Vol. 4, bk. 1, *Suspil'no-politychni tvory,* edited by Svitlana Pan'kova, 225–66. L'viv: Svit, 2007.
Hughes, James, and Gwendolyn Sasse. "Power Ideas and Conflict: Ideology, Linkage, and Leverage in Crimea and Chechnya." *East European Politics* 32, no. 3: 314–34.
Huk, V'iacheslav. "Liuds'ke zhyttia ..." In *Qırım inciri,* edited by Mar'iana Savka, 135–7. L'viv: Vydavnytstvo Staroho Leva, 2017.
Humesky, Assya. "Text and Subtext in Roman Ivanychuk's *Mal'vy.*" In *Cultures and Nations of Central and Eastern Europe,* edited by Zvi Gitelman, Lubomyr Hajda, John-Paul Himka, and Roman Solchanyk, 283–92. Cambridge, MA: Harvard University Press, 2000.
Hunt, Lynn. *Inventing Human Rights: A History.* London: W.W. Norton, 2007.
Iefremov, Serhii. *Korotka istoriia ukraïns'koho pys'menstva.* Berlin: E. Wyrowyj, 1924.
– "U poiskakh novoi krasoty." In *Literaturno-krytychni statti,* edited by E.S. Solovei, 48–120. Kyïv: Dnipro, 1993.
"Infografika po nasyl'nyts'kym znyknenniam v okupovanomu RF Krymu." *KrymSOS,* 18 October 2018. https://krymsos.com.
International Council on Monuments and Sites (ICOMOS). "International Charter for the Conservation and Restoration of Monuments and Sites (The Venice Charter of 1964)." https://www.icomos.org.
"Iosif Brodskii v zashchitu Maramzina." *Khronika zashchity prav v SSSR* 10 (July–August 1974): 9–11.
"Ipchi, Dzhevair Umerovna." In *Deportatsiia krymskikh tatar 18 maia 1944 goda: Kak eto bylo,* edited by R. Kurtiev, Iu. Kandym, and E. Muslimova, 58–9. Simferopol': Odzhak", 2004.
İpek, Yucel. "Vatanda Gurbet." *Kalgay* 7 (January–March 1998): 17.
Iser, Wolfgang. *The Fictive and the Imaginary: Charting Literary Anthropology.* Baltimore, MD: John Hopkins University Press, 1993.
– *The Implied Reader: Patterns of Communication.* Baltimore, MD: John Hopkins University Press, 1974.
– *Prospecting: From Reader Response to Literary Anthropology.* Baltimore, MD: John Hopkins University Press, 1989.
Ivanets', Andrii. *Pershyi Kurultai.* Kyiv: Klio, 2018.
Ivanova, Mariya. *The Black Sea and the Early Civilizations of Europe, the Near East and Asia.* Cambridge: Cambridge University Press, 2013.
Ivanychuk, Roman. "Iak ia shukav svoï «Mal'vy»." In *Chystyi metal liuds'koho slova,* edited by V.D. Muza, 193–200. Kyiv: Radians'kyi pys'mennyk, 1991.
– *Mal'vy (Ianychary): Orda; Romany.* Kyiv: Evroekspres, 2000.

Jakobson, Roman. "The Metaphoric and Metonymic Poles." In Roman
Jakobson and Moris Halle, *Fundamentals of Language*, 2nd rev. ed., 90–6.
Berlin: Mouton de Gruyter, 2002. First published in 1956.
– *O cheshkom stikhe preimushchestvenno v sopostavlenii s russkim*. Berlin:
Opoiaz-MLK, 1923.
– "Studies in Comparative Slavic Metrics." *Oxford Slavonic Papers* 3 (1952): 21–66.
James, Henry. *Art of the Novel*. New York: Charles Scribner, 1970.
Jameson, Fredric. "Third World Literature in the Era of Multinational
Capitalism." *Social Text* 15 (1986): 65–88.
Jaspers, Karl. *The Question of German Guilt*. Translated by E.B. Ashton. New
York: Fordham University Press, 1965.
Jenny, Hans. *Cymatics: A Study of Wave Phenomena and Vibration*. Epping, NH:
MACROmedia, 2007.
"Joint Meeting to Hear an Address by His Excellency Petro Poroshenko,
President of Ukraine." *Congressional Record*, vol. 160, pt. 11. Washington,
DC: US Government Publishing Office, 2014.
Jones, Polly. *Myth, Memory, Trauma: Rethinking the Stalinist Past in the Soviet
Union, 1953–70*. New Haven, CT: Yale University Press, 2013.
– "'A Symptom of the Times': Assigning Responsibility for the Stalin Cult
in the Soviet Literary Community, 1953–64." *Forum for Modern Language
Studies* 42, no. 2 (2006): 151–67.
Jouve, Pierre Jean. *Lyrique*. Paris: Mercure de France, 1956.
Kalaycı, Suzan Meryem. "Interview with Professor Jay Winter." *Tarih* 1, no. 1
(2009): 29–36.
Kalkay, Tuncer. "2014 'ün bıraktıkları!" *Kırım bülteni* 77 (July–December
2014): 4.
Kalytko, Kateryna. "Nastupnoho roku v Bakhchysaraï." Opinionua.com,
27 October 2018. https://opinionua.com.
– *Zemlia zahublenykh, abo malen'ki strashni kazky*. L'viv: Vydavnytstvo Staroho
Leva, 2017.
Kant, Immanuel. *Critique of Pure Reason*. Translated by Werner S. Pluhar.
Indianapolis, IN: Hackett, 1996.
Kaplan, Mehmet. *Kültür ve Dil*. İstanbul: Dergâh Yayınları, 1999.
Kappeler, Andreas. "Mazepintsy, malorossy, khokhly: Ukraintsy v
ethnicheskoi ierarkhii rossiiskoi imperii." In *Rossiia–Ukraina: Istoriia
vzaimootnoshenii*, edited by A.I. Miller, 125–44. Moscow: Shkola "Iazyki
russkoi kul'tury," 1997.
Karas'-Chichibabina, Liliia. "Predislovie." In Chichibabin, *Pered zemleiu
krymskoi sovest' moia chista*, 5–11.
Karatay, Zafer. "Başyazı." *Emel* 246/249 (2014).
– "Demirel'in Tarihî Ziyaretinin Kırım İçin Önemi." *Emel* 226 (May–June 1998).
– "Yansılar, Cengiz Dağcı ve Kırım." *Emel* 167 (July–August, 1988).

Karavans'kyi, Sviatoslav. "Pisnia ianychariv." In *Sutychka z taifunom*. New York: Smoloskyp, 1980.

Karpat, Kemal H. *Çağdaş Türk Edebiyatinda Sosyal Konular*. 2nd ed. İstanbul: Varlık Yayınevi, 1971.

– *Ottoman Population, 1830–1914: Demographic and Social Characteristics*. Madison: University of Wisconsin Press, 1985.

Kas'ianov, Heorhii. *Nezhodni: Ukrains'ka intelihentsiia v rusi oporu 1960–80kh rokiv*. Kyiv: Lybid, 1995.

Keen, Suzanne. *Empathy and the Novel*. Oxford: Oxford University Press, 2007.

Kemal, Namık. *Cezmi*. Ankara: Alter Yayıncılık, 2010.

Kerim, İsmail Asanoğlu. *Gasprinskiyniñ "Canlı" tarihi 1883–1914: Qırımtatar tili, edebiyatı ve medeniyetinden malümat desteği*. Aqmescit: Mejdunarodnıy fond "Vidrocennâ", 1999.

– "Poeticheskii genii Asana Chergeeva (1879–1946)." *Golos Kryma* 13, no. 5 (April 2019). http://goloskrimanew.ru.

Kermençikli, Cemil. "Tatarym." In *Ma-bih il ifitharım qırımlıqtır: menim ğururım*. Aqmescit: Qırımdevoquvpedneşir, 2005.

Khabarova, Zoia. *Dnevnik* [19 May 1944]. Prozhito. https://prozhito.org/person/73.

"Khanskii dvorets v Krymu: Unichtozhenie pod prikrytiem restavratsii." YouTube, 26 December 2017. https://www.youtube.com.

Khazanov, Anatoly. *After the USSR: Ethnicity, Nationalism, and Politics in the Commonwealth of Independent States*. Madison: University of Wisconsin Press, 1995.

Khronika tekushchikh sobytii 2 (30 June 1968). http://www.memo.ru.

Khvyl'ovyi, Mykola. "Ostap Vyshnia v svitli livoï balabaiky." *Prolitfront* 4 (July 1930): 309–12.

Kidd, David Comer, and Emanuele Castano. "Reading Literary Fiction Improves Theory of Mind." *Science* 342 (October 2013): 377–80.

Kılıç, A. "Kırım Türkleri ile niye ilgilenmiyoruz?" *Milliyet*, 12 June 1969.

King, Charles. *The Black Sea: A History*. Oxford: Oxford University Press, 2004.

Kırım Mecmuası 1, no. 13 (October 1918).

"Kırım Türkleri hala insanca yaşayamıyor." *Emel* 52 (May–June 1969).

Kırımal, Edige. "Kırım Türkleri." *Emel* 59 (July–August 1970).

– "Sürgündeki Kırımlılara dair." *Emel* 54 (September–October 1969).

Kirimca, Seyit Ahmet. "Symbols: The National Anthem and Patriotic Songs by Three Poets." In *The Tatars of Crimea: Return to the Homeland*, edited by Edward A. Allworth, 71–83. 2nd ed. Durham, NC: Duke University Press, 1998.

Kırımer, Cafer Seydahmet. *Bazı hatıralar*. İstanbul: Emel, 1993.

– *Gaspıralı İsmail Bey: Dilde, fikirde işte birlik*. İstanbul: Avrasya Bir Vakfı Yayınları, 1997.

Kırımlı, Hakan. "The Activities of the Union for the Liberation of Ukraine in the Ottoman Empire during the First World War." In *Turkey before and after Atatürk: Internal and External Affairs*, edited by Syliva Kedourie, 177–200. London: Frank Cass, 1999.

– *National Movements and National Identity among the Crimean Tatars, 1905–1916.* Leiden: E.J. Brill, 1997.

– ed. "The Ottoman Empire and Ukraine, 1918–21." In *Turkey before and after Atatürk: Internal and External Affairs*, edited by Sylvia Kedourie, 201–39. London: Frank Cass, 1999.

– "The Young 'Tatar' Movement in the Crimea, 1905–1909." *Cahiers du monde russe et soviétique* 34, no. 4 (Octobre–Décembre 1993): 529–60.

Kırımman, Halil. "Kırımlı Sürgünler." *Emel* 52 (May–June 1969).

Kirişçioğlu, Nusret. *12 Mart (İnönü—Ecevit) ve 1960 Tahkikat Encümeni raporum.* İstanbul: Baha Matbaası, 1973.

Kıvanç, Halıt. "Kampta." *Milliyet*, 23 April 1959.

Knott, Eleanor. "Identity in Crimea before Annexation: A Bottom-Up Perspective." In *Russia Before and After Crimea: Nationalism and Identity, 2010–17*, edited by Pål Kolstø and Helge Blakkisrud, 282–305. Edinburgh: Edinburgh University Press, 2018.

Kofman, Michael, Katya Migacheva, Brian Nichiporuk, Andrew Radin, Olesya Tkacheva, and Jenny Oberholtzer. *Lessons from Russia's Operations in Crimea and Eastern Ukraine.* Santa Monica, CA: Rand Corporation, 2017.

Kökçe, Seyare. "Bizim evlerimiz nasıl qurula?" In *Qırım inciri*, edited by Mar'iana Savka, 285–6. L'viv: Vydavnytstvo Staroho Leva, 2017.

Komaromi, Ann. "The Material Existence of Soviet Samizdat." *Slavic Review* 63, no. 3 (Autumn 2004): 597–618.

– "Samizdat and Soviet Dissident Publics." *Slavic Review* 71 no. 1 (Spring 2012): 70–90.

Komarova-Nekipelova, Nina. *Kniga liubvi i gneva.* Paris: Izd. avtora, 1994.

Kononenko, Danylo. "Povernennia." In *Sontsia i moria na mezhi: Proza ta poeziia pys'mennykiv Krymu*, edited by Danylo Kononenko. Simferopol': Tavriia, 2004.

– "Slovo do kryms'kykh ukraïntsiv." *Kryms'ka svitlytsia* 52, 29 December 2017. https://upload.wikimedia.org

Korsovets'kyi, Orest. "Chokrak." In *Suchasni ukraïns'ki pys'mennyky Krymu*, edited by Oleksandr Hubar. Simferopol': Krymnavchpedderzhvydav, 1997.

Körüklü, Refet. "Bırakın a dağlar." *Toprak* 4 (March 1955).

Kosiv, Mykhailo. "Zhyttia korotke, mystetstvo – vichne." Zakhid.net, 26 October 2016. https://zaxid.net.

Kösoğlu, Nevzat, ed. *Türkiye dışındaki Türk edebiyatları antolojisi: Cilt 13; Kırım Türk-Tatar edebiyatı.* Ankara: Kültür Bakanlığı, 1999.

Kostenko, Lina. *Vybrane.* Kyiv: Dnipro, 1989.

Kotsiubyns'kyi, Mykhailo. "Lyst do Ivana Franka" (16.2.03). In *Tvory v tr'okh tomakh*, vol. 3. Kyiv: Dnipro, 1979.

– "Lyst do Ol'hy Kobylians'koï" (25.10.02). In *Tvory v tr'okh tomakh*, vol. 3. Kyiv: Dnipro, 1979.

– "Lyst do Ol'hy Kobylians'koï" (2.7.03). In *Tvory v tr'okh tomakh*, vol. 3. Kyiv: Dnipro, 1979.

– *Pid minaretamy*. In *Tvory v dvokh tomakh*, vol. 1. Kyiv: Naukova dumka, 1988.

Kotyhorenko, Viktor. *Kryms'kotatars'ki repatrianti: Problema sotsial'noï adaptatsiï*. Kyiv: Svitohlad, 2005.

Kozak Mamai. Edited by Stanislav Bushak, Valeriy Sakharuk, and Rostyslav Zabashta. Kyiv: Rodovid, 2008.

Kozlov, Denis. *The Readers of "Novyi Mir."* Cambridge, MA: Harvard University Press, 2013.

Kozlov, Ivan. *V krymskom podpol'e*. Moscow: Sovetskii pisatel', 1947.

"Kratkie soobshcheniia." In *Khronika tekushchikh sobytii* 8 (1969), published in *Sobranie dokumentov Samizdata*, vol. 10-A. Munich: Radio Liberty Research Department, 1972.

Kreindler, Isabelle. "The Soviet Departed Nationalities: A Summary and an Update." *Soviet Studies* 38, no. 3 (July 1986): 387–405.

Krym: Put' na rodinu. Directed by Sergei Kraus, 2015. Russia: All-Russia State Television and Radio Broadcasting Company.

"Krymskie tatary pomogaiut sem'e Sentsova." *Argumenty nedeli – Krym*, 10 August 2017. https://an-crimea.ru.

"Krymskie tatary stali geroiami komiksov." *ATR*, 3 April 2014. https://atr.ua/.

Krymskii klub. *Nashkrym: Axis aestheticus mundi tauricam transit*. New York: Kryk, 2014.

Kryms'kyi, Anatanhel. "Literatura kryms'kykh tatar." In *Studiï z Krymu I–IX*, edited by A.E. Kryms'kyi, 165–91. Kyiv: Filolohichna katedra pid keruvanniam akad. A.E. Kryms'koho, 1930.

– *Tvory v p'iaty tomakh*. Vol. 5, bk. 1. Kyiv: Naukova dumka, 1973.

Kucher, Vasyl'. *Chornomortsi*. In *Tvory v p'iaty tomakh*, vol. 2. Kyiv: Dnipro, 1970.

Kudusov, Eric. "Ethnogenez korenogo naseleniia Kryma." *Kasavet* 24, no. 1 (1995): 14–25.

Kuku, Emir-Usein. "Poslednee slovo v sude." Facebook, 8 November 2019. https://www.facebook.com.

Kul'chyts'kyi, Stanislav, and Larysa Iakubova. *Kryms'kyi vuzol*. Kyiv: Klio, 2019.

Kulichenko, M.I. *Natsional'nye otnosheniia v SSSR i tendentsii ikh razvitiia*. Moscow: Mysil', 1972.

Kulish, Panteleimon. "Kazky i baiky z susidovoi khatky, perelyts'ovani i skomponovani prydnipriantsem." In *Istoriia ukraïns'koï literaturnoï krytyky ta literaturnoznavstva: Khrestomatiia u tr'okh knyhakh*, bk. 1, edited by P.M. Fedchenko, M.M. Pavliuk, and T.V. Bovsunivs'ka, 303–10. Kyiv: Lybid', 1996.

Kuzio, Taras. "Ukraine: Muddling Along." In *Central and East European Politics: From Communism to Democracy*, edited by Sharon L. Wolchik and Jane Leftwich Curry, 335–69. Lanham, MD: Rowman & Littlefield, 2008.

Kyrylenko, V'iacheslav. "Zaiava 'Nashoï Ukraïny' z pryvodu provokuvannia kryms'koiu vladoiu ta militsiieiu mizhnatsional'nykh konfliktiv (7 lystopada 2007 r)." https://maidan.org.ua.

Kyrymohlu [Dzhemilev], Mustafa A. "Noman Chelebidzhikhan z namy." In Iunus Kandym, *Ne zaroste travoiu pole boiu*, 9–12. Ichnia: Format, 2017.

Laclau, Ernesto. "Politics and the Limits of Modernity." In *Universal Abandon?: The Politics of Postmodernism*, edited by Andrew Ross, 63–82. Minneapolis: University of Minnesota, 1989.

Landau, Jacob. *Pan-Turkism: From Irredentism to Cooperation*. Bloomington: Indiana University Press, 1995.

– "Ultra-Nationalist Literature in the Turkish Republic: A Note on the Novels of Hüseyin Nihal Atsız." *Middle Eastern Studies* 39 no. 2 (2003): 204–10.

Landsberg, Alison. "Prosthetic Memory: The Ethics and Politics of Memory in an Age of Mass Culture." In *Memory and Popular Film*, edited by Paul Grainge, 144–61. Manchester, UK: Manchester University Press, 2003.

Laub, Dori. "Truth and Testimony: The Process and the Struggle." In *Trauma: Explorations in Memory*, edited by Cathy Caruth, 61–75. Baltimore, MD: Johns Hopkins University Press, 1995.

Layton, Susan. *Russian Literature and Empire: Conquest of the Caucasus from Pushkin to Tolstoy*. Cambridge: Cambridge University Press, 2004.

Lazzerini, Edward J. "The Crimea under Russian Rule: 1783 to the Great Reforms." In *Russian Colonial Expansion*, edited by Michael Rywkin, 123–38. London: Mansell Publishing, 1988.

– "Ismail Bey Gasprinskii (Gapirali): The Discourse of Modernism and the Russians." In *The Tatars of Crimea: Return to the Homeland*, 2nd ed., edited by Edward Allworth, 48–70. Durham, NC: Duke University Press, 1998.

– "Local Accommodation and Resistance to Colonialism in Nineteenth-Century Crimea." In *Russia's Orient: Imperial Borderlands and Peoples, 1700–1917*, edited by Daniel R. Brower and Edward J. Lazzerini, 169–87. Bloomington: Indiana University Press, 1997.

Lenin, Vladimir. "O rabote Narkomprosa." In *Polnoe sobranie sochinenii*, vol. 42, 322–32. Moscow: Gos. izd-vo polit. lit-ry, 1970.

Leonovich, Vladimir. "Mezh rozovykh barkhanov." In *Vsemu zhivomu ne chuzhoi: Boris Chichibabin v stat'iakh i vospominaniiakh*, 226–31. Khar'kov: Folio, 1998.

Levitin-Krasnov, Anatolii. "Müslüman Dünyasına Çağrı." Translated by F. Yurter. *Emel* 93 (1976).

Lewis, Bernard. *The Emergence of Modern Turkey*. Oxford: Oxford University Press, 1968.

Lewis, Helen. *Shame and Guilt in Neurosis*. New York: International Universities Press, 1971.

Lienhardt, R.G. *Social Anthropology*. 2nd ed. London: Oxford University Press, 1966.

"Liudmila Ulitskaia pro 'krymnash'." Hromadske.radio, 17 September 2014. https://hromadske.radio/ru.

"Liudy ekranu: H. Tasin." *Kino* 3, no. 15 (February 1927): 6.

Liusyi, A.P. *Krymskii tekst v russkoi literature*. Saint Petersburg: Aleteiia, 2003.

Lopatin, V.S., ed. *Ekaterina II i G. A. Potemkin: Lichnaia perepiska 1769–1791*. Moscow: Nauka, 1997.

Lotman, Iu. M. "Mezhdu veshch'iu i pustotoi." In *Izbrannye stat'i v trekh tomakh*, vol. 3, 294–307. Tallinn: Aleksandra, 1993.

– *Struktura khudozhestvennogo teksta: Semioticheskie issledovaniia po teorii iskusstva*. Moscow: Iskusstvo, 1970.

Luckhurst, Roger. *The Trauma Question*. London: Routledge, 2013.

Lukomnikov, German. "Moe uchastie v sbornike stikhov o Kryme ..." *Livejournal*, 30 October 2014. https://lukomnikov-1.livejournal.com.

Lur'e, Lev, and Irina Maliarova. *1956: Seredina veka*. Saint Petersburg: Izdatelskii dom "Neva," 2007.

"Lyst tvorchoï molodi m. Dnipropetrovs'ka." In Viacheslav Chornovil, *Ukraïns'kyi visnyk, 1970–72*, 88–99. Vol 3 of *Tvory v desiaty tomakh*. Kyiv: Smoloskyp, 2006.

Magocsi, Paul Robert, and Yohanan Petrovsky-Shtern. *Jews and Ukrainians: A Millennium of Co-existence*. Toronto: University of Toronto Press, 2017.

Maksimovich, Mikhail. *Sbornik ukrainskikh pesen*. Kiev: V tipografii Feofila Gliksberga, 1849.

Mamai. Directed by Oles' Sanin. 2003. Ukraine: Dovzhenko Film Studio.

Mandel'shtam, Osip. "Tatarskie kovboi." In *Sobranie sochinenii v 4 tomakh*, vol. 2, 432–4. Moscow: Art-Biznes-Tsentr, 1993.

Margalit, Avishai. *The Ethics of Memory*. Cambridge, MA: Harvard University Press, 2002.

Markov, Evgenii. *Ocherki Kryma: Kartiny Krymskoi zhizni, prirody i istorii*. Saint Petersburg: Tipografiia K.N. Plotnikova, 1872.

Martin, Terry. *The Affirmative Action Empire: Nations and Nationalism in the Soviet Union, 1923–1939*. Ithaca, NY: Cornell University Press, 2001.

Marynovych, Myroslav. "Kryms'ka kryza i tsyvilizatsiini shansy Ukraïny." *Den'*, 7 April 2014. https://day.kyiv.ua.

Maximenkov, Leonid, and Leonid Heretz. "Stalin's Meeting with a Delegation of Ukrainian Writers on 12 February 1929." *Harvard Ukrainian Studies* 16, no. 3/4 (December 1992): 361–431.

Mazus, Izrail'. *Istoriia odnogo podpol'ia*. Moscow: Prava cheloveka, 1998.

McGinn, Colin. *Ethics, Evil, and Fiction*. Oxford: Clarendon, 1997.

Mearsheimer, John J. "Don't Arm Ukraine." *New York Times*, 8 February 2015. https://www.nytimes.com.

Medvedev, Roy, and Guilietto Chiesa. *Time of Change: An Insider's View of Russia's Transformation*. Translated by Michael Moore. New York: Pantheon Books, 1990.

Meerson-Aksenov, Michael. "The Dissident Movement and *Samizdat*." In *The Political, Social and Religious Thought of Russian "Samizdat": An Anthology*, edited by M. Meerson-Aksenov and B. Shragin, 19–43. Belmont, MA: Nordland, 1977.

Meerson-Aksenov, Michael, and Boris Shragin. Preface to *The Political, Social and Religious Thought of Russian "Samizdat": An Anthology*. Edited by M. Meerson-Aksenov and B. Shragin, 13–15. Belmont, MA: Nordland, 1977.

Memmi, Albert. *The Colonizer and the Colonized*. Translated by Howard Greenfield. London: Earthscan, 2003.

Miranda, Fransisko de [Francisco de]. *Puteshestvie po Rossiiskoi Imperii: Dnevniki Fransisko de Mirandy*. Translated by M.S. Al'perovich, V.A. Kapanadze, and E.F. Tolstaia. Moscow: MAIK "Nauka/Interperiodika," 2001.

Miroshnychenko, M., and and Iu. Kandym, eds. *Küneşten bir parça / Okrushyna sontsia: Antolohiia kryms'kotatars'koï poeziï XIII–XX st.* Kyiv: Holovna spetsializovana redaktsiia literatury movamy natsional'nykh menshyn Ukraïny, 2003.

"Molytvy i povitriani kuli: V Krymu prokhodiat' provladni aktsiï do richnytsi." *Krym.Realii*, 18 May 2019. https://ua.krymr.com.

Moore, David Chioni. "Is the Post- in Postcolonial the Post- in Post-Soviet? Toward a Global Postcolonial Critique." *PMLA* 116, no. 1 (January 2001): 111–28.

Morgan, Michael Cotey. *The Final Act: The Helsinki Accords and the Transformation of the Cold War*. Princeton, NJ: Princeton University Press, 2018.

Mostafa, Saleh Lamei. "The Cairene Sabil: Form and Meaning." *Muqarnas* 6 (1989): 33–42.

"Muhacir Türküleri." *Emel* 56 (January–February, 1970).

Mukha, Renata. "O pervom vystuplenii Borisa Chichibabina." *Universitates* 1 (2013): 42–5.

Mukorovský, Jan. "Standard Language and Poetic Language." In *A Prague School Reader on Esthetics, Literary Structure, and* Style, edited by P. L. Garvin, 17–31. Washington, DC: Georgetown University Press, 1964.

Musaeva, Sevgil'. "Oleg Sentsov: Eto ne bol', eto prosto zhelanie sdelat' vse pravil'no – vernut' Krym i nakazat' agressora." *Ukraïns'ka Pravda*, 17 February 2020. https://www.pravda.com.ua.

"Mustafa Kemal Paşanın Lenin'e Mektubu (4 ocak 1922)." In *Atatürk ve Komünizm*, by Rasih Nuri İleri, 2nd ed. İstanbul: Sarmal Yayınevi, 1994.

Muzafarov, Refik, ed. *Krymskotatarskaia entsiklopediia*. Simferopol': Vatan 1993.

Nadinskii, P.N. *Ocherki po istorii Kryma*. Vol. 1. Simferopol', 1951.

Nakashima, Ellen. "Inside a Russian Disinformation Campaign in Ukraine in 2014." *Washington Post*, 25 December 2017. https://www.washingtonpost.com.

Nazar, Yaroslav. "Mystetstvo pro viinu: Mizh tvorchistiu ta ahitkoiu." BBC Ukraïna, 22 February 2016. https://www.bbc.com.

Nechui-Levyts'kyi, Ivan. "Ukraïns'ka dekadentshchyna." In *Zibrannia tvoriv u 10 tomakh*, vol. 10, 187–223. Kyiv: Naukova dumka, 1968.

Nekipelov, Viktor. "Ballada ob otchem dome." In *Stikhi: Izbrannoe*. Boston: Memorial, 1992.

– "Chufut-Kale." In *Stikhi: Izbrannoe*. Boston: Memorial, 1992.

– "Gurzuf." In *Stikhi: Izbrannoe*. Boston: Memorial, 1992.

Nekrich, Aleksandr. *The Punished Peoples: The Deportation and Fate of Soviet Minorities at the End of the Second World War*. Translated by George Saunders. New York: W.W. Norton, 1978.

"Novi viddili VUFKU." *Kino* 10 (August 1926): 19.

Novosel'skii, A.A. *Bor'ba moskovskogo gosudarstva s Tatarami v pervoi polovine XVII veka*. Moscow: Akademiia nauk SSSR, 1948.

"Novosti samizdata: T. Franko, M. Lysenko." *Khronika tekushchikh sobytii* 13 (30 April 1970). http://www.memo.ru.

Nucci, Larry P. *Education in the Moral Domain*. Cambridge: Cambridge University Press, 2001.

Nussbaum, Martha. *Love's Knowledge: Essays on Philosophy and Literature*. Oxford: Oxford University Press, 1990.

– *Poetic Justice: The Literary Imagination and Public Life*. Boston: Beacon Press, 1995.

– *Upheavals of Thought: The Intelligence of Emotions*. Cambridge: Cambridge University Press, 2001.

Obertas, Oles'. *Ukraïns'kyi samvydav*. Kyiv: Smoloskyp, 2010.

"Obrashchenie krymskikh tatar k K. Val'dkhaimu." *Arkhiv Samizdata*, no. 1881 (January 1973).

"Obrashchenie pisatelia A.I. Pristavkina v Prezidium Verkhovnoho Soveta SSSR" (15 July 1987). In *Krymskotatarskoe natsional'noe dvizhenie*, edited by Mikhail Guboglo and Svetlana Chervonnaia. Vol. 2, *Dokumenty, materialy, khronika*, 218. Moscow: TsIMO, 1992.

"Ob uprazdnenii Checheno-Ingushskoi ASSR i preobrazovanii Krymskoi ASSR v Krymskuiu oblast'." *Izvestiia*, 26 June 1946.

O'Connor, Lynn E., and Jack W. Berry. "Interpersonal Guilt: The Development of a New Measure." *Journal of Clinical Psychology* 53, no. 1: 73–89.

The Office of the Prosecutor of the International Criminal Court. *Report on Preliminary Examination Activities, 2016*. https://www.icc-cpi.int.

Ognev, Aleksandr and V.A. Red'kin, eds. *Akhmatovskie chteniia: Sbornik nauchnykh trudov*. Tver': Tverskoi gosudarstvennyi universitet, 1991.

Okudzhava, Bulat. "Ia rad by byl pokoem voskhitit'sia." In *Milosti sud'by*. Moscow: Moskovskii rabochii, 1993.

Olgun, Hüsamettin. "Şevçenko'nun ülkesinde." *Ihlamur* 53 (April 2017).

"O priznanii nezakonnymi i prestupymi repressivnykh aktov protiv narodov, podvergshikhsia nasil'stvennomu pereseleniiu, i obespechenii ikh prav (14 noiabria 1989 g)." In Server Tairov, *Krymskie tatary s drevneishikh vremen do nashikh dnei*. Simferopol': Dolia, 2011.

Ortaylı, İlber. *Ottoman Studies*. 3rd ed. İstanbul: Bilgi University Press, 2010.

Orwell, George. *Nineteen Eighty Four*. New York: Signet, 1981.

Otar, İbrahim. "İstanbul Gazetelerinde Kırım." *Emel* 6 (September 1961).

Oushakine, Sergei. "The Terrifying Mimicry of Samizdat." *Public Culture* 13, no. 2 (2001): 191–214.

Özcan, Kemal. *Kırım Dramı*. Istanbul: Babıali Kültür Yayınılıği, 2010.

"O zhurnalakh 'Zvezda' i 'Leningrad' iz postanovlenie TsK VKP(b) ot 14 avgusta 1946g." *Pravda*, 21 August 1946.

Öztürkmen, Arzu. "Folklore on Trial: Pertev Naili Boratav and the Denationalization of Turkish Folklore." *Journal of Folklore Research* 42, no. 2 (2005): 185–216.

Paradzhanov, Sergei. *Dremliushchii dvorets*. Saint Petersburg: Izd-vo "Azbuka-klassika," 2004.

Parla, Taha. *The Social and Political Thought of Ziya Gökalp, 1876–1924*. Leiden: E.J. Brill, 1985.

Pavlenko, Petr. "Rassvet." In *Sobranie sochinenii*, vol. 3. Moscow: Gos. izd-vo khudozh. lit-ry, 1953.

Pavlychko, Solomea. "Modernism vs. Populism in *Fin de Siècle* Ukrainian Literature: A Case of Gender Conflict." In *Engendering Slavic Literatures*, edited by Pamela Chester and Sibelan Forrester, 83–103. Bloomington: Indiana University Press, 1966.

– *Natsionalizm, seksual'nist', oriientalizm: Skladnyi svit Ahatanhela Kryms'koho*. Kyiv: Osnova, 2000.

Pavlyshyn, Marko. "Ia Bohdan (spovid' u slavi) Pavla Zahrebel'noho." In *Kanon ta iconostas*, 62–70. Kyiv: Chas, 1997.

– "'Sobor" Olesia Honchara ta 'Orlova Balka' Mykoly Rudenka." In *Kanon ta iconostas*, 44–61. Kyiv: Chas, 1997.

Perevodchik (Tercüman) 32 (26 September 1893).

Perevodchik (Tercüman) 33 (4 October 1893).

Perevodchik (Tercüman) 40 (26 November 1893).

Perlman, Mişel. "Bütun Müslümanlar Mustafa Cemiloğlu'nu savunmali." *Milliyet*, 15 February 1976.

Perventsev, Arkadii. *Chest' smolodu*. Moscow: Molodaia Gvardiia, 1949.

– *Sobranie sochinenii*. Vol 4. Moscow: Khudozhestvennaia literatura, 1979.

"Pete Buttigieg: 'Shortest Way Home.'" YouTube, 19 February 2019. https://www.youtube.com.

Petrenko-Pod"iapol'skaia, Mariia. "Biografiia Viktora Nekipelova." In Viktor Nekipelov, *Stikhi: Izbrannoe*. Boston: Memorial, 1992.

Petro and Zinaida Grigorenko Family Papers [PGFP]. Series II and IV. Amherst Center for Russian Culture, Amherst, MA.

Pinker, Steven. *The Better Angels of Our Nature: A History of Violence and Humanity*. London: Penguin, 2011.

– "The Seed Salon: Steven Pinker and Rebecca Goldstein." *Seed* 10 (May 2004).

Pişkin, Mehmet, and Mehmet Coşar. *Kırım Kurbanları*. 3rd ed. İstanbul: Yağmur Yayınevi, 1976.

Pleshakov, Constantine. *The Crimean Nexus: Putin's War and the Clash of Civilizations*. New Haven, CT: Yale University Press, 2017.

Pliushch, Leonid. *Na karnavale istorii*. London: Overseas Publications, 1979.

Plokhy, Serhii. *The Gates of Europe*. London: Basic Books, 2017.

– *Ukraine and Russia: Representations of the Past*. Toronto: University of Toronto Press, 2008.

Polian, Pavel. *Against Their Will: The History and Geography of Forced Migrations in the USSR*. Budapest: Central European University Press, 2004.

Pope, Alexander. *An Essay on Man*. Edited by Tom Jones. Princeton, NJ: Princeton University Press, 2016.

"Poroshenko zaiavyv pro hotovnist' vnesty zminy do Konstytutsiï shchodo kryms'kotatars'koi avtonomii." Radio Svoboda, 14 May 2017. https://www.radiosvoboda.org.

"Poslednee slovo Andreia Siniavskogo." *Grani* 60 (June 1966): 154–60.

Posner, Richard A. "Against Ethical Literature, Part Two." *Philosophy and Literature* 22 (1998): 394–412.

Potemkin, Grigorii A. "Rasporiazheniia svetleishago kniazia Grigoriia Aleksandrovicha Potemkina-Tavricheskago kasatel'no ustroeniia Tavricheskoi oblasti s 1781 po 1786-i god [16 October 1783]." *ZOOID* 12 (1881): 249–329.

"Povernennia Krymu: Analitychna zapyska do resul'tativ opytuvan' hromads'koi dumky." Fond demokratychni initsiatyvy imeni Il'ka Kucheriva, 22 October 2018. https://dif.org.ua.

Povinelli, Elizabeth A. "The Cunning of Recognition: A Reply to John Frow and Meaghan Morris." *Critical Inquiry* 25, no. 3 (Spring 1999): 631–7.

"'Povtoriu na dopyti shche raz: Krym – tse Ukraïna' – zastupnyk holovy Medzhlisu." 24 kanal, 15 May 2016. http://24tv.ua.

"Prem'ernyi pokaz dokumental'noho fil'ma E.M. Kozhokina «Ismail i ego liudi»." MGIMO, 3 June 2018. https://mgimo.ru.

"President Erdoğan Congratulates Jamala on Her Eurovision Victory." Yeni Şafak, 16 May 2016. https://www.yenisafak.com.

Prezydiia zakordonnoho predstavnytstva ukrains'koï holovoï vyzvol'noï rady. "U spravi povernennia tatar na Krym." *Suchasnist'* 7, no. 103 (July 1969): 91–2.

Prytula, Volodymyr. "Krym vidviduie turets'kyi prem'ier." Radio Svoboda, 12 September 2012. http://www.radiosvoboda.org.

"Public Opinion Survey: Residents of the Autonomous Republic of Crimea, May 16–30, 2013." International Republican Institute, May 2013. https://www.iri.org.

Pulatov [Pulat], Timur. "Ölümge 'Yoq' dep ayt." In *Qırım: sailama.* Simferopol': Tezis, 2018.

– "Vsem mirom – pomoch bratiam." In *Meskhetinskie turki, i prochie sovetskie narody,* 125–8. Vol. 3 of *Tak eto bylo: Natsional'nye repressii v SSSR 1919–1952 gody,* edited by Svetlana Alieva. Moscow: Rossiiskyi mezhdunarodnyi fond kul'tury "Insan," 1993.

Pushkin, Aleksandr. *Bakhchisaraiskii fontan.* In *Polnoe sobranie sochinenii v 16 tomakh,* vol. 4. Moscow: Akademiia nauk SSR, 1949.

– *Eugene Onegin: A Novel in Verse by Aleksandr Pushkin in Four Volumes.* Translated by Vladimir Nabokov. Vol. 3. New York: Pantheon Books, 1964.

– "Otryvki iz puteshestviia Onegina." In *Polnoe sobranie sochinenii,* vol. 5. Moscow: Izd-vo AN SSSR, 1949.

– *Pushkin on Literature.* Translated and edited by Tatiana Wolff. London: Athlone Press, 1986.

Putin, Vladimir. "Obrashchenie Prezidenta Rossiiskoi Federatsii (18 marta 2014 goda)." Prezident Rossii, 18 March 2014. http://kremlin.ru.

Rakhlin, Feliks. *O Borise Chichibabine i ego vremeni.* Khar'kov: Folio, 2004.

Raskina, E. Iu. "Natal'ia Gorbanevskaia." In *Russkaia literatura XX veka: Prozaiki, poety, dramaturgii,* edited by Nikolai Skatov, 523–4. Moscow: OLMA, 2005.

Ravliuk, Nikolai. "Istoricheskii roman bez istorii." *Pravda Ukrainy,* 7 February 1970.

Reddaway, Peter. "The Crimean Tatar Drive for Repatriation." In *The Tatars of Crimea: Return to the Homeland,* 2nd ed., edited by Edward Allworth, 226–36. Durham, NC: Duke University Press, 1998.

– "The Crimean Tatars." In *Uncensored Russia: The Human Rights Movement in the Soviet Union,* edited and translated by Peter Reddaway, 249–318. London: Jonathan Cape, 1972.

"Rehional'nymy shtabamy DSNS zareiestrovano ponad 1 mln. 70 tysiach vnutrishn'o peremishchenykh osib." Dsns.gov.ua, 25 April 2017. https://www.dsns.gov.ua.

"Reizova, Shadie Dzhaferovna." In *Deportatsiia krymskikh tatar 18 maia 1944 goda: Kak eto bylo*, edited by R. Kurtiev, Iu. Kandym, and E. Muslimova, 90. Simferopol': Odzhak", 2004.

Ricoeur, Paul. *Time and Narrative*. Vol. 1. Translated by Kathleen McLaughlin and David Pellauer. Chicago: University of Chicago Press, 1983.

Rilke, Rainer Maria. "Brief an Witold Hulewicz, 13.11.1925." In *Briefe*, vol. 3. Frankfurt: Insel Verlag, 1987.

Rodichkina, Anna. "Dyvyshsia na suchasnu Ukraïnu …" Gazeta.ua, 19 October 2016. https://gazeta.ua.

Roditi, Edouard. Review of *A Last Lullaby* by Talat S. Halman. *World Literature Today* 65, no. 4 (1991): 763.

Rollberg, Peter. *Historical Dictionary of Russian and Soviet Cinema*. Lanham, MD: Rowman & Littlefield, 2016.

Rorty, Richard. *Contingency, Irony, Solidarity*. Cambridge: Cambridge University Press, 1989.

– "Human Rights, Rationality, and Sentimentality." In *The Politics of Human Rights*, edited by Obrad Savić, 67–83. London: Verso, 1999.

Rose, Deborah Bird. *Hidden Histories: Black Stories from Victoria River Downs, Humbert River and Wave Hills Stations*. Canberra, Australia: Aboriginal Studies Press, 1991.

Rosenfeld, Gavriel. "Why Do We Ask 'What If'?: Reflections on the Function of Alternate History." *History and Theory* 41 (December 2002): 90–103.

"Rossiiskie voennye shturmom vziali bazu morpekhov v Feodosii." RBC, 24 March 2014. https://www.rbc.ru.

Rubenstein, Joshua, and Alexander Gribanov, eds. *The KGB File of Andrei Sakharov*. New Haven, CT: Yale University Press, 2005.

Rudenko, Anzhelika, and Elina Sardalova. "Pro Putina, svobodu i Tsemakha: Velyke interv'iu z Sentsovym. Chastyna druha." Radio svoboda, 26 September 2019. https://www.radiosvoboda.org.

Rudenko, Mykola. "Donbas." In *Sto svityl*. Kyiv: Dnipro, 1970.

– *Naibil'she dyvo – zhyttia*. Toronto: Canadian Institute of Ukrainian Studies, 1998.

– "Slovo pro druha." In *Vsemu zhivomu ne chuzhoi: Boris Chichibabin v stat'iakh i vospominaniiakh*, 209–10. Khar'kov: Folio, 1998.

– "Tataryn." In *Poezii*. Kyiv: Dnipro, 1991.

– "V Donets'ku." In *Poezii*. Kyiv: Dnipro, 1991.

Rudnytsky, Ivan L. "Political Thought of Soviet Ukrainian Dissidents." In *Essays in Modern Ukrainian History*. Edmonton, AB: Canadian Institute of Ukrainian Studies Press, 1987.

Russkie druz'ia krymskikh tatar. "Sudiat krymskikh tatar." In "'Delo' krymskikh tatar." *Novyi zhurnal* 97 (1969): 172–8.

Rustow, Dankwart A. "Political Parties in Turkey." In *Political Parties and Democracy in Turkey*, edited by Metin Heper and Jacob M. Landau, 10–23. London: Routledge, 2016.

"Rus ve komünizm." *Türk Birliği* 3 (June 1966).

Rywkin, Michael. *Moscow's Lost Empire*. Armonk, NY: M.E. Sharpe, 1994.

Saburov, Evgenii. "Sviatye Kirill i Mefodii kak ideologi avangarda." *Iunost'* 4 (April 1995): 7–9.

Şahin, İbrahim. *Cengiz Dağcı'nın Hayatı ve Eserleri*. Ankara: T.C. Kültür Bakanlığı Milli Kütüphane Basımevi, 1996.

– "Kırım Mecmuasında Neşredilen Kırım Konulu Şiirler Üzerine Bir İnceleme." *Türk Dünyası İncelemeleri Dergisi* 2 (1998): 173–90.

Said, Edward. *After the Last Sky: Palestinian Lives*. New York: Pantheon Books, 1986.

– *Culture and Imperialism*. New York: Vintage Books, 1994.

Sakharov, Andrei. *Vospominaniia*. Vol. 2. Moscow: Vremia, 2006.

Salyha, Taras. *Vidlytyi u strofy chas*. L'viv: L'vivs'kyi natsional'nyi universitet imeni Ivana Franka, 2001.

Samar, Valentyna. "Mustafa Dzhemilev: 'Tsia trahediia mene ne zlamaie. Sim'ia Fevzi – moia sim'ia.'" *Dzerkalo tyzhnia*, 31 May 2013. https://dt.ua.

Samokhvalov, Vsevolod. *Russian-European Relations in the Balkans and the Black Sea Region: Great Power Identity and the Idea of Europe*. London: Palgrave Macmillan, 2018.

Sandler, Stephanie. *Distant Pleasures: Alexander Pushkin and the Writing of Exile*. Stanford, CA: Stanford University Press, 1989.

Sanin, Oles'. "Khto boïtsia Mamaia." *Kino-Kolo*, February 2003. http://www .kinokolo.ua.

Saraçoğlu, Cenk. "Ülkücü Hareketin Biliçaltı Olarak Atsız." *Toplum ve Bilim* 100 (2004): 100–24.

Sarıkamış, Fevzi. "Sana Hasret Gideriz Güzel Kırım." *Pınar* 4 (April 1972): 22–4.

Sasse, Gwendolyn. *The Crimea Question: Identity, Transition, Conflict*. Cambridge, MA: Harvard University Press, 2007.

Savchenko, Viktor. "Khronika odnoho kryminal'noho protsesu." *Suchasnist'* 9 (1993): 153-163.

Savchuk, Alena. "Semeinoe delo. Siloviki v Krymu presleduit nesoglasnykh tselymi sem'iami." Open Democracy, 10 September 2019. https://www .opendemocracy.net.

Savka, Mar'iana. "Khoch rizni my, brate, liniia doli spil'na." Facebook, 18 May 2020. https://www.facebook.com.

Schamiloglu, Uli. "Tatar or Turk? Competing Identities in the Muslim Turkic Word during the Late Nineteenth and Early Twentieth Centuries."

In *The Turkic Speaking Peoples: 2,000 Years of Art and Culture from Inner Asia to the Balkans*, edited by Doğan Kuban, 232–43. Munich: Prestel, 2006.

Schimmelpenninck van der Oye, David. *Russian Orientalism: Asia in the Russian Mind from Peter the Great to the Emigration*. New Haven, CT: Yale University Press, 2010.

Schlögel, Karl. *Ukraine: A Nation on the Borderland*. Translated by Gerrit Jackson. London: Reaktion Books, 2018.

Schönle, Andreas. "Catherine's Appropriation of the Crimea." *Slavic Review* 60, no. 1 (Spring 2001): 1–23.

Schwarz, Daniel. "A Humanistic Ethics of Reading." In *Mapping the Ethical Turn: A Reader in Ethics, Culture, and Literary Theory*, edited by Todd F. Davis and Kenneth Womack, 3–15. Charlottesville: University Press of Virginia, 2001.

Ségur, Louis-Philippe de. *Mémoires; ou, Souvenirs et anecdotes*. Vol. 3. Bruxelles: A. Lacrosse, 1825.

Selim, Şakir. "Ev." In *Şair bolsan*. Aqmescit: DOLA, 2014.

Semeniuk, Hryhorii. *Nikoly ne smiiavsia bez liubovi*. Kyiv: Biblioteka ukraïntsia, 2001.

Sentsov, Oleg. "Odniieiu z velykykh hrup." Facebook, 21 May 2020. https://www.facebook.com.

"Sentsov: 'Stal namnogo luchshe ponimat' krymskikh tatar posle togo, kak menia vygnali s Rodiny.'" *Krym.Realii*, 6 November 2019. https://ru.krymr.com.

Sereda, Viktoriya. "'Social Distancing' and Hierarchies of Belonging: The Case of the Displaced Population from Donbas and Crimea." *Europe-Asia Studies* 72, no. 3 (2020): 404–31.

"Sergei Aksenov: Referendum nikto ne otmenit." Vesti.ru, 8 March 2014. https://www.vesti.ru.

"Serhii Zhadan v hostiakh u 503 OBMP, Chastyna 2." YouTube, 12 May 2020. https://www.youtube.com.

Seutova, Sabrije. "Creating a Crimean Tatar National Movement: The Role and Impact of Literature." In *The Reemergence of Civil Society in Eastern Europe and the Soviet Union*, edited by Zbigniew Rau, 113–28. Boulder, CO: Westview Press, 1991.

Sezer, Duygu Bazoglu. "Balance of Power in the Black Sea." In *Crimea: Dynamics, Challenges and Prospects*, edited by Maria Drohobycky, 157–95. London: Rowman & Littlefield, 1995.

Shafak, Elif. "The Silencing of Writers in Turkey." *New Yorker*, 10 December 2016. https://www.newyorker.com.

Shakespeare, William. *Macbeth*. In *The Complete Works*. London: Collins, 2006.

Sharma, Yojana. "Scholars Targeted as Uighur Purge Engulfs Universities." *University World News*, 28 September 2018. https://www.universityworldnews.com.

Sheehy, Ann. *The Crimean Tatars and Volga Germans: Soviet Treatment of Two National Minorities.* London: Minority Rights Group, 1971.

Shentalinsky, Vitaly. *The KGB's Literary Archive.* Translated by John Crowfoot. London: Harvill, 1995.

Shevchenko, Taras. "Kavkaz." In *Povne zibrannia tvoriv u dvanadtsiaty tomakh,* vol. 1, edited by M.H. Zhulyns'kyi, 343–7. Kyiv: Naukova dumka, 2001.

– "Khmel'nyts'kyi pered Kryms'kym khanom." In *Povne zibrannia tvoriv v desiaty tomakh,* vol. 10. Kyiv: Akademiia nauk URSR, 1963.

Shevel', Oksana. "Kryms'ki tatary ta ukraïns'ka derzhava: Pytannia polityky, pravozastosuvannia ta znachennia rytoryky." *Kryms'ki studiï* 7 (January 2001).

Shevel'ov, Iurii. "Trunok i trutyzna." In *Vasyl' Stus v zhytti, tvorchosti, spohadakh ta otsinkakh suchasnykiv,* edited by Osyp Zinkevych and Mykola Frantsuzhenko, 368–401. Baltimore, MD: Smoloskyp, 1987.

Shkadov, I.N., and A.A. Babakov, eds. *Geroi Sovetskogo Soiuza: Kratkii biograficheskii slovar'.* Vol. 1. Moscow: Voeniz, 1987.

Shklovsky, Viktor. "Art as Technique." In *Russian Formalist Criticism: Four Essays,* edited by Lee T. Lemon and Marion J. Reis, 3–24. Lincoln: University of Nebraska Press, 1965.

Shore, Marci. *The Ukrainian Night: An Intimate History of Revolution.* New Haven, CT: Yale University Press, 2017.

Sid, Igor'. *Geopoetika: Punktir k teorii puteshestvii.* Saint Petersburg: Aleteiia, 2017.

Sinyavsky, Andrei. *Strolls with Pushkin.* Translated by Slava I. Yastremski and Catharine Theimer Nepomnyashchy. New York: Columbia University Press, 2016.

Skrypnyk, Mykola. *Statti i promovy z natsional'noho pytannia.* Munich: Suchasnist', 1974.

Smet, Ingrid A.R de. *Menippean Satire and the Republic of Letters, 1581–1655.* Geneva: Droz, 1996.

"SMI: Aktivistov rossiiskogo ob"edineniia 'Edinstvo Kryma' priglasili v Prazhskii grad." TASS, 30 October 2019. https://tass.ru.

Smith, Adam. *The Theory of Moral Sentiments.* 2nd ed. London: A. Millar, 1761.

Smolii, V.A., and V.S. Stepankov. *Bohdan Khmel'nyts'kyi: Sotsial'no-politychnyi portret.* Kyiv: Lybid', 1993.

Snow, C.P. *The Two Cultures.* Cambridge: Cambridge University Press, 1993.

Snow, David A., and Doug McAdam. "Identity Work Processes in the Context of Social Movements: Clarifying the Identity/Movement Nexus." In *Self, Identity, and Social Movements,* edited by Sheldon Stryker, Timothy J. Owens, and Robert W. White, 41–67. Minneapolis: University of Minnesota Press, 2000.

Snyder, Timothy. "The Causes of the Holocaust." *Contemporary European History* 21, no. 2 (May 2012): 149–68.

Sokil, Vasyl. "Nichto ne zabyto, nikto ne zabyt!" *Kontinent* 45 (1985): 345–60.

Sokul's'kyi, Ivan. "Bakhchysarai (Tsykl)." In *Oznachennia voli: Vybrane poezii*. Dnipropetrovs'k: Sich, 1997.

– "Kredo." In *Oznachennia voli: Vybrane poezii*. Dnipropetrovs'k: Sich, 1997.

– "Planovanyi – tut." In *Oznachennia voli: Vybrane poezii*. Dnipropetrovs'k: Sich, 1997.

Solzhenitsyn, Aleksandr. *Arkhipelag GULag 1918–1956: Opyt khudozhestvennogo issledovaniia*. Vols. 1 and 3. Paris: YMCA Press, 1973–5.

– *Nobelevskaia lektsiia po literature 1970 goda*. Paris: YMCA Press, 1972.

– *Sobranie sochinenii v deviaty tomakh*. Vol. 6. Moscow: Terra, 2000.

– *Zhit' ne po lzhi: sbornik materialov, avgust 1973–fevral' 1974*. Paris: YMCA Press, 1975.

Sonevytsky, Maria. "Radio Meydan: 'Eastern Music' and the Liminal Sovereign Imaginaries of Crimea." *Public Culture* 31, no. 1 (2018): 93–116.

Sontag, Deborah. "The Erdogan Experiment." *New York Times Magazine*, 11 May 2003. https://www.nytimes.com.

Sontsia i moria na mezhi: Tvory pys'mennykiv Krymu. Edited by Danylo Kononenko. Simferopol': Tavriia, 2004.

"Soobshchenie TASS" (23 July 1987). In *Krymskotatarskoe natsional'noe dvizhenie*, edited by Mikhail Guboglo and Svetlana Chervonnaia, 219–20. Moscow: TsIMO, 1992.

Spivak, Gayatri Chakravorty. "Ethics and Politics in Tagore, Coetzee, and Certain Scenes of Teaching." *Diacritics* 32, no. 3/4 (Autumn–Winter 2002): 17–31.

Stalin, I.V. "Marksizm i natsional'nyi vopros." In *Sochineniia*, vol. 2, 290–367. Moscow: OGIZ, 1946.

Starozhyts'ka, Mariia. "Nashe korinnia v Krymu." *Tyzhden'*, 6 June 2008. https://tyzhden.ua.

Statiev, Alexander. "The Nature of Anti-Soviet Armed Resistance, 1942–44: The North Caucasus, the Kalmyk Autonomous Republic, and Crimea." *Kritika: Explorations in Russian and Eurasian History* 6, no. 2 (Spring 2005): 285–318.

"Stenogramma zasedaniia Prezidiuma Verkhovnogo Soveta SSSR" (14 fevralia 1954 g.). *Istoricheskii arkhiv* 1 (1992): 48–53.

Stevenson, Alexandra. "Facebook Admits It Was Used to Incite Violence in Myanmar." *New York Times*, 6 November 2018. https://www.nytimes.com.

Stus, Vasyl'. "Sto dzerkal spriamovano na mene." In *Palimpsesty: Virshi 1971–1979*. Munich: Suchasnist', 1986.

Subbotin, Vasilii. "Bor'ba s istoriei." *Literaturnaia gazeta* 4 (31 January 1991).

Subtelny, Orest. *Ukraine: A History*. 3rd ed. Toronto: University of Toronto Press, 2000.

– "The Ukrainian-Crimean Treaty of 1711." *Harvard Ukrainian Studies* 3/4 (1979–1980): 808–17.

"Sud nad Mustafoi Dzhemilevym." *Khronika tekushchikh sobytii* 40 (20 May 1976). http://www.memo.ru.

Şukur, Samad. "İqrarlıq." In *Küneşten bir parça / Okrushyna sontsia: Antolohiia kryms'kotatars'koï poeziï XIII–XX st*, edited by M. Miroshnychenko and Iu. Kandym. Kyiv: Holovna spetsializovana redaktsiia literatury movamy natsional'nykh menshyn Ukraïny, 2003.

Suny, Ronald Grigor. "The Contradictions of Identity: Being Soviet and National in the USSR and After." In *Soviet and Post-Soviet Identities*, edited by Mark Bassin and Catriona Kelly, 17–36. Cambridge: Cambridge University Press, 2012.

"Sürgünü açlık greviyle protesto eden Kırım Türkü Cemiloğlu öldü." *Milliyet*, 7 February 1976.

Svitlychna, Nadiia. "Interv'iu z Nadiieiu Svitlychnoiu." *Moloda natsiia* 2 (2006): 31–43.

Svitoch, Ievheniia. "Pro shcho lysty Nasymy." In *Qırım inciri*, edited by Mar'iana Savka, 235–64. L'viv: Vydavnytstvo Staroho Leva, 2017.

Swoboda, Victor. "The Evolution of Mykola Rudenko's Philosophy in His Poetry." *Studia Ucrainica* 4 (1988): 76–84.

Symonenko, Vasyl'. "Kurds'komu bratovi." In *Bereh Chekan'*. Kyiv: Naukova Dumka, 2001.

– "Odynoka matir." In *Bereh Chekan'*. Kyiv: Naukova Dumka, 2001.

Sysyn, Frank. *Between Poland and the Ukraine: The Dilemma of Adam Kysil, 1600–1653*. Cambridge, MA: Harvard University Press, 1985.

Szymborska, Wisława. *Monologue of a Dog*. Translated by Clare Cavanagh and Stanisław Barańczak. New York: Harcourt, 2006.

Tangney, June Price. "Recent Advances in the Empirical Study of Shame and Guilt." *American Behavioral Scientist* 38, no. 8. (August 1995): 1132–45.

Tanpınar, Ahmet Hamdi. *19uncu asır Türk edebiyatı tarihi*. İstanbul: Çağlayan kitabevi, 1976.

Taraniuk, Irena. "Lider Medzhlisu: 'Krym povernet'sia ranishe, nizh dumaiut' u Kremli." BBC Ukrainian, 25 March 2016. http://www.bbc.com.

Tarnawsky, Ostap. "Dissident Poets in Ukraine." *Journal of Ukrainian Studies* 6, no. 2 (Fall 1981): 17–27.

Taylor, Charles. *Sources of the Self: The Making of Modern Identity*. Cambridge, MA: Harvard University Press, 1989.

Temirkaya, Yunus. "Taras Şevçenkoğa." *Lenin bayrağı*, 9 March 1961.

Terts, Abram [Andrei Siniavskii.] "Iskusstvo i deistvitelnost'." *Sintaksis* 2 (1978): 111–19.

Thomas, Brook. "*The Fictive and the Imaginary: Charting Literary Anthropology*, or, What's Literature Have to Do with It?" *American Literary History* 20, no. 3 (Fall 2008): 622–31.

Toktargazi, Hüseyin Şâmil [Toktargazy, Üsein Şamil]. "Fi-medkh-i-Qırım." In Kösoğlu, *Türkiye dışındaki Türk edebiyatları antolojisi*, 395–6.

– *Mollalar proyekti* (excerpt). In Kösoğlu, *Türkiye dışındaki Türk edebiyatları antolojisi*, 396–401.
– "Nale-i Kırım adlı eserin önsösü." In Kösoğlu, *Türkiye dışındaki Türk edebiyatları antolojisi*, 394–5.
– "Para." In *Küneşten bir parça / Okrushyna sontsia: Antolohiia kryms'kotatars'koï poeziï XIII–XX st*, edited by M. Miroshnychenko and Iu. Kandym. Kyiv: Holovna spetsializovana redaktsiia literatury movamy natsional'nykh menshyn Ukraïny, 2003.
– "Satma saqın." In Kösoğlu, *Türkiye dışındaki Türk edebiyatları antolojisi*, 396.
Trotskii, Lev. *Predannaia revoliutsiia*. Moscow: NII kul'tury 1990.
Tsentr Razumkova. *Identychnist' hromadian Ukraïny v novykh umovakh: Stan, tendentsiï, rehional'ni osoblyvosti*. Kyiv: Tsentr Razumkova, 2016.
Tsur, Reuven. *Toward a Theory of Cognitive Poetics*. 2nd ed. Brighton, UK: Sussex Academic Press, 2008.
Tuan, Yi-Fu. *Space and Place: The Perspective of Experience*. Minneapolis: University of Minnesota Press, 2001.
– *Topophilia: A Study of Environmental Perception, Attitudes, and Values*. New York: Columbia University Press, 1974.
Tumanskii, V.I. "Elegiia." In *Stikhotvoreniia i pis'ma*, edited by S.N. Brailovskii. Saint Petersburg: Izdanie A.S. Suvorina, 1912.
Türk Birliği 1, no. 1 (April 1966).
Türk Birliği 14–15 (May–June 1967).
Türk Birliği 33 (December 1968).
Tvardovskii, Alexandr. "Po pravu pamiati." In *Dom u dorogi: Poemy, proza*. Voronezh: Tsentral'no-Chernozemnoe knizhnoe izd-vo, 1991.
– *Za dal'iu – dal'*. Moscow: Sovetskii pisatel', 1961.
Ubiria, Grigol. *Soviet Nation-Building in Central Asia: The Making of the Kazakh and Uzbek Nations*. London: Routledge, 2015.
Uehling, Greta. *Beyond Memory: The Crimean Tatars' Deportation and Return*. New York: Palgrave Macmillan, 2004.
– "A Hybrid Deportation: Internally Displaced from Crimea in Ukraine." In *Migration and the Ukraine Crisis: A Two-Country Perspective*, edited by Agnieszka Pikulicka-Wilczewska and Greta Uehling, 62–77. Bristol, UK: E-International Relations Publishing, 2017.
"Ukraina i Krym." *Golos Tatar* 2 (29 July 1917).
"Ukraine Seeks Closure of Turkish Straits after Russian Aggression." UNIAN, 30 November 2018. https://www.unian.info.
Ukraïnka, Lesia. "Bakhchysarais'kyi dvorets'." In *Zibrannia tvoriv u dvanadtsiaty tomakh*, vol. 1. Kyiv: Naukova dumka, 1975.
– "Do A. Iu. Kryms'koho (6 May 1912)." In *Zibrannia tvoriv u 12 tomakh*, vol. 12. Kyiv: Naukova dumka, 1979.
– "Do M.P. Drahomanova (3 September 1891)." In *Zibrannia tvoriv u 12 tomakh*, vol. 10. Kyiv: Naukova dumka, 1978.

– "Do sestry Ol'hy (11 September 1897)." In *Zibrannia tvoriv u 12 tomakh*, vol. 10. Kyiv: Naukova dumka, 1978.

– "Nad morem." In *Zibrannia tvoriv u dvanadtsiaty tomakh*, vol. 7. Kyiv: Naukova dumka, 1975.

Ukraïns'ka hromads'ka hrupa spryiannia vykonanniu hel'sinks'kykh uhod. *Ukraïns'kyi pravozakhysnyi rukh: Dokumenty i materiialy kyïvs'koï Ukraïns'koï hromads'koï hrupy spryiannia vykonanniu hel'sinks'kykh uhod*. Toronto: Smoloskyp, 1978.

"Ukrayna Eurovision 2016 – Jamala 1944 (Türkçe Altyazılı)." YouTube, 22 February 2016. https://www.youtube.com.

Ukrayna, Rusya ve Türkiye: Makaleler mecmuası. İstanbul: Ukrayna Halaskâr Cemiyet-i İttihadiyesi Neşriyatından, 1915.

Ulitskaia, Liudmila. *Medeia i ee deti*. Moscow: Astrel', 2011.

Ulusoy, Halık Bikes. "Gelsin." *Toprak* 1 (December 1954).

Umerov, Ervin. *Chornye poezda*. Moscow: Sovetskii pisatel', 1991.

Ünal, Uğur, and Kemal Gurulkan, eds. *Osmanlı belgelerinde Kırım Hanlığı*. İstanbul: T.C. Başbakanlık Devlet Arşivleri Genel Müdürlüğü, 2013.

Urcosta, Ridvan Bari. "Prospects for a Strategic Military Partnership between Turkey and Ukraine." *Eurasia Daily Monitor* 15, no. 170 (4 December 2018). https://jamestown.org.

Ursu, Dmitrii. *Ocherki istorii kul'tury krymskotatarskogo naroda: 1921–1941*. Simferopol': Krymuchpedgiz, 1999.

Üseyin, Emine. "Saqın mennen vedalaşma." *Emel* 270 (January–February– March 2020).

Uytun, Göktürk Mehmet. "Gelsin." *Toprak* 16 (March 1956).

"U Zelens'koho khochut' obhovoryty kryms'kotatars'ku avtonomiiu z narodom." *Ukraïns'ka Pravda*, 13 November 2019. https://www.pravda .com.ua.

Velichko, Samoil. *Letopis' sobytii v Iugo-zapadnoi Rossii v XVII veke*. Kyiv, 1858.

Vendler, Helen. *The Given and the Made: Strategies of Poetic Redefinition*. Cambridge, MA: Harvard University Press, 1995.

Verba, Lesya, and Bohdan Yasen, ed. and trans. *The Human Rights Movement in Ukraine: Documents of the Ukrainian Helsinki Group, 1976–1980*. Baltimore, MD: Smoloskyp, 1980.

Vilenskii, E. "Novye fil'my." *Novyi zritel'* 36, no. 139 (September 1926).

"V krymskom nebe." *Pravda*, 12 May 1944.

Vlasenko, Ivan. "Formula sontsia Mykoly Rudenka." *Uriadovyi kur'ier* 4 (11 January 2007): 11–12.

Voloshin, Maksimilian. "Dom poeta." In *Sobranie sochinenii*, vol. 2. Moscow: Ellis Lak 2000, 2004.

– "Kul'tura, iskusstvo, pamiatniki Kryma." In *Zhizn' – beskonechnoe poznan'e: Stikhotvoreniia i poemy*. Moscow: Pedagogika-Press, 1995.

Vozgrin, V.E. *Istoriia krymskikh tatar.* Vols. 1, 2, 3, and 4. Simferopol': Tezis, 2013.

"V Turechchyni znialy fil'm pro istoriiu kryms'kykh tatar." Krymtatar.in.ua, 10 September 2012. http://krymtatar.in.ua.

Vul', P.M., ed. *Nemetskie varvary v Krymu: Sbornik materialov.* Simferopol': Krasnyi Krym, 1944.

Vyshnia, Ostap. "Tatarynove zhyttia." In *Vyshnevi usmishky kryms'ki.* Kharkiv: Derzhavne vydavnytstvo Ukraïny, 1925.

– *Tvory u p'iaty tomakh.* Vol. 2. Kyiv: Dnipro, 1974.

– *Usmishky.* Vol. 1. Kyiv: Dnipro, 1969.

– *Vyshnevi usmishky: Zaboroneni tvory.* Kharkiv: Klub simeinoho dozvillia, 2011.

– "Zhyttia Tatarynove." *Visti VUTsVK i KhHVK: Literatura, nauka, mystetstvo* 25 (29 June 1924).

Wachtel, Andrew. *Remaining Relevant after Communism: The Role of the Writer in Eastern Europe.* Chicago: University of Chicago Press, 2006.

Wachtel, Michael. *The Development of Russian Verse.* Cambridge: Cambridge University Press, 1998.

Waters, William. *Poetry's Touch: On Lyric Address.* Ithaca, NY: Cornell University Press, 2003.

Weaver, Carol. *The Politics of the Black Sea Region: EU Neighbourhood, Conflict Zone or Future Security Community.* London: Ashgate Publishers, 2013.

Wellek, René. *Concepts of Criticism.* Edited by Stephen G. Nichols, Jr. New Haven, CT: Yale University Press, [1963] 1969.

White, Hayden. *The Practical Past.* Evanston, IL: Northwestern University Press, 2014.

White, Paul J., and Joost Jongerden. *Turkey's Alevi Enigma: A Comprehensive Overview.* Leiden: Brill, 2003.

Wilder, Thornton. *The Bridge of San Luis Rey.* London, New York, and Toronto: Longman, Green, 1929.

Williams, Brian G. *The Crimean Tatars: The Diaspora Experience and the Forging of a Nation.* Leiden: Brill, 2001.

– "Hidden Ethnocide in the Soviet Muslim Borderlands: The Ethnic Cleansing of the Crimean Tatars." *Journal of Genocide Research* 4, no. 3 (2002): 357–73.

Wilson, Andrew. *Ukraine Crisis: What It Means for the West.* New Haven, CT: Yale University Press, 2014.

Wolfe, Patrick. *Settler Colonialism and the Transformation of Anthropology: The Politics and Poetics of an Ethnographic Event.* London: Cassell, 1999.

Wong, Julia Carrie, Michael Safi, and Shaikh Azizur Rahman. "Facebook Bans Rohingya Group's Posts as Minority Faces 'Ethnic Cleansing.'" *Guardian,* 20 September 2017. https://www.theguardian.com.

Yaltirik, Mehmet Berk. *Yedikuleli Mansur.* İstanbul: İthaki yayınları, 2017.

Yanardağ, Merdan. *MHP değişti mi? Ülkücü hareketin analitik tarihi.* İstanbul: Gendaş, 2002.

"Yeniden Çıkarken." *Emel* 1 (November 1960).

Yurchak, Aleksei. *Everything Was Forever Until It Was No More: The Last Soviet Generation.* Princeton, NJ: Princeton University Press, 2006.

Yurdakul, Mehmet Emin. "Çar'a." In *Mehmed Emin Yurdakul'un Eserleri: Şiirler,* vol. 1, 250–1. Ankara: Türk Tarih Kurumu Basımevi, 1969.

– "Ey Türk Uyan!" In *Mehmed Emin Yurdakul'un Eserleri: Şiirler,* vol. 1, 129–42.

– "İsmail Gaspirinski'ye." In *Mehmed Emin Yurdakul'un Eserleri: Şiirler,* vol. 1, 123–5.

– "Nifâk." In *Mehmed Emin Yurdakul'un Eserleri: Şiirler,* vol. 1, 106.

– "Petersburg'a." In *Mehmed Emin Yurdakul'un Eserleri: Şiirler,* vol. 1, 251.

"Zaiava z'izdu na pidtrymku prahnen' kryms'ko-tatars'koho narodu." *Suchasnist'* 12 (1989): 216–17.

Zaitsev, Iurii. "Bezzbroinyi opir totalitarnomu rezhymovi." In *Istoriia L'vova u tr'okh tomakh,* vol. 3. L'viv: Tsentr Evropy, 2007.

Zakharov, Yevhen. "History of Dissent in Ukraine." Virtual Museum of the Dissident Movement in Ukraine. 21 September 2005. http://archive .khpg.org.

– "S'ohodni – 72 roky, iak deportuvaly kryms'kykh tatar." Facebook, 18 May 2016. https://www.facebook.com.

Zarubin, A.G., and V.G. Zarubin, eds. *Skazky i legendy krymskikh tatar.* Simferopol': Dar, 1991.

"Z dopovidnoï zapysky holovy KDB pry PR URSR (8 travnia 1975r)." In *Kryms'ki tatary: Shliakh do povernennia,* pt. 2, edited by V.A. Smolii, 22–8. Kyiv: Instytut istoriï Ukraïny, 2004.

Zeyrek, Yunus. "Şehit Ahmed Cevad." *Bizim Ahıska* 26 (Spring 2012): 24–8.

Zhadan, Serhii. "Iak my buduvaly svoï domy." In *Tampliiery.* Chernivtsi: Meridian Czernowitz, 2016.

– "Pivostriv svobody." *Reflect* 25, no. 32 (2007). https://polutona.ru.

Zhylenko, Iryna. "Homo Feriens." *Suchasnist'* 10 (October 1997): 16–70.

Zorin, Andrei. *By Fables Alone: Literature and State Ideology in Late Eighteenth- and Early Nineteenth-Century Russia.* Brighton, MA: Academic Studies Press, 2014.

"Z redaktsiinoï poshty." *Ukraïns'kyi visnyk* 11–12 (January–March 1988): 361–93.

Zubkovych, Alina. "Language Use among Crimean Tatars in Ukraine: Context and Practice." *Journal of Soviet and Post-Soviet Politics and Society* 6, no. 1 (2020): 159-178.

Zunshine, Lisa. *Why We Read Fiction: Theory of Mind and the Novel.* Columbus, OH: Ohio State University Press, 2006.

Zürcher, Erik J. *Turkey: A Modern History*. 2nd ed. London: I.B. Tauris, 2005.

Zwarun, Andrew. Preface to *The Human Rights Movement in Ukraine: Documents of the Ukrainian Helsinki Group 1976–1980*. Edited by and translated by Lesya Verba and Bohdan Yasen, 9–15. Baltimore, MD: Smoloskyp, 1980.

Index

Sürgün (deportation of the
Crimean Tatars in 1944, Stalin's
Crimean atrocity): demographic
consequences of, 16, 250n87;
events of, 4, 9, 14–16, 249n81; as
most enduring centripetal event
of the Black Sea region, 18; public
commemoration of, 222–3; as Qara
Kün (The Black Day), 91, 236
Svitlychna, Nadiia, 100
Svitlychnyi, Ivan, 143
Svitoch, Yevheniia, 232
Svydnytsky, Anatoly, 152
Symonenko, Vasyl, 143–5, 268n32;
"Kurdskomu bratovi," 143–5; as
"poet of the birth of the Ukrainian
resistance," 143
Szymborska, Wisława, 56

tamizdat, **124**
Tangney, Judith Price, 109
Tanin (newspaper), 69
Tanpınar, Ahmet Hamdi, 45, 183
Tarasov, Mikhail, 16
Tasin, Heorhy, 80–1, 86, 229, 258n31.
See also Alim (film)
Tasvir-i Efkâr (newspaper), 12
Tatteatr, 79
Temirkaya, Yunus, 91
Tercüman (Perevodchik, periodical), 50,
52–4, 77, 174. See also Gasprinsky,
Ismail
Terkibi-bend (verse form), 45
Toktargazy, Üsein Şâmil, 20, 54, 61–3,
65, 79, 210, 257n26; "Fi-medkh-i-
Qırım," 61–2; intertexuality with
Mykhailo Kotsiubynsky, 63–7;
"Para," 63
Tolstoy, Lev, 29, 33
Toprak (journal), 174–5, 188
trauma: elusiveness of literature of
Stalinist trauma, 91; "perverse
double bind" of Stalinist
trauma, 91
Treaties of Brest-Litovsk, 75
Trotsky, Lev, 76
Tsentralna Rada (Central Council),
69, 76, 141; relations with the
Crimean Tatar Qurultay, 69, 141.
See also Qurultay

Tuan, Yi-Fu, 27, 275n38
Tuğaybey (Tugai-Bey or Tuhai-Bey),
82, 210–11
Tumansky, Vasily, 42
Turan, 48, 174, 176, 274n24
Türk (journal), 47
Türk Birliği (journal), 176, 188, 274n22,
275n33
Türkçülük. See pan-Turkism
Turkestan Legion, 181, 183
Turkish-Islamic Synthesis, 170–1,
273n13
Turkish Workers' Party, 188
Türk Konseyi (Turk Congress), 53
Tvardovsky, Aleksandr, 99, 124–5,
133, 135, 155, 263n57; "Po
pravu pamiati," 124–5;
"Za daliu – dal," 124
Tykhy, Oleksa, 164

Ukrainian Helsinki Group (UHG),
163–5, 272n123. See also Rudenko,
Mykola
Ukrainian People's Republic, 75
Ukrainization (ukrainizatsiia), 80, 83.
See also korenizatsiia
Ukraïnka, Lesia, 20, 54, 56–7, 59–63,
67, 79, 130, 157, 232, 255n20;
"Bakhchysaraiskyi dvorets" (The
palace of Bakhchysarai), 56–7;
intertextuality with Aleksandr
Pushkin, 56–7; intertextuality
with Hasan Çergeyev, 56–7, 59–61;
Kaminnyi hospodar (The Stone
Host), 56, 255n; Krymski spohady
(Crimean Reminiscences), 56; "Nad
morem" (At the sea), 59–61, 67;
views of Crimea as "Tatar land," 56
Ukraïnskyi visnyk (journal), 102, 144,
165, 262n24
Ukrayna, Rusya ve Türkiye (collection),
67, 68
Ulitskaia, Liudmila, 205, 278n27;
Medea i ee deti (Medea and Her
Children), 205
Ülküsal, Müstecib, 174
Ulusoy, Halik Bikes, 175
Umerov, Ervin, 90, 259n68
Umerov, Ilmi, 18
Undervud (band), 19